Foundations for Designing User-Centered Systems

Frank E. Ritter · Gordon D. Baxter
Elizabeth F. Churchill

Foundations for Designing User-Centered Systems

What System Designers Need to Know about People

 Springer

Frank E. Ritter
College of IST
The Pennsylvania State University
University Park, PA
USA

Elizabeth F. Churchill
eBay Research Labs
eBay Inc.
San Jose, CA
USA

Gordon D. Baxter
School of Computer Science
University of St Andrews
St Andrews, Fife
UK

ISBN 978-1-4471-5133-3   ISBN 978-1-4471-5134-0   (eBook)
DOI 10.1007/978-1-4471-5134-0
Springer London Heidelberg New York Dordrecht

Library of Congress Control Number: 2013957359

Cover Image: Badrul Sarwar

Printed on acid-free paper

Springer is part of Springer Science+Business Media (www.springer.com)

Foreword

Our core Masters in Software Engineering course at the University of Southern California is a 2-semester course in which students form into about 15–20 teams of six people to define, design, develop, and deploy working software systems for clients in the local South Los Angeles community. The clients range from IT startups, neighborhood small businesses, local government and local community service organizations, to USC doctors, faculty members, librarians, administrators, and student organizations. The student developers come from many countries and cultures: mostly from the US, India, and China; but also from Europe, Latin America, and other parts of Asia.

One concept that seems to be common among all of their cultures is a version of the Golden Rule: "Do unto others as you would have others do unto you." One of the first things that we now teach the students is that this rule carries a dangerous assumption. How, we originally wondered, could such a universally accepted tenet be dangerous? However, we found that it carries the assumption "Everyone is like me," and that many of the students would follow it to create programmer-friendly user interfaces, and say, for example, "Hard to use? What do you mean? Its tight syntax minimizes keystrokes. It gives you the power of direct access to the operating system. It doesn't need to pinpoint errors because they're obvious from scanning the erroneous command."

We now teach them the Platinum Rule, "Do unto others as others would be done unto," emphasize development and exercise of user prototypes, and provide readings, user domain models, exercises, and win–win negotiation capabilities to help them learn how their clients would like to be done unto.

As we've evolved the course over the last 16 years, we've learned a lot about developers and users the hard way, by trying things out and rethinking approaches that didn't work very well.

We could have avoided a great deal of this learning-the-hard-way if we'd had access to the book that you're holding now. *Foundations for Designing User-Centered Systems: What System Designers Need to Know about People* is a well-organized treasure trove of useful insights and case studies about the characteristics of users and how to develop systems that best fit their strengths and avoid their weak spots.

The book begins with some good motivation, context, underlying science, and conceptual frameworks for human-systems integration. It covers considerations of users' physiology (Chap. 3), senses (primarily vision and hearing) (Chap. 4), a strong coverage of users' memory, attention, and learning aspects (Chap. 5), and several good chapters on how to improve human–computer interaction. These provide useful information and guidance on human cognitive capabilities and their implications for considerations such as organizing text and menus, mental models (for problem solving and decision making), groupware and social processes, types of users and their design implications (age, gender, disabilities), error avoidance, task analysis, human-system evaluation considerations, and process models supporting human-systems integration, such as the incremental commitment spiral model.

Just to elaborate on one of these, the book is particularly strong in an area most frequently in need of improvement: groupware and social processes. Most computer systems have been developed to help individuals perform individual tasks, and tend to focus on improving individuals' performance. A lot of groupware also gets developed using such systems, so that the individual-focus gets supported more strongly than the group-focus.

An example of the consequences of this has been our series of win–win requirements negotiation tools we've developed and used in our project course mentioned above. Our first three versions of the tools began by enabling stakeholders to enter and classify the win conditions they wanted from the project, after which efforts were made to identify and resolve conflicts among the win conditions. This was often difficult after they had bought into the things they wanted.

Our fourth version of the negotiation toolset was built on top of a group-oriented support system (the Ventana/GroupSystems infrastructure). There, once stakeholders entered a win condition, they did not stay in their own space, but were presented with another entry window showing some win conditions entered by the other stakeholders. This often shifted their thinking to focus on understanding and accommodating others' win conditions (oh, they want this to run on Windows, Mac, and Unix platforms; we'd better not use any one-platform COTS (commercial off-the-shelf) products; maybe we should use a Java virtual machine or make this a Web application; and do they have all three platforms for us to test on?). This opened our eyes to the differences between individual-focused and group-focused user interfaces, but it left us wondering how many other dimensions of group-oriented user interfaces we needed to consider.

At that point, if we could have had Chaps. 8 and 9 of *Foundations for Designing User-Centered Systems*, we would have been way ahead. It covers various cooperation settings (zero-sum, nonzero-sum, and behavioral games); techniques for promoting cooperation; social networking; critical influence factors for group performance (group size, group composition, social distance, spatial distance, collaboration support, leadership capabilities, task attractiveness); types of motivation to contribute to solutions; and social responsibility effects (demotivators to contribute to solutions).

The section on What Leads to Good Teamwork makes another distinction between the knowledge, skills, and abilities (KSAs) traditionally used to measure individual performance and those needed for group performance. "Knowledge" focuses not only on technical and domain knowledge, but also on knowledge of team objectives and team-mate awareness. "Skills" focuses not only on analysis and synthesis skills, but also on shared situational awareness and conflict resolution skills. The "A" does not represent Abilities but Attitudes, such as mutual trust, team cohesion, and collective orientation. The chapter also has valuable sections on models of social processes and general implications for system design (e.g., structuring user measurement on contributions to mission effectiveness vs. user efficiency as a computer peripheral).

Other strengths of the book are its inclusion of stories, good and bad usage snapshots, puzzles to stimulate learning and make it fun, and many references to helpful sources of further information. A nice observation was "A year in the laboratory can save an hour in the library."

As a bottom line, getting the user interface right can make a fundamental difference (just consider Apple Computer's Fall 2011 quarterly sales of $46 billion and profits of $13 billion). This book may not make you the next Apple, but I believe that it can help make most people and organizations perceptibly better at understanding and satisfying user needs.

Barry Boehm
TRW Professor of Software Engineering
Computer Science Department
University of Southern California

Member, Committee on Human-System Design
National Academy of Sciences' National Research Council

Former Director of the Information Science and Technology Office, and
Director of the DDR&E Software and Computer Technology Office
DARPA

Fellow ACM, AIAA, IEEE, INCOSE
Member U.S. National Academy of Engineering

Preface

Many books on user centered design and HCI focus on the way people interact with technology. This is an important issue, because people routinely interact with technology on a daily basis—personal computers, mobile phones, airplane cockpits, or even more mundane things like electric kettles and toasters. Despite everything that we know about interaction, however, technology still does not always support what we, as *users*, are trying to do, or behave in the way we expect it to. This can be exasperating for us: as users, as designers, *and* as developers.

In *Foundations for Designing User-Centered Systems* we help you to understand *why* people behave and interact with technology in the way they do. By helping you understand both *how* and *why* people behave in the way they do, and by helping you to develop a more systems oriented perspective, we provide you with a framework that will enable you to develop technologies that are both useful and usable. These technologies will also be more acceptable to users because they will be better suited to the way users work in their normal environment.

Our Approach

The people who use technology must be considered to be part of the systems they use. Although people–"users"–are diverse, they also have many characteristics in common. Not all of these characteristics are directly visible or available to system designers without much closer investigation. By understanding the characteristics of users, designers are better able to create safer, more usable, and more acceptable systems.

We have designed *Foundations for Designing User-Centered Systems* to encourage you to ask critical and reflective questions throughout the design process about how your users will work with your technology. Whilst we provide key facts and characteristics about people as users, we have resisted creating a source book filled with lists of endless facts about human characteristics. We have also avoided the temptation of promoting design by rules, so we do not provide lists of guidelines that must be rigidly followed, or known problems that must be avoided.

Our goal is to help you understand the process of designing interactive technologies and to introduce you to a user-centered, systems oriented approach to design. We present a detailed, theoretically grounded approach to understanding people: how they accomplish the things they do and how they work out what they need to do (their tasks) in particular situations.

We have tried to select the most important things you should know about people, based on our experience of working in industry and academia. *Foundations for Designing User-Centered Systems* will help you develop a principled model of users, based on regularities of human behavior, which encapsulates this information so that you can predict how users will behave in different situations. This model will incorporate aspects of how perception, action, cognition, and social processes all contribute to human behavior.

We believe it is important to have the grounding for innovation as well as the ability to evaluate existing systems. Our approach will give you a solid foundation for dealing with a wide range of situations and provide you with the analytical skills to design in innovative ways—including introducing you to computational and cognitive models of how users think. We build on existing methods and techniques, providing you with the basic knowledge that will let you invent your own methods for design and evaluation based on the different settings that you find yourself in.

For Practitioners

As the book has developed, many of our colleagues and collaborators from industry have reiterated the importance of the issues that we address, and how much they support the idea of *Foundations for Designing User-Centered Systems*. They often find that they have to train their staff about users, their tasks, and the context in which they perform those tasks. To address this we provide an extensive theoretical information about design-relevant user characteristics to make practitioners aware of the important issues. In addition, throughout the book we consider the implications for system design, where we offer concrete examples of how the information we present can be applied.

For Teachers and Advanced Students

Our book provides enough material for a semester-long course on users, human–computer interaction, human factors, interface design, or human behavior modeling where users are an inherent part of the envisaged systems. While much more is known about users than we present here, we have intentionally limited ourselves to what can be covered in a semester. We provide follow-up reading for those who wish to take things further at the end of each chapter. More resources on the topics we cover are continually becoming available online and these could be used to extend our material to support longer or more advanced courses. You will also find some useful resources on the *Foundations for Designing User-Centered Systems* web site (www.frankritter.com/fducs).

Acknowledgments

The book has evolved over time as we and our erstwhile colleague, David Gilmore, have taught human–computer interaction, human factors, user interface design, cognitive ergonomics, and cognitive modeling at the University of Nottingham, Penn State, the University of York (UK), and the University of St Andrews. Collating the material was made possible through the original web site created by David as a way to help support students. The idea of turning it into a book emerged as the web site expanded, and as the material has been updated.

While any mistakes remain ours, we need to thank the many people who have offered feedback and encouragement along the way. In particular, we would like to thank the following people. Peter Lonsdale prepared a talk for a class that turned into lecture notes on the application of our approach to the web, and the students at Penn State (Andrew Freed) and at the University of Nottingham helped refine many of the exercises. Dan Gao, Soo Yeon Lee, and B. S. Sowmyalatha (PSU/UP) provided great feedback on improving this text, constantly encouraging more examples. Alexander Daise, Mark Kozlowski, David Kaethner, Lars Guenther, and Marcel Richter (TU/Chemnitz) also offered many good suggestions on how to improve the presentation.

Our colleagues (and where they used it to teach) provided useful feedback based on use. These include Mithu Bhattacharya (PSU/UP), Michael Qin (NSMRL, U. of Connecticut/WPI), Mark Ackerman (Michigan), Kuo-Chuan (Martin) Yeh (Penn State/World Campus), Marcela Borge (PSU/UP), Pat Clemson (PSU/Beaver), and Olivier Georgeon (PSU/UP).

We received comments from several people at PSU, notably Andrew Freed, C. Lee Giles, Alexander Ororbia II, James Wang, and Luke Zhang. Rob St. Amant (NCSU) and Magy Seif El-Nasr (Northeastern) provided useful comments to improve the direction of this book. Simon Robbie (CMU, Apple) provided extensive suggestions throughout the book after a chance meeting at a pterodactyl ride. Jack Sparks (MCWL) read each chapter and the breadth and depth of his biting but not hurtful comments were encouraging. Lisa Dow (University of St Andrews), Ben Dyson (Ryerson University), David Grayson (Fluent Interaction), Chandra Harrison, Junya Morita (JAIST), Les Nelson (PARC), and Margaret Ritter all provided encouragement and support as well as useful feedback on multiple chapters as the book developed. General discussions with Bill Webber (Erlbaum) and Rajal Cohen (PSU) improved the presentation. We should also note that books by John R. Anderson, Boff and Lincoln, Don Norman, and Chris Wickens and his colleagues have helped shape this work, and some of the ways they organize topics are reflected here. Don Meeker (PSU) provided photos and useful comments about the use of his photos.

Many people provided feedback on individual chapters which has greatly helped the book as well, including Jennifer Bittner (Indiana), Shawn Clark (PSU/UP), Georgious Christous (European University Cyprus), Ed Glantz (PSU/UP), David Golightly (University of Nottingham), Kate Hone (Brunel University), M. Cameron Jones (Google), Bill Kennedy (GMU), Russell Lock (Loughborough University), Faidon Loumakis (Fluent Interaction), Naomi Malone (UCF), Sylvie Noel (Communications Research Centre Canada/Centre de recherches sur les communications Canada), Shamil Parbhoo (Fluent Interaction), Ling Rothrock (PSU/UP), Marco de Sa (Twitter), Joe Sanford (PSU/UP), Elaine Seery (Science Editing), Sarah Sharples (University of Nottingham), Tim Storer (University of Glasgow), and Fiona Woodcock (Fluent Interaction).

Gordon Baxter's work on the book was supported by funding from the UK EPSRC's Large Scale Complex IT Systems project. Frank Ritter has drawn on material developed with support from ONR and DTRA and applied this material to their projects, having been influenced by these projects and having used this material to help train researchers on those projects. A Senior Fulbright Fellowship provided support to teach this material at TU/Chemnitz, and the College of IST has been supportive.

Finally, Beverley Ford, Ben Bishop, Jake Kirby, and a copyeditor at Springer have been very helpful and encouraging. They helped us push this book over the finish line with their kind words and support. Figures and pictures used with permission by their authors. Unattributed figures are copyright by the authors and are available for use by instructors on an instructors' web site.

Citations are done in Springer house style; references are done in APA format.

Contents

Part III Methods

Part IV Summary

Overview of Book

Foundations for Designing User-Centered Systems is organized into four parts, as shown in the Table of Contents. The first part has two chapters. Chapter 1 introduces the approach of understanding people (commonly referred to as "users"), their tasks, and their context. It motivates when to study the user, including examples and some risks that arise when you do not. This chapter also notes some ways to organize this knowledge, including risk-driven design and the use of cognitive models.

Chapter 2 provides an overview of the fields that contribute to our approach to designing user-centered systems. This chapter will help readers understand the relationship between different research communities and point to relevant literature and to where further information can be found.

The second part of the book describes what we consider to be the core, design relevant characteristics of users. These chapters build up the foundations for describing users using what we refer to as the ABCS framework: A for anthropometrics, B for behavior, C for cognition, and S for social aspects that underlie human activity. Chapter 3 describes important aspects of users' bodies, *anthropometrics*, including how they sit at terminals, how they type, and how they touch. Chapter 4 deals with the underpinnings of human *behavior*, describing the basic senses used to interact, particularly sight and hearing, as well as why individuals are motivated to behave in particular ways. Chapters 5–7 address *cognition*. Chapter 5 describes the foundations of cognition, that of memory, attention, and learning, particularly the aspects that apply to system design. Chapter 6 describes higher level cognitive capabilities related to system design, that of mental representations influencing mental models, problem solving, and decision making. Chapter 7 examines communication between users and technology. These aspects include some fundamental factors of language related to interfaces, how users read, and typical information-seeking behaviors. Chapters 8 and 9 look at *social* aspects of users. Chapter 8 examines social effects on decision making and factors affecting teamwork. Chapter 9 looks at larger scale, network effects, and provides some models to summarize behavior in this area.

Chapter 10 introduces the study of errors—errors are often a good source of information about human behavior when interacting with technologies. We can ask several questions. What went wrong? Why did it go wrong? How can we prevent the same thing happening again? Chapter 10 provides some background knowledge on errors, including error rates and how technological and human factors interact to cause system errors. The chapter also provides some tools for studying and ameliorating the effects of errors.

The third part of the book provides some methods for studying users in systems. Chapter 11 introduces task analysis. We note several uses for task analysis and illustrate how it can be a very cost-effective method. Worked examples are provided for each method.

Chapter 12 provides two additional methods for improving the design of systems. These methods also help to summarize and apply what we know about users. Cognitive Dimensions (CDs) is a way to summarize how users interact with systems. CDs also offer a framework for making predictions about potential errors; these predictions can provide the groundwork for directed usability tests and for formal or informal quality testing. The chapter also describes Norman's Gulfs of Evaluation and Execution. The Gulfs offer a framework for understanding where users need to be helped to understand and to interact with systems.

Chapter 13 describes empirical evaluation focusing on *user studies*. This chapter describes how to start to run a usability study, and provides suggestions about what to do and what to measure.

Chapter 14 provides a summary of users and how to design user-centered systems. We first summarize the ABCS and then offer an introduction to user modeling as a way to encapsulate the detailed knowledge we have about users as a quick way to generate predictions. We conclude by describing the Risk-Driven Incremental Commitment model as a way to apply what we know about users to system design.

The Appendix describes an air accident that occurred several years ago, known as the Kegworth accident because it took place near the small town of Kegworth in the midlands of the UK. Although a simple diagnosis of *pilot error* was offered as the cause of the accident, on closer analysis this accident resulted from multiple issues which transpired at a number of system levels. The Kegworth accident is used as an example in several places in the book to illustrate how many levels and aspects of a system can influence system performance—and to underscore the complexity of systems that are made up of people and of interactive and interacting technologies. This complexity means we often cannot and should not come up with simple assertions about errors, but rather look for weak points in the overall system and deal with those weak points systematically and in a grounded way.

We believe knowing more about people will help you develop the kind of grounding you need. We also believe that developing a systems approach will protect you from erring toward simple design assumptions and narrow solutions.

Each chapter includes an abstract, an introduction, and a summary to orient the reader and to increase understanding. We include consideration of what the implications are for system design at the end of each major section. There are also lists of other resources for those people who want to find out more.

Endorsements

For all of us who have been 'put on hold,' recorded for quality purposes, been forced to talk to a mindless, uncaring voice non-recognition system, or simply beaten at the computer keyboard in sheer frustration, hope and help are at hand. For Ritter and his colleagues are injecting rational, user-centered design into such systems development. It is a timely contribution, devoutly to be wished. Their text is a shining example of their advocated principles. Readable, informative, easy to use, and innovative, this works puts into practice what it preaches. It should be on the desk of everyone who looks to conceive, design, fabricate, and manufacture any modern technological system—no matter how hard, no matter how soft. Even if only a proportion of designers and users read this book we will be so much better off. If it gets the circulation it deserves it could change our world—and that very much for the better. If not, technorage will only grow and the Luddites will once again become a viable social Party!

Peter Hancock
Provost Distinguished Research Professor
Pegasus Professor, and University Trustee Chair
University of Central Florida

As a software engineer, I've been advocating for the past 20 years that we will only see real improvements in our software when we move away from a technocentric view and adopt a wider perspective that takes into account what users really do. Too many software engineers consider this to be a 'CHI issue' and believe that they can focus on the technology and leave the 'soft stuff' to designers of the user experience.

Well, they are wrong. Not only is it the case that most companies don't employ specialist UX designers, all too often these designers don't understand the underlying technological issues that have to be taken into account if our software is to work effectively, efficiently, and securely. The only way forward in my view is for software engineering education to include education in the human, social, and organizational factors that influence the ways in which software is designed and used.

Up till now, this has been very difficult. Conventional texts on CHI have a different audience and, all too often, focus on current technology rather than underlying fundamentals. This book is different and it's one we've been waiting for. It explains in depth fundamental human capabilities, cognitive strengths, and cognitive limitations that influence the way that we choose, understand, and use software systems. It explains how we communicate and how that affects the ways that interfaces are used; it discusses collaborative working, factors that support and inhibit collaboration, and methods that can be used to understand how people work.

Most importantly, I think, it doesn't just present these fundamentals in isolation. Every chapter in the book has a section discussing the implications for design so that readers not only learn fundamentals but understand why these are important and how they might influence their work. These bring unfamiliar material to life for software engineers and clearly demonstrate why this is important for practical systems design.

This is both a textbook and a reference book. It would be a great basis for a course in human-centered software engineering but, as well as this, practicing engineers can access and learn from the individual chapters and the follow-up material that is suggested. The lack of accessible and comprehensive material on human factors for software engineers has been an important barrier to more widespread acceptance of a human-centered approach to systems design. This book has broken down that barrier and I can thoroughly recommend it to all engineers.

Ian Sommerville
Professor of Computer Science
University of St Andrews, and Author of *Software Engineering*

This is the book I really needed when I developed a course on Applied Cognitive Science within our Master's program in HCI with Ergonomics at UCL. At the time, I had to improvise with a mix of texts on cognitive psychology, engineering psychology, and HCI. *Foundations for Designing User-Centered Systems* fills an important gap in the space of texts for students and practitioners of HCI, focusing, as it does, on understanding people and their interactions (both social and with technology). Critically, it also draws out the implications of this understanding for design. It manages to cover all the key topics in this space while also being engaging and, at times, quirky. A textbook that makes one smile and want to read more is a textbook that works.

Ann Blandford
Professor of Human–Computer Interaction
University College London

I really enjoyed the reading of this lively book that I believe can be appreciated by different kinds of readers. A useful publication written with wit, helping the reader to discover the human capabilities and limitations, the patterns of user's attention and the fundamental principles to adopt at the early stages of system design.

The authors take into consideration not only the usefulness of the artifacts, but also the impact they have on safety. In fact, the main cause of accident nowadays in aviation is the loss of control of the aircraft, often induced by a poor human–machine interaction. This is due, mainly, by poorly conceived interfaces, as the result of a lack of understanding of who the final user is. The overall problem lies in the very fact that the one who produces the artifacts is not the one using them. Eventually, after many years, the study of the human factors as a discipline at the cross-road between medicine, psychology and engineering is addressing the design of the interfaces.

As a human factor specialist, involved in flight operations, I think this book should become a 'must' even in the flight safety domain.

Antonio Chialastri
Senior Captain and Independent Human Factors
Consultant in Aviation and Medicine, Italy

This broad ranging survey of user-centered design techniques provides an effective introduction for designers into what people do, why and when they do it, and what motivates those behaviors.

If you ever wanted to know what a 'steep learning curve' actually looks like and how the user will interact with your system at different points along this curve then this is the book for you!

Through well-illustrated examples, it considers a wide range of topics from traditional ergonomics, through user behavior, cognitive models, and social factors. Many of the examples take off the traditional 'blinkers' of user centred design and show how a human decision at the 'sharp end' may well have its roots in a much wider and blunter context.

As a chief architect for large programs, this book has given me access to a variety of new techniques and an extended vocabulary that I look forward to introducing my design teams to.

Richard Hopkins
Chief Architect and IBM Distinguished Engineer
Co-author of *Eating the IT Elephant*

The HCI profession emerged when psychologists teamed with developers. Design was missing. Today, good teams have strong designers and technologists—but psychological insight is often in short supply. This book fills that gap with a fresh look at established and new knowledge and approaches.

Jonathan Grudin
Principal Researcher at Microsoft Research
ACM Fellow

If you want to design or build interactive systems that are both useful and usable, *Foundations for Designing User-Centered Systems* is an excellent place to begin.

Philippe Palanque
Head of Interactive Critical Systems Group
Universite Paul Sabatier Toulouse
Co-chair of CHI 2014

The "Who, What, When, Where and Why of Human-Systems Interaction"—a practitioner's primer for Systems Designers looking to advance human computer symbiosis in their designs. The book provides a straightforward, easy-to-read introduction to the process of designing interactive technologies using human-centered approaches that avoid the cookie-cutter, simplistic recipes all too common in other publications. Also worth noting is that this guide not only covers foundations for beginners, but also includes practical, real-word examples, as well as emerging essential topics for the design of systems, for more advanced practitioners. The reader will quickly discover that this book provides essential, innovative, and targeted tools for designers who are focused on enabling seamless interactions between humans and technologies. For anyone looking to advance human-computer-symbiosis, this book will not gather dust on your shelf!

Dylan Schmorrow, Ph.D.
Chief Scientist, Soar Technology, Inc.

Anything that helps software developers think more about the mental states of their users and how that affects the utility and usability of their software is a good thing. Even if you don't plan to become a human factors expert, you will find good ideas in this book to help make your applications more successful.

William A. Woods
Research Scientist and Software Engineer

The foundations for designing user-centered systems really delivers on its title. The book succinctly captures the key anthropometric, behavioral, cognitive, and social concepts that are the foundations for designing user-centered systems. Furthermore, the authors artfully imbedded human factors principles into the manner in which materials are presented, turning the book into a demonstration of good practices. I find the structure and layout of the book make it an excellent introductory text for a course in HCI as well as a useful initial reference source.

Michael "Q" Qin
Adjunct professor, WPI

Part I
Introduction: Aims, Motivations, and Introduction to Human-Centered Design

Chapter 1
Introducing User-Centered Systems Design

Abstract If designers and developers want to design better technologies that are intended for human use they need to have a good understanding of the people who are or who will be using their systems. Understanding people, their characteristics, capabilities, commonalities, and differences allows designers to create more effective, safer, efficient, and enjoyable systems. This book provides readers with resources for thinking about people—commonly called "users"—their tasks and the context in which they perform those tasks. Our intention is to enable you to make more informed decisions when designing complex interactive systems. This chapter thus introduces this argument through example design problems. We then present the benefits and costs associated with understanding the user. Two approaches for understanding users are introduced. The first is a framework called the ABCS for understanding, in broad strokes, different aspects of users. The second is user knowledge and action simulation for developing and testing how users approach tasks in more detail. After reading this chapter you should be able to appreciate why it is important to understand users, and the associated benefits and costs of doing so.

1.1 Introduction

Most of us use interactive technologies every day—cell phones, TVs, alarm clocks, cars, vending machines, computers, cameras, microwaves, ovens, ticket machines—the list is endless.

Technology can help us achieve what we desire to do or need to do, but it can also hinder us. When we cannot get something done, when our expectations are not met, or when technology is too hard to use, we get frustrated. When technologies and systems are unpredictable, delays and unforeseen problems can occur.

This book is about designing technology and systems for use by people. We offer an introduction to what we know about why humans do what they do when they do it as users of technology. The book has one central premise:

F. E. Ritter et al., *Foundations for Designing User-Centered Systems*,
DOI: 10.1007/978-1-4471-5134-0_1, © Springer-Verlag London 2014

Understanding people will help you build better interactive technologies and systems.

When we say "understanding people" we mean:

- Knowing how to observe and document *what* people do

  - Using appropriate methods to get credible results and differentiate anecdotes from reliable data

- Understanding *why* people do what they do

  - Developing insights into people's conscious and unconscious motivations for doing things

- Understanding and predicting *when* people are likely do things

  - Understanding people's patterns of behavior

- Understanding *how* they choose to do things the way they do them

  - Understanding what options people actually have and/or perceive they have available to them, understanding the constraints they are under and assessing what the resources they have available to them.

We propose that systems should be designed in a user-centered way. Being user-centered means considering human characteristics and capabilities during system design. It means explicitly asking: who is going to use the system/technology and why; what are they hoping to achieve in using the system/technology; how much effort are they willing to put into learning how to use the system/technology; whether they will be operating the system alone or with others…. Being user-centered means knowing why, as well as how, users do what they do when they do it. We propose that consideration of users' basic human characteristics should be in place before system development begins. Reflection and experimentation with potential users of the system should take place throughout the design and development process using methods like brainstorming, storyboarding, low to high fidelity prototyping, and, as the system gets closer to full functionality, with more formal use testing.

This book assumes no previous knowledge; it is designed to be accessible to those without a background in psychology or computer science; if you have already taken a traditional human–computer interaction (HCI) course, this material may be a quite easy read and help you organize your thoughts. If you have taken several psychology courses, you are likely to recognize much, but perhaps not all, of the material here.

1.2 Starting to Understand Users

Many designers and developers make two fundamental errors. They assume that understanding how a technology will be used can be derived from introspection: from imagining how it will be used. This assumption is based on a second

Fig. 1.1 a Rank order the quality of these switch to light mappings. **b** Note how long, on average, it will take to push a button on each panel. (Adapted from Payne 1995)

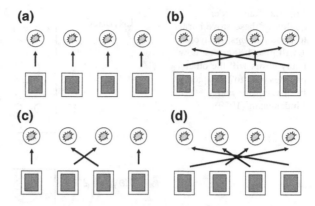

error—that everyone is the same. We know the second assumption is not true from simply observing that the world is made up of very different people with different motivations, different backgrounds, and different skill sets.

To illustrate how our intuitions about people may be incorrect, and why it is always worth testing your designed system with people who will use that system, we offer the following examples.

1.2.1 Designing Mappings Between Buttons and Lights

It is generally claimed that the better designs are those that offer simple, clearer mappings between an action and a response. However, the question is: what is a clearer mapping? Consider Figs. 1.1 and 1.2 taken from a study by Payne (1995) on how well naive subjects could judge the quality of interface designs for a simple system. Payne's experiment assessed what design people predicted would rank best to worst on a very simple interface, where a number of different mappings between the controls and resulting system state were compared (what is called "stimulus-response compatibility" in the scientific literature). In the following example, study participants were able to rank order the designs in Fig. 1.1 from best to worst. They were asked two questions: (1) what is the mapping of lights to switches that gives the fastest response time? and (2) can you give a prediction of how long they will take on average?
Sixty out of 70 subjects got the top ranked one correct. However, only four out of 70 got the complete order correct. The results of the study suggest that, when confronted with anything but the most obvious choices, designers without training may make poor design choices. Before going on, you may wish to try this task yourself. The correct order is given in the exercises at the end of this chapter.

Fig. 1.2 Rank order the quality of these stove burner to knob pairings. If layout 1 will give 100 errors, how many errors will the other pairings lead to? Adapted from Chapanis and Lindenbaum (1959)

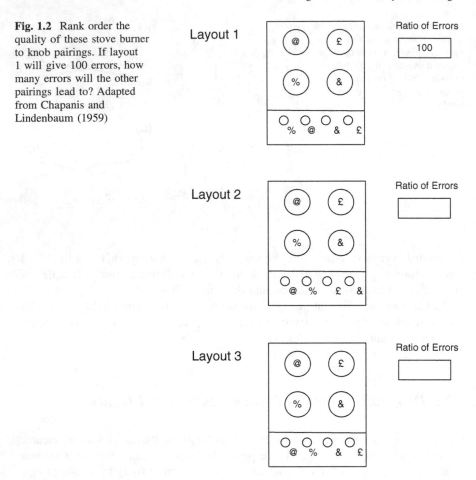

1.2.2 Designing Stove-Top Mappings

For our second example, take a look at the stove-top designs in Fig. 1.2. Which is the best burner to control knob mapping? If you think you know the best mapping, can you provide a quantitative measure of how much better? If layout 1 has 100 errors for a given amount of use, how many errors will the other two have?

For the examples in Fig. 1.2, only four out of 53 subjects selected the correct order of layout to be layout 3 (76 errors per 1,200 trials), layout 2 (116 errors per 1,200 trials), and then layout 1 (129 errors per 1,200 trials), and only 15 out of 53 could correctly identify the best design.

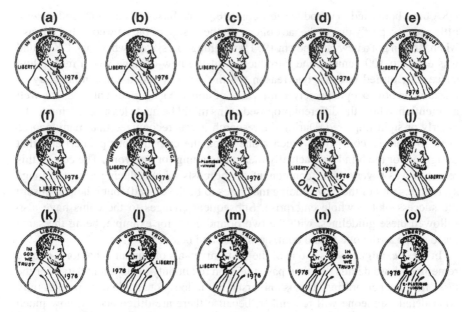

Fig. 1.3 Possible views of a US penny. Without looking in your pocket choose the correct one. Taken from a study by Nickerson and Adams (1979). (Used with permission of Elsevier)

1.2.3 Designing Coins

For our third example, we would like to look at coins. Can you pick out which is a US penny in Fig. 1.3 without looking at a real one?

Most Americans would think that they could recognize a US penny, but more than half of Nickerson and Adams' (1979) American subjects shown the pennies in Fig. 1.3 could not pick out the penny from a set of 15 examples. The correct answer is given at the end of this chapter in Exercise 1.2.

We all know well enough what a penny looks like—relative to the other coins we might encounter—but not in any more detail than is necessary. With the set of alternatives provided by Nickerson and Adams, the choice has to be based on recalling specific features of a penny, which most people have never memorized and have never needed to memorize. You can see similar effects in computer interfaces where users cannot recall which commands are located on which menus (Exercise 1.2 explores this question further).

Although coinage systems may appear a long way removed from the design of user interfaces, they provide good examples of how and why we can benefit from considering the users' perspective in design to avoid system failure. France and the

USA have both tried to introduce new coins (e.g., the Susan B. Anthony dollar) with little success, partly due to the lack of care in the design of the new coin. In contrast, when Britain got a new currency in 1971, switching to a system where one UK pound was equal to 100 pennies, the introduction of the new coinage was a resounding success. It turned out that one reason for the success was a substantial body of research on how people perceived the value of coins (e.g., Bruce et al. 1983) as well as attention to how the different proposed coins might be made least confusing to the elderly or sight impaired. During the research it was recognized that many people need to identify coins from touch alone (e.g., the coin in your pocket) and that designing for the blind user actually meant designing for everyone. The cost of this research was a very small component of the costs of introducing a new coinage system (e.g., all of the new vending machines to be developed), but it helped ensure the success of the whole enterprise. Subsequent changes to the coins have also followed these guidelines, with the two pound coin, for example, being the same basic shape as the one pound coin, but larger and heavier.

In these examples we see one of the first universals of human behavior—people remember those details that they pay attention to but only in sufficient detail for the tasks they are performing. This is universal, but it does not enable us to predict fully what details someone will remember, because there are differences in how much attention people have to spare, what tasks they are performing, and thus what details they will remember. The first two problems in Figs. 1.1 and 1.2 are difficult because the differences in performance of the tasks are not particularly available to consciousness, and most people's representation of how they think they perform these tasks in this area do not reflect how people actually perform the task. The penny question (and the menu question) represent the difference between recognition and recall memory. Usually identifying a penny just requires being able to discriminate between it and other coins. With the set of alternatives provided by Nickerson and Adams, the choice has to be based on recalling the features of a penny, which most people have never bothered to commit to memory (why would they?).

Another classic example is remembering your new cell phone number. It takes a long time to learn it because you, personally, never need to use it (unless you misplace your phone, in which case calling it is a good strategy for finding it!). However, if someone asks you for it, you either have to recall it or have to go through the menus on your phone to find it, eventually recognizing the steps that enabled you to find the number.

This disconnection between how we think we behave and how users *really* behave is common and there are plenty of reasons for it. In most cases we are too busy doing a task to properly observe how we are doing it. When we can observe how we are doing it, it is rare that we can correctly and completely infer why we are doing the task—the observation of behavior is separate from the generation of it. Ericsson and Simon (1993) provide a full explanation of why it is hard for people to examine their own thinking processes. Their explanation includes that when we recognize how we behave, we rarely make written notes and thus any

Table 1.1 Summary of some of the causal factors in the Kegworth air accident and lessons to note

---

- The Engine Instrument System (EIS) used digital displays. A survey of the airline's pilots after the Kegworth accident showed that nearly two-thirds of them believed that the new EIS was not effective in drawing their attention to rapid changes in the engine parameters. If it had, the accident might have been avoided. Thus, the design of the interface for the EIS did not present data in a format that could easily be perceived by the pilots

  Lesson: You need to understand how people look at the user interface to extract information which they then use to make decisions and take actions

- Neither pilot could recall having seen any indication of the abnormally high vibration levels on the EIS. The Captain noted that he rarely scanned the vibration gauges because he had found them to be unreliable in other aircraft in the past. Experts, such as pilots, have a highly developed mental model of the world in which they normally operate, which helps them carry out their tasks. The Captain appears to have excluded the vibration gauges from his mental model because he believed the readings were unreliable

  Lesson: You need to understand how people create and use mental models to help them use a system

- The B737-400 was a glass cockpit aircraft, in which the information is presented on digital displays, rather than on analogue instruments and electro-mechanical displays. The airline (BMA) did not have a glass cockpit flight training simulator for the B737-400, so pilots could only gain experience through actually flying it (i.e., on the job). The only training the pilots were given for the B737-400 was a 1-day audio-visual conversion course

  Lesson: You need to understand how people learn to use new and, particularly, complex systems

- Three members of the cabin crew said they saw evidence of the fire in the #1 engine, but they did not report this to the pilots. The flight crew believed that the problem was with the #2 engine. This seems to have been a failure in what is called Crew Resource Management, a procedure designed to ensure that all the members of a flight crew (pilots and cabin crew) communicate with one another and work together as a team

  Lesson: You need to understand how social issues, including communication, can affect how people use a system

- The B737-400 was fitted with a new type of engine. The engine was thoroughly tested on the ground before being certified by the appropriate authorities. The engine was not tested either in an altitude test cell (which simulates the conditions of flying at high altitudes) or in flight, however. This scenario illustrates how decisions that are made at remote distances from the user interface in a system can have an impact on the way that the users behave. Emergency events, like engine failures, are normally covered by checklists in the QRH (Quick Reference Handbook) that is used by all pilots to deal with known situations

  Lesson: You need to understand that decisions taken at a place and time that are greatly removed from where the system is used can affect the way the system will behave

---

memories of how we behaved are subject to the inherent frailties of human memory. We are also not very good at estimating time accurately and have trouble keeping track of successes and failures. Finally, there are some particular aspects of our own behavior that are very hard to observe, such as basic perception, and some that are hard to describe and reason about verbally, such as performing some spatial reasoning tasks.

1.2.4 What Happens If You do not Take Proper Account of Users, Tasks, and Context?

The Kegworth Air Accident (see the Appendix for a detailed account) was, like many air accidents, the result of several events. Many of these events happened in a short space of time, but some were more distant both in time and in space. From the point when a problem was detected with one of the engines, to the point at which the plane crashed took less than 8 min. Table 1.1 lists some examples of the types of things that went awry and contributed to the accident and the lessons you should note.

This book will help you to understand the underlying issues, and show how you can analyze them. Once you understand that these issues arise at different levels, and how they can interact, you can start to take appropriate steps to make sure they are prevented (or their effects are at least mitigated) when designing systems.

1.3 The Benefits and Costs of Understanding Users

Assuming that your users are just like you can be described as a fundamental attribution error of design. This error is essentially the inverse of what is called the *fundamental attribution error* in social psychology (described in Chap. 8). In the fundamental attribution error you assume that people are not like you when, in fact, they are.

In the fundamental attribution error of design, you assume that your users are like you when, in fact, they are not! Users often can't use the systems as well as the designers because they do not know as much. Sometimes the opposite is true. Users can to be quite resourceful and innovative, and will often use technology in ways that the designer had never fully contemplated; for example, spreadsheets were originally designed for use by accountants, but many people now use them for processing all forms of tabular data. Similarly, the short messaging system (SMS) was originally designed to help engineers debug mobile phone communication systems, but now it is widely used by everyone with a mobile phone as a means of general communication.

If you understand your users and take appropriate account of them when designing your system, there are three main types of benefits (or payoffs) that can result: more usable products (which can lead to wider adoption and more accelerated adoption rates), cost savings, and safer systems. There are some caveats, however, which can be seen as costs: understanding and taking appropriate account of the user in your design does not necessarily guarantee success, and knowing how much you need to understand about your users is a hard question to answer. We discuss all of these below.

1.3.1 Benefit 1: More Usable Products

Understanding people can help you design systems that are more usable, more learnable, and more efficient. For example, the adoption of email has become more widespread because of wider availability of devices and infrastructure but also because email interfaces have progressed from requiring in-depth computer science and systems administration knowledge to manage installation and use to relatively easy-to-use web interfaces with help documentation, message management and retrieval, directly usable features like formatting, and the ability to easily attach or embed multimedia.

Web design provides another example. Changes in the costs of hardware and bandwidth have made it faster and cheaper to develop web pages, but many people and businesses would not be generating as many web pages if they still had to use raw HTML. The rise of special purpose, easy-to-use HTML editors (e.g., Webbly) is one reason for the massive uptake of the web (Holmes 2005). AOL and the initial Netscape browser were both successful products because they made an existing service more usable and more widely accessible. Work in eCommerce suggests that ease of use of existing products and the expected cost of learning to use a new interface can also lead to a type of brand recognition and later to loyalty (Johnson et al. 2003).

Sometimes the usability of a tool does not increase directly through improving an interface but because its utility increases and its frequency of use increases. The decreasing weight (and size) of cell phones has made them easier to carry around, and thus always available. Part of the success of the web arises out of the creation of search engines: Bing, Google, DuckDuckGo, Ask, and the more specific search engines like Citeseer and DBLP (dblp.uni-trier.de) increase the usability of the web by helping users find information based on the topic they are looking for rather than by the location of the information. This increase of usability is not driven by the visual interface, but at a deeper level of supporting the user's tasks.

Users sometimes have problems in understanding what they are looking at. Norman (2013) refers to this as the Gulf of Evaluation. Users also encounter problems in knowing or being able to discover what they have to do to execute their task using a particular interface. Norman describes this as the Gulf of Execution. The Internet examples above are examples where the Gulf of Execution has been made smaller, and thus made more tractable for a wider range of users. We will return to Norman's Gulfs in Chap. 12.

More often, lack of understanding of users leads to some groups of users being excluded. We have worked with web sites that now make sure that they have text versions available to support not only the visually impaired (through text readers and descriptions of pictures), but also two types of users that do not come to mind easily in a US college environment with ubiquitous broadband—those users separated from the site via dialup lines or by vast distances (Ritter et al. 2005).

1.3.2 Benefit 2: Financial Savings

Designing to support users can save companies money, even of the order of millions of dollars. One case is Nynex, the New York telephone company, in the early 1990s. The toll and assistance operators (TAO) are the people who help you when you dial "0". They help customers with collect calls, billing, and other more complex calls. In the early 1990s Nynex was considering upgrading their TAO workstation. They had a room with about 100 of these operators; it was believed that new graphical user workstations could improve productivity. The cost of upgrading all the workstations was going to be about $500,000 (in 1990s dollars). The company engaged a team of applied psychologists to look at how much faster the new workstations would be. The results of a task analysis (using a form of GOMS which is described in more detail in Chap. 11) suggested that the new workstations would not be faster, but would, in fact, be 4% slower to operate. This may seem like a small difference, but a 4% reduction in productivity was going to cost Nynex $2.4 million a year—in addition to the cost of the workstations.

Nynex ran a study to discover how much faster the new workstations would really be. After allowing time for the operators to learn to use the workstations, the operators' performance plateaued about where it was predicted—4% slower. NYNEX now claims that this study saved them $2.4 million per year. The user study paid for itself in the first week (see Gray et al. 1992, 1993 for more details). The slowdown in operator performance was not caused by the fact that the new workstations simply required the user to take more steps to achieve the same goal. The reason was the new interface did not allow multi-tasking; the operators could not type while waiting for the caller to speak which they could with the old. Improved computer processor speed could not compensate for the loss in parallel activity the users had with the previous design.

The NYNEX example reveals the benefits of considering people—in this case the operators—even when there does not appear to be a problem. In many instances the main advantage of studying people using systems—that is, conducting "user studies"—is to identify where people make errors, so that we can prevent them or mitigate their consequences in the final product. People often do not type what they want to type, and sometimes push buttons that they did not intend to push. Strangely enough, this problem can be more prevalent amongst highly-skilled expert users, than amongst beginners. Errors that occur when someone knows the right thing to do, but accidentally does something different, are commonly referred to as 'slips' to distinguish them from mistakes, where the action is taken on the basis of an incorrect plan (Norman 1981; Reason 1990).

These slips can also occur on well-practiced interfaces that do not attempt to catch such slips. These slips can also be very expensive. A local paper (Centre Daily Times, 15 Feb 2002, p. C38) reported that a financial services firm lost up to $100 million because it executed a sell order of 610,000 shares at 16 yen instead of the correct order of 16 shares at 610,000 yen (approximately 100 yen/US$).

In a review of the application of user models to evaluate Army systems, Booher and Minninger (2003) report many instances where millions of dollars over the course of a device's lifetime were saved by better interface design, through reduced training, for example. They also highlight several cases where systems had to be scrapped or modified at great expense because they were not usable.

Use of machines that have different modes can often mislead users into making errors. Photocopier machines that can be used to send faxes have a common problem. The default mode of these machines is to copy, but users may not realize this. Users may type in the area code (say, the U.S. area code 415) as the starting point for sending a fax, but the copier interprets this as a request to make 415 copies of the document that the user intended to send as a fax! More explicit displays and more intelligent systems might attempt to catch this type of error. Photocopies may be relatively cheap, but this type of problem with airline tickets, machine tools, or photographic films quickly become expensive.

1.3.3 Benefit 3: Safer Systems

Much of the work that has made airplanes the safest transportation per passenger mile (Gigerenzer 2004) has gone into supporting pilots and air traffic controllers to avoid and, more importantly, catch and recover from errors. This has led to a drastic decrease in accidents previously ascribed to 'pilot error'. As the cause of these accidents were typically attributed to well-trained and alert pilots, it is fairer to diagnose these errors as poor fits between the pilot's capabilities and the machine at particular times and for particular sets of tasks. Improving this fit thus improved airplane safety.

Medicine provides a rich source of examples too. For instance, interfaces that allow users (e.g., nurses) to type in the digits of a drug dose are inherently more dangerous than those that force users to dial them in using a wheel for each digit (Pew and Mavor 2007). When typing, a repeated digit can increase the dosage by a factor of ten. This type of mistake is not possible with a dial-based interface.

Medical X-ray machines are powerful devices and often offer little margin for error. In addition to their technical requirements, they can have usability problems because their effects are not directly and immediately visible. In the case of radiation treatments for cancer, multiple professionals are involved in their use, from the oncologists and radiologists who specify the treatment, the technicians who administer it, to the physicists who maintain it. There are many examples of where interface design for treatment using X-ray machines and other medical devices have ignored the user's capabilities, tasks, context, or some combination of these, and this has led to loss of life. Perhaps the most famous case is the Therac 25 (Leveson and Turner 1993). Between 1985 and 1987 there were six known accidents involving massive radiation overdoses with the Therac. Notably, such accidents rarely arise from a single cause. The user interface was only one of several contributory factors. In addition to problems with the technology and safety interlocks, the system (including the technician) was poorly prepared to deal with typing mistakes by the technician, and in many installations the level of feedback from the Therac to the radiation technician was not sufficient to help them catch the mistakes sooner.

1.3.4 Cost 1: Understanding the Users Does Not Guarantee Success

Although improving the usability of a system can save lives, lead to product success, and save money, usability is neither a necessary nor sufficient condition for success, nor is it a protection against loss of money or life. Systems with poor usability can still be successful for a variety of reasons. For example, they may offer a functionality that is unique and useful. The earliest versions of planes, computers, printing presses, and satellite phones were all difficult to use, but successful because of their unique functionality.

Products that are well designed with the user in mind may still not be successful. Most or all aspects must be right for a product or system to succeed. Making the usability right does not make the time to market right, it does not make the price appropriate, and other critical aspects such as reliability or marketing may fail.

The system also has to be acceptable to the users. The interface may be well designed on a local level, but if it clashes too much with existing practice (even if the new system is correct) it can quickly fall into disuse (e.g., see Baxter et al. 2005). Similarly, if management does not appropriately support the transition to the new system, it may also fall into disuse. Glashko and Tabas (2009) argue that to understand success you need to understand the user, the business model, and the technology.

The lack of usability can be a sufficient reason for *failure* and this is sometimes overlooked. For some systems, however, usability is not the biggest risk to success. Indeed there are many factors that contribute to success, and none of them on their own are necessary or sufficient to guarantee success. Pew and Mavor (2007) suggest taking a risk driven spiral-based approach to development to deal with this; we describe this approach later in the book.

1.3.5 Cost 2: Knowing When to Stop Analyzing the Users can be Difficult

Knowing when you should stop analyzing the users and start building your system is a difficult problem to address. It is an ongoing issue for HCI (and system design in general) that should be able to demonstrate a worthwhile return on investment. Nielsen (1993), for example, argues that many usability-related design problem issues can be identified by studying a small numbers of users (about five to eight). The caveats are that the results of this approach are highly dependent on the types of users involved and the particular interface. As yet there are no hard and fast rules that can be applied to all systems which will tell you when to stop the user analysis and start building.

The traditional approach to systems deployment largely focused on making the users fit the system. In other words, companies employed the right people (selected using psychometric testing, qualifications, and so on) and, where necessary, trained them as a way to bridge any remaining gaps between the system and the users. This approach has become increasingly unacceptable as people have become better informed about technology and now expect to use it out of the box, In addition, there have been recent political changes which require that systems are accessible to more people (e.g., the Americans with Disabilities Act), rendering the idea of fitting the user to the system less unacceptable.

It is now generally the case that you should design (or re-design) your system to make it fit your users. We would strongly argue that you need to think right from the very start of the project about your users, the tasks they will perform using your system, and the context in which your system will be used. In other words, when you are defining the system's functional requirements, you should also be defining the usability requirements.

The level of detail required here should be guided by the associated risks involved. If you only talk to developers as proxy users to determine usability requirements, for example, there is a large risk that the delivered system will not be acceptable to the real end users because the proxy users will not understand how the real users will carry out their work using the system in a work context that may constrain how the system can be used. If your system will be used in extreme or safety critical environments (e.g., in space or aviation), for example, your users will be highly skilled practitioners making decisions and performing actions in a limited time frame, where the results may have life or death importance. These risks are increased if the designers are unlike the users (Casper and Murphy 2003 provides a nice case study). In these cases we recommend that you do some background work in the domain, looking at existing systems similar to the one you are designing and consulting appropriate resources such as books, as well meeting the users and seeing their context and tasks and running some studies to test out your ideas and develop your understanding of the system's context.

For simple, straightforward systems developed for your own purposes (like many systems that are used in research, for example), you may not need to worry too much about the design of the user interface. Even for very small numbers of expert users it may not be worthwhile spending large amounts of time and effort on developing the user interface because the costs may well exceed the benefits.

Often your population of users will be heterogeneous, and if you are not aware of this heterogeneity you could end up disenfranchising large sections of your users. We have worked with web sites that now incorporate text versions so that they can also support the visually impaired (through screen readers and descriptions of pictures), and users that access the web via low speed connections, such as dialup lines or from very remote locations (Ritter et al. 2005). Neither of these types of users is likely to be the same as many designers.

Although there is no general solution to the question of when to stop analyzing the user and start building the system, Pew and Mavor's (2007) approach provides a subjective answer. In their risk driven approach, the risks to success are re-evaluated as the design process progresses. In some cases, progress with the technology is the largest risk to success; in others, not knowing the user and their tasks will be the largest risk. So Pew and Mavor's answer is that you should study the user and their tasks until the risk of not knowing more about them is lower than the other risks to success. As noted above, we will return to describe this approach in more detail in the final chapter, Chap. 14.

1.4 Summarizing Design Relevant User Characteristics: The ABCS Framework

The purpose of this book is to help you to come up with principled opinions about what designs are most likely to be effective. We introduce the idea of *design relevant user characteristics*. Attempts to define a complete list of human characteristics stretch from hundreds (e.g., Brown 1988) to thousands of pages (Boff and Lincoln 1988; Salvendy 1997). Table 1.2 offers some examples that are often discussed, taken from Brown (1988).

To help organize design relevant human characteristics, we offer a framework that we call the ABCS. The abbreviation represents four aspects of users that often need to be examined when designing systems:

A   Anthropometrics: the shape of the body and how it influences what is designed; consideration of the physical characteristics of intended users such as what size they are, what muscle strength they have, and so on

B   Behavior: perceptual and motivational characteristics, looking at what people can perceive and why they do what they do

C   Cognition: learning, attention, and other aspects of cognition and how these processes influence design; users defined by how they think and what they know and what knowledge they can acquire

S   Social factors: how groups of users behave, and how to support them through design; users defined by where they are—their context broadly defined including their relationships to other people.

We now briefly explain each of these areas in more detail.

Table 1.2 Human characteristics relevant for system design

* Physical characteristics, limitations, and disabilities
* Perceptual abilities, strengths, and weaknesses
* Frequency of product use
* Past experience with same/similar product
* Activity "mental set" (the attitude toward and level of motivation you have for the activity)
* Tolerance for error
* Patience and motivation for learning
* Culture/language/population expectations and norms

1.4.1 Anthropometrics Approach

Anthropometrics is concerned with the physical aspects of the user and the system. For example, Fig. 1.4 shows an input glove. How do people use this? What are their natural movements in it, and do these movements change with a glove on? How long can they use it before becoming fatigued or hurt by it? The answers to questions like these would involve resolving the issues in Table 1.3.

These physical aspects are often studied in the area of human factors and ergonomics and applied to standard office equipment like desks and chairs. A lot is known about how to improve the fit of the hardware to the user's body, including back, knees, waist, and arms (Pheasant and Haslegrave 2006). The optimal work surface height, for example, varies by the individual concerned but also by the task to be performed.

It is also important that we consider whether we need to design for individuals (e.g., desk setups need to be specifically tailored to avoid upper limb disorders), for the average (e.g., seats in buses and trains are designed for averages), or for extremes (e.g., plane ejector seats). For example, Ted Williams, the famous American baseball player and fighter aircraft pilot, reportedly crash-landed a plane rather than eject so that he would be able to play baseball again after the Korean war—the design error was that ejector seats were designed for the average height of a pilot, which left those in the upper 5–10% of the height range in danger of damaged or removed kneecaps if they ejected.[1]

In computer systems these problems include making sure that controls (knobs, dials, buttons, and so on) are of a size that can be manipulated by a wide range of users. Weight and button size are important for their usability and the perceived usability for their marketing. For example, the release of many different sizes of interactive tablet computers into the market over recent years suggests the physical sizes of these devices matter for different use scenarios. Early mobile phones were

---

[1]   http://www.tedwilliams.com/index.php?page=burnjet

Fig. 1.4 An input glove.
(Photo taken by and used
with permission of Georgios
Christou)

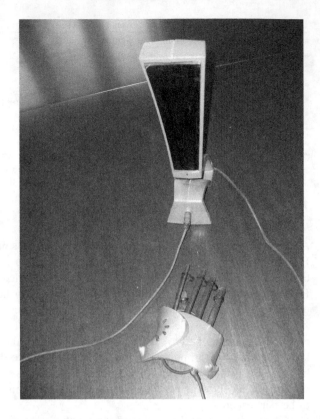

Table 1.3 Example usability issues arising from the anthropometric level

- Providing normative data on limb sizes, body weight/height, and so on
- Providing descriptions of how sensitive touch is for input and output, particularly for the hands
- Measurement of muscle strain (to assess length of time on a particular job)
- Measurement of posture during particular tasks (to facilitate redesign of equipment)

the size of briefcases, and laptops weighed 30 pounds; these failed to be as popular as expected partly because they were not small enough.

These issues are equally important in the design of mobile devices. Weight and button size are important for their usability and the perceived usability for their marketing. These issues will be more important for reality-based interfaces, where computing is embedded into objects such as passports, children's toys, and objects that have RFID tags which allow them to be tracked. These interfaces include both computational aspects as well as the physical nature of the objects and the opportunities and constraints that physical realization provides.

Table 1.4 Example usability issues arising from the behavioral level

Car interfaces—questions of legibility of characters, avoidance of glare in bright sunlight, avoiding parallax problems with different heights of drivers, and making sure that the dials are not obscured by the steering wheel

Making knobs and levers tactually discriminable to enable them to be used without looking to check whether the correct control is being used (e.g., putting a wheel on the landing gear lever in a plane)

Problem of ascertaining the physical actions of how something is used, to see whether it can be made quicker/safer/more productive, and so on

Looking at simple errors (slips of action) that are made, to see how they can be mitigated or prevented

Table 1.5 The original Fitts (1951) list

Humans appear to surpass present-day (i.e., 1951) machines with respect to:
- Ability to detect small amounts of visual or acoustic energy
- Ability to perceive patterns of light or sound
- Ability to improvise and use flexible procedures
- Ability to store very large amounts of information for long periods and to recall relevant facts at the appropriate time
- Ability to reason inductively
- Ability to exercise judgment

Present-day machines appear to surpass humans with respect to:
- Ability to respond quickly to control signals, and to apply great force smoothly and precisely
- Ability to perform repetitive, routine tasks
- Ability to store information briefly and then to erase it completely
- Ability to reason deductively, including computational ability
- Ability to handle highly complex operations, that is, to do many different things at once

1.4.2 Behavioral Aspects

When we discuss the behavioral aspects of the user, we refer to the basic behaviors users can produce. The behavioral level builds on the anthropometric level as the physical aspects of the body are used to produce simple behaviors. Table 1.4 provides several examples, drawing on a wide range of application areas.

Behavioral analysis has supported and led to the creation of checklists of those tasks best performed by humans and those best performed by machines. Table 1.5 shows an example of such a list, where human and machine tasks could be assigned on the basis of better fit. Such lists have been critiqued for being too static (Sheridan 1992), but the exercise of making such lists, updated according to technological innovations and changes in human expectations and abilities through training, can be useful. An excellent example of the evolution of the way we think about task allocation is the recent success of IBM's Watson system. Historically, because humans reason creatively and inductively through association and using mnemonics, they could easily beat computers on standard general knowledge tests. However, since the advent of the Internet, which represents a massive database of general knowledge that has been supplied through untold hours of human content contribution and improvements in computational processing power and search algorithms, it is possible for a machine, Watson, to beat a human at such tests. What we see in this example is that the notion of even what a *machine* is can change over time. Therefore, when considering allocation of processing activities between humans and computational devices, we need to ensure we are using the most appropriate sense of the term *machine*.

We also include simple interaction at the behavioral level. For example, Norman (2013) has written about "forcing functions". These are aspects of devices that suggest particular uses or styles of interaction. In some cases, affordances force a particular style of interaction. One of Norman's favorite examples is door design. Doors with handles suggest that they should be pulled, while doors without handles suggest that they should be pushed. A *forcing function* would be where the door with the handle cannot be pushed, thus forcing that it be pulled. Violation of these affordances (doors that can only be pushed yet have handles) leads to confusion. Perceptual issues sit between the behavior and cognition. For example, PowerPoint presentations where the font is too small means people cannot read the content unless they move physically closer (Kosslyn 2007).

In addition to noting the basic foundations that explain *how* people behave, we also have to consider *why* people behave in the way that they do. The motivation that people have for performing particular tasks will vary, partly depending on internal factors, but also partly on external factors (e.g., is it a work task, is it being carried out in an informal setting, and so on.)

1.4.3 Cognition

The cognitive level uses the previous two levels and builds upon them. On this level, how the user thinks about their task and the system is considered, as well as both basic and higher level cognitive capabilities. These capabilities include a variety of memory systems that the user has available, as well how these memories are organized and how they are used by a central processor. Higher level constructs include how attention and learning affect these structures and processes. Some example cognitive issues are shown in Table 1.6.

Work on the cognitive level will often involve observation of the tool/environment in use, asking the question of why and when is it used? This is necessary because users will vary more on this level of analysis than on the previous two levels. On this level, people will vary based on previous experience, which can include training, formal education, previous use, personal style, and strategy choice.

Table 1.6 Example cognitive level issues

How do users decide where to look for information?

What information do users need to develop a strategy for performing a particular task? Do they need absolute or relative values?

How much experience do the users have with the task and with the interface?

What is the user's mental model of the interface and task (which will often differ from the designer's or the observer's mental model of the same interface and task)?

Is there so much noise and interruption that users cannot process information, for example, the interruptions in the Kegworth aircraft crash?

How can users tell if things are not going well? What feedback do they get? What strategies are available to the user when the system goes wrong?

How can we ensure that users do not lose their ability to perform the task manually as a result of automation?

How can word processors be made more accessible to novice users or casual users? How do these factors change when the systems considered are more complex?

A better understanding of how users think and feel can be used to create better designs. An improved system can come from understanding the mental effort involved in tasks in terms of the information processing mechanisms (architecture) that support our thinking, including constraints such as how many arbitrary symbols users can remember. These issues may help us to understand how complex devices with high functionality (e.g., personal video recorders) can be made more accessible to non-expert users by providing information, by guiding the user, and by not asking them to perform difficult tasks (like remembering more than their short-term memory can hold).

For example, consider the fairly common task of determining differences between two or more items. Imagine you had two dials to read, each with a different number, and these numbers varied randomly. Your task is to press a button when the difference between the two numbers exceeds 10. This task would require you to process the information from both dials, make a mental calculation and evaluate whether the difference exceeds 10. The existence of a third dial which just showed the difference would make your task easier and faster, removing the need for the mental calculation (the cognitive effort).

1.4.4 Social Factors

The final level is the social level. How do users interact with other people in relation to their task? In some cases this interaction will be to work on the task jointly with others using the computer to support and mediate their communication. In other cases, users will ask other users for help in understanding systems, or will use the system for, or with others (such as bank tellers, loan officers, and airline pilots), or the interaction could be constrained by some regulatory authority (as in aviation and the nuclear power industry).

Table 1.7 Example issues on the social level

- A crew distracted by interruptions that failed to complete a safety checklist did not confirm that the aeroplane's flaps were extended, causing the plane to crash on take-off
- A co-pilot failed to get the attention of a more senior captain about concerns that take-off thrust was not properly set, causing the aircraft to crash into a river
- A communications breakdown between captain, co-pilot, and air traffic control on the amount of fuel in the plane caused a crash when the fuel ran out
- You want to buy the same video game as your best friend so you can play him at your house, and so you can practice to beat him!

Like the previous levels, this level builds upon and uses the constructs and theories of the previous level. In this case, the cognitive level, including the mental models of others, is particularly important.

The motivation that people have for performing particular tasks and working in teams will vary, partly depending on internal factors but also partly on external factors (e.g., is it a work task, is it being carried out in an informal setting, and so on).

The social level can be very important. Many of the accidents in safety–critical systems, for example planes, have their roots in the dynamics of the social processes between people controlling various parts of the systems, and their social environment. Perhaps the most typical failure is for a subordinate not to tell a superior or not to tell them forcefully enough about an impending problem, which then becomes unmanageable because of the delay. Simple failures in inter-personal communications can also cause accidents. Table 1.7 lists some further examples of issues on the social level.

Flowers (1997) explains how the task of moving the London ambulance dispatching system from paper to computer went wrong. The designers seriously misunderstood how the dispatchers worked, how the drivers worked, and how the two groups worked together. There were also software development and implementation problems. While no loss of life was reported, ambulance response times were seriously compromised, the director was sacked, and about 3 million pounds ($4.5 million) worth of development was written off. This is an example where social factors were ignored in system design.

Organizational, professional, and national cultural issues—how users from different cultural backgrounds have different characteristics—are also grouped under this heading in this book. Examples of these differences include how colors can mean different things in different cultures: green does not always mean go, and white may be the traditional color for funeral dress rather than black. Other examples include how the most natural ordering of objects may be left to right in many cultures but right to left in others, and how some cultures encourage appropriate questioning of people in responsible positions (such as aircraft pilots), whilst others frown upon it.

As can be seen from the Kegworth air disaster (described in the Appendix), the cabin crew (as well as the passengers) knew that the wrong engine may have been turned off, but did not interrupt the pilots, possibly because of the high social status accorded to the pilots. This type of cultural issue, where someone knows something that could help a team or a project and does not raise the issue, is a well documented problem. How to adjust appropriately the social dynamics to fix problems like this remains an important and interesting problem.

Another example comes from a nuclear power plant in Europe. A reporting system was set up to allow staff to report incidents (near misses) so that the company could learn from them to try and prevent the same thing happening (Masson 1991). This was all working fine, and management and staff had settled into using the system. Staff were happy to report incidents and were not blamed when the incidents did occur. The management then decided that they would change the (negotiated) culture, in which the emphasis had been on reporting incidents, to one that focused on incidents as a measure of safety, and decided that the shift that reported the least incidents would be regarded as the safest shift and would receive some reward.

The net effect was that staff stopped reporting incidents in a bid to make their shift appear to be the safest. In the end a new incident reporting system had to be developed, and all the data about the unreported incidents was lost because the management had unwittingly changed the culture from one that was designed to use reported problems as a way of learning and improving safety to one that was effectively designed to reward the lack of reporting of problems.

1.5 Simulating User Characteristics: Cognitive Architectures

One of the main aims of this book is to help you to develop a better understanding of why users do things the way they do. Understanding the way users think and behave will help you design systems that support users. The ABCS framework, described above, provides one way of organizing this information about user characteristics. It is also possible to encapsulate relevant details in a model. For example, if one is interested specifically in human information processing, cognitive architectures provide a convenient way of modeling human information processing under different conditions, because they include mechanisms that are specifically designed for modeling human cognition.

Figure 1.5 is a schematic of the major components of a computer model of a user. The major components in this model are designed to mimic the major components of users. The top box, ACT-R, refers to a simplified form of the ACT-R cognitive architecture (Anderson and Lebiere 1998). (There are other architectures, but they are similar for our purposes.) In this instance the architecture has been combined with an extension that allows it to interact effectively with the external world. So the combined cognitive architecture takes the bitmap from a computer screen and, in a process approximating vision, computes the objects and some of their features in the image and puts the results into a perceptual buffer.

Fig. 1.5 A representation of
the ACT-R cognitive
architecture with the SegMan
extension to allow it to
interact with interfaces
through computer bitmaps

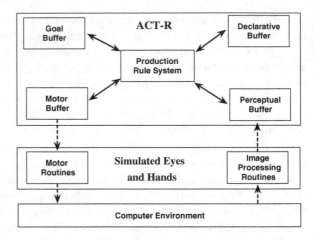

This perceptual buffer represents many of the aspects of the human vision system. Similar buffers should be created for hearing and the other senses.

At the center of the architecture is a reasoning system that can access information in the perceptual buffer and access and modify information in the declarative memory and goal buffers. It uses the information in these buffers to guide its processing, using a process that mimics human behavior. Output actions to the external world are put into a motor buffer, where motor routines generate the results.

This representation is somewhat generic and far from complete, but illustrates a theory of the major information processing components of the user. There are other theories of how users process information, and even the ACT-R theory has changed over time. Work is ongoing to apply this approach to create models of users that can be used to test interfaces (e.g., Byrne 2001; Freed and Remington 2000; Kieras et al. 1997), to serve as intelligent colleagues (Weiland et al. 2002) and opponents in computer-based games and simulations (e.g., Jones et al. 1999; Laird and van Lent 2001; Tambe et al. 1995), and to summarize our knowledge of human behavior (e.g., Anderson et al. 2004; Jones et al. 2000; Lovett et al. 2000).

1.6 Summary

This chapter has introduced the study of people who use artifacts (i.e., *users*), given you some definitions and useful terms, and provided an overview to organize your further reading. We have also highlighted some common (mistaken) pre-conceptions about what makes for good design and noted why studying users is important. In particular, we have introduced the concept of the fundamental attribution error of design, where designers think that users are like themselves, which is very often not the case.

We believe that understanding users is fundamentally important and often leads to more *usable* systems. There are costs as well as benefits associated with studying and understanding users, however, and it is important to realize when you should decide to stop analyzing the users and start building your system. A risk-based approach to development can help inform this decision. We explain this more fully in the Chap. 14 that you might wish to preview.

The information about users' design related capabilities can be organized using the ABCS framework to encapsulate people's physical shape, how they perceive, how they think, and how they interact with other people. This simple abbreviation can be used to remember the information and to guide your considerations during system design. Chapters 3–10 cover these levels.

We also introduced the idea of cognitive architectures, which can be used to develop models that simulate how people perceive, think, and act. Although we used the ACT-R architecture as an exemplar, other cognitive architectures could also be used to organize and apply knowledge about users. We take up this approach again in the Chap. 14.

1.6.1 Structure of the Rest of the Book

You can think of the book as being divided into four parts. The first two chapters introduce the notion of user centered design and examine the underlying history.

The second part of the book (Chaps. 3–10) examines specific characteristics of the user. Our perspective draws heavily on psychology. We focus on the sensory and cognitive, information processing, aspects of the user, partly because this is where our expertise lies, but also because much interaction requires people to sense, understand, communicate, and learn. We limit our discussions to the topics that are most relevant to designers while also offering pointers to those people who want to read more about these topics.

The third part of the book (Chaps. 11–13) introduces some methods that can be used to inform and evaluate design. This is an active area of application and research, and there are now so many different approaches that it would be impossible to cover them all here.

The book concludes with a short summary (Chap. 14). This highlights how you can organize what you have learned about users and notes some possible directions that are currently being explored to apply it.

On completing this book you will have acquired an understanding of humans and their behavior when interacting with complex, interactive systems. You will have sufficient grounding to be better able to design systems that take appropriate account of your users, their tasks, and the context in which they perform those tasks. You will be able to justify how (and why) a particular design is appropriate from a conceptual level down to a practical level, using the toolbox of methods and techniques that we have placed at your disposal.

Table 1.8 Some remaining problems in contemporary system design

- The size of systems and diversity of users and tasks are increasing. How are we to find, represent, and use this information?
- The complexity of the systems is increasing: users do not always get adequate feedback on what is going on, and cannot see the internal state of the system. Norman (2013) provides further examples. How are we to keep users informed without overwhelming them with information?
- The nuances of social and organization factors and the communication of these nuances through computer supported communication are not fully understood and predictable. How can designers get and use this information? How can it be represented?
- How can we improve the usability of designer's tools to help them improve usability for users?
- Studies of the user need to go beyond recommendations about the design of technology—can we offer a conceptual basis for these recommendations? One approach is to create a unified theory of how users behave, but this theory has not yet been fully created or made available for automatic application
- With further understanding come questions about lower and higher levels. Once we know how users work in small groups we can see that larger groups also have influence as do previous groups who used the system. What is this information and how do we include this information?
- Esthetics and emotions are difficult factors to explain and quantify. Users, particularly users of personal and home technologies, generally care about how the system looks and what pleasure it gives them, sometimes irrespective of how it works or how well it works. In these areas, then, esthetics is closely related to acceptability, and there is some evidence of a high correlation between esthetics and usability (e.g., Tractinsky 1997). The inter-relationship between usability, functionality, emotional responses, and esthetics, however, still needs to be worked out

1.6.2 Future Work

You should now be aware that there is a lot to be learned about users. While technology can change rapidly basic user capabilities and characteristics change slowly, if at all. It is important to be aware of critical user characteristics, their relative importance for a design, and their likelihood of change over time.

There is also much more that needs to be learned. As you read the rest of this book, you should become aware of the remaining problems, some of which are listed in Table 1.8.

1.7 Other Resources

Here we note some further books and online resources.

The books by Christopher Wickens (Wickens et al. 1998; Wickens and Hollands 2000) provide more details than this book does. These books focus more on human factors and physical engineering of workplace.

The books by Preece et al. (2002) and Dix, Finlay, Abowd, and Beale, both titled *Human–Computer Interaction*, and *Interaction Design: Beyond Human–*

Computer Interaction, 3rd Edition, by Sharp, Rogers, and Preece are all worth a closer look. These books include more on technology and on designing interface technology rather than focusing in detail on the various aspects of the users that affect interaction. Clayton Lewis and John Rieman's shareware book: *Task-Centered User Interface Design*, hcibib.org/tcuid/ covers similar material but focuses more on design and task analyses, and does not include as much psychology. It helps put the material in this book into perspective for design purposes.

Descriptions of design failures often make interesting reading, and their lesson can sometimes be generalized to other systems. For large systems, Petroski's (1985) book is one of the most popular. Petroski's observation that engineering has progressed over the centuries by learning from failure also applies to interface design. The ACM Committee on Computers and Public Policy's Risks Digest at catless.ncl.ac.uk/Risks/ provides numerous examples of where poor usability has led to problems.

There are many online resources available on HCI and human factors. The HCI Bibliography Project, hcibib.org, provides an online bibliography of papers in journals and conferences related to HCI. The Computer–Human Interaction Special Interest Group of the Association for Computing Machinery (ACM-SIGCHI) has a very useful web site at www.acm.org/sigchi/ They organize the CHI conference every year, as well as producing a magazine, *interactions*.

You can also examine the design and graphic design literature to understand esthetics better. There are books on the design of graphic information (e.g., Tufte 1990), on the design of pages (e.g., White 2002), on the design of fonts, page layouts, graphics, and so on. If you are interested in this area, consider looking through libraries (personal, institutional, and public), using search engines, and consulting academic course catalogues, all of which can provide you with much more information.

Don Norman's books, including the classic *The design of everyday things*[2] (1988/2013), provide a useful set of examples of why design matters. At times the examples may seem small, but in nearly every case their impact is magnified by the number of people affected, the possible severity of the consequences, or their clarity. Many people have been convinced of the importance of HCI as a result of reading this book.

The importance of esthetics should not be underestimated, even though we do not cover it in any great detail here. Jordan (2000), for example, argues that esthetics of devices will increase over time. When systems are equivalent, it may be the case that their users differentiate between them on the basis of how pleasing their appearance is. Some researchers have found that pleasing interfaces work better (Helander and Tham 2003), and Norman (2006, 2009) argues this position repeatedly, including that esthetics and functionality should be considered equally important.

---

[2]   Also published sometimes as *The psychology of everyday things*.

[3]   A millisecond is a thousandth of a second, and is abbreviated ms.

1	File	Home	Insert	Page Layout		References		Mailings	Review		View	

1   File   Home   Insert   Page Layout   References   Mailings   Review   View

2   Home   Insert   Page Layout   References   Mailings   Review   View   Add-Ins

3   [OS Icon] Word   File   Edit   View   Insert   Format   Font   Tools   Table   Window   Work   Help

4   File   Edit   View   Insert   Format   Tools   Table   Window   Help

5   Home   File   Insert   Page   References   Layout   Review   View   Help

6   Home   File   Edit   View   Insert   Font   Tools   Review   Window   Help

7   [OS Icon]   File   Edit   View   Insert   Font   Tools   Review   Window   Help

8   [OS Icon]   Home   View   File   Insert   Review   Layout   Table   Work

9   Word   Home   File   Insert   Page Layout   References   Review   View   Help

10   [OS Icon]   File   Edit   View   Format   Arrange   Inspectors   Stencils   Window   Help

Fig. 1.6 Possible views of the top menu on MS Word. Without looking at Word, which of the ten menus is the one you use?

1.8 Exercises

1.1 The correct ranked order for the buttons in Fig. 1.1 is as follows: (a) (411 ms[3]), (d) (469 ms), (b) and (c) (each 539 ms). The lights in D have a simple rule that users can follow– look to the diagonal. The lights in B and C have two rules (or at least a more complex rule): if the lights are in the middle, hit the button below; if the lights are on the end, hit the diagonal button. The extra conditions, or rules, take extra time to learn and extra time to perform. They would also lead to more errors.

Ask some of your friends and or family to choose the best designs in Figs. 1.1 and 1.2. How do they compare to your performance and to Payne's subjects? If you have access to interface designers, ask them. How does your own stove compare to these mappings? What do your results mean for interface design?

1.2 In Fig. 1.3 the correct coin is Penny A. The point is, most people do not memorize the features of objects in detail, they memorize just enough to recognize and differentiate the coin from typical distracters, like other legal coins, or to find the right menu item when it is in front of them. Try this simple test for the penny with your friends, and also ask computer users to identify the correct Word menu in Fig. 1.6.

1.3 Consider a mobile device (such as a smartphone or tablet). What difficulties might people encounter in using the device for the first time? What difficulties might people have in understanding how to use it and what to do with it? How would they go about learning how to use it?

---

[3] A millisecond is a thousandth of a second, and is abbreviated ms.

Write short notes (about one side of a page) on some of these issues you have identified, classifying them as anthropometric, behavioral, cognitive, or social. Think about what design changes you might make to the device to make it easier for novices to use.

1.4 Consider an airplane crash like Kegworth, the Asiana in San Francisco, or another one where you can obtain some of the details. Classify the problems that led to the disaster with respect to the four levels introduced here. Summarize what level was the most important and could have stopped the disaster.

1.5 Select something you use every day that you think is well designed. Think about why this is well designed. You may wish to consider esthetics, mappings of actions to responses, how you learned to use it, and what kinds of mistakes or errors you still make.

1.6 What are some other payoffs from studying the user? As ways to brainstorm, consider the types of outputs the various fields related to users would provide. As another hint, consider fields that study users or aspects of users, and consider what they might want from interfaces or from interactions with interfaces or systems.

References

Anderson, J. R., & Lebiere, C. (1998). *The atomic components of thought.* Mahwah, NJ: Erlbaum.

Anderson, J. R., Bothell, D., Byrne, M. D., Douglass, S., Lebiere, C., & Qin, Y. (2004). An integrated theory of the mind. *Psychological Review, 111*(4), 1036–1060.

Baxter, G. D., Monk, A. F., Tan, K., Dear, P. R. F., & Newell, S. J. (2005). Using cognitive task analysis to facilitate the integration of decision support systems into the neonatal intensive care unit. *Artificial Intelligence in Medicine, 35,* 243–257.

Boff, K. R., & Lincoln, J. E. (Eds.). (1988). *Engineering data compendium (User's guide).* Wright-Patterson Air Force Base, OH: Harry G. Armstrong Aerospace Medical Research Laboratory.

Booher, H. R., & Minninger, J. (2003). Human systems integration in army systems acquisition. In H. R. Booher (Ed.), *Handbook of human systems integration* (pp. 663–698). Hoboken, NJ: John Wiley.

Brown, C. M. L. (1988). *Human-computer interface design guidelines.* Norwood, NJ: Ablex.

Bruce, V., Gilmore, D., Mason, L., & Mayhew, P. (1983). Factors affecting the perceived value of coins. *Journal of Economic Psychology, 4*(4), 335–347.

Byrne, M. D. (2001). ACT-R/PM and menu selection: Applying a cognitive architecture to HCI. *International Journal of Human-Computer Studies, 55*(1), 41–84.

Casper, J., & Murphy, R. (2003). Human-robot interactions during the robot-assisted urban search and rescue response at the World Trade Center. *IEEE Transactions on Systems, Man, and Cybernetics Part B, 33*(3), 367–385.

Chapanis, A., & Lindenbaum, L. E. (1959). A reaction time study of four control-display linkages. *Human Factors, 1*(4), 1–7.

Ericsson, K. A., & Simon, H. A. (1993). *Protocol analysis: Verbal reports as data* (2nd ed.). Cambridge, MA: MIT Press.

Fitts, P. M. (1951). Engineering psychology and equipment design. In S. S. Stevens (Ed.), *Handbook of experimental psychology* (pp. 1287–1340). New York, NY: John Wiley.

Flowers, S. (1997). *Software failure: Management failure... Amazing stories and cautionary tales.* New York, NY: Wiley.

Freed, M., & Remington, R. (2000). Making human-machine system simulation a practical engineering tool: An APEX overview. In *Proceedings of the 3rd International Conference on Cognitive Modelling* (pp. 110–117). Veenendaal, The Netherlands: Universal Press.

Gigerenzer, G. (2004). Dread risk, september 11, and fatal traffic accidents. *Psychological Science, 15*(4), 286–287.

Glushko, R. J., & Tabas, L. (2009). Designing service systems by bridging the "front stage" and "back stage". *Information Systems and e-Business Management, 7*(4), 407–427.

Gray, W. D., John, B. E., & Atwood, M. E. (1992). The precis of project Ernestine or an overview of a validation of GOMS. In *Proceedings of the CHI'92 Conference on Human Factors in Computer Systems*. New York, NY: ACM Press.

Gray, W. D., John, B. E., & Atwood, M. E. (1993). Project Ernestine: Validating a GOMS analysis for predicting and explaining real-world task performance. *Human-Computer Interaction, 8*(3), 237–309.

Helander, M. G., & Tham, M. P. (2003). Hedonomics: Affective human factors design. *Ergonomics, 46*(13/14), 1269–1272.

Holmes, N. (2005). The Internet, the Web, and the Chaos. *IEEE Computer, 38*(108), 106–107.

Johnson, E. J., Bellman, S., & Lohse, G. L. (2003). Cognitive lock-in and the power law of practice. *Journal of Marketing, 67*, 62–75.

Jones, G., Ritter, F. E., & Wood, D. J. (2000). Using a cognitive architecture to examine what develops. *Psychological Science, 11*(2), 93–100.

Jones, R. M., Laird, J. E., Nielsen, P. E., Coulter, K. J., Kenny, P., & Koss, F. V. (1999). Automated intelligent pilots for combat flight simulation. *AI Magazine, 20*(1), 27–41.

Jordan, P. W. (2000). *Designing pleasurable products*. London: Taylor & Francis.

Kieras, D. E., Wood, S. D., & Meyer, D. E. (1997). Predictive engineering models based on the EPIC architecture for a multimodal high-performance human-computer interaction task. *Transactions on Computer-Human Interaction, 4*(3), 230–275.

Kosslyn, S. M. (2007). *Clear and to the point: 8 psychological principles for creating compelling Powerpoint presentations*. New York, NY: Oxford University Press.

Laird, J. E., & van Lent, M. (2001). Human-level AI's killer application: Interactive computer games. *AI Magazine, 22*(2), 15–26.

Leveson, N. G., & Turner, C. S. (1993). An investigation of the Therac-25 accidents. *IEEE Computer, 26*(7), 18–41.

Lovett, M. C., Daily, L. Z., & Reder, L. M. (2000). A source activation theory of working memory: Cross-task prediction of performance in ACT-R. *Journal of Cognitive Systems Research, 1*, 99–118.

Masson, M. (1991). Understanding, reporting and preventing human fixation errors. In T. W. v. d. Schaaf, D. A. Lucas & A. Hale (Eds.), *Near miss reporting as a safety tool* (pp. 35–50). Oxford, UK: Butterworth-Heinemann.

Nickerson, R. S., & Adams, M. J. (1979). Long-term memory for a common object. *Cognitive Psychology, 11*, 287–307.

Nielsen, J. (1993). *Usability engineering*. Chestnut Hill, MA: AP Professional Press.

Norman, D. A. (1981). Categorization of action slips. *Psychological Review, 88*, 1–15.

Norman, D. A. (2006). *Emotional design: Why we love (or hate) everyday things*. New York, NY: Basic Books.

Norman, D. A. (2009). *The design of future things*. New York, NY: Basic Books.

Norman, D. A. (2013). *The design of everyday things*. NY: Basic Books.

Payne, S. J. (1995). Naive judgments of stimulus-response compatibility. *Human Factors, 37*, 495–506.

Petroski, H. (1985/1992). *To engineer is human: The role of failure in successful design*. New York, NY: Vintage Books.

Pew, R. W., & Mavor, A. S. (Eds.). (2007). *Human-system integration in the system development process: A new look*. Washington, DC: National Academies Press. http://books.nap.edu/catalog.php?record_id=11893. Accessed 10 March 2014.

Pheasant, S., & Haslegrave, C. M. (2006). *Bodyspace: Anthropometry, ergonomics, and the design of work* (3rd ed.). Boca Raton, FL: Taylor & Francis.

Preece, J., Rogers, Y., & Sharp, H. (2002). *Interaction design*. New York, NY: Wiley.

Reason, J. (1990). *Human error*. Cambridge, UK: Cambridge University Press.

Ritter, F. E., Freed, A. R., & Haskett, O. L. (2005). User information needs: The case of university department web sites. *ACM interactions, 12*(5), 19–27. acs.ist.psu.edu/acs-lab/reports/ritterFH02.pdf

Salvendy, G. (Ed.). (1997). *Handbook of human factors and ergonomics* (2nd ed.). New York, NY: Wiley.

Sheridan, T. B. (1992). *Telerobotics, automation, and human supervisory control*. Cambridge, MA: MIT Press.

Tambe, M., Johnson, W. L., Jones, R. M., Koss, F., Laird, J. E., Rosenbloom, P. S., et al. (1995). Intelligent agents for interactive simulation environments. *AI Magazine, 16*(1), 15–40.

Tractinsky, N. (1997). Aesthetics and apparent usability: Empirically assessing cultural and methodological issues. In *CHI '97* (pp. 115–122). New York, NY: ACM. http://sigchi.org/chi97/proceedings/paper/nt.htm. Accessed 11 March 2014.

Tufte, E. R. (1990). *Envisioning information*. Cheshire, CT: Graphics Press.

Weiland, W., Szczepkowski, M., Urban, G., Mitchell, T., Lyons, D., & Soles, R. (2002). Reusing cognitive models: Leveraging SCOTT technology in an LCAC virtual training environment. In *Proceedings of the 11th Computer Generated Forces Conference*, 02-CGF-115. Orlando, FL: U. of Central Florida.

White, A. W. (2002). *The elements of graphic design: Space, unity, page architecture, and type*. New York, NY: Allworth Press.

Wickens, C. D., Gordon, S. E., & Liu, Y. (1998). *An introduction to human factors engineering*. New York, NY: Addison-Wesley.

Wickens, C. D., & Hollands, J. G. (2000). *Engineering psychology and human performance* (3rd ed.). Upper Saddle River, NJ: Prentice-Hall.

Chapter 2
User-Centered Systems Design: A Brief History

Abstract The intention of this book is to help you think about design from a user-centered perspective. Our aim is to help you understand what questions to ask when designing a technology or a system or when you are evaluating a design that already exists. We focus on physiological, cognitive, and social aspects of the human user, aspects that will affect how someone will use what you design. This chapter introduces some historical background to the field of User Centered System Design, and introduces current themes.

2.1 Introduction

It has long been recognized that we need to consider human capabilities and characteristics when designing technologies and systems. As Nickerson summarized in 1969, when the potential for computer-based technologies was first being fully recognized: "the need for the future is not so much computer oriented people as for people oriented computers" (Nickerson 1969, p. 178 in the IEEE version).

Since then a number of fields have grown up, expitly concerned with how to design effective technologies and systems that are intended for human use. User-Centered Systems Design (UCSD or HCSD or when the word "human" is used instead of "user"), User Experience (UX), User-Centered Design (UCD), Interaction Design (IxD) and Human–Computer Interaction (HCI) are areas of research that have taken up that call and are concerned with improving how people interact with computers. Each of these has a slightly different focus and breadth, and each encompasses many different approaches. What they all have in common is that they grow their methods and deliverables in response to changes in the technological landscape.

In this chapter we offer an overview of the intellectual roots of these areas of research and development. Early work focused on the learning and use of command-line interfaces and on programming languages. Following the development of now familiar) WIMP interfaces (Windows, Icons, Menus, Pointer) and

F. E. Ritter et al., *Foundations for Designing User-Centered Systems*,
DOI: 10.1007/978-1-4471-5134-0_2, © Springer-Verlag London 2014

Graphical User Interfaces (GUIs), the focus shifted to understanding how to design visual layouts and the optimization of input devices. Developments in the technology of the devices (e.g., mobile computing, embedded computation, and sensor technologies), and in input methods (e.g., sound, vision, and gesture), have led to a proliferation of design and evaluation methods and a focus on the effects of context on user's experiences of devices, applications, and services. Further, as the uses of technology have been ever more democratized—computers are no longer only available to a few expert users—the effects of individual differences or divergences in use by different user populations have also been increasingly of interest (e.g., differences between children and adults, cultural differences in uptake and use, gender differences in use). Research has also focused on much broader concerns, such as the effects of technology design and uptake in terms of social impact and cultural/global sustainability.

2.2 Influential and Related Research Fields

The intellectual roots of User-Centered Design (UCD, also sometimes called User-Centered System Design, UCSD) lie in several areas of basic and applied research. These include:

- Cognitive and social psychology
- Linguistics
- Mathematics
- Computer science
- Engineering
- Human factors and ergonomics
- Socio-technical systems design
- Scientific management
- Work, industrial, and occupational psychology
- Human relations
- Organizational behavior.

User-centered systems designers also draw on basic research in anthropology, sociology, and information science, and in recent years there has been considerable overlap with ideas flowing between UCD researchers and practitioners and those in research areas such as user experience (UX), human–computer interaction, computer supported cooperative work, computer-mediated communication, and ubiquitous/pervasive computing.

Figure 2.1 presents a simple summary of roots of UCD and how they are related. It is deliberately simplistic but should provide you with some insights into how UCD came about.

Fig. 2.1 A pictorial
summary of some of the
fields related to the user. The
major fields are shown with
solid lines

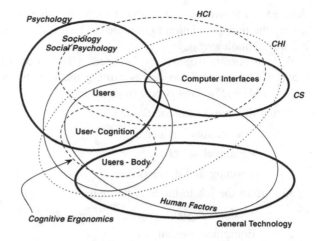

In this section we offer a brief introduction to the fields we consider to be most influential to our approach in this text. These include various branches of human factors and ergonomics, user-centered design, and human–computer interaction.

2.2.1 *Ergonomics and Human Factors*

Derived from the Greek word *ergon* for work and *nomos* for natural laws, ergonomics draws on a number of research areas including anatomy, engineering, physiology, and psychology. The purpose of ergonomics and human factors research and practice is to maximize the safety and healthiness of work environments and work practices, and to ensure the usability of tools, devices, and artifacts in general. More specifically, ergonomics and HF are concerned with providing a good fit between people and their work or leisure environments. There are a number of sub-fields in ergonomics that have arisen as a result of the increasing penetration of technology into everyday lives. We give a short overview of each of these below. First, however, it is worth considering the notion of "fit."

Many of us are familiar with ergonomic assessments in the workplace; these assessments are conducted to minimize the risk of hazards to health and to prevent ailments such as upper limb disorders. In the UK, however, human factors have embraced the broader context of work practices, going beyond physical environment considerations and biomechanics to include selection and training. Thus, fitting the person to the environment is the responsibility of selection and training, whilst ergonomists fit the environment to the person. Although in this book we are not concerned with selection and training, it is worth noting that there is a complementary relationship between these activities–user groups may be selected or required by the working environment and/or training and selection are employed to modify the user population to provide the most advantageous fit between the user and the technology.

We can borrow from Rodger's (cited in Holloway 1991) encapsulation in the 1950s which was summarized as "fitting the man to the job and the job to the man"[1] (FMJ/FJM). This is broken down into:

Fitting the man to the job through

> Occupational guidance
>
> Personnel selection
>
> Training and development

and fitting the job to the man through

> Methods design
>
> Equipment design
>
> Negotiation of working conditions and (physical and social) rewards.

Although Rodger's definition is limited, as it does not take into account the organization in which the person works, we can see this useful encapsulation for occupational psychology as extended by consideration of issues dealt with by human factors.

The concept of 'fit' is a useful one. For physical devices and designed environments, the term *fit* is used literally. For example, on amusement park rides there are height restrictions—children have to wait till they are a certain height and weight before they are allowed on rides. However, the concept of fit is also used when people need to conform the way they act and think to accommodate how tasks are laid out in interfaces. Sometimes this is appropriate, but sometimes alternative designs which modify themselves to accommodate human traits would be more effective. For example, Figs. 2.2 and 2.3 show two example web sites that invite the user to fit themselves to the interfaces, suggesting they modify their behavior to the interfaces. In Fig. 2.2 the web site can recognize that users often put their email address in (e.g., fer2@psu.edu), but rather than remove the domain for the user (@psu.edu), it instructs the user to do so. Figure 2.3 shows a low-cost airline web site where the user is trying to find a cheap flight from Edinburgh to Naples in the run up to Christmas. The results on the *3 day view* and *3 week* view tabs simply show there is nothing available. Even the *Year view* tab only shows the cheapest prices against the months when flights take place. The user then has to infer from the results on the *Year view* tab that the last flights take place in October. The problem arises because the user is thinking in terms of flight dates—

---

[1] We note that the language at the time used the word *man* to include both genders, a practice that, appropriately, is no longer acceptable.

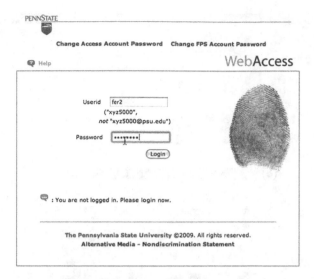

Fig. 2.2 An example interface that attempts to "fit the user to the machine". In the top entry field the user is expected to remove the domain rather than have the system do that (many sites, including GMail, will let users login with either user-name or user-name@domain, this one does not)

they do not care about dates when there are no flights—but the web site only works in terms of calendar dates.

2.2.1.1 Classical Ergonomics

Classical ergonomics has also been called interface ergonomics. The interface referred to is the person/machine interface of controls and displays, and the principle contribution of the designer is the improved design of dials and meters, control knobs, and panel layout. Notably people are usually referred to as *users* or *operators* in this literature. The expert's concerns can extend beyond the design of chairs, benches, and machinery to specify at least partly the optimum physical work environment, including temperature, humidity, and location of work surfaces.

This classical approach started with the design of military equipment, but now considers the design of items and workspaces in civilian contexts. This approach often takes a consultancy mode, with advice usually being delivered in the form of principles, guidelines, and standards. This can cause problems for two reasons: (1) classical ergonomists are only called in at the end of development and asked to advise on the final product, rather than being involved throughout the development process—this means that ill-thought out design decisions with poor rationale may already be "baked into" the design, and no easy fix (or no fix at all) is possible; and (2) guidelines and prescriptions for design activity are usually generic, and lack context specific details. We return to this issue in Sect. 2.3.

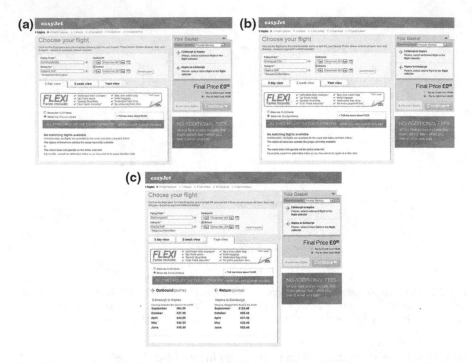

Fig. 2.3 In this interface the airline presents flight information using calendar dates. On the *left* is the 3 day view, in the *center* is a 3 week view, and on the *right* is a year view. Whereas the user most likely wants to view flight dates (with a pointer to the last, or next available flight, e.g., something like "there are no flights available for the period you have selected, the nearest available dates are October xx 2013 and April yy 2014"). This interface offers hints and encourages the user to search repeatedly rather than do the search for the user

2.2.1.2 Error Ergonomics

Error ergonomics is the study and explanation of human error in systems. The zero defects approach assumes that human error is the result of inadequate motivation, c.f. the examples of accidents and error attribution including the official report on Kegworth noted in the Appendix. Reason (1997) describes this as the person model or person approach. This approach tends to result in campaigns for safety procedure training and for safety oriented materials. These drives attempt to raise awareness and incentives for the workers. Even during the World War I, where the work force was *highly* motivated, error ergonomists discovered that fatigue was a major cause of errors.

Similarly, the error data store approach, which forms a part of methods like THERP (Technique for Human Error Rate Prediction, Swain & Guttman, 1983) assumes that human error is inevitable (this is discussed further in Chap. 10). This approach produces data banks of error probabilities for a variety of tasks executed under various conditions. It is therefore necessary to predict the incidence and consequences of human errors in any given situation. The results inform the design of systems in a way that minimizes the occurrence and effects of errors.

2.2.1.3 Systems Ergonomics

This approach was developed in the USA in the 1950s, and takes a more holistic approach to understanding users and systems as they work in concert. That is, the user and the system are seen as a single interacting system that is placed within a work context. Within this approach, system design involves parallel development of hardware and personnel issues, with training and selection issues considered. The ergonomist acts as an integral member of the design team, working throughout the life cycle to inform the system design. Therefore, in addition to the physical, behavioral and cognitive considerations of the finished product itself, the human factors expert (or "ergonomist") is involved in: (1) determining the required task functions (by activity and task analysis in conjunction with the consideration of the task requirements) and allocating the functions between the user and the system (2) the design of personnel subsystems, and (3) the design of job descriptions and job support materials (e.g., manuals and training schemes).

The approach differs from user-centered design as the designers and human factors experts still view the user as just one part of the system, whereas user-centered design focuses more on the user's needs and perspective than those of the system, tasks, and activities per se. In computer system development, for example, a systems approach would consider the task from a logical, syntactic perspective and then the computer system implementation issues with a view to allocating function between the user and the computer system. A user-centered approach would consider the processing capabilities of the human user and analyze tasks from the perspective of the user.

2.2.1.4 Cognitive Ergonomics/Cognitive Systems Engineering

Since the mid-1960s and the development of integrated circuits and third generation computer systems, research has been carried out in user-centered aspects of data processing, management information systems, information systems, and information technology. The 1970s saw a rapid increase in the use of computer-based technologies, resulting in the body of knowledge about user-centered design methods in areas such as Office Information Systems, industrial process control systems, and transportation systems. The role of people changed from one of directly controlling machinery and equipment to one in which they were interacting with computer based technology. In industrial systems this was characterized by a change in the operator's role from one of hands-on control to one of monitoring and supervisory control. This change from *doing* to *thinking* meant that it became more important to understand the way that people perceived problems, made decisions, and took actions. This led to the development of the field of cognitive ergonomics, which is nowadays more frequently described as cognitive systems engineering (CSE), or just cognitive engineering.

Originally developed in the 1970s and early 1980s (Hollnagel and Woods 1983), cognitive systems engineering has continued to evolve since that period

(Hollnagel and Woods 2005; Woods and Hollnagel 2006). Cognitive ergonomics is concerned with *human–machine systems*. Here, *machine* is taken to represent any artifact that is designed for a specific purpose. There are technological aspects to these systems, which are investigated from the perspective of how they affect use. These systems are always embedded in a socio-technical context because people are involved in the design, construction, testing, and use of these systems. Although CSE practitioners regard all systems as *socio-technical systems*, they usually draw a distinction between the *technological* system, in which the technology plays the central role in determining what happens, and the *organizational* system, in which people mainly determine what happens.

CSE is concerned with applicable, approximate models of how people perceive, process, attend to, and use information to achieve their goals. Aimed at designers, instructors, and users, CSE draws on many areas of psychology that are often taught separately, such as planning, language, problem solving, learning, memory, and perception. However, CSE addresses how such processes work together. It is different to the direct application of cognitive psychology in that it does not look at cognitive processes in isolation, but at their integration and how they are involved in particular activities or situations. CSE also differs from cognitive psychology in focusing on theories which can predict behavior in what have been called real world settings, rather than laboratory settings, although results from laboratory settings are considered informative. Real world settings may require a more detailed treatment of, for example, individual differences, uncertainty, ad hoc problem solving, and so on, than many other branches of psychology. CSE also places greater emphasis on the co-agency of action between the user and the machine, but, again, this is a difference in emphasis and these fields overlap to a great extent.

CSE is thus largely concerned with applications in complex dynamic domains, such as aviation, industrial process control, healthcare, and so on. It normally starts by attempting to understand the issue at hand, using observation to try to understand the patterns of work. It then uses this understanding to guide the search to identify what would be useful to support the types of work that have been observed. These insights are then used as a basis for (innovative) design, in participation with others, to support the work, the processes of change, and optimizing the process.

2.2.2 Socio-Technical Systems Design

The term *socio-technical systems* was originally coined by Emery and Trist (1960) to describe systems that involve a complex interaction between humans, machines, and the environmental aspects of the work system—something that is true of most systems in the workplace. The corollary of this definition is that all of these factors—people, machines, and context—need to be taken into account when developing socio-technical systems using so-called socio-technical system design (STSD) methods such as ETHICS (Effective Technical and Human Implementation of Computer-based Systems; Mumford 1983, 1995). In reality, these methods are more like guiding philosophies than design methods that are usually associated with systems engineering (Mumford 2006). In other words, the STSD methods tend to provide a process and a set of guiding principles (e.g., Cherns 1987; Clegg 2000) rather than a set of detailed steps that have to be followed.

From its inception in the period immediately after World War II, by what is now called The Tavistock Institute, until the present day, there have been several attempts at applying the ideas of STSD, although these have not always been successful (e.g., see Mumford 2006 for a critical review of the history of STSD methods). Early work in STSD focused mostly on manufacturing and production industries such as coal, textiles, and petrochemicals. The general aim was to investigate the organization of work and to see whether it could be made more humanistic, incorporating aspects such as the quality of working life. In other words, the idea was a move away from the mechanistic view of work that is usually associated with Taylor's principles of scientific management, which largely relied on the specialization of work and the division of labor.

The heyday of STSD was probably the 1970s. This was a time when there were labor shortages, and companies were keen to use all means available to keep their existing staff. This was also the period where more and more computer systems were being introduced into the workplace. Apart from the usual cultural and social reasons, companies could also see good business reasons for adopting socio-technical ideas. As just one of many such examples, Digital Equipment Corporation (DEC) had a family of expert systems that were developed using STSD (e.g., see Mumford and MacDonald 1989) to support the configuration and location of DEC VAX computers that saved the company tens of millions of dollars a year (Barker and O'Connor 1989).

There was a downturn in the use of STSD in the 1980s and 1990s as lean production techniques and business process re-engineering approaches dominated system development. STSD is, however, still widely advocated in the field of health informatics for the development of health care applications (e.g., Whetton 2005). Many medical systems are still never used because they introduce ways of working that conflict with other aspects of the user's job, or they require changes to procedures that affect other people's responsibilities. By focusing on the underlying work structure, STSD approaches facilitate the development of medical systems that are acceptable to the users (Berg 1999, 2001; Berg and Toussaint 2003).

Socio-technical ideas pervade a lot of thinking around information systems, although they may not always be explicitly referred to as such (Avgerou et al. 2004). The ideas appear in areas such as participatory design methods, computer supported cooperative work (CSCW), and ethnographic approaches to design. Recently, Baxter and Sommerville (2011) have outlined the need for socio-technical systems *engineering*, which integrates the ideas that have been developed in these different areas.

2.2.3 Cognitive Modeling and Programmable User Models

A cognitive model is an approximation of how people reason. The goal of a cognitive model is to explain scientifically very basic cognitive processes, explain how these processes interact, account for errors and breakdowns in these processes, and derive predictions about how those reasoning processes will proceed under different conditions.

Cognitive modeling is a method developed from early work in the late 1950s when psychologists realized that computational processes may be a good analog of human reasoning processes: like humans, computers take input in the form of symbols, require memory for information storage, and manipulate those symbols with algorithms to produce output. It was therefore proposed not only that human reasoning could be an inspiration for thinking about computational processes but also that computers may be a good way for us to simulate human reasoning and therefore derive deeper understandings of how humans think (Newell et al. 1960; Newell and Simon 1972).

Cognitive models in the late 1960s, the 1970s, and the 1980s focused on how people solved problems *symbolically*: humans take input in and form symbols, require memory for information storage, and use algorithms to manipulate those symbols to produce output. The models were usually limited to one task (or one type of task) and usually simulated reasoning in terms of what was going on in the user's mind. They addressed *human information processing* but did not address how information is taken in from the external world, how actions are performed in the world, and the ways in which real world settings impact the pace at which those processes take place. Each model was essentially a micro-theory of how some part of behavior occurred, and it was independent of other micro-theories. Over time, the need to integrate the micro-theories increased, which led to the idea of *unified theories of cognition* (UTCs; Newell 1990).

These theories are implemented as cognitive architectures available as computer simulations that constrain how models (based on task knowledge) can perform tasks in psychologically plausible ways. So, for example, often when humans perform two tasks simultaneously, the performance on one is affected by the performance on the other. Cognitive models are essentially programs written in a specific language to run on particular cognitive architectures. The models can perform complex tasks including perception, learning, reasoning, problem solving, remembering, decision making, proprioception (how people manage their bodies in space), and ambulation (how people move around physical spaces).

There has long been an overlap between cognitive modeling and human–computer interaction. Drawing on these developments in psychological theory and in simulation modeling, design researchers started investigating the possibility of building models of how people reason and problem solve when using complex interfaces, so that predictions about the pros and cons of different interface and information representation choices could be tested prior to investing in any interface or interaction development (e.g., Pew and Mavor 2007). Models force the designer to consider psychological factors systematically and explicitly as they make usability predictions. Examples of some influential approaches in the world of human–computer interaction are the Model Human Processor (MHP), GOMS (which stands for Goals, Operators, Methods, and Selection rules), the Keystroke Level Model (KLM) (see Card et al. 1983), and Programmable User Models (PUMs: Young et al. 1989). We will discuss this further in Chap. 11 on task analysis.

In recent years we have become more and more familiar with concepts such as Artificial Intelligence (AI) and Machine Learning (ML). These fields share roots with these cognitive modeling efforts. It has also been more recently acknowledged that cognitive models can combine symbolic and *sub-symbolic* processes–such as neural net modeling, for example. These hybrid models allow us to consider the characteristics and constraints of the brain's architecture of neurons and how the neural underpinnings of cognition impact cognitive processes (Busemeyer and Dieterich 2010) on both a symbolic and sub-symbolic and also an emergence level.

In the first part of the book we introduce several ideas and theories about the way that people behave. These ideas and theories are all encapsulated in cognitive architectures like ACT- R (Anderson 1993, 2007; Anderson et al. 2004) and Soar (Laird 2012; Newell 1990). There are still active research communities for both of these architectures. We introduced ACT-R in Chap. 1 and return to use it to help summarize design relevant user characteristics in Chap. 14.

2.2.4 User-Centered and Human-Centered Design

Through the 1980s, user-centered design (UCD, Norman and Draper 1986) came to the fore. User-centered design involves focusing on the user's needs, carrying out an activity/task analysis as well as a general requirements analysis, carrying out early testing and evaluation, and designing iteratively. As in the systems approach, this has a broader focus than the other approaches, but here there is a greater emphasis on the user and less of a focus on formal methods for requirements gathering and specification, and a move from linear, rigid design processes to a more flexible iterative design methodology.

A related movement, Human-Centered Design (HCD), expanded the focus from the user in interaction with the system to considering how human capabilities and characteristics are affected by the system beyond direct interaction with the interface or system itself. Humans should be seen as the most important element of information systems and should be *designed in*. The people context of information systems must be studied and understood. In more recent work, dimensions such as gender, race, class, and power are also being explicitly considered with respect to people's interactions with interactive technologies.

This sensibility surfaces in three ways. First, consideration is given to the fact that the introduction of a new system engenders changes in the organization of peoples' behaviors and activities—that is in how people do things. These behavioral changes also affect others. So, user needs and demands, situational effects, and technological requirements are considered in tandem. The boundaries between which issues are defined as *technical* and which are *organizational* or *social* are considered to be malleable, not fixed, and need to be negotiated. This kind of approach is also prevalent in socio-technical systems design, described above.

Second, human-centered design addresses the fact that more and more systems are being built where users do not interact directly with the technology as "users." Examples may be telecare assistive technologies—bed sensors which are programmed to track automatically when a person gets out of bed and to raise an alarm if they are not back in bed within a programmed time limit.

Finally, human-centered design tends to look to the longer-term effects, as well as the immediate, task-related issues that occur at human-system "touchpoint" moments. New applications of technology should be seen as the development of permanent support systems and not one-off products that are complete once implemented and deployed. In other words, the way in which technological change alters the organization of activities, and what are likely ongoing interventions, need to be considered.

User-centered (and human-centered) design methods tend to emphasize user participation in the design process for ideation and evaluation of design options. In this book, we have adopted the user-centered perspective, but we do not focus on the interaction with the interface; our intention is to broaden the scope of analysis to the user + technology system in the task context. Hence we have adopted the term "user-centered system design".

2.2.5 User Experience

User experience has been described as "a person's perceptions and responses that result from the use or anticipated use of a product, system, or service" (ISO 9241-210). According to this definition, *user experience* goes beyond interface design to address a person's emotions, beliefs, preferences, perceptions, physical and psychological responses, behaviors, and accomplishments that occur before, during, and after use. Three factors that influence user experience are considered—the system, the user and their characteristics, and the context of use of the technology or system. User experience is often used interchangeably with *usability* but there is clearly a different focus that is signaled: usability and *usability engineering* focus on task related aspects (getting the job done); user experience and *experience design* focus on and foreground the users' feelings, emotions, values, and their immediate and delayed responses.

2.2.6 Human–Computer Interaction

Human–computer interaction (HCI) is the study of interaction between people (user) and computers. Although often confused with interface design, the remit of HCI is considerably broader. Further, while HCI draws insights from the foundations of interfaces design (design sciences and graphics), the roots of HCI lie in the social sciences.

The Association for Computing Machinery (ACM), the major professional association for computer science, has a subgroup, a special interest group (SIG) on Computer–Human Interaction (full name SIGCHI). SIGCHI was fundamental in creating, nurturing, and defining HCI as a field. There are a number of excellent texts that summarize the history and current activities in HCI that are shown below. SIGCHI (Hewett et al. 1996) defined HCI as:

> … a discipline concerned with the design, evaluation and implementation of interactive computing systems for human use and with the study of major phenomena surrounding them.

It is worth noting that HCI as a field is constantly changing in response to technological innovations and consequent emerging user needs and demands, and this response is also updated in the ACM's recommended curriculum where HCI is a core area of computer science (http://www.acm.org//education/curricula/ComputerScience2008.pdf).

In 2006, Suzanne Bødker (2006) outlined three "waves" in the development of HCI as a field. The first wave drew insights from cognitive theory and human factors predominantly (see also Bannon 1991). We believe this perspective is still relevant while the perspectives of the second and third waves broaden HCI's remit, increasing its influence. The second wave that developed through the late 1980s into the early 2000s focused on groups working with collections of applications, drawing on theories of "situated action," "distributed cognition," and "activity theory." Scholars wrestled with how to capture the effects of context on activity. Bødker suggests that at this point "rigid guidelines, formal methods, and systematic testing" were no longer the central focus as HCI researchers and practitioners moved to "proactive methods such as a variety of participatory design workshops, prototyping, and contextual inquiries…". Finally, the third wave of HCI acknowledges that computers are increasingly being used in private and public spheres, moving out of workplace contexts and into everyday life for "nonwork, non-purpose, and non-rational" uses. This third wave necessarily addresses the "expansion of the cognitive" to include emotional and esthetic aspects of experience, but also the pragmatic and cultural-historical.

A recent report summarizes current and future teaching in HCI and documents some of the changes that have occurred in the field since its beginnings in the early 1980s (Churchill et al. 2013). It is also worth noting that the role and involvement of the HCI expert varies in design. The nature and level of involvement depends on the ethos of the design setting (the relative importance of usability issues and the degree of focus on supporting the user). We will deal with more HCI research in upcoming chapters.

2.3 Standards, Principles, and Guidelines

All of the disciplines mentioned above have a goal of answering specific research questions using experimental and observational methods. For example a research project may ask:

- Is this chair comfortable over an 8 h working day?
- Can the user get their task done with this application?
- Is the font used in this interface readable?
- Have we made the most important information in this interface stand out?
- Is this interface esthetically appealing to the user demographic I am interested in?
- Will the user get the information they need in a timely fashion if there is an emergency?

It is not always possible to carry out this research to answer questions of this sort oneself, so researchers turn to lessons learned from previous studies that are codified as *standards, principles, and guidelines* that can be applied to the problem situations they encounter.

Formal standards are generated by experts. They are intended to capture the agreed-upon wisdom and best practices of the field. Once created, they offer a common vocabulary for designers/developers and, ideally, result in systems that are more consistent for users, more easily inter-operable, and easier to integrate. In the design world, standards tend to be concerned with human adaptability and human variability. They are prescriptions for safe, acceptable designs, detailing the limits outside which the user may suffer from stress, and accidents may be caused. Standards are and can become part of the law. For example, British Standard BS 5330 deals with the relationship between sound levels in the workplace and the incidence of hearing loss.

Principles are prescriptive and specify general theoretical ideas that can underpin design decisions. They do not specify the limits of human capabilities like standards do and tend to be more general than guidelines. (Note that although we make this distinction between guidelines and principles, the ergonomics literature generally does not.) Ideally, such principles are encapsulations of theoretical insights that have been derived from extensive data gathering and testing. For example, Norman (1988, 2013) outlines a set of principles that designers should consider, e.g., making things visible and providing feedback. Norman's principles are based on his theory of action and interaction (noted further in Chap. 12). In particular, he emphasizes that the state of the system should be visible, that feedback on user's actions should be

Table 2.1 Principles for design to avoid exasperating users (Hedge 2003)

- Clearly define the system goals and identify potential undesirable system states
- Provide the user with appropriate procedural information at all times
- Do not provide the user with false, misleading, or incomplete information at any time
- Know thy user
- Build redundancy into the system
- Ensure that critical system conditions are recoverable
- Provide multiple possibilities for workarounds
- Ensure that critical systems personnel are fully trained
- Provide system users with all of the necessary tools
- Identify and eliminate system "Gotchas!"

provided, and that the system should be consistent across its subsystems. Similarly, Hedge (2003) offers the principles shown in Table 2.1.

Guidelines are prescriptive and offer some general guidance for making design decisions. They tend to be more specific than principles, but still relate existing theory and knowledge to either new design or established design problems (e.g., Brown 1988; Mosier and Smith 1986; or the Apple design guidelines, available online). Below we offer a number of principles and guidelines that we have found useful in our own work. In designing and evaluating systems we ask questions about the design's *functionality, usability, learnability, efficiency, reliability, maintainability*, and *utility* or *usefulness*. These are all discussed below.

(1) Functionality, what something does, is often the first thing to be considered while consideration of usability issues is sometimes tacked on at the end of development. This can lead to poorly designed artifacts that are hard to use but that offer new functionality. Sometimes this is enough. Sometimes it is not. Often, with more thoughtful design, one can have both (Pew and Mavor 2007).

(2) Usability is a complex concept that can be defined in several ways. For example, Ravden and Johnson (1989) specify the following as all relevant to an assessment of whether a system or technology is usable or not:

Visual clarity
Consistency
Informative feedback
Explicitness
Appropriate functionality
Flexibility and control
Error prevention and control
User guidance and support.

Eason (1984) offers the following definition of usability: the "major indicator of usability is whether a system or facility is used." However, this is patently not the case as many devices that are used are hard to use. More usefully, Eason notes that usability is not determined by just one or two constituents, but is influenced by a number of factors. These factors do not simply and directly affect usability, but interact with one another in sometimes complex ways. He focuses on three elements in particular that need to be taken account of explicitly: system function-task match, task characteristics, and user characteristics. Eason argues that these are independent variables that lead to changes in user reaction and scope of use that could be restricted, partial, distant, or constant.

In 1991 the ETSI (European Telecommunications Standards Institute) proposed two kinds of usability dimensions, those linked to performance and those related to attitude, where performance is measured objectively and attitude represents subjective dimensions (see http://www.etsi.org).

Although Shackel (1991) maintains the distinction between performance and attitudinal dimensions, he defines four distinguishable and quantifiable dimensions which can assume varying degrees of importance in different systems: effectiveness, learnability, flexibility, and attitude. These dimensions are not mutually exclusive in the sense that measures of effectiveness, for example, can at the same time also give some indication of system learnability. However, they provide a good starting point.

Finally, Booth (1989) says that usability is usefulness, effectiveness, ease of use, learnability, attitude, and likeability. A useful system is one that helps users achieve their goals. This more pragmatic approach is also taken by the International Standards Organisation (ISO) in their 9241 series of standards: "the usability of a product is the degree to which specific users can achieve specific goals within a particular environment; effectively, efficiently, comfortably, and in an acceptable manner."

(3) Learnability is how easy the system is to learn. This is affected by a number of factors: for example, how complex it is, how well the system behaviors are signaled in the form of feedback, how consistently the system behaves, how mode changes which may lead to different kinds of behavior are signaled to the user, and so on. Learnability can also be affected by how well the system is documented, either formally (though instructions) or informally through the availability of other users who may be more expert and can help the novice learner.

Learnability is also affected by how similar the new system is to other systems that the users know, because there may be transfer of knowledge from previous system use. How similar it is to previous systems not known to the user can also be important because, if there are other users, they may be able to help novices with new systems if the new systems are similar to previous systems, and existing consultants and teachers may be available if the systems are similar.

(4) Efficiency of a system can be measured through the use of resources such as processor time, memory, network access, system facilities, disk space, and so on. Programmers tend to focus mostly on efficiency, because it ensures that systems work fast and do not frustrate users by keeping them waiting. Note that this is a *computer* not a *human* centric view of efficiency. It is a relative concept in that one system can be evaluated as more efficient than another in terms of some parameter such as processor use, but there is no absolute scale on which to specify an optimum efficiency with regard to people's experience of a system when carrying out a task. Optimum efficiency from a human-centric perspective requires consideration of the task, the task-context, and the characteristics of the users. One needs to consider the users' knowledge level and disposition, including their motivation. It is also important not to confuse efficiency with speed of execution; speed may be important, or it may also be ultimately inefficient.

In the early days of computers, when programs were small and computer time was relatively expensive, efficiency of computer time was considered to be of paramount importance, and it probably was. With today's faster machines, designers need to consider the effects of choices upon all resources and the consequences of different kinds of efficiency. For example, when considering Internet sites, slow download times are an efficiency issue caused by site/application design and connectivity bandwidth. Users can get frustrated if they are in a hurry to complete a transaction. However, the opposite also occurs—when a transaction is *too* efficient, users can get disoriented and dissatisfied (e.g., one-click payments without asking the user to review orders before placement). Thus efficiency must be calculated in terms of technical efficiency that matches user efficiency expectations for the task at hand.

(5) Reliability is concerned with the dynamic properties of the eventual system and involves the designer making predictions about behavioral issues. We need to know whether the system is going to be complete (in the sense that it will be able to handle all combinations of events and system states), consistent (in that its behavior will be as expected and will be repeatable, regardless of the overall system loading at any time, and across components of the system), and robust (when faced with component failure or some similar conflict, for example, if the printer used for logging data in a chemical process-control plant fails for some reason, the whole system should not crash, but should instead follow a policy of *graceful degradation*).

As systems get larger the problems of ensuring reliability escalate. For safety critical systems where this factor is most important, various techniques have been developed to help overcome limitations in design and implementation techniques. For example, in a system used in a fly-by-wire aircraft in which the control surfaces are managed by computer links rather than by direct hydraulic controls, the implementation will be by means of multiple computers, with a strong likelihood that each will have been programmed by a separate development team and tested independently. Any operational request to the control system will then be processed in parallel by all the computers and only if they concur with the requested operation will it be carried out.

(6) Maintainability is how easy a system is to maintain and upgrade. As systems get larger and more costly, the need for a life-long time in service increases in parallel. To help achieve this, designs must allow for future modification. Designers need to provide future maintainers with mental models of the system and the design rationale so that future maintainers can gain a clear understanding of the system and how it is put together (Haynes et al. 2009). Development of modular designs helps, but larger systems present further problems. While small systems can be modeled with a structural model (i.e., laying out the component parts of the system), as systems get larger it is important to develop functional models that simulate what the component parts do themselves and in interaction with each other.

(7) Utility/Usefulness is an important concept always to consider when designing systems. Is it ultimately useful for users and how long is its likely usefulness? Is this something that will become an everyday system or an infrequently used system? When it is used, how useful do users find it or are there other workaround that users would rather engage with? Usefulness can be measured both in terms of how often and in what way something is used, but can also be measured with subjective scales like 'how much do you like this?' People may find something useful because it makes them feel good about themselves rather than because it is an efficient, reliable system with a highly usable interface from our perspective as designers.

2.4 Summary

In this chapter we have provided an overview of research areas that have contributed to our understanding of user-centered design. User-centered design draws on *multiple* sources of knowledge to support creating systems that are based on users' abilities, capabilities, and task. What all these approaches have in common is the perspective that when designing we need to consider variation and similarity in the contexts, people, and tasks that characterize different design situations and settings. A one-size-fits-all approach seldom works to achieve the most productive, safe, and enjoyable design solution. We summarize this perspective by inviting you to remember that design is about considering *particular* people doing *particular* tasks in a *particular* context—our focus in this book is people doing tasks using technologies, but this perspective can be more generally applied.

It is worth highlighting at this point that, in order to comply with ISO standard 9241-210 (which now refers to *Human*-Centered Design, rather than *User*-Centered), the following four activities are now *requirements* (previously they were recommendations):

1. Understanding and specifying the context of use (including users, tasks, environments)
2. Specifying the user requirements in sufficient detail to drive the design
3. Producing design solutions that meet these requirements
4. Conducting user-centered evaluations of these design solutions and modifying the design to take into account the results.

Our aim in this book is to provide you with the foundations that will help you to meet these requirements. In the first part of the book we focus on the capabilities of users. We categorize these capabilities into anthropometric, behavioral, cognitive, and social aspects. Although we separate issues into these categories, we acknowledge that the boundaries between them are somewhat blurred: our bodies affect how we act, and our behaviors affect how we participate socially. Thus, all these factors interact. A key skill for effective human-centered system design is to understand which factors are central or primary in any design situation and which are peripheral or secondary.

In the latter part of the book we provide introductions to some methods that can be used to guide design and evaluation. These include task analysis, evaluation methods, and the notation of cognitive dimensions. These methods differ in terms of their preferred unit of analysis, the kinds of data collected, and the analyses that are conducted. We finish the book by providing a framework that will allow you to integrate your knowledge of the user with the methods in a systematic way.

2.5 Other Resources

There are a lot of helpful texts that can give you some background to the field of user-centered system design. Some of the texts that we have cited above are particularly helpful. For more on the history of this field read this book:

Shachtman, T. (2002). *Laboratory warriors: How Allied science and technology tipped the balance in World War II*. New York, NY: HarperCollins.

A classic text that laid many of the basics out for the field of user-centered systems design is Don Norman and Steve Draper's 1986 text:

Norman, D. A., & Draper, S. W. (Eds) (1986). *User centered system design: New Perspectives on human–computer interaction*. Hillsdale, NJ: Erlbaum.

Jack Carroll's summary of Human Computer Interaction in the *Encyclopedia of Human Computer Interaction* is a great place to start if you want an overview:

Carroll, J. M. (2009). Human computer interaction (HCI). In *Encyclopedia of Human–Computer Interaction*. M. Soegaard & R. F. Dam (Eds.). Aarhus, Denmark: The Interaction Design Foundation.

Two good textbook style overviews are:

Sharp, H., Rogers, Y., & Preece, J. (2011). *Interaction design: Beyond human–computer interaction* (3rd ed.). Chichester, UK: John Wiley and Sons Ltd.

Shneiderman, B., & Plaisant, C. (2009). *Designing the user interface: Strategies for effective human–computer interaction* (5th ed.). Reading, MA: Addison Wesley.

One of the best introductions to the practice, the how-to's, of user-centered design is by Elizabeth Goodman, Mike Kuniavsky, and Andrea Moed. They cover basic techniques and methods that will help you design better interactions. They also offer case studies and examples that you can compare to your own design situations:

Goodman, E., Kuniavsky, M., & Moed, A. (2012). *Observing the user experience: A practitioner's guide to user research*. San Francisco, CA: Morgan Kaufman

For more formal methods and models of interaction programming, read Harold Thimbleby's text *Press On*:

Thimbleby, H. (2007). *Press on—Principles of interaction programming*. Cambridge, MA: MIT Press.

If you want to know more about field based and participatory requirements gathering, a well known method is Contextual Design. This is described in this text:

Beyer, H., & Holtzblatt, K. (1997) *Contextual design: Defining customer-centered systems*. San Francisco, CA: Morgan Kaufmann.

Finally, cognitive modeling can offer enormous gains when you are thinking about how users think. An excellent introduction to this area of research and application is:

Gray, W. D. (Ed.). (2007). *Integrated models of cognitive systems*. New York: Oxford University Press.

2.6 Exercises

2.1 Consider a smartphone, either a specific one or a composite one, and consider the human factors of using it. What are the issues that each field of HCI, human factors, and cognitive ergonomics address?

Write short notes (about one side of a page in total) noting the issues on these three types of analyses.

2.2 Pick a company's web site or a university department's web site. Summarize in note form how each of the major fields noted in this chapter would analyze it and its users. Note what would be the outputs and typical recommendations. Which approach would you prefer to apply to the web site you choose? Note the relative value and the absolute value of each. That is, which gives the best results for the amount of inputs, and which gives the best value without regard to cost?

2.3 When you go home tonight, take a look at your kitchen. Look at all the displays in the kitchen and summarize what information they contain and when you would use that information. Look at the layout of the kitchen and think about whether things are placed in the most convenient place to make your movements through the kitchen when you are cooking as efficiently as possible. Make your favorite snack and draw a picture of how you move through the kitchen. Note how the kitchen can be improved based on your analysis, including both no-cost and expensive changes. This exercise is designed to make you think more deeply about the physical, cognitive, behavioral, and information issues that go into how optimized your kitchen is for you to use.

2.4 Analyze Hedge's (2003) set of design principles in Table 2.1. These principles arose out of installing a popular operating system.

(1) For each principle, note the support it has in general, when it would be true, and exceptions where it would not be true.

(2) Comment on the usefulness and usability of the principles as a set.

(3) Compare these principles with another set of HCI design principles that you find (and note and reference).

References

Anderson, J. R. (1993). *Rules of the mind*. Hillsdale, NJ: Erlbaum.

Anderson, J. R. (2007). *How can the human mind exist in the physical universe?*. New York, NY: Oxford University Press.

Anderson, J. R., Bothell, D., Byrne, M. D., Douglass, S., Lebiere, C., & Qin, Y. (2004). An integrated theory of the mind. *Psychological Review, 111*(4), 1036–1060.

Avgerou, C., Ciborra, C., & Land, F. (2004). *The social study of information and communication technology*. Oxford, UK: Oxford University Press.

Bannon, L. (1991). From human factors to human actors: The role of psychology and human–computer interaction studies in systems design. In J. Greenbaum & M. Kyng (Eds.), *Design at work: Cooperative design of computer systems* (Vol. 25–44). Hillsdale, NJ: Erlbaum.

Barker, V. E., & O'Connor, D. E. (1989). Expert systems for configuration at Digital: XCON and beyond. *Communications of the ACM, 32*(3), 298–318.

Baxter, G., & Sommerville, I. (2011). Socio-technical systems: From design methods to engineering. *Interacting with Computers, 23*(1), 4–17.

Berg, M. (1999). Patient care information systems and healthcare work: A sociotechnical approach. *International Journal of Medical Informatics, 55*(2), 87–101.

Berg, M. (2001). Implementing information systems in health care organizations: Myths and challenges. *International Journal of Medical Informatics, 64*(2–3), 143–156.

Berg, M., & Toussaint, P. (2003). The mantra of modelling and the forgotten powers of paper: A sociotechnical view on the development of process-oriented ICT in health care. *International Journal of Medical Informatics, 69*(2–3), 223–234.

Bødker, S. (2006). When second wave HCI meets third wave challenges. In A. Mørch, K. Morgan, T. Bratteteig, G. Ghosh, & D. Svanaes (Ed.), *NordiCHI Nordic Conference on Human-Computer Interaction October 14–18*, (pp. 1–8). Oslo, Norway.

Booth, P. (1989). *An introduction to human-computer interaction*. Hove, UK: Erlbaum.

Brown, C. M. L. (1988). *Human-computer interface design guidelines*. Norwood, NJ: Ablex.

Busemeyer, J. R., & Dieterich, A. (2010). *Cognitive modeling*. Thousand Oaks, CA: Sage Publications.

Card, S. K., Moran, T., & Newell, A. (1983). *The psychology of human-computer interaction*. Hillsdale, NJ: Erlbaum.

Cherns, A. (1987). Principles of socio-technical design revisited. *Human Relations, 40*(3), 153–162.

Churchill, E., Bowser, A., & Preece, J. (2013). Teaching and learning human-computer interaction: Past, present, and future. *Interactions, 20*(2), 44–53.

Clegg, C. (2000). Sociotechnical principles for system design. *Applied Ergonomics, 31*, 463–477.

Eason, K. (1984). Towards the experimental study of usability. *Behaviour and Information Technology, 3*(2), 133–143.

Emery, F. E., & Trist, E. L. (1960). Socio-technical systems. In C. W. Churchman & M. Verhulst (Eds.), *Management science models and techniques* (Vol. 2, pp. 83–97). Oxford, UK: Pergamon.

Haynes, S. R., Cohen, M. A., & Ritter, F. E. (2009). Designs for explaining intelligent agents. *International Journal of Human-Computer Studies, 67*(1), 99–110.

Hedge, A. (2003). 10 principles to avoid XP-asperation. *Ergonomics in Design, 11*(3), 4–9.

Hewett, T. T., Baecker, R., Card, S., Carey, T., Gasen, J., Mantei, M., et al. (1996). *ACM SIGCHI curricula for human-computer interaction.* New York, NY: Association for Computing Machinery. http://sigchi.org/cdg/index.html

Hollnagel, E., & Woods, D. D. (1983). Cognitive systems engineering: New wine in new bottles. *International Journal of Man-Machine Studies, 18*, 583–600.

Hollnagel, E., & Woods, D. D. (2005). *Joint cognitive systems: Foundations of cognitive systems engineering.* Boca Raton, FL: CRC Press.

Holloway, W. (1991). *Work psychology and organizational behaviour: Managing the individual at work Thousand Oaks.* CA: Sage.

Laird, J. E. (2012). *The Soar cognitive architecture.* Cambridge, MA: MIT Press.

Mosier, J. N., & Smith, S. L. (1986). Application of guidelines for designing user interface software. *Behaviour and Information Technology, 5*, 39–46.

Mumford, E. (1983). *Designing human systems for new technology—The ETHICS method.* Retrieved March 10, 2014, from http://www.enid.u-net.com/C1book1.htm

Mumford, E. (1995). *Effective systems design and requirements analysis: The ETHICS method.* Basingstoke, UK: Macmillan Press.

Mumford, E. (2006). The story of socio-technical design: reflections in its successes, failures and potential. *Information Systems Journal, 16*, 317–342.

Mumford, E., & MacDonald, W. B. (1989). *XSEL's progress: The continuing journey of an expert system.* New York, NY: Wiley.

Newell, A. (1990). *Unified theories of cognition.* Cambridge, MA: Harvard University Press.

Newell, A., Shaw, J. C., & Simon, H. A. (1960). Report on a general problem-solving program for a computer. In *International Conference on Information Processing*, (pp. 256–264). UNESCO: Paris.

Newell, A., & Simon, H. A. (1972). *Human problem solving.* Englewood Cliffs, NJ: Prentice-Hall.

Nickerson, R. (1969). Man-Computer interaction: A challenge for human factors research. *Ergonomics, 12*: 501–517. (Reprinted from *IEEE Transactions on Man-Machine Systems, 10*(4), 164–180).

Norman, D. A., & Draper, S. W. (Eds.). (1986). *User centred system design.* Hillsdale, NJ: Erlbaum.

Norman, D. A. (1988). *The psychology of everyday things.* New York, NY: Basic Books.

Norman, D. A. (2013). *The design of everyday things.* New York, NY: Basic Books.

Pew, R. W., & Mavor, A. S. (Eds.). (2007). *Human-system integration in the system development process: A new look.* Washington, DC: National Academies Press. http://books.nap.edu/catalog.php?record_id=11893. Accessed 10 March 2014.

Ravden, S., & Johnson, G. (1989). *Evaluating usability of human-computer interfaces: A practical method.* Chichester, UK: Ellis Horwood.

Reason, J. (1997). *Managing the risks of organizational accidents.* Aldershot, UK: Ashgate.

Shackel, B. (1991). Human factors for informatics usability book contents. In B. Shackel & S. J. Richardson (Eds.), *Usability—context, framework, definition, design and evaluation* (pp. 21–37). New York, NY: Cambridge University Press.

Swain, A. D., & Guttman, H. E. (1983). *A handbook of human reliability analysis with emphasis on nuclear power applications.* Washington, DC: US Nuclear Regulatory Commission.

Whetton, S. (2005). *Health informatics: A socio-technical perspective.* South Melbourne, Australia: Oxford University Press.

Woods, D. D., & Hollnagel, E. (2006). *Joint cognitive systems: Patterns in cognitive systems engineering.* Boca Raton, FL: CRC Press.

Young, R. M., Green, T. R. G., & Simon, T. (1989). Programmable user models for predictive evaluation of interface designs. In *Proceedings of CHI'89 Conference on Human Factors in Computing Systems*, (pp. 15–19). ACM Press: New York, NY.

Part II
Design Relevant User Characteristics: The ABCS

Chapter 3
Anthropometrics: Important Aspects of Users' Bodies

Abstract This chapter addresses factors that arise from basic characteristics of the human body. While bodies vary in their size, shape, capabilities, and limitations, there are some common factors that are shared and some general guidance that we can apply to design better interfaces and systems. This is a broad topic: the influence of bodies on usability applies to all systems, and is illustrated with examples from desktop, laptop, mobile, and handheld systems. After briefly providing an overview of the issues involved, this chapter covers the importance of the physical setup for computers. We also introduce and discuss the importance of touch and tactile feedback, better known as haptic perception. Haptic perception has become increasingly important with the widespread uptake of touch screen devices and gaming interfaces. We illustrate the importance of haptic perception by considering how people interact with a wide range of devices and systems. The chapter concludes with some implications of the need to consider anthropometric factors when designing interactive systems.

3.1 Introduction

People have bodies. Human bodies have certain characteristics and capabilities: they take up space and are designed to move in certain ways. This means that the extent of our reach when static and our range of motion are limited. Human bodies are designed for certain kinds of movement—we crawl, walk, run, and reach for things. Thanks to a complex sensorimotor system, we can perceive and manipulate objects, and to issue and sense tactile feedback. Human bodies also need certain forms of nourishment and can become fatigued. Understanding the characteristics and capabilities of the human body can both inspire and constrain design options.

Obviously, users need their bodies to interact with interfaces. In some cases the path from the user's intention to the desired action appears effortless and error free. These situations encourage us to forget the situations where the user is tired, the timing of the task is demanding, or the user has difficulty performing the required

F. E. Ritter et al., *Foundations for Designing User-Centered Systems*,
DOI: 10.1007/978-1-4471-5134-0_3, © Springer-Verlag London 2014

Fig. 3.1 The steering wheel from the Caterham 2012 Formula 1 car. The wheel contains multiple controls to adjust traction, suspension, and aerodynamics (reproduced with permission of Caterham F1 Team, UK)

Fig. 3.2 Outfits designed to reproduce the effects of age on younger users (reproduced with permission from Nathan Fried-Lipski and the MIT AgeLab)

physical actions. Designers of interfaces and of larger systems need to give appropriate consideration to the user's body in order to take advantage of its capabilities and to mitigate against the limitations and constraints it imposes. The size of the cockpit in a Formula 1 racing car, for example, is limited for obvious reasons. This restricts the things that the driver can physically reach to control the car. The steering wheel in Formula 1 cars (like that of the Caterham 2012 Formula 1 car shown in Fig. 3.1) has therefore evolved into an interface that brings within easy reach all of the systems that drivers need to interact with.

People vary and their physical dimensions and capabilities also vary. Figure 3.2, for example, shows a suit designed to mimic the effects of age when worn by younger people. The suit leads users to modify how they walk, how they look around the environment, and how they see. Similarly, the gloves and goggles in Fig. 3.3 can be used to mimic the effects of arthritis and poor vision, which will affect how people interact with computer technology.

The appearance or structure of a physical object can suggest how it should be used, or support a particular use. These physical affordances—after Gibson (1979)—are useful, because they make it easier for people to determine how to use the object: handles on doors, for example, afford pulling. Some affordances build

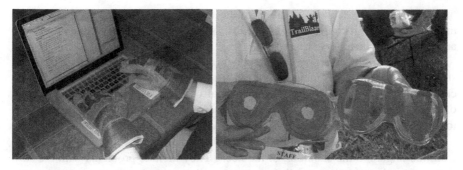

Fig. 3.3 Easy to create modified gloves (they have wooden popsicle sticks in the fingers) and goggles (with paint on them) that give the user restricted hand mobility and restricted vision respectively

on existing knowledge—you learn to double click using a mouse button, for example—but the most powerful and primitive affordances support direct interaction with the object. Norman's (1988, 2013) book provides many examples of useful affordances, as well as several that are confusing or even useless, such as putting a pull handle on a door that you have to push open!

The objects in computer interfaces that can be manipulated (clicked, dragged, rotated, and so on) by the user should also provide appropriate affordances. This is why buttons, for example, should look like they need to be pressed (or clicked on) even if they appear on a flat surface. Similarly, the use of a hand icon as a mouse cursor in applications such as Adobe's Acrobat Reader is designed to afford the action of scrolling through a document on the display.

3.2 Physical Aspects of Interaction

There are two main anthropometric issues that need to be considered when designing interactive systems. The first relates to *how the users will interact with the system*: will they be sitting (which is still most prevalent) or standing (which is becoming more prevalent)? Note, however, that as computational artifacts are increasingly embedded in our physical environment, the repertoire of possible body positions is correspondingly increasing. The second, which is becoming increasingly important, relates to *how much weight the user can carry and support* if the device or artifact is intended to be carried by the user, as with mobile and portable devices.

3.2.1 Posture

The posture adopted by users when they interact with systems is important. If users adopt an incorrect posture or stay still too long, this can lead to performance problems, such as reduced attention to the task over time, or an increase in the number of errors. It can also lead to health issues including eye-strain, back pain, and upper limb disorders (ULDs).

ULDs are quite common. Many people who use display screen equipment suffer from ULDs. ULDs include conditions such as repetitive strain injuries (RSI), cumulative trauma disorder, and occupational overuse syndrome. Although most of these conditions are not indicative of any serious ill health, it makes sense to try to avoid them as far as possible.

ULDs are aches, pains, tension, and disorders that involve any part of the arm from the fingers to the shoulder, or the neck. They include problems with the soft tissues, muscles, tendons, and ligaments, as well as with the circulatory and nerve supply to the limbs. ULDs are often caused or exacerbated by work and particularly repetitive work.

There are several risk factors that contribute to the chance of suffering from ULDs. These include task-related aspects, such as uncomfortable working postures, continuous use of excessive force, and long tasks. Other risk factors include organizational aspects, such as a poor working environment (lack of temperature regulation, poor lighting, and so on) and job demands, such as time pressures, and a lack of rest breaks or task rotation. There are suggestions that lack of control of one's time or task exacerbates the situation, encourages reporting of the problem, or helps accelerate the process. In addition, some people are more susceptible to some of these risks than other people. It is now a legal requirement in most countries to make sure that workstations are appropriately set up for people who regularly use such equipment for extended periods of time, as shown in Fig. 3.4. It is important to make sure that the keyboard is placed appropriately with respect to the hands and the wrists, that the display is positioned correctly, that the display is appropriately illuminated, and that the angle of the head, neck, back, hips, and feet when using the workstation are considered.

The recommended sitting posture is to be more upright and avoid pressure on wrists, hands, and elbows. Posture will naturally change across tasks, however, with some people leaning forward to type on a touch screen device, for example, but leaning back to read from the screen of the same device. English and Andre (1999) identified several postures that should generally be avoided; some of the at-risk postures observed during web browsing are shown in Fig. 3.5.

There are situations where people deliberately choose to ignore the risks, however. Hand-held game consoles, for example, include information about the potential risks of extended use in their instruction manuals. In spite of this, some people persist in playing games for excessive periods of time without a break, and often hunched over the console.

It is most important to be aware of the risks and to take appropriate steps to mitigate the effects of these risks. The UK's Health and Safety Executive developed the Assessment of Repetitive Tasks (ART) tool to help in this area. ART is designed to assist health and safety inspectors in assessing those repetitive tasks

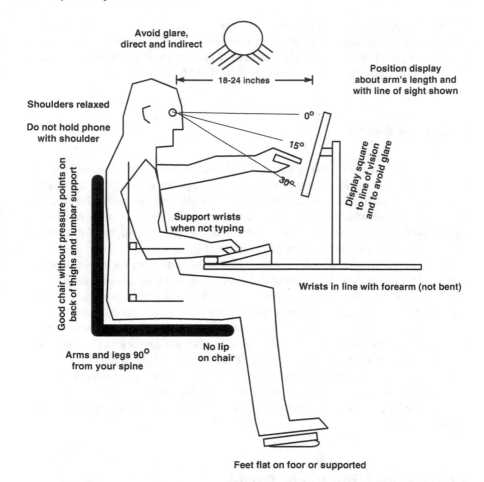

Fig. 3.4 Useful information about how to arrange a computer display and work area to avoid wrist and upper limb disorders (ULDs). Contains public sector information published by the Health and Safety Executive and licensed under the Open Government Licence v1.0

Fig. 3.5 Postures to be avoided when web browsing. Placement of non-mousing (e.g., *left*) elbow on chair armrest or workstation desk, results in direct contact pressure (reproduced with permission from English and Andre 1999)

that involve the use of upper limbs. It focuses on the common risk factors that contribute to the development of upper limb disorders in situations that involve repetitive work. The tool is freely available from the Health and Safety Executive's website (http://www.hse.gov.uk/msd/art-tool.htm).

3.2.2 Load Bearing

More and more people are using portable and mobile devices (phones, tablets, and so on). With these devices the user often has to support the weight of the display (and hence the interface) during interaction. Normally the user will have to carry the device around with them too. The net result is that the user must be able to support both the weight of the device when using it and the weight of the device whilst carrying it around for extended periods of time.

At this point, all we can encourage you to do is to note what the device weighs, to study existing standards and similar devices, and to observe and talk to users. Simply asking users to complete a survey about the device is unlikely to generate much useful data, because they may not be able to judge weights abstractly or to consider their desire to carry an object without knowing and understanding its functionality. It probably makes more sense to give the devices to the users and observe how they explore and use them. If the device is for regular, routine use, you should observe them over a realistic period of time that includes the variety of environments in which the device will be used. The technology and functionality is rapidly changing in this area, which may change what users think is an acceptable weight to carry.

3.3 Interacting with Haptic Devices

Touch is usually regarded as the third most important sense after vision and hearing (which are both covered in the next chapter). What most people refer to as the sense of touch, however, is really a combination of two senses: the skin (or cutaneous sense) and kinesthesis (Loomis and Lederman 1986). The cutaneous sense is responsible for creating the feeling that the outer surface of the human body has been stimulated, which it does using receptors in the skin together with the associated nervous system. Kinesthesis (or the kinesthetic sense) generates an awareness of static and dynamic body posture based on information coming from the muscles, joints, and skin (afferent information), along with a copy of the signal sent to the motor system (an efferent copy). The efference copy is used to help distinguish between information coming from within the body and information coming from outside the body, and helps to explain why you do not laugh when you tickle yourself (there is a match between the afferent information and the efference copy)!

The mechanisms for the two senses are separate, but functionally they are much more difficult to separate, and they usually operate in tandem. For this reason, the two senses are associated with three types of tactual perception:

- *Tactile perception*, which is solely mediated by changes in cutaneous stimulation. Tactile perception always occurs within the context of a particular static posture, and may depend on that posture.
- *Kinesthetic perception*, which is (mostly) mediated by variations in kinesthetic stimulation. This includes situations where the cutaneous sense only indicates contact with the stimulus, and does not provide any spatial or textural information about the stimulus.
- *Haptic perception*, which is the most common type of tactual perception. It involves using information from the cutaneous sense and kinesthesis to understand and interpret objects and events in the environment.

In the rest of this section, when we refer to touch, we will be referring to haptic perception, unless otherwise specified. Most devices that are used to provide input to computer-based systems make use of haptic perception. In general, however, most haptic devices only support interaction using the hands or fingers, even though users could (theoretically, at least) use any part of their body. There is, however, a growing number of devices that support input using the feet, such as the highly sophisticated da Vinci surgical system[1] which has been successfully used in cancer surgery. The feet are also used to move around in virtual reality systems. The mouth and other parts of the body tend to be supported somewhat less, but they can be critical in interfaces for people with disabilities who cannot use their limbs, and increasingly for the military in unusual situations or circumstances.

In this section we will focus our discussions on how people use hands and fingers to interact with systems. These discussions will consider the most common types of haptic devices that support interaction with computer-based systems. The future may include other devices, such as pens (e.g., Tian et al. 2008), multi-touch interfaces on a wider variety of objects (e.g., Jiang et al. 2012), or gestures, but these could be analyzed in a similar way.

3.3.1 Physical Keyboards

Physical keyboards—we use the term here to distinguish them from the soft keyboards that are used on touch screen devices—have a haptic interface. The feel of the key clicks provides you with haptic feedback about whether a keypress has been detected (and hence whether the corresponding character will appear on the associated display screen). Sometimes people will complain about the feel of a particular keyboard. Usually they are referring to the position and shape of the

---

[1] http://www.intuitivesurgical.com/products/davinci_surgical_system/

keys but they may also be describing a keyboard that requires too much or too little pressure to operate the keys. You may also hear users talk about a *soggy* feel to the key action, which means that they cannot clearly tell whether a particular key has been pressed or not, based on the key's motion.

Typing is still the most common way of entering data into computer-based systems (including mobile devices). It is thus useful to briefly consider typing in more detail and to identify some of the regularities of behavior in this area. Card et al. (1980, 1983) provide a good overview of the general issues of human typing, whilst Salthouse (1986) focuses on transcription typing.

Users' typing speeds range from a few words per minute (wpm) to over 100 wpm, although there is often a trade-off between speed and accuracy. It is sometimes said, for example, that expert typists achieve speeds of 90 wpm with 90% accuracy. The differences in speed are primarily due to practice—those that type more tend to get faster at it, using two hands rather than single-finger or hunt-and-peck typing styles.

Typical typing speeds tend to occupy relatively narrow ranges for different categories of typist: novices can generally type at least 10 wpm; good journeyman programmers are closer to 30–60 wpm; and users whose jobs includes large amounts of typing are more likely to achieve rates above 60 wpm. We can extrapolate from these numbers to find keystroke times of about 750 ms per keystroke for slow typists ranging down to 125 ms per keystroke for fast typists. These numbers are useful for predicting reaction times and for working out how fast the computer has to respond.

Many users can type some keys faster than others. For example, the "n" key (average typing time 221 ms) takes longer to type than the space bar (155 ms), as shown in Fig. 3.6 (Card et al. 1983, p. 62). This result suggests that when you design interfaces you should consider associating keys that are faster to type with actions that have to be performed frequently. There are exceptions to this rule, however, which include situations where you deliberately want to slow down the user so that they have time to consider the effect of their actions (such as in safety critical systems), and where memorability is important.

Keyboard users make errors. Salthouse's (1986) review of transcription typists reports error rates in the range 1–3.2%, noting four types of observable errors: (1) substitution of letters ("work" for "word"), (2) intrusions ("worrd" for "word"), (3) omissions ("wod" for "word"), and (4) transpositions ("wodr" for "word"). These categories are not exclusive, and sometimes may be mistaken for each other. Only about half (40–70%) of these errors are caught by the typist and can account for 35% of expert typists' time (Landauer 1987b, p. 151).

The Typist model (John 1996) summarizes many of the behavior regularities of typing noted above. Typist can be used to explain how typing occurs and how errors arise. Its structure and behavior can also be examined to identify where interfaces for typing could be improved, and where changes would not make a difference. In transcription typing, for example, providing the typists with an additional paragraph of material to be typed is not useful because transcription typists do not look that far ahead.

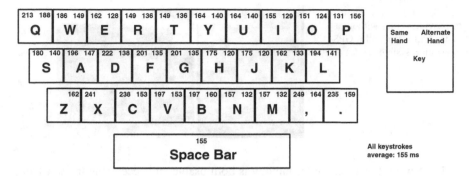

Fig. 3.6 The time (in milliseconds) to type different keys on the keyboard based on 155,000 keystrokes. Times taken from Kinkead (1975) cited in Card et al. (1983). Same hand times are for keys typed with the same hand; alternate hand is for keys typed after a key typed by the other hand

3.3.2 Touch Screens

Probably the best-known and most widely used devices that support haptic input are touch screens. These are now commonplace on many mobile devices (smartphones, tablet computers, and so on) and in information and ticket sales kiosks. Feedback for these devices is mostly provided through visual and audio channels. Figure 3.7 shows two examples of touch screen applications, one of which is static (an e-voting system), and the other highly portable (a handheld GPS satellite navigation system).

Touch screen displays are electronically more complicated than normal displays because they use either pressure or electrical conductance to determine where the screen is being touched. If the interface is well designed, it will be very clear to the user what actions they have performed on the screen (selection, scrolling, and so on), and the interface will be easy to use, and easy to learn to use. There are many examples of videos online, for example, that show young children figuring out how to use touch screen devices without any instruction.

The end of the finger is of the order of ten times the size of the normal arrowhead cursor that you see on most systems. You will need to take this, and individual variations in finger size, into account when designing touch screen interfaces to avoid *fat finger* problems. These occur when people touch more than one button at a time, or accidentally touch the wrong button. It has been calculated that about 9% of clicks on adverts on mobile devices are accidental![2] So, if you need to accommodate many buttons on a small touch screen, you will need to have a deeper understanding of how the technology works and the ways in which users use small buttons.

---

[2] http://econsultancy.com/uk/blog/10649-mobile-s-biggest-ad-challenge-fat-fingers

Fig. 3.7 A touch screen used to provide voting without a paper trail (*left*), and a GPS navigation system (*right*)

Even when touch screen technology is both usable and acceptable to the users, there can be other risks that mitigate against its use in some situations. The touch screen voting system shown on the left side of Fig. 3.7, for example, was removed within a year of being introduced because it could not produce a voter-verifiable paper audit trail. In other words, there was no way for a voter to tell that their vote had been properly recorded rather than discarded after they had pressed the appropriate buttons. The public and public officials believed that the risk of potential corruption—the voter gets feedback from the device saying the vote has been cast, but the vote never gets processed to include it in the count—made the system unacceptable.

3.3.3 Pointing Devices

People still widely use mice as a way of interacting with systems and applications, although usage may decline as the uptake of touch screen technology continues to rise. Although the mouse is still the most common form of pointing device, there are others, such as trackpads, graphic tablets, tracker balls, and light pens. Recently released devices, such as Google Glass, are increasingly exploring the pros and cons of gaze as a means of pointing. However, for the time being, the dominant mode of interaction with desktop computers is still the mouse.

The movement of on-screen cursors using pointing devices generally follows Fitts' (1954) law. In its most general form, Fitts' law states that the time to point to an object is related to the distance from the object and inversely related to the size of the object, as shown in Fig. 3.8.

There are several variants of Fitts' law. The simplest is shown in Eq. (3.1):

$$\text{time} = \text{intercept constant} + \text{slope constant} * \log_2(2 \times d/w) \qquad (3.1)$$

Card et al. (1983) variant shown in Eq. (3.2) is slightly easier to use:

$$\text{time} = 70\,\text{ms} * \log_2(d/w + 0.5) \qquad (3.2)$$

Fig. 3.8 Description of the variables in Fitts' Law. X is where the user starts to point from, d is the distance to the target, and w is the width of the target

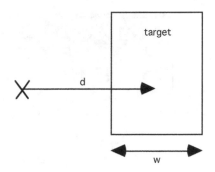

The argument to the $\log_2$ function in these equations is a measure of the difficulty of the move, measured in bits of information (Shannon 1948). It is sometimes called the index of difficulty. As shown in Fig. 3.8, the target distance, d, is measured from the point where the movement starts, X, and the target size, w, is the width of the target. If the movement was from above or below the target, the target size would be based on the height of the target (MacKenzie and Buxton 1992). The *intercept constant* and *slope constant* vary across tasks and across input modalities. Typical values for the *intercept constant* are about 100 ms. The *slope constant* varies from about 20 ms for very good input devices like using fingers directly, to 105 ms for using arms directly as well as for mice.

Fitts' law is less accurate where the size of the object, or the distance that has to be moved, are very large, for example, where the user's mouse reaches the edge of the desk before the mouse pointer has reached the edge of the screen, so the user has to pick up the mouse and move it back across the desk before the pointer can be moved any further. Some versions predict a negative reaction time for large or close objects (where d/w is 0, for example), and time to move to distant objects tends to be underestimated. Also note that the units are arbitrary, as it is the ratio of the target size to target distance that is used. Fitts' law is, however, a fairly robust law, and has been usefully applied to many interfaces because it makes good suggestions for interface design.

There are at least two implications for designing user interfaces that arise out of Fitts' Law. The first is that larger objects lead to faster pointing times than smaller objects. The second is that shorter distances also lead to faster reaction times. Indeed, the fastest time is to move a very small distance towards an infinitely large target. Moving the cursor to the screen's edge (with effectively an infinite target size) is much faster than moving the cursor to a bounded (finite) box that is more centrally located. So, menu bars at the very top of the screen are much faster to access than menu bars that are offset from the edge. These implications have to be traded off against other factors though, such as the size of the other objects in a display, the size of the display itself, sequencing of tasks, and how often the objects and commands are used.

Fig. 3.9 A screen shot of an application (Word11 for Macintosh) with several menus

Fig. 3.10 Word 2010 for Window's menu bar with offset from display edge

Figure 3.9 shows several example menu bars. The top menu (starting with the Apple and Word) will be the fastest because it is next to the screen edge. Being next to the edge makes the target size very large. The other menus below that will be slower to access. The icons on the far left (the dashed box with a pointer, the grid, the circular line, picture, etc.) will, however, be relatively fast to point to, because they are on an edge, if the user is approaching them from the center of the window. However, they are not because they are offset from the edge by Word.

Figure 3.10 shows Word 2010's menu in Windows in which the menu items (File, Home, etc.) are offset from the top edge. The time to switch to a menu bar item in Fig. 3.9 is (assuming from the middle of the screen) limited by the constant time and time to click because the target size is infinite, so the user can move the mouse without regard to the target. So, about 100 ms + 1,100 ms or 1,200 ms. The time to switch to a menu bar item in Fig. 3.10 is about 100 ms + 100 ms × $\log_2$ (8 cm/1 cm) or 1,500 ms. In other words, at least 25% longer.

Figure 3.11 shows the Eclipse integrated development environment (IDE), including some aspects for writing user models. In this interface the menus are also offset from the top of the window, which might not even be flush with the top of the display. Selecting buttons and panels will thus be slower and more error prone with this menu.

Fitts' law yields some more sophisticated suggestions when combined with Hick's law, which predicts how long it takes to choose one item from a list of several options (Landauer 1987a). When combined, these two laws suggest that

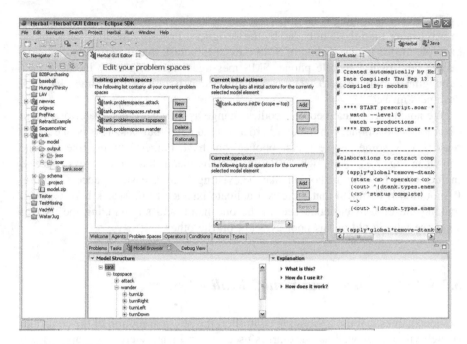

Fig. 3.11 The Eclipse workspace

broader and shallower menus will be faster to use than narrower and deeper menus (multiple movements take more time than choosing), although the size of the effects are moderated by the naturalness of the categories of the menu items (Landauer 1987b, pp. 146–147).

It is also worth noting that Fitts' Law also applies to moving to a particular key on a keyboard, although the constants in the equation are different. The results here would advocate making frequently used keys bigger and possibly putting them close to the edge of the keyboard, depending on how they are used. The sequence in which keys are regularly used is also an important factor to consider in working out the layout of the keys.

3.3.4 Mobile Phones

Thumbing is an important area of interface interaction (see, for example, James and Reischel 2001; MacKenzie and Soukoreff 2002). Many mobile phone users interact using their thumbs rather than their fingers. In some cases they use one hand, particularly when using those parts of the screen that can be used more easily one handed. In other cases, they cradle the phone in the fingers of both hands, and then enter data using both thumbs. Phones that have full keyboards, rather than just numeric keypads, are particularly suited to using both thumbs for text input.

The use of thumbing is an important reminder that users will often use devices in ways other than those intended by the designers. Probably the most widespread example of this is the sending of SMS messages, a task that is performed by most people who own a mobile phone. SMS messages were originally included as a debugging feature to help telephone engineers; it is one of the things that HCI designers missed.

We noted earlier that people's bodies change as they get older. Deterioration in eyesight, for example, can make it harder to read small buttons. This is one of the reasons why some people prefer phones that have bigger buttons, like the one shown in Fig. 3.12. Although the larger buttons mean that there is less space to include other features, it should make the existing features easier to access and use. It should also be noted that there is a delicate balance to be struck here between making the buttons easier to see on the one hand, and stigmatizing the user as someone who is old or has poor eyesight on the other.

3.3.5 Video Games and Virtual Reality Systems

In video games that use a vibrating controller, the physical motion of the controller (which vibrates as well as buzzing) is used as a primary source of (haptic) feedback. In car driving games, for example, the vibration may indicate that the car has left the road surface (see also Fogtmann et al. 2008 and Bau and Poupyrev 2012 for two examples of their use). Video games are becoming increasingly sophisticated in this area.

Haptic feedback in virtual reality systems provides a useful way to help the user feel immersed in the virtual environment. In some cases it is easier to communicate particular types of information in virtual environments, such as the forces that exist between objects and those that are needed to manipulate objects. Force has also been used, for example, in virtual surgery to represent different parts of the body, and to illustrate the forces involved in manipulating atoms within a molecule when designing drugs (e.g., Zonta et al. 2009).

One way of providing haptic interaction is through a force feedback glove, which is instrumented and has force feedback pads in the fingers. The user wears the glove, and as they move their hand and fingers in the glove, the movements are applied to modify the relevant objects in the interface. If an object in the interface is not movable, or requires a significant force to move it, this is fed back to the user by providing a greater force on feedback pads and hence onto the user's fingers. Data gloves are often perceived as being quite cumbersome, however, which is an issue that is now starting to be addressed through the development of devices that support gesture-based interaction such as Microsoft's Digits[3] which utilizes a wrist-worn gloveless sensor.

---

[3] http://research.microsoft.com/apps/video/dl.aspx?id=173838

Fig. 3.12 An example phone interface (Jitterbug Plus) designed with larger buttons and a simpler interface. Taken from www.greatcall. com (used with permission)

In immersive environments users still receive most of their feedback on their actions and movements through the visual channel. Where there is a mismatch between the visual scene and the inner ear's movement, however, this can lead to nausea. Full motion simulators attempt to provide some of this information by providing initiating cues to the motion. How to provide this information to a user remains a technical problem that is informed by knowledge about the user.

3.3.6 Other Devices

Other devices have introduced some other novel methods of interaction. Apple's iPod, for example, incorporated the idea of using a dial which, when rotated, produces behavior similar to that of a scroll bar, as shown in Fig. 3.13. When it was introduced this was quite novel, and many users liked it.

Fig. 3.13 Apple iPod, showing the novel (at the time) circular dial control

Fig. 3.14 The Samsung TicToc music player

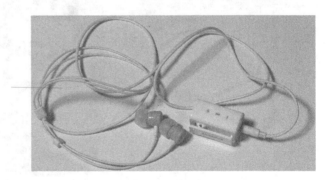

Another music player, the Samsung TicToc mp3 player (Fig. 3.14), takes a different approach to interaction. The TicToc has only one button, and feedback is obtained through a combination of three LEDs, which backlight the three icons on the body of the player, and speech. You press and hold the button (located on the end of the player) to turn the TicToc on. This causes all three LEDs to illuminate, and the player tells you how much battery capacity is left and then starts playing automatically. To increase the volume, you hold the player with the "+" icon uppermost and press the button several times until you get the desired level. To reduce the volume you turn the player the other way up and repeat the process. If you want to turn the player off you press and hold the button. Again, all the lights illuminate before the player switches off.

Moving between tracks is relatively straightforward: you hold the player horizontally, and press the button once to skip to the next track, or twice if you want to skip to the previous track. If you want to skip to the next album, you press it three times. The novel interaction involves shaking the device. If you shake it once it tells you the artist name followed by the name of the track that is currently playing (as long as you have added the music using the TicToc program). You also shake the player (three times) if you want to change the mode, which cycles through Normal, Shuffle, Fast (tempo), and Slow (tempo): it then tells you which mode you have switched to.

The Samsung TicToc may not be to everyone's tastes, but the interaction methods can actually be quite useful. If you listen to music when you go out exercising, for example, you can operate the TicToc without having to stop and look at the interface to locate the correct button, and read the display, as you would with other digital music players.

3.3.7 Advantages and Disadvantages of Haptic Interfaces

Touch-based interfaces are important for a wide range of users and will be particularly important for users without sight as the technology to provide haptic interfaces improves. Explorations include: a computer mouse that can provide tactile feedback via a series of electric motors (Göbel et al. 1995); computers that let users feel the texture of, for example, a fabric on their screens (Dillon et al. 2001); and mobile phones made with latex that enable people to communicate by touch as well as speech (Park et al. 2013). Table 3.1 notes the range of applications that are possible, and illustrates the range of users and tasks that can take advantage of haptic interfaces.

Tactile feedback is already used by many interfaces to convey important information about the status of a system, particularly that a given operation has been accomplished. For example, using a switch is confusing if there is no obvious tactile or audible sensation that it has been operated. If there is no obvious visual or auditory indication of the switch being operated, then touch is the next most likely means of providing that feedback. Keyboards are designed to provide this type of feedback.

Kaczmarek and Bach-y-Rita's (1995) list of advantages to using touch (Table 3.1), can be extended further:

(1) Users have a lot of skin. Several parts of it are sensitive enough to provide a useful communication media.
(2) Skin has several functional similarities to the eye, including the ability to map from a two-dimensional display of the environment to the user's skin, and to integrate the signal over time.
(3) Representations learned visually can be recognized tactilely.
(4) The inputs required can be quite low and easily achievable with current technology. In particular, the fingertips are very sensitive to changes in pressure.

Table 3.1 Types of users and tasks that can use a haptic interface

---

Users with poor vision

Teleoperators in areas where vision is not possible or not clear, such as muddy sea floors or areas with high radiation or poor light

Drivers (cars, buses, tractors, miners) at night

Aircraft pilots and car drivers in fog

Users with poor or temporarily degraded sense of touch

Astronauts (and others, such as first responders) wearing gloves

People with insensate feet or hands (a common complication of diabetes) or who have reduced sensitivity due to age

Teleoperators who would like more feedback about what is in their gripper

Users who need an additional input channel or need touch as the input channel

Cellular phone users in situations where audio ringing is not acceptable

Surgeons who need to know the elasticity and shape of organs during virtual surgery

Game players who could feel that they are being hit or are bumping a wall

---

Expanded from Kaczmarek and Bach-y-Rita (1995)

(5) Touch provides another input modality. This is useful as primary modality for users without sight. For sighted users, communication through touch does not interfere materially with motor or other sensory functions.

(6) For telepresence, such as virtual reality applications, tactile feedback is very important for obtaining the sense of immersion.

Many of the barriers to using haptic interfaces such as cost, power requirements, safety, and usefulness have now been overcome. This explains why there are now so pervasive in smartphones and tablet computers.

3.4 Implications for System Design

System performance is a result of particular users doing particular tasks (using a particular technology) in a particular context. When you are thinking about designing interactive systems, you will need to consider all of these aspects together.

Your users may have limited vision or even no vision at all. This can be a permanent physical characteristic: they may be blind, for example. It may also be a constraint of the task environment, for example when operating motor transport at night or in foggy weather conditions. Currently, interfaces that make use of auditory information are most important to people with visual impairment, but haptic interfaces are becoming more important as the technology improves, and the associated costs fall.

If your users will include older people, you may need to give consideration to the type of technology that you will use. As people get older, or if they have diabetes, their skin loses its sensitivity. This means that if you are going to use a touch screen interface it may need to utilize resistive technology rather than capacitive technology.

If the user's task has to be carried out remotely, or requires wearing gloves (ranging from those used outdoors to those used in space), then you may want to augment visual (and auditory) feedback with haptic feedback. Teleoperators, for example, often like to have feedback about what they are holding in their grippers, and surgeons performing operations remotely need to know about the shape and elasticity of the organs that they are dealing with.

One aspect of haptics which we have not considered here, but which can be important, is the feel of a device and the materials it is made from, its esthetics. A smooth, shaped surface, for example, may help to lead to a positive emotional experience of using a particular device. This is one of the reasons why mice evolved from relatively square devices to something that is now much more rounded and better suited to the shape of the hand when using it.

If your system will be installed in an environment where there is limited space, this may determine how the users can interact with the system. It is always worth going to look at the installation location beforehand. One of the authors was involved in putting in a system that normally used a mouse. The system was to be installed alongside another system which meant that there was very limited desktop space available. As a result, a trackerball interface was used instead of the mouse because it requires less space to operate.

If your system includes manual controls, it is important to provide haptic feedback to indicate that these controls have been operated. This is particularly true when there is no obvious visual or auditory feedback when a button has been pressed or a switch has been activated, for example.

If you are developing a mobile application or system, you will need to think about all the contexts in which it may be used. If it can be used in a situation where visual and auditory feedback are not allowed, for example, then you may want to give the device a haptic interaction capability. Most mobile phones, for example, provide a silent mode in which the phone vibrates rather than rings.

3.5 Summary

This chapter has introduced the fact that at least some aspects of users' bodies are involved in interacting with devices and systems. Although the fields of human factors and ergonomics routinely consider this aspect of work, it tends to be less explicitly represented in HCI. Users' bodies provide capabilities and constraints on what tasks they can perform, the loads that they can support and carry, and how quickly and accurately they can provide input to a system. Using this information can help us make effective choices about which input modality to use, and how to design menus and dialog boxes.

Human capabilities and constraints vary between users, and within users they vary across time and across context. The best interfaces are those that take all of these differences into consideration so that they can support as wide a range of use—people, technology, and context—as possible.

3.6 Other Resources

There are many texts that are available for deepening understanding of design relevant aspects of the body. Although not explicitly focused on the human body nor on technology, we strongly recommend Don Norman's excellent text, *The Psychology of Everyday Things*, to get you into a way of thinking about people interacting with designed objects of all kinds. An extremely readable text, we think you will find many examples that relate to your everyday world (many related to anthropometrics) and that will get you thinking about design from a different perspective.

Norman, D. A. (1988). *The psychology of everyday things*. NY: Basic Books. (2013 ed. *The design of everyday things*)

Further information on the range of users' bodies and how they move can be found in engineering handbooks. We recommend looking at:

Boff, K. R., Kaufman, L., and Thomas, J. P. (1986). *Handbook of perception and human performance* (Vol. I, II, and III). New York: John Wiley & Sons.

Industrial engineering explores this area in much more depth, and knows about how best to support users that stand, squat, and assume a variety of other postures. Wickens et al. (1998, Chaps. 10 and 11) provide a useful introduction to these topics.

The International Standards Organization (ISO, you may see this acronym on a variety of technical measures and standards) has been developing standards for usability for several years. The most relevant series here is ISO 9241, Ergonomics of Human System Interaction (http://en.wikipedia.org/wiki/ISO_9241).

It is also worth thinking about new forms of interaction beyond the current keyboard layout. There are a number of research projects addressing new forms of input beyond the keyboard. This edited special issue gives some pointers to future thinking research work:

Schmidt, A., and Churchill, E. F. (2012). Interaction beyond the keyboard, *IEEE Computer, 45*(4). 21–24.

3.7 Exercises

3.1 Consider a smartphone, either a specific one or a composite, general one. Attempt to come up with a trade-off function between a set of features (which you create) and weight. Describe how to choose a reasonable point on that curve. Is your smartphone more like a phone, tablet, or laptop?

3.2 Choose an existing interface and make five suggestions how touch could change or improve its usability. Interfaces where this is easy to do include CAD/CAM systems and data mining systems. Interfaces that are more difficult include online learning environments and simple web sites.

3.3 Describe five systems where anthropometrics make a difference. To get you started, consider small systems for playing music, and also consider how these systems can be integrated with other capabilities (e.g., cellular phones).

3.4 Write a short report on the quality of your own desk and work area. Compare it with an ergonomically suggested design as well as with what is available in the place where you use a computer for study or work purposes.

3.5 Compute the constants for Fitts' law based on a thumb. This can be done by creating a set of targets for the thumb and measuring the time for the thumb to move to those targets. In the case where video analysis is not available, a useful approach is to have the thumb move to the target multiple times and then move back, or to type in a series of actions and then use linear regression to compute the best predicted time per action. The resulting constants and times can then be compared with other constants for pointing approaches.

3.6 Compute the time it would take to select an Eclipse menu item from the application's top menu in Fig. 3.11, like "Refactor," and a menu from the window's panels, like "Target.java." You should compute this for the middle of the screen (as shown) and from the actual location of the mouse pointer.

3.7 Given a 15″ diagonal touch screen, how many buttons could you put on it?

    (a) Note your assumptions.
    (b) Describe how many buttons you could fit on the screen.
    (c) Note any lessons you found while doing this task.

3.8 On a Penn State online course system, similar to many online course systems, the web page shown on the top of Fig. 3.15 appears. If you click on the link next to the pointer (Template for the Team Contract), the page on the bottom comes up. This page notes that if you do not move the mouse over the target phrase (blank_team_contract.doc) in 5 s, the file will automatically download (presumably to your default download directory). It is often much better to download into your course directory, so you have to quickly move your mouse over the target phrase.

    Comment on what would be a reasonable default time to move the mouse using Fitts' law. Is 5 s a reasonable time, or could it be much less, or should it be more?

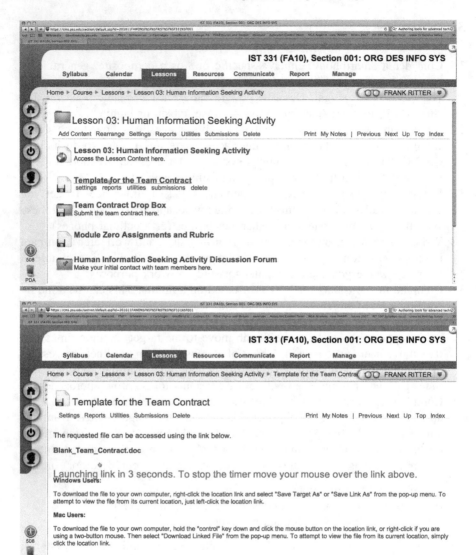

Fig. 3.15 File downloading in the Angel course management system. How long should the user have to move their mouse to stop a download?

References

Bau, O., & Poupyrev, I. (2012). REVEL: Tactile feedback technology for augmented reality. *ACM Transactions on Graphics, 31*(4), Article 89, 1–11.

Card, S. K., Moran, T. P., & Newell, A. (1980). The keystroke-level model for user performance time with interactive systems. *Communications of the ACM, 23*(7), 396–410.

Card, S. K., Moran, T., & Newell, A. (1983). *The psychology of human-computer interaction.* Hillsdale, NJ: Erlbaum.

Dillon, P., Moody, W., Bartlett, R., Scully, P., Morgan, R., & James, C. L. (2001). Sensing the fabric: To simulate sensation through sensory evaluation and in response to standard acceptable properties of specific materials when viewed as a digital image. In *Haptic human-computer interaction, First international workshop* (pp. 205–218). Berlin: Springer.

English, J., & Andre, A. D. (1999). Posture and web browsing: An observational study. In *Proceedings of the 43rd annual meeting of the Human Factors and Ergonomics Society* (pp. 945–949). Santa Monica, CA: Human Factors and Ergonomics Society.

Fitts, P. M. (1954). The information capacity of the human motor system in controlling amplitude of movement. *Journal of Experimental Psychology, 47*(6), 381–391.

Fogtmann, M. H., Fritsch, J., & Kortbek, K. J. (2008). Kinesthetic interaction—Revealing the bodily potential in interaction design. In *OZCHI'08: Proceedings of the 20th Australasian conference on computer–human interaction: Designing for habitus and habitat* (pp. 89–96). New York, NY: ACM Press.

Gibson, J. J. (1979). *The ecological approach to visual perception.* Boston, MA: Houghton Mifflin.

Göbel, M., Luczak, H., Springer, J., Hedicke, V., & Rötting, M. (1995). Tactile feedback applied to computer mice. *International Journal of Human-Computer Interaction, 7*(1), 1–24.

James, C. L., & Reischel, K. M. (2001). Text input for mobile devices: Comparing model prediction to actual performance. In *CHI '01 Proceedings of the SIGCHI conference on human factors in computing systems* (pp. 365–371). New York, NY: ACM.

Jiang, Y., Tian, F., Zhang, X., Liu, W., Dai, G., & Wang, H. (2012). Unistroke gestures on multi-touch interaction: Supporting flexible touches with key stroke extraction. In *ACM conference on Intelligent User Interfaces (IUI)* (pp. 61–70). New York, NY: ACM.

John, B. E. (1996). TYPIST: A theory of performance in skilled typing. *Human-Computer Interaction, 11*(4), 321–355.

Kaczmarek, K. A., & Bach-y-Rita, P. (1995). Tactile displays. In W. Barfield & T. A. Furness III (Eds.), *Virtual environments and advanced interface design* (pp. 349–414). Oxford: Oxford University Press.

Kinkead, R. (1975). Typing speed, keying rates, and optimal keyboard layouts. In *Proceedings of the Human Factors Society 19th annual meeting* (pp. 159–161). Santa Monica, CA: Human Factors Society.

Landauer, T. K. (1987a). Relations between cognitive psychology and computer systems design. In J. M. Carroll (Ed.), *Interfacing thought: Cognitive aspects of human- computer interaction* (pp. 1–25). Cambridge, MA: MIT Press.

Landauer, T. K. (1987b). Relations between cognitive psychology and computer systems design. In J. Preece & L. Keller (Eds.), *Human-computer interaction* (pp. 141–159). Englewood Cliffs, NJ: Prentice-Hall.

Loomis, J. M., & Lederman, S. J. (1986). Tactual perception. In K. Boff, L. Kaufman, & J. Thomas (Eds.), *Handbook of perception and human performance* (Vol. II, pp. 31-31–31-41). New York, NY: Wiley.

MacKenzie, I. S., & Buxton, W. A. S. (1992). Extending Fitts' law to two-dimensional tasks. In *Proceedings of ACM CHI 1992 conference on human factors in computing systems* (pp. 219–226).

MacKenzie, I. S., & Soukoreff, R. W. (2002). Text entry for mobile computing: Models and methods, theory and practice. *Human-Computer Interaction, 17*, 147–198.

Norman, D. A. (1988). *The psychology of everyday things.* New York: Basic Books.

Norman, D. A. (2013). *The design of everyday things*. New York: Basic Books.

Park, Y. W., Baek, K. M., & Nam, T. J. (2013). The roles of touch during phone conversations: Long-distance couples' use of POKE in their homes. In *Proceedings of the 2013 ACM annual conference on human factors in computing systems*, (pp. 1679–1688). New York, NY: ACM.

Salthouse, T. A. (1986). Perceptual, cognitive, and motoric aspects of transcription typing. *Psychological Bulletin, 3*(3), 303–319.

Shannon, C. E. (1948). A mathematical theory of communication. *Bell System Technical Journal, 27*, 379–423; 623–656.

Tian, F., Xu, L., Wang, H., Zhang, X., Liu, Y., Setlur, V., et al. (2008). Tilt Menu: Using the 3D orientation information of pen devices to extend the selection capability of pen-based user. In *ACM SIGCHI annual conference* (CHI) 2008, (pp. 1371–1380). New York, NY: ACM.

Wickens, C. D., Gordon, S. E., & Liu, Y. (1998). *An introduction to human factors engineering*. New York, NY: Addison-Wesley.

Zonta, N., Grimstead, I. J., Avis, N. J., & Brancale, A. (2009). Accessible haptic technology for drug design applications. *Journal of Molecular Modeling, 15*(2), 193–196.

Chapter 4
Behavior: Basic Psychology of the User

Abstract This chapter examines what are described as user behavioral characteristics. These are characteristics that are related to perception in broad terms. The
chapter starts by defining some behavioral terms and concepts that are used in this
and subsequent chapters. We then describe in detail several aspects of the two
main perceptual systems that are involved in interacting with computer-based
systems: vision and hearing. For each of these aspects we consider some of the
implications they have for system design. We finish by introducing the topic of
motivation to help explain why individual users may behave in a particular way
when carrying out a task.

4.1 Introduction

When we refer to behavioral characteristics we are really talking about things that
are linked to sensation and perception, in general terms. We know that people have
five basic senses: sight, hearing, touch, smell, and taste. Sensation occurs when the
sense organs (eyes, ears, and so on) are stimulated, and they generate some form of
coding of the stimuli. Perception occurs when this coded information is further
interpreted using knowledge of the current context (physical, physiological, psychological, and so on) to add meaning. The process of perception is subjective:
simply presenting designed stimuli in such a way that they will be sensed accurately does not necessarily mean that they will be perceived in the way that the
designer intended.

Sight, hearing, and smell all sense stimuli that appear at some distance from the
body. In other words they detect distant (distal) stimuli. Touch and taste, however,
rely on contact being made with the stimuli. This means that the stimuli have to be
very close to the body, which is why they are described as proximal stimuli.

We need to think about the user's behavioral characteristics when designing
systems because we want to make sure that the system fits the user. A well-designed
system will take into account the user's ability to detect changes in an interface, for
example, and we can use this information to inform the design of screen layouts to

F. E. Ritter et al., *Foundations for Designing User-Centered Systems*,
DOI: 10.1007/978-1-4471-5134-0_4, © Springer-Verlag London 2014

help the user make the most of that ability. It is also important to remember that these abilities will vary across users, tasks, and contexts. If your system will be deployed in a brightly lit office, for example, then reflected light and glare are likely to affect the user's ability to read what is displayed on the screen.

In most computer-based systems we tend to privilege vision and hearing over the other senses, although the rapid uptake of smartphones and tablet computers has increased the importance of considering touch (described in Chap. 3). Often it is important to consider how the different sensory modalities can be used together to provide further useful information to the user. In dark, or dimly lit conditions, for example, using different shaped knobs and switches can be used to exploit the sense of touch to impart information to the user. Similarly, if a user has impaired vision, we may want to present information in such a way that it can be exploited by other senses, such as touch and hearing.

Once we have an understanding of how people sense and perceive things, and how the different senses work together, we can start to think about broader design questions such as:

- What is the best way to present information to the user?
- Can the user detect the information that we are presenting to them?
- If we are presenting a lot of information to the user, should we be presenting it using more than one sensory channel (e.g., visual and auditory channels are often both used for alarm information).

Next, we introduce some basic concepts from behavioral psychology that will help you to understand and interpret the rest of the chapter. We then provide quite detailed descriptions of the visual and auditory perceptual systems. There are many aspects of the visual and auditory systems that need to be considered when designing systems. For this reason, we consider the implications for system design at the end of each of the sections in this chapter. Note that we omit the senses of smell and taste here because their use is almost exclusively limited to systems that are dedicated to tasks that only involve detecting particular smells and tastes.

4.2 Behavioral Psychology Terminology

Within psychology many terms have been developed to describe different aspects of behavior, extending far beyond perception. Here we introduce some terms that may help you when thinking about the user and usability with respect to perception.

4.2.1 Thresholds and Just Noticeable Differences (JNDs)

Each sense has a threshold for detecting stimuli. Sounds that are too quiet or visual stimuli that are too faint cannot be sensed. Table 4.1 gives some representative

Table 4.1 Some human sensory thresholds (under ideal conditions)

Sight	A candle flame seen from 50 km on a clear dark night (100 quanta to the eye, or 10 quanta absorbed by the rods)
Sound	The tick of a watch from 6 m in very quiet conditions (0.0002 dynes/cm^2)
Taste	One gram of table salt in 500 L of water (0.0001 M)
Smell	One drop of perfume diffused throughout a three room apartment or 1×10^{-12} mol/L of ethyl merchantman
Touch	The wing of a bee falling on your cheek from a height of 1 cm (10 mg force)

thresholds under ideal conditions for the various senses (taken from Galanter 1962). It should be noted that thresholds can vary across tasks and contexts. In a room full of noisy machinery, for example, you may need to increase the volume of alarm warning sounds, so that they can be heard by users.

The sensitivity of perception can be measured, based on how small a change can be detected. This difference is called a *just noticeable difference*, or JND. In vision, for example, it is how much brighter a scene has to be in order for someone to report it as being brighter; and in hearing it is how much louder a sound must be to be noticeably different. Although JNDs are objectively measured, their magnitude is subjective, varying across users, tasks, contexts, and modality.

4.2.2 Habituation

All living things react to stimuli. If a stimulus occurs repeatedly and is not regarded as salient they will habituate to it. People who live beside a railroad track, for example, grow accustomed to the noise of the trains to a point where they no longer notice it. In other words, people learn which stimuli are not salient (in the current context), and hence do not require further processing. Habituation effectively frees up cognitive resources, which allows people to use those resources to deal with new stimuli as they are presented. Constant "confirm action" boxes, for example, will become habituated to.

4.2.3 Signal Detection Theory (SDT)

Accuracy is an important aspect of performance. In many cases, simple measures of correctness, such as the number of targets that were recognized and the number that were missed, are sufficient. This is too simple a measure, however, when examining performance under conditions where the ability to be correct is difficult, and the types of mistakes are important. Table 4.2 provides a way of summarizing this more complex situation: if you report seeing something when it is there, it is called a hit; if you fail to report seeing something when it is there, it is called a miss. Similarly,

Table 4.2 Types of responses to a signal

Response	Signal present	
	Yes	No
Yes	Hit	False alarm (FA)
No	Miss	Correct rejection (CR)

reporting seeing nothing where there is nothing there is called a correct rejection, whilst reporting seeing something when it is not there is called a false alarm.

Human visual behavior often includes searching, scanning, and monitoring. Vigilance tasks, which are a subset of these tasks, usually involve an extended time period between the signals that the user is supposed to recognize. While it should be possible to moderate the performance of these tasks based on the dimensions used in the table, it is often useful to analyze these situations using Signal Detection Theory (SDT) (Swets 1973; Swets et al. 1961; also see Wickens et al. 2014 or Wickens 2002).

SDT was developed to explain the task of identifying enemy planes on hard to read radar displays. It has been applied to a wide range of classification and decision making tasks. Swets (1973), for example, used SDT to summarize how well doctors could classify cancer tumors from X-ray films. It can also be applied within computer games to explain the potential problems when players search for enemies or resources.

Figure 4.1 shows how the key parameters in SDT relate to the ability to distinguish the object of interest (signal) from distracting items (noise). The set of signals is assumed to be normally distributed about a point some distance away from 0, whilst the set of noise is normally distributed around 0 (indicating no valid signal strength). d' represents the distance between the mean of the noise and the mean of the signal, and is an inherent property of an observer and stimuli. Observers set a threshold (here, beta, β, some authors call this lambda, λ, or yet another Greek character) as a parameter that is inherent in the observer. Observations above the threshold are classified by the observer as signal and observations below are classified as noise. Thus, the parts of the signal above the threshold are hits and the parts of the noise distribution are false alarms (FA). Observations below the threshold are either correct rejections (CRs) if they are noise or misses if they were part of the signal.

Observers can often adjust the threshold to take account of the relative costs of the four responses in Table 4.2. The cost of false alarms and misses will influence where the threshold is set. Where misses are costly, the threshold will be to the left, classifying more signal and more noise as positive responses. Where false alarms are expensive compared to misses, the threshold will be moved to the right, eliminating more of the noise but also part of the signal.

Signal detection theory is often described in terms of sensitivity and bias. The sensitivity (which is the same as d') refers to the separation between the signal and noise distributions. Where the separation is small, and the two distributions

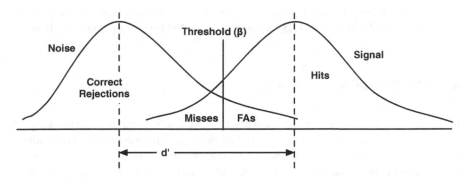

Fig. 4.1 Signal and noise distributions in signal detection theory

overlap considerably, sensitivity is said to be low. Where the separation is large, sensitivity is said to be high. The response bias (which is the same as β) describes how conservative the user is in responding. If the user responds conservatively, this is because a lot of evidence is needed to be sure that what has been observed is really a signal (a true hit), and not just noise.

4.2.4 Implications for System Design

It is important to be aware of the context in which your system will be used. A data indicator on a display, for example, will be sensed differently in a brightly lit location and in a dimly lit location. Users also find it hard to differentiate between elements in an interface that use stimuli that are separated by less than a JND (such as two shades of the same color). If it is important that some elements on a display which are visually similar (such as same shape, but slightly different color) are processed differently, they should be made distinct by separating one or more dimensions of their appearance by several JNDs (several shades of color, for example).

If a system generates lots of false alarms or interrupts, users may habituate to the alarm sounds, like in Aesop's Fable about the boy who cried wolf. Then, when a real emergency happens, users may ignore the alarm. It is therefore crucial to minimize the number of false alarms. Pay close attention to how and where alarm limits are set, and make sure that you take into account how noisy the data values being judged are. This may involve preventing the alarm from oscillating on and off when there are recurrent spikes in the values that are due to artifacts such as measurement error.

For systems where the users have to perform vigilance tasks (like monitoring the screens of hand luggage scanners at airports to identify dangerous and prohibited items), you will need to calculate the costs of false alarms and misses. If the costs are high, there are some measures that you can employ to increase the users' sensitivity, such as showing target examples that they can refer to for comparison, and to change their response bias, such as making clear to them the costs of false alarms and misses (see Wickens et al. 2014 and Wickens 2002 for more complete lists).

4.3 The Physiology of Vision

In the next few sections we examine the details of vision. We start by offering a high-level description of the physical structure of the eye. This should help you understand the basic idea of how vision works and what some of its important limitations are. Unlike a camera snapshot, for example, the eye does not capture everything in a scene equally, but selectively picks out salient objects and features from the current context, and focuses on them so they can be processed in more detail.

4.3.1 Overview of Vision

For normally sighted people, vision is by far the most widely used sense. Vision is important in everyday work because it allows us to use interfaces like those shown in Fig. 4.2. Understanding the basics of how human vision works, including its strengths and weaknesses, will help you to design systems that more closely match your user's visual capabilities.

4.3.2 The Basic Structure of the Eye

Figure 4.3 shows the basic structure of the eye. The important physiological features that you need to be aware of are the lens, the retina, the rod and cone cells (the sensory receptors in the eye which respond to different light waves), the fovea, and the optic nerve.

When you look at an object, an image of it is projected onto the eye. The angle that is subtended by that object at the eye is described as the *visual angle*. The ability to discriminate between two objects that are close together is described as *visual acuity*. This is usually expressed in terms of the minimum visual angle that can be resolved, for which the standard is normally a gap subtending 1 min of arc (1/60 of a degree). Acuity is usually expressed as a fraction which expresses the ratio of the standard distance used in eye-tests (20 ft or 6 m) to the distance at which a gap subtends 1 min of arc. So when you hear someone described as having 20/20 (or 6/6) vision, the numbers refer to their visual acuity.

The light coming from an object is focused by the lens and projected onto the retina at the back of the eye. Muscles attached to the sides of the lens contract in order to thicken the lens and bend the light more to achieve a clear focus when the

Fig. 4.2 An interface that has to be recognized quickly and accurately

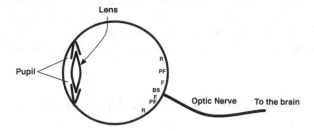

Fig. 4.3 Basic structure of the eye (not to scale). The retina is the area (*roughly circular*) from R to R. The parafovea is from PF to PF. The fovea is from F to F. The blind spot is at BS, where the optic nerve leaves the eye and blood comes in

stimulus is near. These muscles relax when the object is further away. This process of contracting and relaxing is called accommodation. As people age, the lens stiffens, which makes it harder for the muscles to affect its curvature as much, so glasses are prescribed to compensate for the reduced level of accommodation.

The *fovea* constitutes a small part of the retina, about 1–2° of visual arc, which approximately equates to the angle covered by your thumbnail when viewed at arm's length. The receptor systems that permit visual acuity are concentrated only in the fovea, so we need to fixate on an object to have a clear image of it. Surrounding the fovea is the parafovea, which has a lower level of visual acuity than the fovea.

You can demonstrate the existence of the fovea to yourself by staring at a dot in the center of a page. Only the area immediately surrounding it will appear in clear focus, so to clearly perceive a scene of any size the eyes must move around. These semi-conscious movements are called saccades and take approximately 200 ms to program, and last 20–200 ms, which is just about the interval of the persistence of vision.

The *pupil* of the eye reacts to the amount of light falling on the retina by expanding and contracting in such a way as to keep that amount approximately constant. This feedback mechanism operates within a certain fairly narrow range of illumination (about 16–1), but the enormously greater variation in retinal illumination (about 10^9–1) demands an intermediate mechanism to allow the eye to function over the whole range of illumination. This mechanism is called *adaptation*. Adaptation is one of the most profound and pervasive sensory phenomena. Our eyes are prevented from adapting to what they are seeing by continually moving. These normal movements, which are normally unnoticeable, are faster and smaller than saccades, and described as micro-saccades.

You may have had the experience of entering a theatre from the bright outdoors and stumbling to your seat in the darkness, tripping over the feet of people already seated. In a few moments you will have adapted to the darkness, that is, you have become more accustomed to the lack of light. This mechanism applies to the sense of smell too: when walking into a kitchen where someone is cooking you will notice the odors as very strong, but after a few minutes they become less noticeable. These examples illustrate that after exposure to a stimulus the sensitivity to that stimulus reduces; after removal of the stimulus, the sensitivity returns.

4.3.3 Using Eye-Tracking to Measure Eye Movements

A lot has been learned about how people read and use interfaces by using eye trackers (Duchowski 2007; Holmqvist et al. 2011). Eye trackers are electro-optical systems (typically cameras that can be automatically focused and adjusted) that record where a user has focused their eyes. Simple systems measure where a single eye is looking. Better versions of this simple system can do this without the user having their head fixed, and many can now measure this non-intrusively. Figure 4.4 shows a head-mounted eye-tracker and two example summaries of eye-tracking data. More complex systems can measure both eyes and note how the eyes work together (e.g., strabismus, a measure of how much the eyes have focused onto something near to the head by rotating).

Simple eye-trackers can generally tell which line the user is looking at (to an accuracy of typically 0.5–1° of angular measure, which is about a line of 12 point text on a display at 12 in.). Better eye trackers can tell which letter or which part of the letter the user is focusing on (down to 0.25°).

A useful exercise that will help you to appreciate the accuracy of eye-trackers is to compute the size of a 10 point (1/7 in.) letter at 12 in. using trigonometry. When you have done this, you should see that the tolerance in eye-tracker accuracy is less than the size of the fovea. So although we may know where the center of the user's fovea is focused, there could be several other items that are also projecting onto it and to which the user is attending.

Fig. 4.4 A head-mounted eye-tracker and an example analysis showing the order that a user looked at the interface (*top*) and how long they looked at each part (*bottom*) (photo by Ritter, used with permission of the analyst pictured; analyses courtesy of Maik Friedrich 2008)

In addition to being widely used in psycholinguistics to understand how people read text, eye-tracking is increasingly being used in other fields such as HCI and advertising (Moore and Churchill 2011; Navalpakkam and Churchill in press; Nielsen and Pernice 2010). The availability of relatively cheap, non-intrusive trackers has seen them being used more widely in exploring how people process the text on web pages. With the use of appropriate software you can quickly identify the hot spots on a page, which are areas that the users look at for most of the time.

4.3.4 Rods and Cones

The *retina* at the back of the eyeball is composed of two basic types of cells—*rods* and *cones*—organized in layers. The rods and cones sense light, and mark the start of the transition from sensation to perception with light energy being converted into electrical energy.

According to duplicity theory, the differences between the rods and cones result in two different receptor systems in the eye: one that is best suited to daylight, and one best suited to twilight or moonlight. There are 6 million cones, mostly located in the fovea. These function in daylight conditions and are responsible for color vision. The 120 million rods are distributed across the retina beyond the fovea.

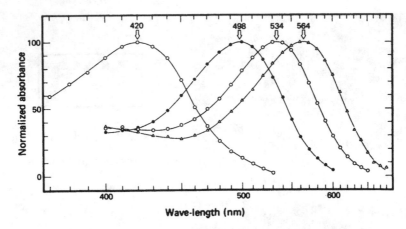

Fig. 4.5 Diagram of sensitivity in nanometers (nm) of rods and cones (reprinted with permission from Bowmaker and Dartnall 1980)

They are much more sensitive to light than the cones and are active in dark conditions; in bright conditions they become overloaded. The distributions of rods and cones overlap in the parafovea. The rods are mostly located beyond the parafovea, in the periphery of the retina, and are very sensitive to movement.

The visual receptors respond to light waves. The term *light* is used to describe electromagnetic energy in the visible range of wavelengths approximately 400–700 nm (see Fig. 4.5). The wavelengths that we see are determined by the physics of the eye and the chemistry of the photoreceptor pigments in the eye. Electromagnetic energy with wavelengths below the visible spectrum includes ultraviolet rays, X-rays, and gamma rays; electromagnetic energy with wavelengths above the visible spectrum includes infrared rays, microwaves, and radio waves.

Our sensitivity to spectral radiation is not constant across the electromagnetic spectrum. Instead, we sample it through a pair of filters. The first filter is provided by the spectral sensitivity of the rods, which have a maximum sensitivity around 500 nm (498 in Fig. 4.5). The second is provided by the pooled responses of the three types of cones (the leftmost and two rightmost curves in Fig. 4.5) and has maximum sensitivity around 555 nm. Below 380 nm (infrared) and above 700 nm (ultraviolet) we are effectively blind to electromagnetic waves. Therefore, there is a wide range of information that meets our eyes which falls outside our window of visibility.

Although we sense infrared energy as heat, other wavelengths outside the visible spectrum are imperceptible without the aid of devices such as radios or infrared goggles. Ultraviolet energy is destructive to living tissue, so it is filtered out by the yellow pigment in the lens of the eye. People who have had their lenses removed because of cataracts, however, can see ultraviolet energy as light. Rather than experiencing it as a new color sensation, which would require another type of cone, they see it as the same color that people with normal vision would see violet.

Fig. 4.6 Cover your right eye and focus directly on a digit with your left eye. Then move the page away from your head. At about a foot the word blind spot will disappear. The location of the blind spot and screen sizes will vary, so you may have to try different focus points

When you switch from looking at colored objects in bright light to looking at the same objects in dim light, all other things being equal you will notice that one object now seems brighter than the other. If you look at a blue flower and a red flower, for example, first in daylight and then at dusk, you will notice that under low illumination both appear faded, but the blue seems brighter than the red. Likewise, a piece of green paper and a piece of red paper which are matched for brightness in good light will not be matched in dim light. This effect is called the Purkinje Shift, and is based on the fact that long wavelength colors such as red appear duller under low illumination than shorter wavelength colors (such as blue). The effect occurs because of the shift from high illumination vision (cones) to low illumination vision (rods) under different light conditions. The rods are relatively more sensitive to light in the blue region than the cones, hence the apparent greater brightness of the blue flower in dim light. These relationships can be seen in spectral sensitivity curves that illustrate that maximum sensitivity goes from red to blue green (i.e., to shorter wavelengths) when we shift from bright to dim light and from the cones to the rods.

One final point about rods and cones: there is one part of the retina where there are no receptors (rods or cones) present. This is where the optic nerve leaves the retina. When the image of an object falls on this *blind spot*, nothing is seen. You can use Fig. 4.6 to help you find your own blind spot. The blind spot is in a different place for each eye.

4.3.5 Implications for System Design

If your system is going to be deployed in an area where users experience large step changes in lighting conditions on entering that area (from light to dark or vice versa) you will need to take account of the fact that their eyes will need time to adapt to the new lighting conditions. You could consider having gradual changes in lighting levels as they enter the area, for example.

People will often use a relatively large dialog box positioned in the center of the screen to get the user's attention for something that is important. This dialog box is usually large enough to project an image onto the retina that fills a significant portion of the fovea. It would be equally possible to capture the user's attention by make an item on the display screen move, or make it flash or blink, as long as the item is located in a position that projects onto the periphery of the retina. In this way the movement or flashing gets detected by the rods in the eye. There is a negative implication here too: if your user is carrying out an important task that requires high levels of concentration using the display screen, you should try to avoid having items on the screen move or flash, particularly if they would project onto the periphery of the user's eye.

If you are designing a system that has to be operated in light sensitive conditions, such as a photography dark room or a radar operations room, you need to consider how you can help the users see so that they can carry out their tasks in the dimly lit conditions. Usually in these situations, red light is used to illuminate the rooms, albeit at quite low levels. The rods are relatively less sensitive to light at the red end of the visible spectrum, which means that the rods start dark adapting even though there is still some light available.

In most cases people using technology work at arm's length from their display screen. This means that the blind spot is usually not a problem, because the brain processes the images from both eyes together to perceive what is on the screen. If you have a system which requires the user to be much closer to the screen, and they are not detecting some items that are important, you should consider investigating whether those items are in fact located in their blind spot.

4.4 Low Level Visual Perception

Here we consider the low level details of vision. These range from how light is detected, through various aspects associated with color, to flicker and pop-out effects. Several of these aspects of low-level vision have implications for system design.

4.4.1 Vision and the Measurement of Light

There are two important ways in which light gets from an object to the eye: incident light (light falling on an object) and reflected light (light reflected from an object). Incident light is referred to as *illuminance* whereas reflected light is termed *luminance*. White surfaces typically have reflectances of 80% and black surfaces around 10%.

Luminance is measured in candelas per square meter (cd/m^2). As the luminance of an object increases, so does the eye's visual acuity or ability to discern small details. The pupil's diameter decreases and therefore increases the depth of focus in the same way as a standard camera lens when the aperture is adjusted. An increase in luminance of an object or display will also make the eye more sensitive to flicker.

Contrast describes the relationship between light emitted from an object and light emitted from the surrounding background. It is defined as the difference

Fig. 4.7 A Hermann grid on the *far left*. In the *center* a similar effect in a file system. Adding shading and color removes the effect on the *right*

between the luminance of the object and its background divided by the luminance of the background, as shown in Eq. (4.1).

$$\text{(Object Luminance } - \text{ Background luminance)}/\text{Background Luminance} \quad (4.1)$$

The contrast will be positive if the object is emitting more light than the background and negative if the background is emitting more light than the object. Objects can therefore be described as having positive or negative contrast.

Brightness is a subjective response to light. There is no real means of measuring absolute levels of brightness but, in general, a high luminance from an object implies a high brightness. It is possible to experience odd effects at high-to-low brightness boundaries, as shown in the left part of Fig. 4.7, which is called a Hermann grid. Designers should be wary of creating effects like the Hermann grid (in the center of Fig. 4.7) because they can be distracting. Adding color or shading can remove this effect. Indeed, the design of folders on most modern desktops avoids this by increasing the spacing of the icons both vertically and horizontally, but this choice costs display space.

Related to the Hermann grid are the concepts of *figure* and *ground*: figure refers to the objects that are to be attended to; ground refers to the background objects. In Fig. 4.7 the boxes and files are the figure and the white background is the ground. When the objects are placed too close together, however, the perceived gray fill that results can become more prominent and appear to be part of the figure. It is important to consider keeping objects that are figure prominent, and maintaining a useful ground.

The interpretation of Fig. 4.8 is based on figure and ground. If the white is perceived as the figure, it appears to be a vase or a goblet; if the black is the figure, it appears to be two heads.

The objects that you want the users to see or distinguish need to be appropriately sized. In good viewing conditions a minimal perceptible visual angle of about 15 min of arc should be maintained and in poor viewing conditions this should be increased to 21 min. These correspond to a 4.3-mm object and a 6.1-mm object, respectively, viewed from 1 m.

The full *field of view* for a stationary forward looking eye covers about 208° horizontally (although it is blocked by the head and the nose at certain points), and about 120° vertically. This only refers to light falling on the eye, and does not

Fig. 4.8 A Rubin vase that
can be interpreted as a vase or
two heads facing each other

necessarily mean that something will be seen when the signals are further processed. The field of view is an important factor in determining the size of a
particular display screen or the layout of displays and control equipment.

4.4.2 Color Vision

Color is the result of perception, and is not an intrinsic part of an object. The
corollary of this is that, under different lighting or contrast conditions, the apparent
color of an object will change. There are some terms that you should be aware of
when thinking about color vision.

Lightness is a measure on the black–white dimension of how close to white the
color is (100% is white, or bright). The amount of color that there is in the light is
described by its *saturation*, which refers to the purity of the sensation as opposed
to grayness: the higher the saturation, the higher the purity of color. *Hue* is primarily dependent on wavelength; it is closest to the way that the term *color* is used
in everyday language.

If the wavelength of visible light is varied over its range (400–700 nm), with
constant luminance and saturation, a person with normal color vision can distinguish about 1,200 differences in color. If luminance and saturation are also varied,
approximately 8,000 differences in color can be distinguished. When the viewing
is carried out in isolation by a person with normal color vision, however, only 8–10

different colors can be identified accurately without training. If you need more than 8–10 distinct colors you may need to use texture or text to provide features to assist the user in discriminating between them.

People's sensitivity to color is not uniform across their field of view. The eye is not sensitive to color at the periphery of vision. Accurate discrimination of color is only possible to around 60° from the straight ahead position (with the head and the eyes stationary) and the limit of color awareness (as opposed to discrimination) is approximately 90° from the straight ahead position. The eye is best suited to the perception of yellow-green light, and color is only well perceived in foveal (central) vision. It is least sensitive to red, green, and yellow light at the periphery of color vision where it is most sensitive to blue light. This variation in sensitivity arises from the way that the rods and cones are distributed in the fovea.

Perceptions of a particular color are affected by prolonged exposure to other colors—this is because different cones are responsive to different dimensions of color (e.g., red–green or yellow–blue). Looking at red light, for example, causes the red cones to become adapted, so the red light reduces in salience. This is often seen in color after effects, or afterimages. There are also several visual illusions you may have seen where you first stare at a picture or a display until the colors apparently disappear, and then when you look at another picture or a blank piece of paper the complementary colors appear.

Color constancy refers to the situation in which we attempt to perceive colors as being the same even when they are different. Our clothes do not change color when we go indoors, for example. The wavelengths hitting the retina may have changed, however, and the reflected light will be different, although we will still perceive the colors to be the same. Vegetables and meat in supermarkets are one of the most compelling examples of constancy not working—stores tend to be lit so that objects give off particular wavelengths—when you get home with different lighting the colors are substantially duller.

4.4.3 Color Blindness

It is important to be aware of color blindness (or, more strictly color vision deficiency) because around 7% of Western men and 0.5% of Western women are red–green color deficient. In other words they are bichromats, because they can only distinguish two primary colors (typically they cannot tell red from green). Other cues, such as brightness, can be used to help distinguish red from green.

Most of us can discriminate between all three primary colors (red, green, and blue), and are known as trichromats because we have three types of cones for seeing color. Quadchromats appear to have better color discrimination under different lighting conditions, but see the same colors. Many animals are mono-chromats: they cannot distinguish any colors because they have only one set of cones (or just rods). They hence perceive the world in monochrome.

4.4.4 Color Systems

There are many theories of how we perceive color (Sekuler and Blake 2005). There are a lot of technical details and tools available which allow us to make quite strong predictions about color perception. For our purposes, the most important thing to remember is the high level distinction between the two ways that we perceive color: additive and subtractive.

Computer displays use projected light (for the most part) and printed paper uses reflected light. Projected light uses a different set of primary colors, the additive colors of red, green, and blue (often referred to as RGB), while reflected light use the subtractive colors: cyan, magenta, and yellow (with black as the *key* color, which is why they are often referred to as CMYK). The additive colors start from black, no light, and then add colors to get other colors, and then, when all are added, white is produced. The subtractive colors remove colors from white, effectively reducing the amount of light that is reflected, and ending up at black. Thus, with current technology it is hard to get a pure black color on a display screen (at least some of the lights tend to stay on), although it is possible to get closer to pure black using subtractive colors.

The colors from printed materials cannot completely match the colors from a screen because of the way the two different color systems work. There are some tools available that can help you make the two match more closely, however, but in the end the choice of how closely you make them match may be down to personal preference.

4.4.5 Flicker

People are sensitive to flickering lights. The flicker can be made imperceptible, however, by using rates that exceed the flicker fusion rate. In the early days of the movies, cinema films ran at a frame rate below the flicker fusion rate, which is why any movements appear jerky and you can still detect the flicker (which explains why they were often referred to as the flicks). In modern cinema, the flicker problems is overcome by typically showing films at 24 frames per second, with the image being presented twice per frame on two-blade shutter projectors, and three times per frame on three-blade shutter projectors.

It should be noted, however, that lights which flicker at a rate of 7–10 cycles per second[1] can trigger epileptic fits in some people. Series 500 of the ISO 9241 standard on ergonomics of human–computer interaction is a guideline that addresses this issue for display screen equipment, and you sometimes hear warnings about flickering lights and images before they appear during a television

---

[1] You will also see this measure in Hertz: 1 Hz is 1 cycle per second.

C C C C C C C C C   C C C C C C C C C C

C C C C C C C C C   C C O C C C C C C C

C C C C T C C C C   C C C C C C C C C C

C C C C C C C C C   C C C C C C C C C C

C T C C C C C C C   C C C C C C O C C C

C C C C C C C C C   C C C C C C C C C C

Fig. 4.9 The *left half* of the figure shows a bunch of Cs and Ts. The *right half* shows a bunch of Cs and Os. You should be able to see that the Ts pop-out from the Cs whereas the Os do not

program. The effect of flicker in system design is decreasing as the refresh rate of most displays are so fast that flicker is becoming less of a problem.

4.4.6 Pop-Out Effects

One of the most useful applications of vision to interface design is to take advantage of how the eye searches. One of the most useful effects is that certain stimuli 'pop out' from other stimuli. Figure 4.9 shows that with a bunch of Cs, Ts pop-out, and Os do not pop-out. Similar effects can be found for color, and a few other features (Treisman and Gelade 1980).

Figure 4.10 shows an application of this and a few other effects. First, you have some object recognition that occurs—a car and building and perhaps some signs are recognized. Then you have some automatic processes occur, you are expert at reading so words appear as well, and these pop-out to a certain extent. You also have the ability to read words, and these appear. Expertise and previous experience also counts. If you have not heard of French Connection—UK (FCUK), your automatic processes may read it as something else. This result is not a true pop-out effect, but it is a related phenomenon, the word completion effect.

Providing multiple encoding of search items also helps in a visual search (Garner 1974). In Fig. 4.11 targets are encoded in several ways using multiple features. Highlighting visual targets using just two discriminating features often helps users find them, particularly if the encoding is not taught to users but is just inherent in the interface.

Some feature differences will pop-out to users (Treisman and Gelade 1980). Differences in color, when there is not much color, and straight line segments in a set of smooth curves will both pop-out. Partially open circles will not pop-out when mixed with circles and slight changes in size will not pop-out. Figure 4.11

fcuk
Nationwide
VACLENSA PLC

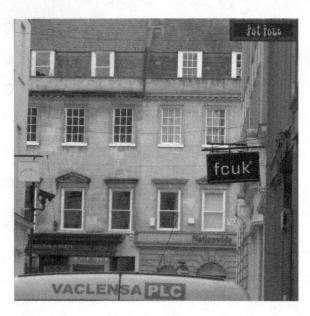

Fig. 4.10 Sign for French Connection-UK, taken in Bath, England. Note the effects of automatic processing, the word completion effect, on multiple sets of letters in this picture

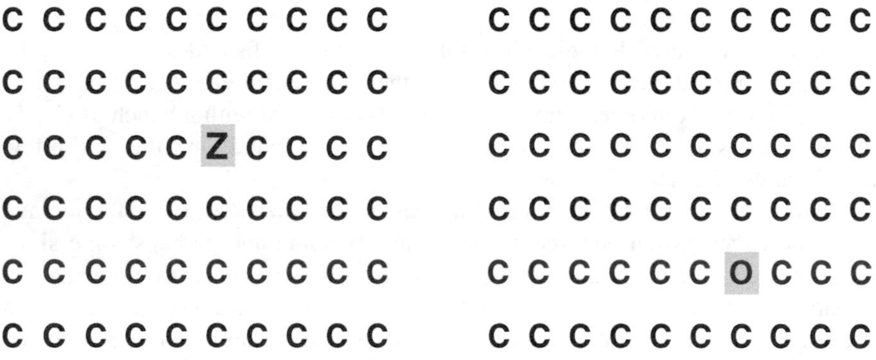

C C C C C C C C C C C C C C C C C C C C
C C C C C C C C C C C C C C C C C C C C
C C C C C Z C C C C C C C C C C C C C C
C C C C C C C C C C C C C C C C C C C C
C C C C C C C C C C C C C C C C O C C C
C C C C C C C C C C C C C C C C C C C C

Fig. 4.11 A picture showing a bunch of Cs and a Z and an O with the Z and O in bold, highlighted, slightly larger to provide three features that can pop-out. The Z has more features different so it will pop-out more easily. The O without the shading would be harder to find

has the targets modified with some differences that will pop-out and some differences that will not pop-out.

Pop-out effects can be used to highlight spelling mistakes (as shown in Fig. 4.12), to highlight a target file within a folder, and to highlight target words on web pages during a search.

(a)   **(b)**

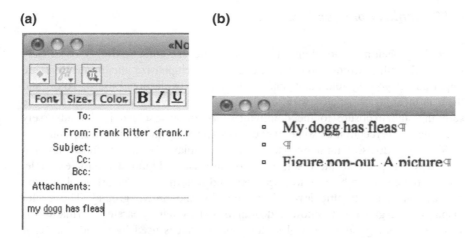

Fig. 4.12 Example uses of visual encoding to highlight spelling mistakes. On the *left*, a mail system underlines and makes the misspelled word appear in *red*; on the *right*, Microsoft Word puts a *wavy red line* under the word

Fig. 4.13 The use of color and luminance on aircraft displays facilitates the finding of particular information (this will be less apparent in b/w versions of this figure!)

4.4.7 Implications for System Design

It has long been a rule of thumb that you should use color sparingly on display screens. In other words, you just use color to emphasize the things that are important. If your system has displays that rely on widespread use of color, and there is meaning associated with the different colors, you should check to make sure that the exposure to the dominant color on the screen is not adversely affecting the perception of some of the other (possibly more important) colors.

When you do use color to encode items on a display, you need to make sure that the users can perceive the colors that you are using. Figure 4.13, for example, shows how color can be used to help users find information. The artificial horizon display above the throttle levers has blue sky and brown ground. The center displays have green and yellow and orange text to help separate information. If you are designing safety critical systems or interfaces used by a wide range of users, you should consider using redundant information to help people with red-green color vision deficiency distinguish between these two colors on the screen.

If you are developing a system which must produce color print-outs, and the colors and the differences between colors are important, you will have to take into account the fact that the colors on the screen and on the print-out will appear somewhat different. You will therefore need to find a way to make the two representations match as closely as possible, which may involve using third party software. This process may be further complicated by the fact that different makes of color printer can produce print-outs of the same screen image that look different.

Nowadays the flicker rate of most display screens is high enough for the flicker to be imperceptible. There is some evidence, however, that the flicker rate can affect how people read, because it changes the size of the saccadic eye movements that take place during reading (e.g., see Kennedy and Baccino 1995). If you are developing a system which requires people to read large amounts of text from the display, you may want to make sure that you choose display screen hardware that has a flicker rate that minimizes the amount of interference on reading.

If you are designing a system where you need the user to focus on one (or more) particular items on a densely populated screen, you should consider whether you can make those items pop-out from the display by appropriately changing some of the items' features. There is a potential downside of working with densely populated displays too, in that there may be some items which pop-out of the display when you do not want them to. In these cases you would have to consider how you could make those items appear more similar to the surrounding items.

4.5 Higher Level Visual Perception

In addition to how low level aspects of the eye influence perception, there are several higher level aspects of vision that influence cognition. Several of the results here have different interpretations, as to whether they are the result of vision or the result of cognition. A comprehensive theory of the user would incorporate this interaction between vision and cognition. Being aware of the higher level perceptual issues can help you design better interfaces.

4.5.1 Movement and Spatial Perception

Movement can be detected either by moving ourselves (even though the image falls on the same part of the retina) or by staying still whilst the image moves across the retina. The processing of the stimuli related to body movements and visual stimuli are combined because we can track a still object with our eyes while moving our bodies and yet be sure that it is still.

Above a certain speed of movement the eye can spontaneously track a moving object. Ask someone to slowly wave a small light (about as bright as a lit match) around in a darkened room and follow it with your eyes. The movement of the light will be seen even though no image is moving across the retina (because your eyes will keep it constantly on the retina). The periphery of the retina is the area most sensitive to movement, but it is very difficult to identify an object at the extreme periphery of the field of view. The detection of a moving object in the periphery of the eye is what usually initiates the movement of the eye in pursuit of that object so that it can be brought into focus on the fovea. Movement may also be perceived as afterimages when both the eye and the retinal image are stationary (this effect is due to adaptation of the motion detectors in the eye). Thus, the eye and the brain combine their results to get this apparent motion.

4.5.2 Depth Cues

Spatial perception is determined from the muscular activity of the two eyes and discrepancies between the two images that are formed. When we want to display a 3D image on a screen, we have to represent the 3D image using just two dimensions, although better 3D displays continue to appear. We can simulate depth perception using the discrepancy between the two images, as well as the perceptual depth cues listed in Table 4.3.

In the real world, motion parallax may be one of the most important cues that enable us to perceive distance and depth. It occurs when we move our heads from side to side and we see objects displaced at different rates. Objects that are further away appear to move more slowly than objects that are closer. In screen design, the trick is to move the viewpoint of the "camera" so that the image on the screen moves according to the principles of motion parallax. This is not used in most non-game interfaces, although virtual reality systems provide it, and video games provide it through motion of objects.

Table 4.3 Perceptual depth cues

Size	The larger of two otherwise identical objects appears to be closer than the smaller one
Interposition	If one object partially occludes a second object then the blocked object is perceived to be behind and beyond the blocking object
Contrast, clarity and brightness	Sharper and more distinct objects appear to be nearer, and duller objects appear to be farther away
Shadow	Shadows cast by an object provide some cues about the relative position of objects
Texture	As the apparent distance increases, the texture of a detailed surface becomes less grainy
Motion parallax	When moving one's head from side to side the objects one sees are displaced at different rates
Stereoscopic depth	Two images of the same object from slightly different angles are presented separately to each eye. Perceived depth is induced through the fusion of the two images. This is often used in virtual reality

Fig. 4.14 The time to count objects as the number of objects varies from one to eight. Counts from one to three are substantially faster per item than for five and greater (reprinted with permission from Peterson and Simon 2000)

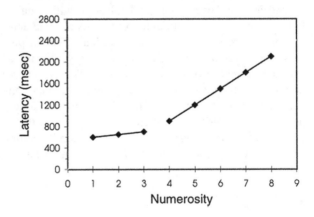

4.5.3 Subitizing

Figure 4.14 shows that the curve for counting objects presented visually in a psychology experiment (not that appear one at a time like train cars or a haptic situation like counting coins in your pocket) has a bend on it at about between 3 and 4. Up to three objects, you recognize the number effectively, with about 50 ms difference per object, above four and certainly at five, you have to count the objects, so the time to respond increases by about 250–300 ms/object. The first part of the curve is called subitizing, and is thought to be an effect of the architecture of the perceptual system.

Given the effect of subitizing, if you are passing sets of information to a user, or giving them things to count, understand that smaller numbers are much faster to recognize and count than larger numbers. In a related effect, if you are counting

Table 4.4 The Gestalt principles of visual grouping

Proximity	Elements that are close together appear as groups rather than as a random cluster of elements
Similarity	Elements with the same shape or color are seen as belonging together
Common fate	Elements which appear to move together are grouped together
Good continuation, continuity	Elements that can be grouped into lines or shapes will be
Closure	Missing parts of the figure are filled into complete it, so that it appears as a whole
Symmetry	Regions bounded by symmetrical borders tend to be perceived as coherent figures
Figure-ground	The geometric organization that is perceived is the one with the best, simplest, and most stable shape. For example, four dots arranged as if they were at the corners of a square will be perceived as a square rather than a triangle plus an extra dot

based on a fixed number of objects you can track, then you cannot expect users to follow more than three or four objects on the screen.

4.5.4 Gestalt Principles of Grouping

The *Gestalt principles of visual grouping* (listed in Table 4.4) can be used to explain how groups of objects are interpreted. The principles were developed as a rebellion against the simplistic notion that perception could be structurally analyzed into its component parts, and that complex ideas were the result of associating together simpler ones. This simplistic view dominated psychology in the late nineteenth and early twentieth centuries. The Gestalt principles allow that the whole can be more than just the sum of the parts.

Gestaltists focused on the fact that there are important aspects of form and structure. We see the world as composed of discrete objects of various sizes that are seen against a background comprised of textured surfaces. The spatial and temporal relationships between elements are as important as the absolute size, location, or nature of the elements themselves, and a sensation-based account of perception fails to capture this. Some of the principles of visual grouping are illustrated in Fig. 4.15.

4.5.5 Other Theories of High Level Visual Perception

There are several other views of visual perception apart from the psycho-physiological one we have described. These views tend to deal more with perception-as-phenomenological-experience or perception-in-information-processing rather than

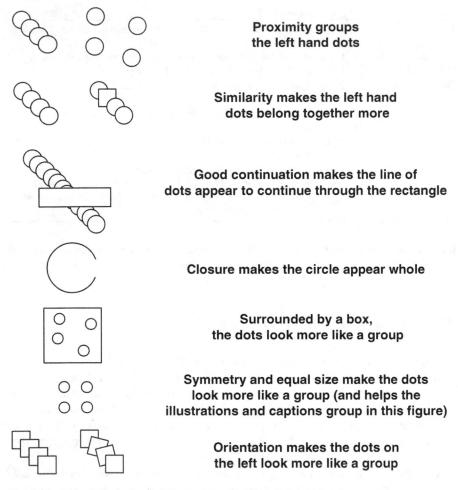

**Proximity groups
the left hand dots**

**Similarity makes the left hand
dots belong together more**

**Good continuation makes the line of
dots appear to continue through the rectangle**

Closure makes the circle appear whole

**Surrounded by a box,
the dots look more like a group**

**Symmetry and equal size make the dots
look more like a group (and helps the
illustrations and captions group in this figure)**

**Orientation makes the dots on
the left look more like a group**

Fig. 4.15 Several illustrations of the Gestalt principles of visual grouping

perception-as-registering-and-coding-sensation. They include the Constructivist, the Ecological, and the Active Vision approaches.

In the Constructivist approach, seeing is regarded as an active process in which our view of the world is constructed from a combination of information in the environment and previously stored knowledge. So, what we get from our eyes is not a 2D visual representation of the world like a photograph. Instead, the visual system constructs a model of the world by transforming, enhancing, distorting, seeking, and discarding information. In doing so, the visual system provides us with a much more constant view of the world than if we were simply to "see" the images produced on our retinas. So, when we move about (e.g., walk down a street), buildings appear stationary and people appear to be approximately the same size and shape—despite the fact that their actual relative images on the retina may be quite different. In the same way, our ability to perceive objects displayed on computer screens, for example, whether they are text or graphics, 2D or 3D representations, is a result of our prior knowledge or our expectations as to what should appear as well as what lands on our retinas.

In the Ecological approach (e.g., Gibson 1979), the process of seeing is greatly influenced by what uses (affordances) the object perceptions suggest. This approach, which is also called direct perception, stems from work with aircraft pilots. It takes as its starting point not a retinal image that is passively sensed, but the ambient optical array that the observer samples. Perception and actions are seen as tightly interlocking and mutually constraining.

In the Active Vision approach, Findlay and his colleagues (e.g., Findlay and Gilchrist 2003) build on the Ecological approach, but emphasize the role of cognition in controlling vision. This view opposes the idea of just taking scenes and analyzing them, and instead incorporates the notion of interacting with scenes. In interacting, the eye (and brain) chooses where to look next based on what has been focused on before and what was seen in those locations.

4.5.6 Implications for System Design

If you are designing a system where the three-dimensional positioning of items on the display is important, you will need to decide which perceptual depth cues you should use. The final choice is likely to depend on the context in which the display screen will be used, as different lighting conditions can affect the way that the displayed image is perceived, so if you only use narrow and quite pale shadows, for example, these may not be very obvious in brightly lit conditions.

For critical systems, if the user has to undertake a task which involves responding to the number of target items that appear on the display screen, you will need to consider how to display those target items. If the number of items is very low, the users will be able to react very quickly. If the number is very large, however, you may need to think about organizing them in some way (using the Gestalt principles, perhaps), or even splitting them across displays to optimize the response time.

At present, most display screens offer one level of resolution, such that all items on the display are presented with that resolution irrespective of their importance. If you are designing a system which requires an increased level of detail for items that are currently being used (perceived) then you may want to consider the possibility of using gaze-contingent multi-resolution displays (Reingold et al. 2003). These displays maximize the resolution at the part of the screen where the user is currently looking. This approach can provide a much more detailed image for a given bandwidth because more pixels (and information) are allocated to what the user is currently looking at, rather than effectively wasting pixels by providing an unnecessary level of detail for items that the user is not currently looking at.

When people are designing displays which involve items that need to be grouped together they often include them within some form of container (usually a box). The Gestalt principles suggest, however, that careful placement of the items will also be sufficient to determine how they are perceived by the user. The laws also suggest that careful attention needs to be paid to how you lay out items on a display, because you can, unwittingly, end up with unrelated items being perceived as being related simply because of their relative placement.

4.6 The Auditory System

For normally sighted and hearing people, hearing is the most important sense after vision in any interaction. Most people can hear sound in the frequency range 20 Hz up to 20,000 Hz, but both the upper and lower frequency limits tend to deteriorate with age and health. Hearing is more sensitive within the range 1,000–4,000 Hz, which in musical terms corresponds approximately to the top two octaves of the piano keyboard, and represents much of the range of the human voice.

Thus, the stimulus for audition is any vibration that will set the ossicles (small bones) of the ear in motion between about 20 and 20,000 Hz. Ordinarily, this means vibrations of the air but vibrations transmitted through other bones (particularly the skull) also contribute to auditory sensation. (Having a tooth extracted or drilled will almost convince you that the jaw was designed to transmit vibrations to the ear in the most efficient manner possible!) There are now headsets available that use direct bone conduction as a way to transmit sound in noisy environments.

4.6.1 Theoretical Description of Sound

It is convenient to consider the stimulus for sound to be made up of successive compressions and rarefactions (expansions) of air that follow a waveform over time. An example is shown in Fig. 4.16.

Waveforms like that in Fig. 4.16 can be summarized as being made up of sine waves (they look a lot like the first part of the waveform in Fig. 4.16 but are smoother and follow the sine function used in trigonometry). There are at least two reasons for using the sine function. The first is that they are easy to create; a pure tone produced by an electronic oscillator or a tuning fork follows a sine wave. The second and more important reason is that theoretically a wave of any shape can be analyzed into component sine waves. This is known as Fourier analysis. Figure 4.17 provides a simple example. Work with sine waves thus provides a standard for comparison across different types of sounds.

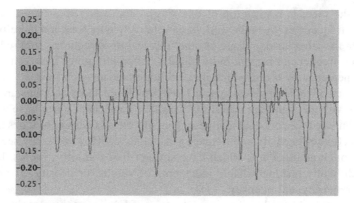

Fig. 4.16 An example waveform from audacity

Fig. 4.17 Example, simplistic, Fourier analysis that might match the waveform in Fig. 4.16

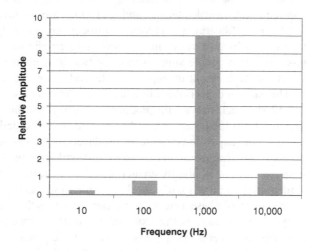

Waveforms with a single sine wave sound purer. Waveforms with different combinations of frequencies sound different. How many of these subwaves there are determine whether you are hearing a piano or an organ, or Frank or Gordon speaking.

Loudness of the sensation is largely dependent on the amplitude of the wave. However, the ear is not equally sensitive to all frequencies, so sounds at different pitches will not have the same loudness. The pitch of the tone depends primarily on the frequency of the sine wave, but not completely. Pitch is also dependent on amplitude. The apparent pitch of high frequency tones will increase with increasing amplitude but the apparent pitch of low tones decreases with increasing intensity. The loudness of a tone will also depend on the phase relationships of the component frequencies of the stimulus (that is, do they all start at once or do they start after each other but offset in time). Timbre is a quality that depends on the purity of the tone; is it made up of one single sine wave frequency or a broad mixture of frequencies? A tuning fork has a relatively pure tone and therefore little timbre. On the other hand, a piano or other musical instrument has timbre because of the other frequencies present in its sounds. Different timbres are often assigned different meanings by users, which may be important for your design.

Low tones of equal loudness appear to occupy more space and thus are said to have more volume than high tones. On the other hand, high tones have a greater density than low tones of equal loudness. The volume and density of tones are each a joint function of intensity and frequency of the tones. However, they seem to be as real as pitch and loudness which have simpler bases. In other words, listeners have no difficulty making reliable judgments of volume or density of tones that differ in frequency and intensity.

Hearing can be likened to carrying out a type of Fourier analysis of the auditory stimulus, separating a complex wave into its sine wave components. There are some situations where this analogy breaks down, such as when two stimuli of approximately equal intensity and frequency are simultaneously presented to the ear. Instead of hearing both tones, as a linear Fourier analysis would allow, a single tone is heard which varies in loudness in a periodic manner. You may have heard this when two people sing together or two instruments are played together. The effect can be pleasant or unpleasant depending on the frequency of the beats.

The basis of beats is the following. If you have a pure tone of 256 Hz and another of 257 Hz, each one would produce a steady pitch that would be difficult to distinguish from the other. When the two are played together the compressions and rarefactions (expansions) of the air produced by the two tones will at some point be in phase (synchronized) and the two tones will add together. However, because the frequency of one is slightly greater than the other, they will get out of phase after a while and their effects will cancel each other out. As this process repeats, they will go in and out of phase as many times per second as the difference between the tones in cycles per second. In this example, it would be once per second and so you will hear one beat per second. This provides a very accurate way of measuring the difference between two tones, far better than the ear could discriminate if the two tones were presented separately. This fact is used to good effect by piano tuners. They tune one note until it no longer beats with the standard tuning fork. Then the other notes are tuned until their harmonics do not beat with the first note.

4.6.2 Measuring Sound

Sound intensity is normally measured using the *deciBel* scale. This is a relative logarithmic scale where 10 decibels (dB) = 1 log unit ratio of energy, or a Bel (name after Alexander Graham Bell). To give some practical examples, the threshold of hearing is 0 dB, a whisper registers 20 dB, and normal conversation registers between 50 and 70 dB.

Fig. 4.18 Example sound levels (in decibels). **a** [140] Rock band (amplified) at close range; **b** [120] Loud thunder or fireworks; **c** [100] Jet plane at 500 ft; **d** [100] Subway train at 20 ft; [90] (not shown) Potential for permanent hearing loss; **e** [80] Busy street corner; **f** [60] Normal conversation; **g** [40] Typical room; **h** [20] Whisper; [0] (not shown) Threshold of hearing

   The intensities of various common sounds are shown in Fig. 4.18. The sensitivity to both frequency and loudness varies from person to person. Generally, though, the ear is insensitive to frequency changes below about 20 dB (i.e., below a whisper). Once levels get above 90 dB (as shown by the line in the table), prolonged exposure can lead to permanent hearing loss. This level is often surpassed by some industrial jobs, and by the iPods and MP3 players of those people who have the volume control turned up excessively high.
   This scale does not describe perceived loudness well. Increasing an auditory stimulus by equal ratios does not produce equal increments in sensation. It is obvious that the difference in loudness between a whisper and a normal conversation is less than the difference between a normal conversation and a subway train. What is said, the context, and background noise also influence perceived loudness. However, the ratio of the energy in a whisper to that in a conversation is about the same as the ratio in conversation to that of the noise of a subway train. This explains why a 100-W stereo is much louder than a 1-W pocket radio, and a 200-W stereo is not much louder than a 100-W stereo. The corollary of this is that when measuring loudness, asking people to directly estimate apparent intensity of

loudness (known as magnitude estimation) is often the best way to quantify sounds, at least for interface design.

4.6.3 Localizing Sound

People are generally poor at using spatial cues to successfully localize sounds (Catchpole et al. 2004; Kubovy and van Valkenburg 2001). The idea that localization is based on inter-aural time differences at low frequencies and inter-aural intensity differences at high frequencies is called the 'duplex' theory and dates back to Lord Rayleigh (1907), a pioneer in perception. This does not hold for complex sounds.

We can identify the location of a sound from the time taken for waves to reach the ears, coupled with information from head and shoulder movements. Sound reaching the far ear will be delayed in time and will be less intense relative to that reaching the nearer ear. Thus, there are two possible cues as to the location of the sound source. Owing to the physical nature of the sounds, these cues are not equally effective at all frequencies.

Low frequency sounds have a wave length that is long compared with the size of the head, and this "bends" the sound around the head very well. This process is known as diffraction, and the result is that little or no shadow is cast by the head. On the other hand, at high frequencies where the wavelength is short compared to the dimension of the head, little diffraction occurs. A "shadow" almost like that produced by a beam of light occurs.

Inter-aural (between-ear) differences in intensity are negligible at low frequencies, but may be as large as 20 dB at high frequencies. This is easily illustrated by placing a small transistor radio close to one ear. If that ear is then blocked with a finger, only the sound bending around the head and entering the other ear will be heard. The sound will be much less "tinny" because high frequencies will have been attenuated more than low; the head effectively acts like a low pass filter (allowing only low frequency sounds). Inter-aural intensity differences are thus more important at high frequencies than at low ones.

If a tone is delayed at one ear relative to the other, there will be phase differences between the two ears (the peaks of the waves will arrive at different times). If nerve impulses occur at a particular phase of the stimulation waveform, the relative timing of the nerve impulses at the two ears will be related to the location of the sound source. This is used to locate "wide" sounds. However, for sounds whose wavelengths are comparable with, or less than, the distance between the two ears there will be ambiguity. The maximum path difference between the two ears is about 23 cm, which corresponds to a time delay of about 690 µs. Ambiguities occur when the half wavelength of the sound is about 23 cm, i.e., when the frequency of the sound is about 750 Hz. A sinusoid of this frequency lying to one side of the head produces waveforms at the two ears that are in opposite phase (phase difference between the two ears of 180°). From the observer's point of view, the location of the sound source is now ambiguous, because the waveform at the right ear might be either a half-cycle behind that at the left ear or a half-cycle ahead. Head movements or movement of the sound source may resolve this ambiguity, so that there is no abrupt upper limit in our ability to use phase differences between the two ears. However, when the wavelength of the sound is less than the path difference between the two ears, the ambiguities increase; the same phase difference could be produced by a number of different source locations.

There are two different mechanisms for sound localization: one operates best at high frequencies and the other at low frequencies. For middle frequencies neither mechanism operates efficiently, and errors are at a maximum. Stevens and Newman (1936) investigated localization of single bursts with smooth onsets and offsets for observers on the roof of a building so that reflection was minimized. The listeners had to report the direction of the source in the horizontal plane, to the nearest 15°. Although left–right confusions were rare, low frequency sounds in front were often indistinguishable from their mirror location behind. If these front–back confusions were discounted, then the error rate was low at very low and very high frequencies and showed a maximum for mid-range frequencies (around 3,000 Hz). Intensity differences are more important at high frequencies, and phase differences provide usable cues for frequencies below about 1,500 Hz.

4.6.4 Discriminating Sounds

Our abilities in discriminating sound depend upon whether we mean absolute discrimination or relative discrimination (this applies to vision too). Absolute discrimination is quite poor (e.g., systems should not rely on remembering a tone or sound), but relative discrimination is very good. With sounds we can remember no more than five to seven items for absolute discrimination unless we can attach meaning to them, such as pitch labels. Also, as we vary more of the dimensions of the stimulus (increasing its complexity), so we increase our ability to discriminate (up to 150 sounds—varying in frequency, rhythm, location, duration, volume, etc.).

4.6.5 Implications for System Design

There are two ways in which sounds are used in current systems. The first is to provide voice output. The second is to provide audible alerts, such as telephone ring tones, and audible alarms.

Voice outputs generally require more processing than plain sounds. They can convey much more information, however, and they are particularly important for people with impaired vision. Blind users, for example, use voice output with screen readers so they can process the text shown on a display screen.

In general it is said that automated female voice output is easier to understand. If you are designing a system that requires voice output, the rule of thumb is usually to prefer a clear, slightly high, female voice if you can only choose one. If you have a system that produces multiple voices in the same task context, however, you will need to think more deeply about your choices. First, and foremost, however, you will need to choose voices that are easily discernible from each other. If your system has a sophisticated speaker system, you may also be able to separate the voices spatially.

You will also need to take account of the geographical context in which your system will be used. If your system is being deployed in the UK, for example, users may prefer the system to use a voice that has a British accent. Personal preferences can play a role too, so you may want to allow your user to select which voice output should be used. Indeed, many motor vehicle satellite navigation (satnav) systems now allow you to choose the voice that will be used to offer you verbal directions on how to reach your travel destination.

Like sight, hearing generally diminishes with age. If you are designing a system for a population that will include older users, you will need to take the possible reduced hearing levels into account when selecting voices and sounds to use as output. Some mobile phones by default include ring tones that can compensate for hearing loss in older people.

Audible alarms are supposed to be designed to alert the user to abnormal or undesirable situations. In many cases the audible alert is used in addition to a visual alert. If you want to quickly attract your user's attention in an emergency situation, the easiest way is to use square-ended, sudden onset waveforms such as klaxons or bells to provide audible alarms. The problem is that they evoke a startle reaction, and if the sound is at high volume it can even cause panic. The design of audible alerts requires great skill because you want to make sure that your users process the meaning of the alert rather than focusing on trying to stop the loud, incessant noise. The alarm sound needs to be distinctive so that users can recognize it and recall its meaning. If you are trying to convey urgency, you should avoid high intensity sounds, and instead consider the speed of the alarm sound: a tri-tone alarm, for example, which doubles in speed, will suddenly sound very urgent.

4.7 Motivation

4.7.1 Introduction

Now that you know some of the basics about *how* humans behave, it is also important to be aware of *why* they behave in particular ways. Generally there are two reasons why people act in a particular way. The first is governed by the central nervous system: if someone blows a puff of air into your eyes, for example, you automatically blink. We have no conscious control over these sorts of actions.

The second reason is where people make a deliberate decision to perform a particular act. One of the influencing factors that determines not only their action, but how well they perform it is their motivation: motivation is something that drives behavior. It cannot be used as a singular explanation for why people do things, however, because behavior is also influenced by needs, incentives, expectations, and the presence of conflicting motivations, as well as unconscious factors.

Motivation is usually considered from three aspects: the physiological, the behavioral, and the psycho-social. Here we provide a brief introductory overview, so that you can start to understand *why* an individual user behaves in a particular way. This may be particularly useful if you are designing gaming software, for example, where you want to keep the user engaged by providing the appropriate motivation for them to carry on playing. We will return to the topic of motivation in Chap. 8 to discuss how it plays out in team settings.

4.7.2 Maslow's Hierarchical Theory

Perhaps the best known theory of motivation is Abraham Maslow's (1943) Hierarchy of Needs. The simplest way to visualize the hierarchy is as a pyramid as shown in Fig. 4.19, although Maslow never presented a figure.

At the bottom of the pyramid are the basic, physiological human needs like breathing, food, sleep, and excretion. These are fundamental to human existence. Above that, in order, are safety, love and belonging, and esteem, with self-actu-alization at the very top. Each level requires that the level below it be mostly satisfied. Maslow also believed in what he called *metamotivation*—the motivation of people for continual personal improvement.

People are orienting towards, and try to satisfy, more than one of these levels at the same time. It is likely that motivations that appear lower in the pyramid will dominate those that appear at a higher level (e.g., eating when you are hungry or going to the bathroom when you feel the need would likely win out over doing something to improve your self-esteem). Whilst there have been many theories of motivation proposed since Maslow's, his basic ideas remain popular.

4.7.3 Extrinsic and Intrinsic Motivation

The basic needs—those towards the bottom of Fig. 4.19—are met for designers and many users, so the higher level needs are the focus of attention from our perspective. In his book, *Drive*, Pink (2009) presents a summary of motivational

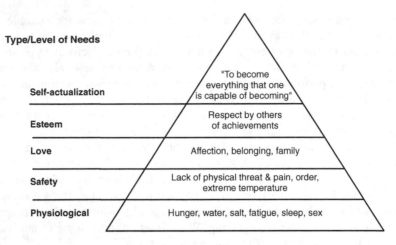

Fig. 4.19 Maslow's hierarchy of needs

psychology research, some of which can be applied to systems design. His work was influenced by that of Deci and others, on Self-Determination Theory (SDT, e.g., Ryan and Deci 2000).

Pink (2009) identifies three versions of motivation:

- Motivation 1.0 is simply about doing what you have to do to survive.
- Motivation 2.0 is associated with the industrial revolution. The underlying assumption is that most people do not want to work, so pressure (both positive and negative) needs to be applied to encourage the right behavior. In other words, extrinsic motivation needs to be supplied, using a carrot and stick approach, such as encouraging work by paying bonuses.
- Motivation 3.0 acknowledges the existence of intrinsic work drives. For many important tasks people want to do the work: they are intrinsically motivated. This includes creative and non-routine work, such as system design, software engineering, and most tasks performed by knowledge workers.

For tasks that are boring or onerous, Pink argues that Motivation 2.0 is still applicable. Where there is little room for creativity, work is generally performed better if the rationale for doing it is provided, the boringness is acknowledged, and people are given some autonomy in how the work is carried out.

For creative and non-routine work, Pink (2009) argues that the keys to high performance are the drives to direct your own life, to extend your abilities, and to live a purposeful life. This sort of work can be hindered by extrinsic motivations. Deci (1971), for example, found that if you paid participants to do a simple puzzle, they were less likely to do it while waiting to take part in the experiment (and hence not being paid), whereas participants who were not paid were more likely to try to solve it while waiting. The argument is that the extrinsic reward focuses attention on that reward, which facilitates the behavior that the reward encourages, and generally damps other related behavior. Extrinsic rewards may work up to a point, but beyond that, performance can start to decrease. Similarly, if people are focused on the extrinsic reward and it is then withdrawn, this can also lead to a reduction in performance.

The problem lies in achieving the right balance between extrinsic and intrinsic rewards. Pink suggests one way is to increase basic payments and reduce or even eliminate bonus payments. His claim is that people will continue to increase performance if they are intrinsically motivated. In other words, they do the task because they like doing it, or they feel a sense of altruism when they do it (Toms Shoes in California, for example, donates a pair of shoes to needy children for every pair that it sells), or they are given autonomy in what they do (Google, for example, allows employees to spend 20% of their work hours on something new).

Based on his analysis of studies from psychology and behavioral economics, Pink identifies three elements of intrinsic motivation:

- Autonomy—the ability to choose what to work on, how to work on it, who to work with, and when to work on it. If you allow people to make these sorts of decisions they become more productive. Pink argues that autonomy leads to engagement, and engagement leads to mastery. It is not possible for every type of situation, however, so some of the attributes are less mutable than others. If someone is operating a safety critical system in a nuclear power plant, for example, you really *do* want them to follow the rules about how they work.
- Mastery—the desire to understand a process or task and to get better at performing it. Achieving mastery is most enjoyable when the task provides the right level of challenge: too easy and it can become boring; too hard and it can create anxiety. The balancing of knowledge to work requirements is what Vygotsky (e.g., Chaiklin 2003) calls *appropriate scaffolding* or the *Zone of Proximal Development*, and Csíkszentmihályi (1990) calls *flow*. It is not always easy to operationalize these concepts, particularly in social settings, such as a classroom with multiple learners. The desire to achieve mastery can be a powerful drive, although it is not universal. Users who want to become experts will want to understand the task and develop the skills needed to do it well. This drive can also be exploited for boring and difficult tasks as long as the user understands the need for repeated drill exercises, or how the difficult tasks fit into the whole task.
- Purpose—this is really the desire to improve things; most people are at least partly purpose-driven. Under Pink's Motivation 2.0 the purpose is related to the extrinsic motivation. In Motivation 3.0, however, the purpose is related to intrinsic motivation: people know why the task is important, and may even do it free of charge. Emphasizing the goal of the task and its purpose can drastically influence performance. Working for the good of the company, your town, your nation, or the planet in this way can be more motivating than working for money.

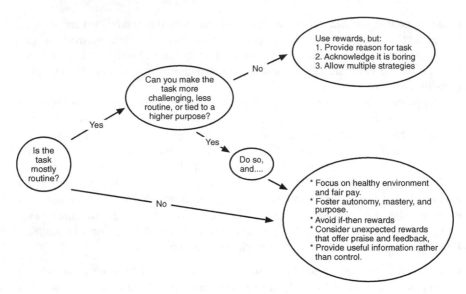

Fig. 4.20 When and how to use rewards based on theories in Pink (2009)

4.7.4 Implications for System Design

How much you need to consider motivation during system design will depend on three things: your particular users, the particular tasks they are doing, and the particular context in which they are working. It is probably best to consider these in reverse order, and think about the context first. If the context is a work setting, then there may be little or nothing that you can do to provide any motivation for your users to do their tasks over and above the motivation they already get from their company. If it is a leisure setting, however, then you will need to look at ways of engaging users in doing their tasks. You could offer virtual monetary rewards, for example, or badges of achievement to show that they had attained a particular level of proficiency at performing the task. Figure 4.20 summarizes this approach.

In terms of the particular tasks they are performing, there are more ways in which you can contribute in work settings. Given what you know about how visual perception and aural perception work, you can now start to think about how to make important items stand out on a crowded screen (using pop-out effects), for example, and how to design audible alarms that can be used to quickly identify a problem (by making them distinctive). In this way you can help your users to improve their task performance, and help them to achieve mastery.

In leisure settings your approach to dealing with the user's tasks may be more perverse, in that you do not want to make it too easy for your users to achieve mastery. You want to make them engage with the game, for example, and spend time and effort to attain any rewards, such as being able to progress to the next level of attainment, on the way to achieving mastery.

Finally, you need to think carefully about your users. People are different: some are driven mostly by extrinsic rewards (particularly money), whereas others may do things for intrinsic rewards, such as the enjoyment or satisfaction they get from doing them.

4.8 Summary

This chapter has provided a more detailed theory of what information users get from their primary perceptual systems. Nearly all users interact through vision and sound, and a deeper understanding of how users get information from these senses provides numerous suggestions for how to improve systems.

Many designers start out with a theory that the eye is like a camera—and so it is in some ways, having a lens and a surface on which the image is registered (the retina). However, as with many metaphors and analogies, the use of the camera metaphor is problematic, and is often called 'naive realism'. It is an inadequate theory of perception.

There are some critical differences between cameras and photography and the eye and visual perception. These differences mean that there is not a simple one-to-one correspondence between the context of a scene and what we perceive. The most important point is that light sensitivity varies across the whole of the retina. It is best in the center of the retina, the fovea, and worst at the edges. The eye thus has to move (saccade) over the visual scene all the time to see the details. Users have to actively do this, and if they do not know where to look or do not know how to interpret an object, they will not see what the designer intends.

If you want to view the eye as a camera, you have to view the eye as a very odd camera. It has a more variable speed film (or sensor) to support wide changes in light than you can buy. It has a poor focusing system (it has to be on the retina to be well developed), and poor quality film over much of the remaining negative (rods). The user has to move the camera to see details. If you view it this way, you probably have a reasonable model of the eye in mind, but a very odd camera.

Hearing is more straightforward. The differences between how the ear works and folk psychology are less drastic. The ear is a little bit more sensitive than most might believe, and can distinguish a wide variety of sounds, but without attention or training some sounds will not be distinguished.

In the future you will see (a) improved displays and (b) more attention given to the integration of types of perception and action. In the first area, of improved displays, you will see continued improvement in the quality of displays. Sound appears to stop improving around 44 kHz sample rates; above that, increasing the quality of the sound is not very noticeable—CDs do not sound a lot different from MP3 files, or so many consumers believe. A similar effect will be found as displays get better, in that the eye can still see more than a display can show. When a display provides the details that the fovea can see across its whole surface, or when the display adapts to provide more details where the fovea is, the quality will reach a maximum.

In the second area, users integrate their senses—motion, sound, and vision. Current displays are not well integrated with users' movements. This integration will be important for virtual reality (VR). Head-mounted displays move with the user, and most do not compensate for this motion. The users feel their motion with their inner ear, and do not see this motion in the display (or, in some cases, see movement but do not feel it with their inner ear). Over periods of time, sometimes even short periods of times, this non-correspondence between eye and ear can lead to nausea. This mismatch can also appear when an interface is stationary and the user is inside a moving vehicle. Examples include reading books in cars as well as using displays in cars, trucks, and ships. The results are not directly dangerous but they are debilitating and dangerous if the display is necessary for the vehicle. Work is ongoing to understand and ameliorate these effects.

Finally, you will need to think about how to motivate your users to do the tasks they need to do. This will involve balancing their individual needs and aspirations with an appropriate combination of extrinsic and intrinsic rewards if you want to get the best out of them.

4.9 Other Resources

For further descriptions of human perception and performance, it is worth consulting this text:

Boff, K. R. and Lincoln, J. E. (1988). *Engineering data compendium: Human perception and performance*. Wright-Patterson Air Force Base, OH: Harry G. Armstrong Aerospace Medical Research Laboratory. This set of three volumes covers the breadth of what was known about these areas of human behavior at that time. It remains useful because of its breadth.

There are several texts that will tell you more about visual perception. Two we recommend are:

Bruce, V., Green, P. R., and Georgeson, M. A. (2003). *Visual perception: Physiology, psychology and ecology*. Hove, UK: Psychology Press.

Sekuler, R. and Blake, R. (2005). *Perception*. (5th ed). New York, NY: McGraw-Hill.

An excellent introduction to eye movements and their relationship to attention if offered by Goldberg and colleagues:

Goldberg, J. H. and Kotval, X. P. (1999). Computer interface evaluation using eye movements: methods and constructs, *International Journal of Industrial Ergonomics, 24*, 631–645. This provides comparative assessment of measures of eye movement locations and scan paths used for evaluation of interface quality.

You can also get a broad overview of eye gaze and its relationship to attention by looking at Navalpakkam and Churchill's chapter available in a general textbook on HCI methods edited by Olson and Kellogg:

Navalpakkam, V., and Churchill, E. F. (in press). Eyetracking: A brief introduction. In J. S. Olson & W. Kellogg (Eds.), *Ways of knowing, HCI methods*. Heidelberg, Germany: Springer.

To learn more about auditory perception, hearing, look at this text:

Moore, B. C. J. (2013). *An introduction to the psychology of hearing. (6th. Ed)*. Bingley, England: Emerald Group Publishing.

Also, a readable text by ex-leader of the band Talking Heads, David Byrne is "How Music Works". It includes a very interesting, and very readable guide to the way that music (as an example of sound) works for the listener. It describes how both analog and digital technology affect the way that we hear sounds, in addition to the context in which the sounds are played.

Byrne, D. (2012). *How Music Works*. Edinburgh, UK: Canongate Books.

To better understand how these basic perceptual capabilities affect how we think, it is worth looking at John Anderson's book on cognitive psychology.

Anderson, J. R. (2009). *Cognitive psychology and its implications* (7th ed.). New York, NY: Worth Publishers. This book includes information about where perception and cognition interact.

The Poynter Institute (http://www.poynter.org) has online tutorials to help designers understand the complexities of color and its use in print and online journalism. These tutorials include page design exercises, which let you experiment with the use of color in magazines, newspapers, and web sites. See also Color, Contrast and Dimension in News Design, https://www.newsu.org/courses/color-news-design (requires free registration).

Clayton Lewis and John Rieman's shareware book: *Task-Centered User Interface Design*, hcibib.org/tcuid, includes discussions about how to visually design an interface to support users. They are familiar with vision, visual cognition, and the application of this knowledge to interface design. Their view helps extend how to apply this knowledge to interface design.

4.10   Exercises

4.1   To study the effects of color on perception you should generate 15–20 stimuli for people to look at on a smartphone. These all have to be items that they have to process in some way, so they could be short paragraphs to read, words to say out loud or to categorize, or objects to name. The items should be prepared in both black and white and color.

Have a group of users do the task with both the black and white and color objects. Record the time it takes them to do the tasks and how many errors they make. You may have to vary the size of the objects to get these measures to vary.

In addition to reporting what you find, you should indicate what the findings mean about displays and the use of color.

4.2 Choose six icons from popular or not so popular software packages. Also choose six menu items that are words (e.g., Format: Frame, File: Save, Insert: Date, Message: Reply, View: Master Document, Tools: Goal Seek, Edit: Copy) or choose icons from an online training system or training system such as Rosetta Stone.

Ask six to ten people to tell you what they think each icon and each menu item will do or represents. Summarize your results in a table as well as a set of suggestions for how to design interfaces. If you have access to a different population of users, people from different cultures, physical abilities, or ages, run the study on that population as well and compare their responses to your classmates.

4.3 Explain how signal detection theory can be used to analyze web site reading and searching. Based on this analysis, provide three suggestions for your favorite search engine or web site that includes search.

4.4 Redraw the signal detection curve in a big format. Either make the curves big, or put the signal and noise on separate lines to that they are easy to work with. Label the parts of the curves that make up hits, misses, false alarms, and correct rejections.

Redraw the curves with the signal being smaller. How does this affect the setting of the threshold, or how does it influence how to set the threshold for a given ratio of hits to false alarms?

4.5 Choose an online, social web site, such as Facebook, YouTube, or Yelp. Sketch several tasks that can be done by users with the site. Describe the intrinsic and extrinsic motivation(s) for users to perform those tasks. Do the same for an online course site, and for an online game. Note some insights that arise.

References

Bowmaker, J. K., & Dartnall, H. J. A. (1980). Visual pigments of rods and cones in a human retina. *Journal of Physiology, 298*, 501–511.

Catchpole, K., McKeown, J. D., & Withington, D. J. (2004). Localizable auditory warning pulses. *Ergonomics, 47*(7), 748–771.

Chaiklin, S. (2003). The zone of proximal development in Vygotsky's analysis of learning and instruction. In A. Kozulin, B. Gindis, V. Ageyev, & S. Miller (Eds.), *Vygotsky's educational theory and practice in cultural context* (pp. 39–64). Cambridge: Cambridge University.

Csíkszentmihályi, M. (1990). *Flow: The psychology of optimal experience*. New York, NY: Harper and Row.

Deci, E. L. (1971). Effects of externally mediated rewards on intrinsic motivation. *Journal of Personality and Social Psychology, 18*(1), 105–115.

Duchowski, A. T. (2007). *Eye tracking methodology: Theory and practice.* London: Springer.

Findlay, J. M., & Gilchrist, I. D. (2003). *Active vision: The psychology of looking and seeing.* Oxford: Oxford University Press.

Friedrich, M. B. (2008). *Implementierung von schematischen Denkstrategien in einer höheren Programmiersprache: Erweitern und Testen der vorhandenen Resultate durch Erfassen von zusätzlichen Daten und das Erstellen von weiteren Strategien (Implementing diagrammatic reasoning strategies in a high level language: Extending and testing the existing model results by gathering additional data and creating additional strategies).* Faculty of Information Systems and Applied Computer Science, University of Bamberg, Germany.

Galanter, E. (1962). Contemporary psychophysics. In R. Brown, E. Galanter, E. H. Hess, & G. Mandler (Eds.), *New directions in psychology* (pp. 87–156). New York: Holt, Rinehart & Winston.

Garner, W. R. (1974). *The processing of information and structure.* Potomac, MD: Erlbaum.

Gibson, J. J. (1979). *The ecological approach to visual perception.* Boston: Houghton Mifflin.

Holmqvist, K., Nyström, M., Andersson, R., Dewhurst, R., Jarodzka, H., & van de Weijer, J. (2011). *Eye tracking: A comprehensive guide to methods and measures.* New York, NY: Oxford University Press.

Kennedy, A., & Baccino, T. (1995). The effects of screen refresh rate on editing operations using a computer mouse pointing device. *The Quarterly Journal of Experimental Psychology, 48A*(1), 55–71.

Kubovy, M., & van Valkenburg, D. (2001). Auditory and visual objects. *Cognition, 80,* 97–126.

Maslow, A. H. (1943). A theory of human motivation. *Psychological Review, 50*(4), 370–396.

Moore, R. J., & Churchill, E. F. (2011). Computer interaction analysis: Toward an empirical approach to understanding user practice and eye gaze in GUI-based interaction. *Computer Supported Cooperative Work, 20*(6), 497–528.

Navalpakkam, V., & Churchill, E. F. (in press). Eyetracking: A brief introduction. In J. S. Olson & W. Kellogg (Eds.), *Ways of knowing, HCI methods.* Heidelberg: Springer.

Nielsen, J., & Pernice, K. (2010). *Eyetracking web usability.* Berkeley, CA: New Riders.

Peterson, S. A., & Simon, T. J. (2000). Computational evidence for the subitizing phenomenon as an emergent property of the human cognitive architecture. *Cognitive Science, 24*(1), 93–122.

Pink, D. H. (2009). *Drive.* New York, NY: Riverhead Books.

Reingold, E. M., Loschky, L. C., McConkie, G. W., & Stampe, D. M. (2003). Gaze-contingent multiresolution displays: An integrative review. *Human Factors, 45*(2), 307–328.

Ryan, R. M., & Deci, E. L. (2000). Self-determination theory and the facilitation of intrinsic motivation, social development, and well-being. *American Psychologist, 55,* 68–78.

Sekuler, R., & Blake, R. (2005). *Perception* (5th ed.). New York, NY: McGraw-Hill.

Stevens, S. S., & Newman, E. B. (1936). The localization of actual sources of sound. *American Journal of Psychology, 48,* 297–306.

Strutt, J. W. (Lord Rayleigh, Third Baron of Rayleigh) (1907). On our perception of sound direction. *Philosophical Magazine, 13,* 214–232.

Swets, J. A. (1973). The relative operating characteristic in psychology. *Science, 182,* 990–1000.

Swets, J. A., Tanner, W. P., & Birdsall, T. G. (1961). Decision processes in perception. *Psychological Review, 68,* 301–340.

Treisman, A. M., & Gelade, G. (1980). A feature integration theory of attention. *Cognitive Psychology, 12,* 97–136.

Wickens, C. D., Hollands, J. G., Banbury, S., & Parasuraman, R. (2014). *Engineering psychology and human performance* (4th ed.). Boston, MA: Pearson.

Wickens, T. D. (2002). *Elementary signal detection theory.* Oxford: Oxford University Press.

Chapter 5
Cognition: Memory, Attention, and Learning

Abstract Memory, attention, learning are intertwined in the user's cognitive processing. These are the basic mechanisms of the user's cognitive architecture and thus provide the basis for cognition. Users have several types of memory that are important for computer use. Attention can be seen as the set of items being processed at the same time and how they are being processed. If there are more items stored in memory or the items in memory are better organized these effects will improve performance and provide the appearance of more attention. Users also learn constantly. The effects of learning lead to more items being stored in memory and allow the user to attend to more aspects of a task.

5.1 Introduction

Memory and attention both play an important role in interaction. Complementing these two facilities is the user's ability to learn things in a variety of ways. Together, these three concepts form the basics of the information processing mechanisms of a user's cognitive architecture. We consider the three concepts together here because of their interdependencies, focusing on the most important aspects with respect to computer users, rather than covering everything that is known about them.

It is worth noting at this point that the term *memory* is used in three different ways. The first refers to the mental function of retaining information about things—stimuli, events, images, ideas, and so on—when those things are no longer present. The second refers to the hypothesized storage system in the brain where this information is stored. The third refers to the information that is stored itself. In order to avoid ambiguities we refer to storage of items in and retrieval (or recall) of items from memory when we want the first meaning; we refer to memory when we want the second meaning; and we refer to items (or information) in memory when we want the third meaning.

F. E. Ritter et al., *Foundations for Designing User-Centered Systems*,
DOI: 10.1007/978-1-4471-5134-0_5, © Springer-Verlag London 2014

Users' initial perceptions of an interface will be influenced by how they store and process information in short-term memory, and by how the information in their long-term memory helps them interpret that interface. The way people use a system will be greatly influenced by how well they can retrieve commands and locations of objects from memory. Similarly, their feelings of success with a system will be influenced by their biases in retrieving information about past successes and failures with the system.

Attention refers to the selective aspects of perception which function so that at any instant a user focuses on particular features of the environment to the relative exclusion of others. It plays a central role in interaction, where it often is not possible to interact with all aspects of the interface at the same time. Some interfaces require less attention from the user and this can be a good thing if it allows them to perform more than one task at a time efficiently.

User performance improves through learning. Learning is the most important process for adapting the user to the machine. There are several ways of describing learning, but for users the most important aspects of learning are probably learning facts and learning skills (or procedures) to perform tasks, but there is also learning to recognize images and perceptual-motor behavior.

5.2 Memory

Memory is one of the most studied areas in psychology. Understanding memory will help you as a designer to make it easier for users to memorize and later remember what they want or need to know. We begin by dealing with the structure of memory, which should enable you to follow the rest of the chapter more easily (this approach of providing a way to organize what you will learn is itself a result of memory research).

5.2.1 Types of Memory

Memory can be categorized in several ways. We will first look at memory based on where it is stored. Then we will examine memories by their content, including memories about a particular time and place (episodic), about object types (semantic), about facts (declarative), and about how to do a task (procedural). While there are other ways to conceptually organize memory, for system design, the set of categories we present here will give you a broad overview of the issues.

5.2.1.1 Iconic Memory

We can start our discussion of memory with perceptual-based information, specifically images. Perception, while fleeting, is not completely temporary. There is an image left when you close your eyes or after an image you have been looking at has disappeared. This is called iconic memory.

Visual iconic memory holds only a few items. Some suggest a limit of two or three items (Zhang and Simon 1985); others suggest a few more. These items also decay (disappear) at a fairly fast rate. Sperling (1961) had subjects view a screen of numbers and then asked them to retrieve items after the items were no longer displayed. He determined that items exist in a temporary memory store for about 500 ms, with an exponential decay rate. If items are not processed, about half of the records of these items disappear in each half second.

Items can be put into short-term or long-term memory by processing them. However, as this takes time, the other items can decay and be lost from iconic memory. Thus items that appear on an interface for a short time have to be noticed and processed to be remembered.

5.2.1.2 Short-Term Memory

Short-term memory (STM) is a temporary memory store. Work by Atkinson and Shiffrin (1968) helped establish STM as a common concept in memory research. It can be considered analogous to the registers in a computer. Cognition writes information into short-term memory but, unlike the computer, the contents decay with time. You might start out across the room knowing the phone number you want to dial, or start to bring up a browser to type in a URL, but by the time you get there, physically or metaphorically, you may have forgotten the number or URL. This type of loss is one of the first ways that people get introduced to short-term memory.

George Miller, in a famous study (Miller 1956) found that, for unrelated objects, users could remember around seven meaningful items (plus or minus two). The estimate of the rate of loss of these items varies somewhat based on who is studied and what they are trying to remember. Some authors have found that half the information disappears in about 5 s if it is not rehearsed (practiced).

Short-term memory is often used to store lists or sets of items to work with. There are several interesting and immediate effects of memory of lists that are worth knowing about. The first effect, called primacy, is that items that appear at the start of a list are more easily retrieved from memory.

The second is that distinctive items in a list are better retrieved (the Von Restorff effect). For example, if they are printed in red ink or a bell goes off when you read them, or they are in some other way distinct or important, they will be better retrieved. The improvement in memorability requires distinctiveness—highlighting a whole text and putting a box around it does not help because nothing stands out. Similarly, writing everything in red does not help, but writing only one word in ten in red will help. This effect is also illustrated later in this chapter by discussing Nepal and encoding.

The third is that items in a list that make more sense, IBM, PDQ and XYZ, are better retrieved than items that do not have associations for everybody, such as

Table 5.1 Abbreviations that are more memorable in one culture than another. (Note that German capitalizes differently compared to English)

For German	For English
MfG = Mit freundlichen Grüßen with kind regards	ABC = American or Australian Broadcasting Company
CDU = Christliche demokratische Union a large German political party	PDQ = Pretty darn quick
SPD = Sozial demokratische Partei Deutschlands. Another German political party	ASAP = As soon as possible
DRK = Deutsches Rotes Kreuz. rescue service/ambulance/Red Cross	PIA = Peoria International Airport
ZDF = Zweites Deutsches Fernsehen. TV Station	TLAs = Three Letter Abbreviations or Acronyms
GmbH = Gesellschaft mit beschraenkter Haftung (Society with limited liability, i.e., a limited company)	CMU = Concrete Masonry Unit

For neither culture: http://us.support.tomtom.com/cgi-bin/tomtom_us.cfg/php/enduser/std_adp.
php?p_faqid=2053&p_created=1092921663&p_sid=lXplZnAj&prod_lvl1=141&prod_lvl2=
2030&cat_lvl1=2356&p_accessibility=&p_redirect=&p_lva=&p_sp=cF9zcmNoPSZwX3Nv
cnRfYnk9JnBfZ3JpZHNvcnQ9JnBfcm93X2NudD01NCw1NCZwX3Byb2RzPTE0MSwxO
DMsMTk1NCwyMDMwJnBfY2F0cz0yMzU2JnBfcHY9MS4xNDE2Mi4xODM3Mi4xOTU
0OzIuMjAzMCZwX2N2PTEuMjM1NiZwX3NlYXJjaF90eXBlPWFuc3dlcnMuc2VhcmNo
X2ZubCZwX3BhZ2U9MQ**&p_li=&p_topview=1

SCE, ORD and PIA. If the user can group items into a meaningful item, to chunk it, the subitems are easier to recover because just the chunk has to be retrieved. These associations or chunks vary across people. We include a few examples in Table 5.1, including an item that would only make sense to a computing system.

Finally, the last items presented in a list are better retrieved as well (the recency effect). The primacy effect and the recency effect can be combined to create a serial position curve, as shown in Fig. 5.1.

These regularities suggest that you cannot increase your short-term memory by trying harder, but you can by presenting items in a particular order. Knowing more can also help. In air travel, for example, if you know that ORD is the airport code for O'Hare Airport, FRA is Frankfurt Airport (am der Main), and PIA is Peoria International Airport, then you only have to retrieve three codes rather than nine letters if you are presented with FRAORDPIA. This process was used in early phone systems in the US where regions were given names from the associated numbers, for example, as immortalized in the song "Pennsylvania 6-5000", which would have been 726-5000 (and would not have been as catchy).

Later theories, such as that embodied in the ACT-R theory (Anderson 1993, 2007), propose that short-term memory is just activated long-term memory. As processing occurs, objects are moved directly from perception into long-term memory. The observed effects for items in short-term memory are just the effects

Fig. 5.1 The Serial Position curve. The primacy effect is that earlier items are better remembered and the recency effect is that items more recently encountered are better remembered

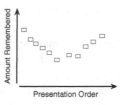

you see with less strong long-term memories. The number of items held in long-term memory that can be worked with at once is working memory, which we cover next.

5.2.1.3 Working Memory

Working memory is considered a more dynamic concept than STM. It is hypothesized as a temporary memory store (an audio or semantic scratchpad) with associated mechanisms for rehearsing, refreshing, and using the stored information. It also includes a mechanism of central or executive attention that regulates the contents of that memory store based on performing a task. This view is based on the models and definitions of Baddeley (1976, 1986). Working memory is seen less as a scratch pad than short-term memory, but it is viewed more within the context of the processing that will use it, and how the scratch pad and processing interact. This view of working memory suggests that increases in working memory can have numerous effects, ranging from more directed attention to better performance in general (Engle 2002).

These items in working memory are often rehearsed in what is called a phonological loop, where the material to be stored is repeated rapidly to oneself. This loop can hold about 2 s of verbal information. The direct implications are that items that are faster to pronounce take up less space. This has been found for numbers in different languages—languages with long names (in syllables) for numbers lead to fewer objects that can be retrieved. "Seven," which is two syllables long, for example, will take up more space than "one." Running through this loop only holds information; it does not alone increase memory for the items.

Working memory for a task is influenced by several factors. Focusing on a single task directly improves the amount of working memory available for that task. There also appear to be individual differences in working memory, with some people having more working memory than others (Daneman and Carpenter 1980; Lovett et al. 2000). Talking while doing a task provides some additional memory (not more traditional working memory, but more memory through the acoustical loop, which is repeating information verbally to yourself and hearing it, temporarily increasing your effective working memory), and in addition to slowing down performance can lead to more insights (Ericsson and Simon 1993). Further work suggests that extreme amounts of practice can lead to a type of increase in working memory (Ericsson and Kintsch 1995).

5.2.1.4 Long-Term Memory

Long-term memory (LTM) contains items that that you have permanently encoded. If items are processed enough they are put into long-term memory. Examples
of different types of items that are typically held in long term memory include your
name, the name of your dog, and how to start up your computer.

Items can be put into long-term memory from short-term memory. These items
can be objects, associations, or procedures for doing a task. Studies in this area
make various suggestions about the amount of time required to move items from
short-term memory into long-term memory.

Encoding is the storing of items in memory so that they can later be retrieved.
Items are put into long-term memory by processing them. More meaningful processing at encoding, such as using rehearsal, seems to make it possible to retrieve
items more reliably over a longer period of time (Tulving 2002).

Declarative knowledge, like knowing the capital of Nepal, requires attention to
put the items into long-term memory. This task is easier if the items are already
known. Being able to retrieve the name of the capital of Nepal from memory
would be harder if you did not know that Nepal was a country in South America.
This fact may help you to be able to recall the role of encoding better.[1]

Procedural skills, such as typing, can get put into long-term memory without
attention to this process (through implicit learning), but are usually best done with
attention and deliberate practice. Procedural skills initially will require attention to
perform; with practice they can require less attention, like driving or typing. The
amount of processing you have to do can also influence how well these memories
get created, which we will cover shortly.

Retention is the interval between encoding and retrieval. Activities during
retention can cause forgetting, such as processing similar items; interruptions; and
so on. Length of retention interval is important, too, which is covered in the section
on learning.

Retrieval depends upon the information available to cue recall. What is
retrieved depends on having information on hand—a request—to start a retrieval.
Retrieval is usually better (within about 10% in accuracy or response time) the
more similar recall circumstances are to the internal and external encoding circumstances (even down to temperature, lighting, mood, etc.).

We can remember much more information when it is meaningful and when its
meaning is processed at encoding time. Later discovery of its meaning does not
especially help when trying to retrieve it. Failure to process meaningful information also makes it harder to later retrieve that information. Ability to recall is
thus affected by success at each step—encoding, retention, and retrieval.

---

[1] This perverse statement is explained in a later section. Most students remember this part of the
book.

There is some debate about how long items in long-term memory are stored. Some theories propose that items decay to the point that they are no longer retrievable, and other theories propose that the items are still there, but no longer retrievable because they are no longer unique enough to be retrievable. The implications of these two different approaches may be basically the same for system design.

5.2.1.5 Declarative Versus Procedural Memory

Descriptions of memory often divide memory into two types to illustrate different effects. Perhaps the most common is the difference between declarative and procedural memory, which is used to categorize their contents based on how they are used.

The contents of declarative memory are facts or statements about the world, such as "The hippy is in the park," "the star is above the square," and "Colleen's hair is auburn." Retrieval of items from declarative memory is improved by practice, and the items are intentionally generated for sharing and verbalizing. One study estimated that it takes about 6 s of processing to encode an item for subsequent retrieval (Simon 1974), although the time required is context dependent: more complex items may take longer.

Declarative memory is used to store and retrieve information such as simple user instructions, user passwords, and to understand materials in interfaces.

The contents of procedural memory are acts, or sequences of steps that describe how to do particular tasks. These items can be viewed as a type of programming language for cognition. Examples of items that would be stored in procedural memory include how to type, how to ride a bicycle, and many aspects of how to program or use an interface.

Items in procedural memory are generally more robust against decay, and retrieval is often less context sensitive than items in declarative memory (Jensen and Healy 1998). Like declarative memory, retrieval and application gets faster with practice.

The ACT-R theory (a unified theory of cognition, or "UTC," realized as a computer program, and explained earlier in the introduction and used in the concluding chapter) uses these two types of memory explicitly, both procedural (rules) and declarative (chunks). The Soar theory (another UTC) represents declarative information as the result of a procedure to retrieve information from memory, and is thus a type of procedural memory.

5.2.1.6 Implicit Versus Explicit Memory

Memories can also be categorized as explicit or implicit: items stored in explicit memory are reportable, whereas items in implicit memory are not. Most declarative information is explicit in that it can be reported, whereas most procedural information is implicit in that the precise details are not reportable.

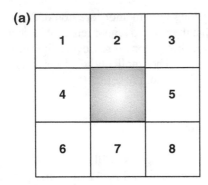

Type in the tile to move [1-8]: _____   **Click on the tile to move into the empty space.**

Type in direction to move [N/S/E/W]: _____

Fig. 5.2 Two types of interfaces for the 8 puzzle that lead to different types of learning. **a** Interface leading to more explicit representation. **b** Interface leading to more implicit representation

Some procedural information, such as how to use the Emacs text editor, a keystroke driven editor, starts out fairly explicit in that the user can describe what they are doing and why. Over time procedural information, or skills learned through trial and error without explicit, declarative reflection, can become implicit. In this case, the user can recognize objects, can have a way of performing a task but without being able to note why or how, and in some cases cannot even be able to recognize that they can do the task well. If the information remains in explicit memory users can perform tasks more robustly and, because they can describe how to do the tasks, they can help others more readily.

Users can be encouraged to store information in explicit memory by helping them develop a mental model of a task, and by providing them with time to reflect on their learning. Information gets put into implicit memory when the user works without a domain theory and learns through trial and error.

Work with the 8-puzzle (see Fig. 5.2) has illustrated this effect in interfaces. In this puzzle there are eight tiles and nine spaces. The task is to arrange the tiles in numerical order (left to right, top to bottom). The interface in Fig. 5.2a requires users to note the tiles that had to be moved and where to move them to, as a way of encouraging users to plan and think ahead. It also provided them with an explicit representation of steps for their reflection. Users that saw the interface that required only clicking on the tile to move it into the adjacent blank space (Fig. 5.2b) needed less explicit input and appeared to encourage behavior that led to less information being stored in memory.

In the first interface subjects reflected on their moves and developed an explicit representation of the problem. They took fewer moves to perform the task than those who used the second, direct manipulation, interface (although they took more time).

The subjects in the second interface were less able to describe how to solve the puzzle, but were slightly faster at solving it (Golightly et al. 1999; O'Hara and Payne 1998). This effect, of increased response time leading to fewer, more thoughtful, commands has been seen before (in a study by Forgie cited in Nickerson 1969, p. 171).

These results raise interesting questions about interface design. If learning is an important feature of the system, then interfaces that encourage reflection and learning about the domain may be more suitable, even though it takes more time to do the task. Tutoring systems that support the development of more explicit representations, for example, will help learners be able to explain and later teach how to do a task.

5.2.1.7 Prospective Memory

Prospective memory is also important for users. It is a form of memory that involves remembering to do something at the appropriate time based on either events or absolute times. The storage of information for future activities (both in the short- and long-term) is prone to failure and appears limited. There have been tools for centuries to help with retrieving these items from memory (strings tied around fingers), but there are also now computational-based tools to support prospective memory, such as time schedulers, calendars, and To Do lists, particularly on smartphones.

5.2.2 Mnemonics and Aids to Memory

There are several ways of improving memory performance—both storage and retrieval—which exploit the way that memory is arranged and operates. The use of mnemonics, for example, is a technique that helps to increase the amount or quality of information, or the speed at which it is retrieved.

One of the first mnemonics is the method of loci (in Latin, 'places'). In this mnemonic, a speaker (typically) would store in memory something familiar to them, like a set of locations in their house. They would then associate the items that they later wanted to with these locations. Retrieving a set of items in this way is much more robust than trying to recall each item individually without any associated, structured context. Users are not particularly likely to use this method, but you might when giving a talk, by placing the major points you want to make one per room in a familiar house. Expert memory demonstrations often use either this technique, or a similar one based on making up a story using the objects. One notable subject increased their memory span to 80 digits over a course of 230 h of practice by using athletics running times to group the digits (Ericsson et al. 1980).

Another popular mnemonic is to have a phrase to cue the retrieval of a set of things. For example, "Active Penguins Seek the Nearest Deep Pool" is a mnemonic for the seven layers of the Open Systems Interconnection (OSI) model of networks, and "Richard Of York Gave Battle In Vain" is a mnemonic for the colors of the rainbow in sequence.

Probably the most useful aid to recalling items for users is recognition. Recognition memory is more robust than recall memory. It is easier to recognize something that you have previously seen than it is to recall what it was that you saw. Many interfaces take advantage of recognition memory by putting objects or actions in a place where they can be recognized instead of requiring the user to recall them. Dialogue boxes and explicit links in web pages are the most overt form of this. Menus hide the cues one level or more, but the same process is at work.

The trade-off here is that for experts the recognition process and its application in an interface is often much slower than the recall process. For example, looking for and then recognizing objects on a menu to perform a file manipulation task is typically slower than recalling and using keystroke commands to do the same task. More expert users, or those doing a task quite often, will be able to use recall memory, and most likely will want to for greater efficiency. The use of recognition memory appears to require offering the user multiple, related items from which the user has to recognize (and select) the one they want. This represents a design trade-off, which will be best addressed if you know your user's tasks as well as the available technologies. A simple solution is to provide shortcuts of some kind, and provide the user with access to them as they use the interface, almost turning the interface into a tutor of itself.

Anomalous or interesting things are better retrieved from memory. As noted earlier, the learning of declarative information is influenced by the content. For example, Nepal is not in South America, so if you knew this when you were reading a previous section of this chapter, you are likely to recall that section better because it stood out. This von Restorff effect was originally seen when looking at learning lists of words. If a bell was rung when a word was presented, that word was subsequently better recalled. This effect applies in general to things that are distinctive. For example, a word in red will be easier to recall if it appears in a list of words in black. (Putting all the words in red will not work nor will highlighting all of a section to memorize; the point is for objects to stand out from similar items, so highlighting the entire book does not work!)

Finally, practice and repetition of the target task helps. This is another example of the Von Restorff effect. You should now be able to recall it better because you have seen it and, more importantly, processed it more often. Practice and repetition help to increase the amount of information stored for later retrieval from memory, but only if attention is paid to the stimuli and the stimuli are elaborated. A basic and early theory in memory research was about levels of processing. Greater processing of stimuli leads to better subsequent retrieval of those stimuli. Counting the number of vowels in a piece of text does not lead to very good retention of that text. Reading the text leads to better retention, and arguing with the text or another reader helps even more; rewriting in your own words is even better. This is one reason that teachers ask you about what you have read and encourage you to process it actively.

These aids to improving memory performance are presented more formally in study guides. Another method, PQ4R, is described below.

5.2.3 PQ4R: A Way to Improve Reading Comprehension

A common question about memory is how to apply what we know about it to learning. One approach to integrate what we know about memory and learning into a study method is the PQ4R method (preview, question, read, reflect, recite, review). In this method, the learner first previews the material. This helps with distributing the learning, and it also starts to form a structure for learning, a type of elaboration (Thomas and Robinson 1972).

The next step is to generate questions that the reading should answer. These can come from the preview, and from your goals and previous knowledge.

The four Rs come quickly then. The reading is done with the preview and questions in mind. This should be a more situated experience in that the point of the reading and scope of the reading are clearer.

After reading, the material is reflected upon. This is canonically done by writing up a short summary and explicitly writing out answers to the questions from the second set.

Then the material is recited, that is, spoken out loud. This helps form different memories (verbal ones), and also adds to the distributed learning approach that has been set up.

Finally, all the materials are later reviewed, or studied. This allows another pass and also allows any questions arising during the break to be answered.

This book is designed to help support the use of PQ4R and similar learning methods that emphasize multiple passes and reflection during learning. On the book level, it does this by providing a detailed table of contents that can help with previews, introductory chapters that note why you may be interested in this material, and chapters providing structures (the ABCS, cognitive architectures) that can be used to organize the material. On the chapter level, it provides abstracts for each chapter that can serve as previews, and questions at the end of each chapter than can be used to guide learning.

You may see this sort of behavior exhibited by users when they get multiple chances to learn in the same interface using multimodal output, or when the instructions on how to use the material provide help with these stages by providing an overview, for example.

5.2.4 Memory Biases

There are other aspects of memory that need to be considered when working with and designing for users. Poor decision making, for example, is often influenced as much by the way memory retrieval supports decision making as by how the choices themselves are made. The inherent biases associated with memory can often affect how well it operates.

5.2.4.1 Interference

The retrieval of items from memory can either be hindered or helped by other items in memory. If two items are very similar they can be confused for one other. For example, if you spend a long time knowing someone's name incorrectly, or you type in a command incorrectly a few times, it can take much longer to correct this error. This type of interference has been proposed as one of the primary aspects that makes learning arithmetic difficult (Siegler 1988). The intelligent tutoring systems based on ACT-R, therefore, do not allow the user to practice incorrect knowledge (Anderson et al. 1989). This is likely to be one of the ways that they can help students learn the same material in one-third of the typical time (Corbett and Anderson 1990). Interface designers should thus be mindful of errors and how interfaces help users to not remember them!

5.2.4.2 Retrieval Biases

Items presented towards the beginning of a sequence (primacy) or towards the end of a sequence (recency) are more successfully retrieved from memory. When it comes to reasoning about a situation or a set of activities, the items retrieved to support reasoning will be biased in those two directions. The use of an external memory aid and formal analysis can help.

The von Restorff effect will also apply. Information that is stored in a context that is distinctive will be easier to retrieve. The relative amounts or numbers of items retrieved will thus not support appropriate reasoning, as the items will not be retrieved in proportion to their occurrence in the world.

5.2.4.3 Encoding Effects

The content of an item that is to be stored in memory can be influenced by its encoding. The location of the item, the location of the user, sights, smells, sounds, and mental state can all be included in the way the item is encoded for storage. Examples of this include certain smells bringing back childhood memories, and certain people only recognized well in certain contexts. For example, we find it much harder to recognize students outside the classroom environment in which we met them.

Users will have these same effects. The information that they can retrieve for computer systems may in some cases be tied to aspects of the interface that you did not intend or may not even have control over. The particular terminal or computer they use, their home page, or where they put a manual on a bookshelf may all become part of their knowledge about how to use a system because these aspects can influence the retrieval of items from memory. This also suggests that, for more robust recall of items from memory, users should be supported in building up a variety of retrieval cues and have a chance to practice (i.e., rehearse) these items in a variety of situations before they have to retrieve them in earnest.

5.2.4.4 Priming

Priming refers to how presenting objects before their use, sometimes quite briefly, facilitates their use and the use of items related to them. Typically, primes are presented for short periods of time, under a second, but it applies to all time periods. For example, anything about Nepal or South America would be more recognized by readers of this text because they have been used previously.

This approach can be used to facilitate the retrieval of items from memory. When presented with a list of words to remember, such as "bed rest awake tired dream wake snooze blanket doze slumber snore nap peace yawn drowsy," many subjects will report that "sleep" was included as well. This effect can be explained by noting that many, if not all, of these words prime the word "sleep." When it is time to recall the words, the word "sleep" is also very active, and this is (falsely) used as a cue that it appeared in the list as well. The book by Intons-Peterson and Best (1998) explores this and related topics of distortions in memory.

Users will find it easier to retrieve items from memory that have been recently used. This is a possible mechanism to explain why consistency within a system or between a manual and a system is important. Names of items in the manual will be more quickly identified in the interface if the same name is used. Related concepts will also be helped, but to a lesser extent.

This effect also can lead to retrieving information to support previously held beliefs, rather than generating new ones. It is important then to provide users with external memory aids to help in the retention and analyses of situations.

5.2.4.5 The Loftus Effect

The Loftus effect (e.g., Loftus 1975), also known as the misinformation effect, describes how people take on knowledge implicitly from questions. Asking someone a question often leads them to assume and later learn the facts implicit in the question. Asking someone "What color hat was the suspect wearing?" will lead many people to infer and later recall (without understanding that they just inferred and did not see) that the suspect was indeed wearing a hat. In one of their original studies Loftus and her colleagues asked subjects if they recalled meeting Bugs Bunny at Disney World as a child (Loftus 2003). Depending on the condition, about a third could erroneously recall this (Bugs is with Warner Brothers, not Disney!). Instructions and manuals can suggest capabilities not generally available, or could help support users by noting the interconnected nature of most systems. Multiple choice exams can, with their questions, remind you of components of the answer. For example, a question that asked you "Which of the following is a type of memory?" implies that there are several types. This type of test could help create false memories.

If used directly, this effect can help users. Queries to users that provide context to the question or even a default action can help users.

5.2.5 Implications for System Design

What we already know about human memory provides numerous implications for improving the lot of the user. Users will be able to learn interfaces that are similar to other interfaces or other knowledge structures more easily than completely new interfaces. Users are limited in the amount of new information that they can perceive, comprehend, and learn. A fairly direct implication is to use words that users know, and use the words consistently to strengthen the chances of later successfully retrieving these words from memory.

It has long been known that retrieving names from memory is faster than naming objects. This suggests that, instead of displaying icons, we might be better served by displaying words (Chilton 1996). The approach, of using names instead of icons would also help the visually impaired, who rely on software to translate computer interfaces into verbal representations. Raskin (2000, Sect. 6.3), provides further interesting examples and arguments encouraging the use of words instead of icons. Figure 5.3 shows icons used for translation during international travel, as well as some icons from interfaces that are more difficult to interpret.

Our understanding of memory can and should influence password choice. This knowledge can inform more than "experience and common sense," which is sometimes used. Users will want to choose passwords that are hard to guess, and systems may enforce this. However, many passwords that are hard to guess are arbitrary (that is, not meaningful to users) strings of letters, digits, and punctuation, such as "ouibou94!3"). Thus, some strong passwords are hard to recall when users need them. There have been surveys on what passwords people use when they are not given any guidance (the results are pretty scary from a security standpoint). What needs to happen more is helping users generate mnemonics for remembering the passwords, rather than writing them down on paper or installing them in a computer-based passport (unless you trust the computer company selling the passport, which many state attorney generals do not). The issue of recallable yet strong passwords is one of the topics routinely dealt with under the auspices of the topic of usability of security. Some analysts have argued for word-based passwords, such as 'islandcarekeyboard', which is long and thus hard to guess, but easier to recall as each chunk is several letters rather than a single letter.

There are several poorly understood but important questions relating to the use of memory with respect to system design:

Fig. 5.3 The *top* figure is taken from a Kwikpoint travel guide designed to help communicate in a foreign language (you point at what you mean), used with permission. Icons on the *bottom* are taken from Word 2011 (The icons in Fig. 5.3b mean, from right to left: view field codes, zoom 100%, online layout, page layout, and automatic change. Word is improving in that you can now mouse over the icons to learn their names.)

- The impact of interruptions. Many work environments include numerous interruptions. The effect of these on the way that items are stored in, and retrieved from, memory is just starting to be studied. What work exists suggests to us that the length of interruption is less important than the similarity of material processed.
- Other memory tasks. Most of the memory literature concerns simply learning a list and then recalling it sometime later. Many work-related memorial tasks involve retaining some piece of information for a short time, then replacing it with some similar piece of information ('keeping track' tasks). These have not been studied very often.
- Support for memory. Most of the literature is studies of processes and architectures of memory—but our interest is in preventing the need for memory and providing support for tasks requiring the use of memory. This is an active area for design.

5.3 Attention

Everyone knows what attention is. It is the taking possession by the mind in clear and vivid form, of one out of what seem several simultaneously possible objects or trains of thought…It implies withdrawal from some things in order to deal effectively with others, and is a condition which has a real opposite in the confused, dazed, scatterbrained state.

William James

Fig. 5.4 This picture shows someone (*circled*) doing more tasks than their system (both vehicle and head) were designed for—driving in a crowded urban environment and talking on a hand-held cell phone. The phone in this position takes both verbal and motor attention, and it causes an additional planning load to operate the car one-handed, and leads to poor situation awareness (i.e., they did not see the person on the street who took this picture). Also note the Gestalt effect of the can and tree!

Designing systems to attract, manage, and maintain attention is important. Figure 5.4 shows a user with a task that requires attention (driving), who is also attempting to perform an additional task (talking on a cell phone). If you would like a short demonstration of attention, go to http://www.youtube.com/watch?v= -AffEV6QlyY, which takes advantage of your ability to pay attention. It takes some time to understand, and you should not be too easily shocked.

Attention refers to the selective aspects of perception which function so that at any instant a user focuses on particular features of the environment to the relative (but not complete) exclusion of others. There are several useful metaphors for describing attention. It can be seen as a set of buffers that hold information for processing. It is directly related to that processing as well.

You might imagine attention as the area and process of central cognition, such as work being done on a table. Tasks that take less attention need less of the table or less of the time of the person working at the table. Many processes in human cognition are thus closely tied to the concept of attention as a space for cognition, and various parts of a processor can support attention.

Figure 5.5 shows two common and important uses of attention. Both situations involve aspects of motor control and cognition, and require monitoring the situation and taking corrective action. In both cases performance suffers when the tasks are not given sufficient attention.

There are also other aspects of human behavior that are not based on focal or conscious attention. We can still do some information processing without consciously attending to information—how else would we know to shift our attention

Fig. 5.5 A car dashboard at night (*left*) and a plane's cockpit during the day (*right*). Note similarities and differences, including the use of luminance, color, and some similar interaction devices

to some new information? An example of this is the 'Cocktail-party effect', where you can hear your name in a different conversation even though you are not paying attention to that conversation in a crowded room.

Many researchers believe that our ability to process information without focal attention is limited to surface features, syntactic properties, or similar shallow features. In this view we cannot process the meaning of something without conscious attention. So we cannot remember something in the long-term without paying conscious attention to it. This is thus the difference between hearing and understanding, for example. Some evidence suggests that some meaning can be processed without attention, but not very much, and that any long-term memory that results will almost exclusively be of surface features.

The study of skilled, procedural performance reveals that we can, after extensive practice, perform many things without paying much conscious attention to them. Some of these skills (e.g., driving) are very sophisticated. With practice we do not have to pay attention to as many subparts of the task. This allows us to do another task at the same time (such as talk while drive). It also means that less is actively processed, decreasing our memory for those aspects of the task. This perhaps explains why it is hard to give directions for familiar routes, as the features are no longer processed by attention.

5.3.1 Wickens' Theory of Attentional Resources

There are some more elaborate theories of attention. Perhaps the best known of these is the theory of attentional resources developed by Wickens (e.g., Wickens and Hollands 2000), illustrated in Fig. 5.6. In this theory, Wickens proposes the idea that users have multiple types of resources as a way of explaining how people time-share across tasks and variations across people. Resources affect which part of perception

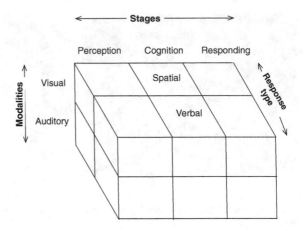

Fig. 5.6 The conceptual components of Wicken's model of the user's processing, modality, and places for attention

is used (visual or auditory), response type (choice of response type, and execution of that response, spatial or verbal), and the stages of processing (perception, cognition, and responding). These define resources for processing and holding information, with some tasks using more of one type of resource than another.

Most of the evidence to support Wickens' model of attentional resources comes from studies of dual task performance. Evidence for two different types of resources, for example, can be found by varying the difficulty of responding to one task and looking at performance on a concurrent (more) perceptual task. The performance on the perceptual task is (more or less) constant, even though more resources are needed for the responding task.

5.3.2 An Information Processing Model of Attention

The ACT-R theory (Anderson and Lebiere 1998) incorporates a model of attention that summarizes one of the common theories in this area, that of attention as a spotlight in the mental world which is directed at what is being thought about. Attention in ACT-R is represented as activation of concepts in its declarative memories. People with more attention have more activation available (Lovett et al. 2000). This activation of memory creates the spotlight that focuses on the mental objects that are being used in processing. These objects may include semantic memories and episodic memories, as well as current goals and processes.

If more activation is available, this allows more objects to be manipulated at the same time. This saves time re-retrieving them from memory and allows larger, more complex objects to be created and used. Each of the objects has an associated strength. Objects that are more familiar have a higher associated strength and, as a result, need less activation to be matched against procedural knowledge than less familiar objects.

Objects in the various perceptual input buffers, such as vision and hearing, need to be brought into memory in central cognition by a transfer process. Moving objects into central cognition does not happen automatically, but has to done intentionally. The amount of time the new memories are processed and how they are processed will determine how strong the resulting memories are.

5.3.3 Divided Attention

Users who are attempting to do two tasks at the same time will have to move more information around. They will start doing one task, and during processing on that task they will have to notice when it is time to swap tasks and work on the second task. In other words, they will need to divide their focus of attention between the tasks they are performing.

How the two tasks interact will depend on several things. Users will perform better if they can spend larger blocks of time on each task. Users that are more practiced with each task will be able to switch more smoothly and will be able to activate the necessary memories to assist in doing the new task faster. Practicing doing the tasks together will also lead to better overall performance. In this case, the user might be learning how to interleave subtasks.

Attention is influenced by both the frequency of access and type of use of items, so dual tasks that use different perceptual buffers will interfere less with each other. People can learn to drive and talk at the same time in normal weather conditions, because driving does not use a lot of audio cues. That leads to the two tasks not using the same perceptual buffers very much. At least one theory in this area, EPIC, proposes that the only bottlenecks in performance are perception and action (Kieras et al. 1997; Meyer and Kieras 1997).

Pairs of dual tasks, such as reading email and web browsing, based on a computer interface will almost certainly interfere with each other to some extent. The user will be using the same resources, including perception, aspects of cognition, and output, typically vision, memory, and motor output, for each task. The perceptual buffer will have to be refocused or directed to a different part of the screen. These factors will make it harder to do each of the tasks when the other is present.

5.3.4 Slips of Action

Attention and skilled behavior have a critical role in the occurrence of slips of action, where people have the right intention but perform the wrong action (Norman 1981; Reason 1990). People essentially work in one of two modes:

1. Using open loop control: behavior is based on anticipation and feedforward rather than feedback, so there is little or no need for them to monitor the result of their actions. Other activities can be performed at the same time—automatized driving and game play and typing are examples.

2. Using closed loop control: performance is mediated using feedback on any actions carried out, so conscious monitoring of behavior is required. Only one activity can be carried out at one time. Learning how to drive, deliberate walking on a rock field, editing a manuscript are examples, or learning how to play a game by mapping commands to a controller.

Very few tasks can be performed completely using open loop control. Slips of action typically occur when open loop control is being used instead of closed loop control, such as:

- When users overlook information that affects behavior. For example, users that do not note the mode of a word-processor or the location of the insertion point and input and modify text in ways that they did not intend.
- When users continue performing a familiar activity even though they intended to do something different. For example, clicking on the "Yes" button in response to the prompt "Do you really want to delete this file?"
- When users fail to correctly discriminate between relevant objects in the world—performing an action on unintended objects. For example, trying to click on an image icon on a web-based form.

Although it is not clear that we can design to always pre-empt these slips, we can predict the kinds of circumstances when they occur. We can also recognize the power of open loop behavior that can foil "Do you really want to...?" dialogues. We will return to discuss slips of action and other types of erroneous behavior in Chap. 10.

5.3.5 Interruptions

Interruptions are becoming increasingly common in interfaces as systems become more advanced and can be given tasks to perform asynchronously. There are also other causes of interruptions, including colleagues, phones, and email systems that beep when you have new messages.

In many ways interruptions can be seen as a secondary task, and hence the work in this area is effectively a subset of the work on dual task performance, where the user is trying to do two tasks at once. Interruptions are effectively the secondary task, which is much less important, generally not regarded as part of the user's main task, and is not under control of the user.

Interruptions do appear to cause real decrements in performance (Bailey and Konstan 2001; McFarlane 1999) and users do not like them because they lead to changes in affect (Bailey and Konstan 2001). McFarlane (1997) has attempted to create a taxonomy of interruption types and their implications for design. His results indicate that the choice of how to deal with interruptions will depend on the importance and types of the main task and of the interruption. Dealing with interruptions immediately disrupts the main task more than taking the interruption between subtasks. Dealing with interruptions at scheduled times leads to better performance on the main task, but poorer performance on the interruptions. Intermediate strategies offered different trade-offs (McFarlane 1999).

Sometimes interruptions are useful. It has been hypothesized that interruptions are useful for solving hard problems (where there is a so-called incubation effect). This effect has been noticed by programmers who get stuck on a problem—coming back to a hard problem later sometimes makes the problem easier. Being interrupted for minutes, hours, or days in these tasks allow the user to forget their mistakes and mis-starts, or to receive suggestions from the environment. Kaplan (1989) found that at least part of the incubation effect came from cues in the environment. One problem he gave subjects was "What goes up a chimney down but not down a chimney up?" Subjects who were called and asked by Kaplan if he had left an umbrella in their office were much more likely to solve the problem, but did not attribute the cause to his call.

As you consider the larger context of your users' tasks, you should keep in mind the possible effects of interruptions. Some interfaces will be less sensitive to the effects of interruptions. We are just starting to be able to predict and measure these effects.

5.3.6 Automation Deficit: Keeping the Human in the Loop

If you want to get funny looks, while you are driving a car, ask your passenger "Do you ever wake up and find out you are driving and wonder where you are going and where the other cars are?" Some find this humorous, and others, if they do not know you well, may be startled. This is similar to what happens when someone has to resume or take over a task at short notice when the system relinquishes control because it does not know what to do. This happens to people such as aircraft pilots and power plant operators who find themselves *out of the loop*, i.e., not being kept up to date by the systems about what it is doing. The user will then allocate their attention to dealing with the task, but they have to spend time and effort trying to understand the current situation before they can diagnose the problem and resolve it.

Generally, the way to avoid this problem is to include more status information to keep the user continually informed before the situation requires their input. This allows one to develop and maintain a mental model of that situation and how it is unfolding, so that users can decide when they may need to take action.

This whole argument about the need to keep the human involved in the control loop was first summarized by Bainbridge (1983), and it remains as an issue today (Baxter et al. 2012). Woods and Patterson (2001) explain some of the effects on users if the technology does not keep them kept informed about what it is doing.

Fig. 5.7 This system shown here included an instant messenger (iChat) text and video chat, a proprietary video conferencing tool, slides of the talk online and printed, as well as paper-based reminders and notes. In this task, however, the subtasks were integrated: to watch the man in the suit talk and ask him questions

5.3.7 Implications for System Design

Interfaces can help users do more than one task. Figure 5.7 shows a workplace where the user is doing multiple subtasks related to listening remotely to a talk (watching the talk, reading the talk slides, looking at the map of where the talk is, timing the talk, reading a paper about the talk, waiting for a snack). Typically, this is by helping them do each of the tasks more easily and by requiring less attention to do each of the tasks. More recent work is attempting to find the times and ways to interrupt the user at more appropriate moments.

Knowing how attention and perception work can help create better indicators of the arrival of another task, such as a beep or flash, or a change in its priority. Knowing about attention also helps with design because you know that attention is not limitless, and is sometimes missing. How and when to best interrupt a task and how to best support various sets of dual tasks remain open problems.

It is possible to increase the user's attention by including multiple modes of input and output. For example, when users need more attention, adding voice input and voice output as interaction modalities to supplant a visual display can provide users with the ability to watch their performance in a flight simulator. That way, they are receiving feedback on it at the same time (Ritter and Feurzeig 1988).

In applied settings, where attention is paid to multiple processes, some that are time critical, it can be important to pay attention to a process before it becomes necessary to control the process. The section on automation deficit explained this more fully.

5.4 Learning and Skilled Behavior

Learning is where performance changes with practice, typically getting faster, becoming less demanding, and generating fewer errors. Learning is important for users. They learn in several ways, including learning new information and new skills. Learning is the primary way for them to improve the strength of their memories. As they retrieve something more often, their memory strengths improve as well. Thus, retrieving a password is faster and more robust after 2 trials than 1, and after 100 trials than 99 (all else being equal), but with ever decreasing improvements with practice.

Users also use learning to help with attention. As they learn more, they can recognize situations and generate responses faster. This gives them more time to pay attention to a task or to a secondary distracting task.

Users can also learn to adjust their behavior to fit to the interface. If the interface does not describe an action the way the user would, the user typically has to learn the new name, which they can and will do. If the interface has steps or substeps to an action, the user has to learn these as well. If objects are not where the user expects, the user has to learn their location. The good news is that learning can often happen without much distress to the user, but woe to the interface that requires the user to learn everything!

We will present here a theory of how users learn. This theory has many implications, including how users' behavior changes with learning, what extreme practice looks like, and what this can mean for interface design. For more information on learning, see Anderson (1982, 1995, 2004) and Lindsay and Norman (1977).

5.4.1   The Process of Learning

A description of the general process of learning (and types of task performance) has arisen in several areas, including behavioral psychology (Fitts 1964), cognitive ergonomics (Rasmussen 1983), and cognitive psychology (Anderson 1982). These theories all start with the learner acquiring declarative information about the domain. At this stage, problem solving is very difficult. The concepts are not always connected to each other. The learning might be seen as learning how to learn more about the task. What has been learned at this point might not be enough to be able to do the task yet. Basic declarative knowledge of the task is learned at this stage, such as the initial problem-solving state and the actions available for problem solving. Problem solving, when it is possible, requires considerable effort, and is not always correct. Problem solvers might not have much confidence in their performance. Anderson calls this the cognitive stage. Rasmussen calls this type of behavior knowledge based, as shown at the top of Fig. 5.8.

When learners are at this first stage, behavior occurs at the most fundamental level, when there are no direct rules to inform the user what to do. Expert users may have to resort to this stage in emergencies or novel situations, such as when birds get ingested into an aircraft engine, or when trying to change Unix permissions on shared files. These conditions require deliberate thought and reasoning about the state of the situation or system based on the user's knowledge (i.e., mental model) of the system, and then about what action to perform next. As you might expect, work proceeds slowly because each step has to be deliberated over from first principles.

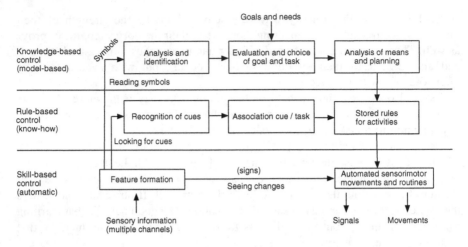

Fig. 5.8 A schematic of Rasmussen's theory of performance. (Adapted from Rasmussen 1983)

With learning and practice, the user progresses to the associative stage, or rule-based stage (as shown in the middle of Fig. 5.8). The learner can solve problems more routinely and with less effort. The declarative knowledge has been compiled into procedures relevant to the task domain that can be performed directly. At this stage users may often be able to just recognize what needs to be done. For users of complex systems, behavior becomes a conscious activity and is based on familiar rules, either dictated or acquired, such as changing lanes when driving a car, or formatting a paragraph in a Word document using styles.

The final stage, called skills or tuning, tunes the knowledge that is applied. At this point the user still gets faster at a task, but the improvements are much smaller, as they are smaller adjustments. New declarative information is rarely learned, but small adjustments to rule priorities happen. At this point users consider themselves, if not experts, to be real users. Rasmussen calls this level of performance skill-based. Anderson calls it the autonomous stage.

At the skill-based level, performance is much more automatic, as shown at the bottom of Fig. 5.8. Skill-based performance usually occurs when users are performing routine functions in their normal operating environment. Much of their behavior is no longer available to conscious thought, or available for verbalization etc. Users not only perform the task faster, they may also appear to have more attention to provide to other tasks. Examples include changing gear in a car with a manual shift gearbox, and cutting and pasting text.

These stages of learning have been noticed in several areas of formal reasoning. Formal reasoning involves problems with known goals (like solve for x), and equations or rules that can transform representations (such as adding 2 to each side of an equation). Formal reasoning is used in areas such as physics problem solving (Larkin 1981; Larkin et al. 1980a, b), geometrical proofs and solving algebraic problems.

In these types of problems the problem solvers (and computer models) start with domain knowledge and the goals for which they are trying to find answers. Novices work backward from the goal. In the case of physics problem solving, the task is to derive a value of a variable (like final speed) given some known variables (like mass, initial speed, and force) and some equations (like Force = Mass × Acceleration). Novices tend to work back from what they are trying to solve for final speed, chaining inference rules together until they find known variables. If they need to compute the final speed then they look for an equation that computes speed. Then they look for more equations to find the variables in the first equation, until they bottom out with known variables. This is known as backward chaining or bottom-up reasoning.

As the reasoning terminates in the answer, how to apply the rules in a forward sense, without search, is learned. More expert behavior is a mix of these approaches. With even more practice experts can reason in a forward sense. "If I have speed and time then I have acceleration, then if I have acceleration I have….." The answer in this case is found more quickly and with less effort. This is known as forward chaining or top-down reasoning.

This type of reasoning difference is seen in computer repair and trouble-shooting, software usage, and other domains where formal reasoning can be applied. Better interfaces will support the novice by providing the appropriate domain knowledge needed to learn the inferences, and support the novice and expert by providing the state information to reason from.

Learning can also occur in the opposite direction, from (implicit) skills back to knowledge about these skills, but this learning is less well understood. Implicit learning can occur when the user is working at the skill level, with knowledge eventually being derived on the cognitive level through the observation of one's own behavior. This type of learning, which is an active area of research in psychology, often leads to or arises from strategy changes.

Whichever way the user learns, some key phenomena survive:

- The ability to recognize correct/incorrect items comes before the ability to generate correct items.
- Knowledge is not acquired in an all-or-nothing way. Novices go through a stage of fragile knowledge, trusting that what has been acquired is correct, whereas sometimes it may be incorrect.
- Experts acquire a rich repertoire of representations of their knowledge. It is not only that experts know more than novices; what they know is much better organized, understood to a greater depth, and more readily available.

5.4.2 Improvements from Learning

Perhaps the biggest regularity of human behavior in general and users in particular is that the changes due to learning leads to them getting faster at performing a task the more they do it. Similar curves showing decreases in performance times have

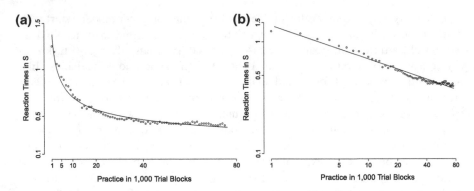

Fig. 5.9 Time to perform a simple task (pushing a combination of buttons) on a linear plot (**a**) and log–log plot (**b**) as well as a power law fit to the data shown as the *solid line* on each plot (adapted from Seibel 1963, and previously used in Ritter and Schooler 2001, reproduced here with permission)

been seen in tasks ranging from pushing buttons, reading unusual fonts or inverted text, doing arithmetic, typing, using a computer, generating factory schedules, all the way up to writing books (Ohlsson 1992). These improvement curves are also found when large groups work together, for example, building cars.

There are huge improvements initially, although users rarely report satisfaction with these improvements. The improvements decrease with time, however, following a monotonically decreasing curve. This is shown in Fig. 5.9 for the Seibel task, a task where you are presented with a pattern of ten lights and you push the buttons for the lights that are on. Each point represents the average for doing 1,000 patterns. Notice that with extended practice, performance continues to improve, but by smaller and smaller increments. Over a wide variety of tasks and over more than seven orders of magnitude (hundreds of thousands of trials), people get faster at tasks.

With data with changes this wide and with small changes becoming important later in the curve it becomes difficult to see the improvements. This is why the data are plotted using logarithmic axes: the difference between two points is based on their logarithms, as shown in Fig. 5.9. Typically, on these log–log plots, learning curves follow pretty much a straight line.

The mathematical representation of this curve is currently somewhat disputed. Some believe that the learning curve is an exponential curve, and others think it is a power equation (thus, called the power law of learning) of the form shown in Eq. (5.1):

$$\text{Time of a trial} = \text{Constant1} \, (\text{Number of trial} + \text{PP})^{-\alpha} + \text{Constant2} \qquad (5.1)$$

where Constant1 is the base time that decreases with practice, PP is previous practice on the task, α (alpha) is a small number typically from 0.1 to 0.5, and Constant2 is the limitation of the machinery or external environment (reviewed in Newell 1990, Chap. 1; see also Anderson 1995, Chap. 6).

PP is either estimated, measured directly, or ignored. In most cases it is ignored because the task is unique enough to the learner. In other cases, such as taking up a familiar task, the equation does not fit as well.

Constant2, the minimum time due to the limitations of the environment, is computed from equations describing the world or using physical equipment. For example, you might measure how long it takes a ball to fall to the ground with a camera if the task involves catching a falling ball, or you might record how fast an interface can accept keystrokes when driven by a computer program.

α is thus found typically by plotting the data on a log–log plot, and fitting a straight line. This fitting is typically done by fitting a linear equation (which has a known closed form solution) to the log of the trials and the log of the time. The more accurate but more computationally expensive approach is to fit the power law equation including the constants that are appropriate using an iterative algorithm.

Having an equation to predict learning is important for several reasons. For science, it helps summarize learning, and comparison of the constants is a useful way to characterize tasks. It also has practical applications. For engineering, design, and manufacturing, it predicts how fast users will become with practice. These equations are used in manufacturing to predict factory output and profitability.

Others believe that the match to a power law is an artifact of averaging the data from multiple people and multiple series, and that the curve is best described as an exponential when the data is examined in its purest form (Heathcote et al. 2000). Both cases have basically the same implications for users with limited lifetimes and physical equipment, but have different implications for the details of how the underlying cognitive architecture is implemented.

The improvement in performance time itself does not appear to delineate the stages of learning noted earlier. This may be because the first stage of learning, where performance might be quite difficult, has to reach a nearly complete level before the task can even be performed. There are hints of this in Fig. 5.9b, where the initial slope is fairly shallow in the log–log plot, perhaps more shallow than would be expected. In complex tasks, the transition of rule learning and rule tuning within task might lead to steady improvement, and be masked by the large number of rules and sub-tasks. Looking at individual users working on well-measured tasks may allow these stages to be seen. When this has been done, strategy changes can be seen (Delaney et al. 1998).

In addition to time reducing with practice, several other aspects of performance improve as well (Rabbitt and Banerji 1989). Errors decrease with practice. The variance in the time to do a task also decreases. That is, with practice the range of expected times decreases. Some think that this decrease in variability is what leads most to the speedup because the minimum time to perform a task generally does not decrease with practice (although there are clearly notable exceptions to this, for example, for tasks that cannot be completed by novices).

There appear to be two places where learning does not get faster. Users cannot get faster when the machinery they are working with cannot keep up with them.

Fig. 5.10 The learning curve for a series of better strategies, showing the initial slow down and then savings due to switching strategies

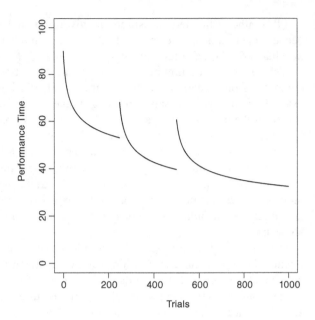

This was first noted when cigar rollers improved up to a point and then stopped. It was found that the users were rolling faster than the machine could pass materials to them (Snoddy 1926).

The second place where users do not get faster is when they change strategies. As a user picks up a new strategy, they will often experience a slowdown, moving back on the practice curve for that strategy. However, with practice, performance on this curve with a lower intercept improves, usually to be much better than the previous strategy (Delaneyet al. 1998). Figure 5.10 illustrates this effect.

If your system supports multiple learning strategies, you should consider helping the user transition between them. In text editors, for example, there are several ways to find a particular text string, including scrolling and searching line-by-line, scrolling and searching by paragraph, and using the inbuilt search function. In one survey (Card et al. 1983), most users were not using the most efficient strategy (searching), but moving line-by-line. Experts use searching, which can be 100 times faster than scrolling.

5.4.3 Types of Learning

Learning can be described in several ways. It can be organized by the types of memories that are created or practiced. One common way to distinguish types of learning is as declarative and procedural. Another common way is as implicit and explicit. The distinctions between these classifications are still being argued over, but they represent useful and interesting differences about users that help with interface design.

Declarative learning is learning facts (declarations). The "power button is on the keyboard" and "the computer manager's office is in 004A" are two examples. Declarative learning can be separated into two subtypes of recognition and recall. Recognition memories are easier to build than recall memories. That's why multiple choice tests seem easier—you just have to recognize the answer. This corresponds to the first stage of declarative learning.

Procedural learning is learning how to do procedures. Using an interface, and playing a computer game are examples of this. Procedural memories are probably more complex than declarative memories in that they generally support the skill being performed in a wide variety of environments and slightly different situations, which thus represent more knowledge. These memories have to come after the declarative representations are available to create them.

These two types of learning have different regularities associated with them. Declarative learning can, by definition, be described and reported. Procedural memories cannot be directly reported (Ericsson and Simon 1993). You cannot directly describe the knowledge you use to ride a bike. You can, however, accurately report the declarative knowledge that you use to generate your procedures (like keep your weight balanced) and what is in your working memory as you are doing the task (there is a parked car ahead). You can also watch yourself do a task and attempt to describe much of what you were paying attention to as you did it. What you think you were paying attention to when doing the task will, however, be dependent on your mental model of the task and how demanding the task is. This approach is called introspection.

There are fundamental problems with introspecting like this. While introspection can lead to useful and helpful insights, it does not lead to complete and valid theories of human thinking (Ericsson and Simon 1993). Just as you can't program a computer to write out the instructions as it does them (the instruction to write out replaces the instruction it copies), you can't think about thinking very accurately while thinking. Mainstream psychology has rejected introspection as a true representation of how people think, but you may find it useful for inspiration for ideas that can be later validated by other approaches. In our experience it is sometimes useful inspiration, but it is sometimes just way off because of our biases about how we would like to think we think.

As an example of this, users think that they cannot learn new key bindings between keys and commands (e.g., <Ctrl-s> to search vs. <Ctrl-f> to search). When key bindings in an editor were changed on users on the second day of a study about learning to use a text editor, for the first hour or two the users felt much, much slower. They were slower than they were at the end of the first day, but faster than when they started. They regained their skill level by the end of the second day (Singley and Anderson 1989). This study illustrates three important things about users. The first is that they are always learning. The second is that introspection often leads to incorrect conclusions. They rather disliked the new interface, but they adapted more quickly than they thought they did. The third is that the users were able to transfer much of

Fig. 5.11 Massed versus distributed practice in relation to time to learn a list. Given exponential decay, which is often assumed for memory, the *solid line* shows a given amount of practice as one block, and the *dashed line* shows the same amount spread out over a longer period. The distributed practice has higher activation after the second practice, and will for the remainder of the curve

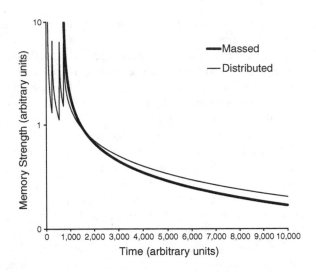

what they had learned from the old interface to the new interface. Only the key bindings changed; the underlying approach and the command structures did not, so the users were able to apply most of what they had learned. Another similar example is that users seem to prefer mice over light pens, even though the light pens were faster to use (Charness et al. 2004).

Another way to represent learning is with the implicit/explicit distinction. Implicit learning seems to be automatic, is based on practice, is not improved by reflection, and produces knowledge that cannot be verbalized. This might be roughly equivalent to the rule tuning stage. If the rules are created based on a simple domain theory, but a more complex domain exists, then additional learning can occur.

Explicit learning proceeds with full consciousness in a hypothesis testing way; it produces knowledge that can be verbalized. This is examined in more detail in a later section on problem solving.

These distinctions become important when teaching users how to use an interface. Some information is reported to them as declarative knowledge to be learned (where things are, who other users are, and what are the objects), and some information consists of procedural skills such as how to do a task.

Learning can be massed or distributed. Massed refers to learning that occurs at a single time, for example, cramming for a test. Distributed learning occurs with breaks in time between the learning episodes. Figure 5.11 shows how much better distributed learning can be. Distributed learning takes less total time (sometimes one-third of the time), and the retention is better, sometimes 50% better. Anything you can do to assist your users to learn in a distributed fashion will help their learning. Some interfaces now put up hints, which appears to be a way to support distributed learning.

Finally, we should note again that learning is rarely complete. It is easy to think that if you have learned to operate a system your learning about that system is complete. This needn't be so; many users can sometimes perform very competently with very little knowledge, and other systems, such as UNIX and the Emacs editor are complex enough that once competent, users can continue to learn new ways to use them and new components for several years.

5.4.4   Skilled Behavior, Users in Complex Environments

Real human skills are a complex mixture of these levels of learned behavior. In most cases, routine users will work with an open-loop behavior at the skilled level. That is, they will be able to perform most tasks in a routine way using existing, well-used knowledge and not check all of their steps. Their behavior will be open-loop, that is, they will not check all of their work. They will not close the loop by checking that things worked correctly because in most cases they no longer need to. If they do make mistakes, they will be able to recognize them quickly. They will continue to get faster with practice, but the improvement will be minor. There will also be some closed-loop behaviors for tasks that are less well practiced, and in these behaviors users will be more careful and check their work.

For example, airplane pilots often operate at all three levels. Some aspects of their behavior are automatic; for others they refer to rules and procedures, whilst for others, particularly in non-routine emergencies, they reason on the basis of their knowledge about the plane and learn. (In routine emergencies they will use checklists.)

Rasmussen's (1983) argument is that good design needs to support all three levels of operation, not just one. We can also note a social human factor here. If there are multiple operators, they may operate at different levels at different times because at the knowledge level they may have different knowledge, which may give rise to conflict or to strength, depending on how these differences in approach are resolved.

The knowledge level implies a certain amount of planning activity, but you will find there are those who believe that people do not engage in planning—arguing that behavior is situated in a context (e.g., Suchman 1983). In other words, they argue that we perceive the situation and decide what to do then, not on the basis of some pre-formed plan.

Two responses can be made to this.

- One can do both—have a plan and allow the situation to change it (e.g., performing actions in a different order from that planned).
- Planning seems best related to Rasmussen's knowledge-level, whereas situated action is 'rule-level' behavior. Again, these are not exclusive options—some people in some skills may function exclusively at one level, whilst others may switch between levels at high speed.

Fig. 5.12 A scene from a fishing port in Massachusetts where knowledge can influence perception (There is a boat that has sunk next to the dock. Only its mast is visible next to the boat on the right. The book's web site provides a more detailed picture showing the missing boat.)

Learning will also influence perception. It was not immediately apparent to the photographer from the photograph in Fig. 5.12 what was wrong with this scene (although it looked 'odd'), but it would be apparent fairly quickly to a boat captain. This is a simple example of where knowledge or learning, can influence other processes, such as vision.

5.4.5 Expertise

With extended practice, users become experts at their task. Generally, to become world class, it takes about 10 years of practice as well as some deliberate reflection and declarative learning, either from extensive self-tutoring or from a coach (Ericsson 1996; Hayes 1981; Simon and Chase 1973; Simonton 1996). There are exceptions, but these researchers argue that exceptions are truly rare. Less time is required to attain local or national prominence in a particular field, or where a task or technology is new. While practice is a usual and necessary condition, simple practice is not enough to guarantee an expert level of performance: coaching and deliberate practice are needed (Ericsson 1996).

This level of performance is interesting to people because it shows how good performance can be. When the practice is on a socially important task, such as flying planes or programming, it can also be quite rewarding to the practitioners.

Some theories suggest that with practice the user gains more than just speed in the task. In some instances they appear to have greater memory for, and can pay more attention to the task at hand (Ericsson and Kintsch 1995). In all cases, they have more knowledge and better anticipation of what will happen in the task, and in nearly all cases they have more accurate perception for and of the task details.

5.4.6 Transfer

Transfer of learning is important. After a skill has been learned, the goal is often to reuse or apply the knowledge to a new situation. If no transfer occurred, then every situation would be a new situation. If transfer was perfect, then few situations would be novel. Studies have shown that transfer is usually far from perfect, that it can be underestimated, and that it is possible to predict transfer effects.

Perhaps the earliest study on transfer had subjects read a story about how a king wished to invade a town, but his army was too big to come through a single gate in the town. So he split his troops up into smaller parties. Subjects then read about the use of lasers to attack cancer, but the problem was that the light was too intense to directly fire through the tissue at the cancer. What to do?

A surprising number did not think to use multiple lasers, which is what the transfer of knowledge would suggest. This lack of obvious (to the experimenter) transfer effect has been repeated many times. Problem solvers have trouble transferring knowledge or strategies where there are structural but not surface similarities. Thus, users do not always transfer useful information.

The second study to keep in mind is that of perverse Emacs. Singley and Anderson (1989) trained users for several hours with a powerful text editor called Emacs. Then, on day 2, some subjects were trained on Perverse Emacs, which was just like Emacs, but the keystroke commands were different. Subjects, we can imagine, did not like this at all, but at the end of the day, their performance was indistinguishable from the people who had used Emacs in day 1 and day 2. Thus, transfer can occur, but users do not always see it, and they do not like it when transfer leads to small mistakes (as would have often happened in the first hour for the users of Perverse Emacs). Thus, changing key bindings is likely to lead to frustration, but might not hurt users in the long run.

Finally, there are some tools to measure potential transfer. Kieras and Polson (1985) created a simple language to express how to do a task, and many task analysis techniques can be used in a similar way. Each instruction in the language, such as how to push a button, takes time to learn. Thus, the number of differences between instruction sets indicate how much knowledge can be transferred and how much must be learned. Analyses of popular operating systems suggest that there are real differences between them, with one being a subset of the other (and one thus being easier to learn).

5.4.7 Implications for System Design

All users will learn and get faster at doing a task as they repeatedly do it. This is an important way that users fit themselves to a task, covering up errors in design or compensating for trade-offs made in interface design that do not favor the user.

Interfaces that are initially too slow will become faster, but will require training (to learn the task) and practice (to get faster), and may not end up fast enough. Time to perform a task can be roughly predicted by comparison with other tasks or after several initial trials to get the slope of the learning curve (this approach is used in industry to predict manufacturing times). There are theories that should provide this information in the future when the theories become more tractable (Anderson 2007; Christou et al. 2009).

Theories also note what should be provided to users at different stages of their learning (Kim et al. 2013; Ohlsson 2008). Users must have some declarative information about a task before they can perform it. This means that interfaces and their associated system, including manuals, online help, web sites, and other users, should provide the new user with enough information to perform the task or at least to start to explore the environment. More generally, you should aim to support user task performance and learning at all levels, from knowledge-based to skill-based.

How procedural and declarative memory are used will depend on how they are represented. If the user has a more general representation and declarative knowledge associated with it, through practice the user can create procedural memories (Kim et al. 2013). The procedural knowledge can transfer to new problems more easily. Interfaces and systems (including instructional materials) that support more general representations and more task-oriented representations (vs. tool specific representations) will allow users to transfer their knowledge both in and out of the interface more readily.

The learning curve that can be created by observing learners can provide insights to system design directly. The start of the curve shows how difficult the interface is for novices. The amount of time to initially perform the task might be seen to be too high or at an acceptable level. Figure 5.13a shows a relatively shallow curve where novices are not so different from experts in performance. Figure 5.13b shows a curve where novices would be less happy, but which might be appropriate for a game. The slope of the curve can also provide insights. If the curve is very steep, and the system will be used often, the initial task times might not be an issue. If the interface is to be used only a few times, then the slope needs to get the user's task time to an acceptable level within that time frame. It can be the case that 150 s is an acceptable time, or it can be that 50 s is not and even the top curve is not fast enough—it will depend on the context.

Some users like to learn. This is probably most often seen in games, which have their explicit goal to teach the user some procedural skill (like driving a racing car), or some declarative knowledge (like the way round a dungeon). Most other users prefer not to learn, but will if the task is important enough.

If the users are likely to encounter situations where they may not have enough expertise to deal with the situation easily (e.g., plane malfunctions), you should consider providing them with instructions at that point (e.g., how to land when out of fuel). These instructions will not always help, but they often can. In computer systems these problems are often now being found on the Internet (e.g., how to repair a bad disk, how to clear a stuck keyboard).

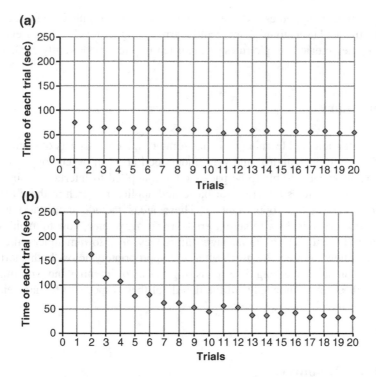

Fig. 5.13 Two learning curves with approximately the same final speed. **a** A relatively shallow learning curve. **b** A relatively steep learning curve

Systems that allow users to recognize actions they want to do will be easier initially to use than those that require users to recall commands. There is a trade-off, however, when the novices become experts. The experts will be able to recall the keystrokes or command names and will not wish to wade through the choices. For example, Linux experts like to use keystrokes in the command shell, while novices on Windows prefer a graphical user interface.

Systems that encourage users to reflect on how to perform the task may lead to different types of learning. Where the learning is incidental and not tied to educational intent or systems, this may not matter. On the other hand, tutoring systems should be careful that what users learn is what is intended. For example, the interface should not encourage users to just try key presses or button clicks to see what happens, which can lead to implicit learning that is tied to the representation of the interface and not to the domain.

Learning in such a situation has been seen in solving the 8-puzzle. Figure 5.2 shows such a puzzle. When users could directly click on the interface to indicate the tile to move, they took a larger number of moves and could verbalize their knowledge less well than users that had to work harder to interact with the interface, such as clicking on the tile and the direction to move, or using a speech interface.

The experimenters hypothesized that the increased cost of typing in the direction to move the tile lead users to think more and learn at a higher level. When users could just click, they created simple rules and learned implicitly (Golightly et al. 1999).

5.5 Summary

Memory, attention, and learning make up some of the core aspects of cognition of users. These are well studied and well understood areas in psychology, and their results are increasingly able to be packaged and applied to interface design.

There remain interesting areas for basic and applied research in these areas as technology creates new opportunities. These areas include multi-tasking, prospective memory aids, how to help users learn from systems, how to avoid biases in memory, how to help users manage things they need to remember (like passwords), and how to direct the user's attention appropriately across both short time spans (e.g., an hour) and long time spans (e.g., years of learning and working with a system like Unix). Knowledge of the details of these aspects of human behavior allow better interfaces to be built.

5.6 Other Resources

If you would like to learn more about the areas covered in this chapter, it is well worth reading the book by Alan Baddeley from 2004 on book on human memory. Baddeley is one of the pioneers of human memory research as we understand it today. This text renders his portfolio of scientific research accessible to a general audience, offering insights that will change the way you think about your own memory and attention:

Baddeley, A. (2004). *Your memory: A user's guide*. Buffalo, NY: Firefly Books.

You may well have heard of the magic number 7 about human memory before. If you'd like to read a paper that shows how this number was demonstrated to apply to human memory, it is worth seeing if you can get a copy of Miller's classic paper, published in a key psychology journal, *Psychological Review*. We note, however, that while this finding is still cited in the popular press as a well-known feature of human memory, subsequent studies have added more nuance to the observation–familiarity with the domain, modality (visual, auditory), and memory enhancement tactics can contribute to how many items are remembered:

Miller, G. A. (1956). The magic number seven, plus or minus two: Some limits on our capacity for processing information. *Psychological Review, 63*, 81–97.

John Anderson's texts on cognitive psychology provide an excellent introduction also. These are more directed at beginning scholars wishing to dive deeper
into this area:

Anderson, J. R. (1999). *Learning and memory* (2nd ed.). New York, NY: John Wiley and
Sons.

Anderson, J. R. (2009). *Cognitive psychology and its implications* (7th ed.). New York,
NY: Worth Publishers.

An excellent introduction to cognitive modeling is Allen Newell's Unified
Theories of Cognition. Although written a while ago, the text offers a nice
introduction to the thinking that launched this field of research, and to a particular
cognitive modeling environment that we mention in passing, Soar:

Newell, A. (1990). *Unified Theories of Cognition.* Cambridge, MA: Harvard University
Press.

Elizabeth Styles' text on attention, perception, and memory offers a very good
starting point and highlights how they are interdependent and interact:

Styles, E. H. (2005). *Attention, perception and memory: An integrated introduction.* Hove,
UK: Psychology Press.

For an accessible book on how reflection and memory affect performance in a
business setting, read Tom Demarco's *Slack*:

Demarco, T. (2001). *Slack: Getting past burnout, busywork, and the myth of total efficiency.* New York, NY: Broadway Books.

There are also many online demonstrations and resources in this area on sites such
as The Exploratorium (http://www.exploratorium.edu/memory) and the EPsych site
(http://epsych.msstate.edu).

5.7 Exercises

5.1 Find a user of a smartphone. It may have to be someone from outside your
class. Ask them to note as many of the menu items on the smartphone as they
can, and the structure of these menus. Have them do it without access to their
phone.

Compare what they remember with the phone itself. It will be useful to do
this for several people and compare the results. What does this tell you about
phone usage and users' memory?

5.2 Find an online tutorial, perhaps from this class or another class, or an online
tutorial to teach you Lisp or Java. Using an informal representation, break
down what you learn from a sample lesson into these concepts: math, theory

of programming, programming constructs, language syntax, programming interface, online tutorial interface.

What are the results, and what do they suggest for the design of online tutorials?

5.3 With respect to a web site for a university department (or your company's), create a list of tasks and information that a user of a university department's web site would be able to retrieve from memory and a similar list that users might not initially be able to recall, but would recognize. An example of the first could include the main phone number, and an example of the second could include special resources or accomplishments of the department.

5.4 Recall of memories is more difficult than recognition. As an example of this, write down the 50 US states. You can adapt this task to your own country, for example, listing the UK counties, the Bundesländer of Germany, or the number of member states in the European Union.

This effect also works for computer interfaces. You could attempt to name the menu bar items for a menu driven interface that you use often.

5.5 Usability of security remains an ongoing active research area. Memory influences the use of computer security. There are several ways that this can happen. One way is in the choice and memorizing strategies for passwords. Read https://www.cs.cmu.edu/~help/security/choosing_passwords.html or find a similar study on how people choose passwords. If you have time, write down your previous passwords, or ask people you know to fill out a small survey on what type of password they have, or have had. What do the results say about human memory and about computer interface design for passwords?

5.6 The first step of this exercise is to prepare a task for users to perform. This task should take people about 2 min on their first attempt, and they should be successful nearly all of the time. Students have used such tasks as card sorting, shoe tying, word processing, paper airplane construction, typing a paragraph, and web navigation. You should prepare instructions, as you will be having someone else perform the task. If the task is longer than 2 min it gets hard to run the necessary number of trials. If it is less than 2 min it may get hard to time as the users get faster. Anywhere from 70 s to 210 s is likely to work easily, and greater or lesser amounts will work to a certain extent. Online tasks may be more appropriate for your course, but what's interesting is that it does not matter what task you choose or whether it is online or not.

To get a good look at the learning curve, you should run 2–5 users on your task, and the subjects should each perform the task at least 15 times. Because of the logarithmic scale, 100 times is twice as good as 10, a 1000 times is three times as good. You may choose to run 5 subjects on the task 15 times (at most, 5 subjects × 2 min × 15 times = 150 min, so you may want to have help), or you might choose to run 2 users over a longer series of trials.

You should record the time taken to perform the task each time, and note whether the user made any minor errors, significant errors, or catastrophic errors. Some of these suggest that something besides normal learning was going on, or that a trial was in some way unusual.

When you graph your results, you should see a power curve or exponential curve. Both linear and log–log plots are interesting ways to plot this data.

You should comment on how your results fit the predictions in this book, other resources, and what your results mean for your task and for related tasks.

References

Anderson, J. R. (1982). Acquisition of cognitive skill. *Psychological Review, 89*, 369–406.

Anderson, J. R. (1993). *Rules of the mind.* Hillsdale, NJ: Erlbaum.

Anderson, J. R. (1995). *Learning and memory.* New York, NY: Wiley.

Anderson, J. R. (2004). *Cognitive psychology and its implications* (5th ed.). New York, NY: Worth Publishers.

Anderson, J. R. (2007). *How can the human mind exist in the physical universe?*. New York, NY: Oxford University Press.

Anderson, J. R., Conrad, F. G., & Corbett, A. T. (1989). Skill acquisition and the LISP tutor. *Cognitive Science, 13*(4), 467–505.

Anderson, J. R., & Lebiere, C. (1998). *The atomic components of thought.* Mahwah, NJ: Erlbaum.

Atkinson, R. C., & Shiffrin, R. M. (1968). Human memory: A proposed system and its control processes. In K. W. Spence & J. T. Spence (Eds.), *The psychology of learning and motivation* (Vol. 2). New York, NY: Academic Press.

Baddeley, A. D. (1976). *The psychology of memory.* New York: Basic Books.

Baddeley, A. D. (1986). *Working memory.* Oxford, UK: Oxford University Press.

Bailey, B. P., & Konstan, J. A. (2001). The effects of interruptions on task performance: Annoyance, and anxiety in the user interface. In *Interact, 2001* (pp. 593–601).

Bainbridge, L. (1983). Ironies of automation. *Automatica, 19*(6), 770–775.

Baxter, G., Rooksby, J., Whang, Y., & Kahajeh-Hosseine, A. (2012). The ironies of automation… still going strong at 30? In *Proceedings of ECCE 2012 Conference* (pp. 65–71). Edinburgh, North Britain.

Card, S. K., Moran, T., & Newell, A. (1983). *The psychology of human-computer interaction.* Hillsdale, NJ: Erlbaum.

Charness, N., Holley, P., Feddon, J., & Jastrzembski, T. (2004). Light pen use and practice minimize age and hand performance differences in pointing tasks. *Human Factors, 46*(3), 373–384.

Chilton, E. (1996). What was the subject of Titchner's doctoral thesis? *SigCHI Bulletin, 28*(2), 96.

Christou, G., Ritter, F. E., & Jacob, R. J. K. (2009). Knowledge-based usability evaluation for reality-based interaction. In G. Christou, E. L.-C. Law, W. Green & K. Hornbaek (Eds.), *Challenges in the evaluation of usability and user experience in reality-based interaction (workshop proceedings). At CHI 2009 Conference on Human Factors in Computing Systems, Boston, MA, 2009. CHI 2009 Workshop: Challenges in Evaluating Usability and User Experience in Reality Based Interaction* (pp. 36–39). Toulouse, France: IRIT Press.

Corbett, A. T., & Anderson, J. R. (1990). The effect of feedback control on learning to program with the LISP tutor. In *Proceedings of the 12th Annual Conference of the Cognitive Science Society* (pp. 796–803). Erlbaum: Hillsdale, NJ.

Daneman, M., & Carpenter, P. A. (1980). Individual differences in working memory and reading. *Journal of Verbal Learning and Verbal Behavior, 19*, 450–466.

Delaney, P. F., Reder, L. M., Staszewski, J. J., & Ritter, F. E. (1998). The strategy specific nature of improvement: The power law applies by strategy within task. *Psychological Science, 9*(1), 1–8.

Engle, R. W. (2002). Working memory capacity as executive attention. *Current Directions in Psychological Science, 11*(1), 19–23.

Ericsson, K. A. (Ed.). (1996). *The road to excellence: The acquisition of expert performance in the arts and sciences.* Mahwah, NJ: Erlbaum.

Ericsson, K. A., Chase, W. G., & Faloon, S. (1980). Acquisition of a memory skill. *Science, 208,* 1181–1182.

Ericsson, K. A., & Kintsch, W. (1995). Long-term working memory. *Psychological Review, 102,* 211–245.

Ericsson, K. A., & Simon, H. A. (1993). *Protocol analysis: Verbal reports as data* (2nd ed.). Cambridge, MA: MIT Press.

Fitts, P. M. (1964). Perceptual-motor skill learning. In A. W. Melton (Ed.), *Categories of human learning* (pp. 243–285). New York, NY: Academic Press.

Golightly, D., Hone, K. S., & Ritter, F. E. (1999). Speech interaction can support problem solving. In *Human-Computer Interaction—Interact '99* (pp. 149–155). IOS Press.

Hayes, J. R. (1981). *The complete problem solver.* Philadelphia: The Franklin Institute Press.

Heathcote, A., Brown, S., & Mewhort, D. J. K. (2000). The power law repealed: The case for an exponential law of practice. *Psychonomic Bulletin & Review, 7*(2), 185–207.

Intons-Peterson, M. J., & Best, D. L. (1998). Introduction and brief history of memory distortions and their prevention. In M. J. Intons-Peterson & D. L. Best (Eds.), *Memory distortions and their prevention.* Mahwah, NJ: Erlbaum.

Jensen, M. B., & Healy, A. F. (1998). Retention of procedural and declarative information from the Colorado Driver's Manual. In M. J. Intons-Peterson & D. L. Best (Eds.), *Memory distortions and their prevention* (pp. 113–124). Mahwah, NJ: Erlbaum.

Kaplan, C. (1989). *Hatching a Theory of Incubation: Does putting a problem aside really help? If so, why?,* Carnegie-Mellon University, University Microfilms International, Catalog #9238813.

Kieras, D. E., & Polson, P. G. (1985). An approach to the formal analysis of user complexity. *International Journal of Man-Machine Studies, 22,* 365–394.

Kieras, D. E., Wood, S. D., & Meyer, D. E. (1997). Predictive engineering models based on the EPIC architecture for a multimodal high-performance human-computer interaction task. *Transactions on Computer-Human Interaction, 4*(3), 230–275.

Kim, J. W., Ritter, F. E., & Koubek, R. J. (2013). An integrated theory for improved skill acquisition and retention in the three stages of learning. *Theoretical Issues in Ergonomics Science, 14*(1), 22–37.

Larkin, J. H. (1981). Enriching formal knowledge: A model for learning to solve textbook physics problems. In J. R. Anderson (Ed.), *Cognitive skills and their acquisition* (pp. 311–334). Hillsdale, NJ: Erlbaum.

Larkin, J. H., McDermott, J., Simon, D. P., & Simon, H. A. (1980a). Expert and novice performance in solving physics problems. *Science, 208,* 1335–1342.

Larkin, J. H., McDermott, J., Simon, D. P., & Simon, H. A. (1980b). Models of competence in solving physics problems. *Cognitive Science, 4,* 317–345.

Lindsay, P. H., & Norman, D. A. (1977). *Human information processing* (2nd). San Diego, CA: Harcourt Brace Jovanovich.

Loftus, E. F. (1975). Leading questions and the eyewitness report. *Cognitive Psychology, 7,* 560–572.

Loftus, E. F. (2003). Our changeable memories: Legal and practical implications. *Nature Reviews Neuroscience, 4,* 231–234.

Lovett, M. C., Daily, L. Z., & Reder, L. M. (2000). A source activation theory of working memory: Cross-task prediction of performance in ACT-R. *Journal of Cognitive Systems Research, 1,* 99–118.

McFarlane, D. C. (1997). *Interruption of people in human-computer interaction: A general unifying definition of human interruption and taxonomy* (Tech Report No. NRL/FR/5510–97-9870): Naval Research Laboratory. (also at infoweb.nrl.navy.mil/htbin/webcat).

McFarlane, D. C. (1999). Coordinating the interruption of people in human-computer interaction. In *INTERACT '99* (pp. 295–303). IOS Press.

Meyer, D. E., & Kieras, D. E. (1997). A computational theory of executive cognitive processes and multiple-task performance: Part 1. Basic mechanisms. *Psychological Review, 104*(1), 3–65.

Miller, G. A. (1956). The magic number seven, plus or minus two: Some limits on our capacity for processing information. *Psychological Review, 63,* 81–97.

Newell, A. (1990). *Unified theories of cognition.* Cambridge, MA: Harvard University Press.

Nickerson, R. (1969). *Man-Computer interaction: A challenge for human factors research. Ergonomics, 12* (pp. 501–517). (Reprinted in 1969 in *IEEE Transactions on Man-Machine Systems, 10*(4), 164–180).

Norman, D. A. (1981). Categorization of action slips. *Psychological Review, 88,* 1–15.

O'Hara, K., & Payne, S. J. (1998). Effects of operator implementation cost on performance of problem solving and learning. *Cognitive Psychology, 35,* 34–70.

Ohlsson, S. (1992). The learning curve for writing books: Evidence from Professor Asimov. *Psychological Science, 3*(6), 380–382.

Ohlsson, S. (2008). Computational models of skill acquisition. In R. Sun (Ed.), *The Cambridge handbook of computational psychology* (pp. 359–395). Cambridge: Cambridge University Press.

Rabbitt, P., & Banerji, N. (1989). How does very prolonged practice improve decision speed? *Journal of Experimental Psychology: General, 118,* 338–345.

Raskin, J. (2000). *The humane interface.* Boston, MA: Addison-Wesley.

Rasmussen, J. (1983). Skills, rules, knowledge: Signals, signs and symbols and other distinctions in human performance models. *IEEE Transactions: Systems, Man, & Cybernetics, SMC-13,* 257–267.

Reason, J. (1990). *Human error.* Cambridge, UK: Cambridge University Press.

Ritter, F. E., & Feurzeig, W. (1988). Teaching real-time tactical thinking. In J. Psotka, L. D. Massey, & S. A. Mutter (Eds.), *Intelligent tutoring systems: Lessons learned* (pp. 285–301). Hillsdale, NJ: Erlbaum.

Ritter, F. E., & Schooler, L. J. (2001). The learning curve. In W. Kintch, N. Smelser, & P. Baltes (Eds.), *International encyclopedia of the social and behavioral sciences* (Vol. 13, pp. 8602–8605). Amsterdam: Pergamon.

Seibel, R. (1963). Discrimination reaction time for a 1,023-alternative task. *Journal of Experimental Psychology, 66*(3), 215–226.

Siegler, R. S. (1988). Strategy choice procedures and the development of multiplication skill. *Journal of Experimental Psychology: General, 117*(3), 258–275.

Simon, H. A. (1974). How big is a chunk? *Science, 183,* 482–488.

Simon, H. A., & Chase, W. G. (1973). Skill in chess. *American Scientist, 61*(393–403), FIND.

Simonton, D. K. (1996). Creative expertise: A life-span developmental perspective. In K. A. Ericsson (Ed.), *The road to excellence: The acquisition of expert performance in the arts and sciences* (pp. 227–253). Mahwah, NJ: Erlbaum.

Singley, M. K., & Anderson, J. R. (1989). *The transfer of cognitive skill.* Cambridge, MA: Harvard University Press.

Snoddy, G. S. (1926). Learning and stability. *Journal of Applied Psychology, 10,* 1–36.

Sperling, G. A. (1961). The information available in brief visual presentations. *Psychological Monographs, 74*(whole No. 498).

Suchman, L. (1983). Office procedures as practical action: Models of work and system design. *ACM Transactions on Office Information Systems, 1,* 320–328.

Thomas, E. L., & Robinson, H. A. (1972). *Improving reading in every class: A sourcebook for teachers.* Boston, MA: Allyn & Bacon.

Tulving, E. (2002). Episodic memory: From mind to brain. *Annual Review of Psychology, 53*, 1–25.

Wickens, C. D., & Hollands, J. G. (2000). *Engineering psychology and human performance* (3rd ed.). Prentice-Hall: Upper Saddle River, NJ.

Woods, D. D., & Patterson, E. E. (2001). How unexpected events produce an escalation of cognitive and coordinative demands. In P. A. Hancock & P. A. Desmond (Eds.), *Stress, workload, and fatigue* (pp. 290–302). Mahwah, NJ: Erlbaum.

Zhang, G., & Simon, H. A. (1985). STM capacity for Chinese words and idioms: Chunking and acoustical loop hypotheses. *Memory and Cognition, 13*(3), 193–201.

Chapter 6
Cognition: Mental Representations, Problem Solving, and Decision Making

Abstract There are several higher level structures built upon the basic structures of memory, attention, and learning in the user's cognitive architecture. These representations and behaviors include mental models, problem solving, and decision making. These structures and processes form the basics of higher level cognition when interacting with technology, and describe some of the ways that users represent systems and interfaces, and how users interact with and use systems. Mental models are used to understand systems and to interact with systems. When the user's mental models are inaccurate, systems are hard to use. Problem solving is used when it is not clear what to do next. Problem solving uses mental models, forms a basis for learning, and can be supported in a variety of ways. Decision making is a more punctuated form of problem solving, made about and with systems. It is not always as clear or accurate as one would like (or expect), and there are ways to support and improve it. There are some surprises in each of these areas where folk psychology concepts and theories are inaccurate.

6.1 Introduction

When people interact with artifacts, even for the first time, they usually have some idea of what to do. If it is a piece of electrical equipment, they may first look for the on/off switch, for example, and then press that. The way that people interact with artifacts is governed by their mental representation of that artifact. These mental models develop over time: as people use the artifact more and more, they learn more about how it works and refine their mental model accordingly. The mental models can be either structural (based on the structure of the artifact in terms of its components) or functional (based on the behavior of the artifact).

As the complexity of artifacts increases, it becomes harder to develop a complete, accurate structural mental model of them. If you are someone who drives a car but takes it to someone else for maintenance, for example, the chances are that you have a relatively simple functional mental model of how the car

F. E. Ritter et al., *Foundations for Designing User-Centered Systems*,
DOI: 10.1007/978-1-4471-5134-0_6, © Springer-Verlag London 2014

operates—when you turn the key, you expect the engine to start, and so on. This model will allow you to carry out limited troubleshooting if the car does not behave as you expect it to. If you are a car mechanic, however, you will have a much more developed structural model of how the car works, which will allow you to diagnose and remedy any problems.

Designers have a functional mental model of how users behave. These models may be naïve and contain several inaccuracies because they have created and refined these models based on their own experiences of how they themselves behave, rather than based on their experiences of how their users really behave. One of the main purposes of this book is to help designers to develop a more sophisticated and more accurate model of users. You should, at this point in the book, know that, while not all users are the same, they are similar in many ways. Users differ in terms of the knowledge they possess, their capabilities, and their attributes. They also share common structures in how they receive and process information, and interact with the world. Understanding how these differences and similarities influence their behaviors will help you to design systems that are better suited to a wider range of users.

You should have learned by this point in the book that users behave unusually when they find themselves in novel or rarely encountered situations. This is because their mental models are not fully developed for those situations. In these situations, users often have to go back to basics, and use their mental model to carry out some problem solving. The way that they problem solve has associated biases, weaknesses, and strengths that you may be able to deal with in your design.

As part of the problem solving process, users will often make decisions about what actions to take next. Decision making, like problem solving, has associated biases, weaknesses, and strengths that can be used to inform system design.

Problem solving and decision making are probably the most widely observable and, arguably, the most important behaviors of users. Many fields of research study these topics, including psychology, economics, and statistics. Here we focus on how people make judgments and decisions, and how to support these processes in system design.

6.2 Mental Representations

Users can make use of several types of representations when they are problem solving or using an interface to perform a task. For example, users can understand an electronic circuit as a series of propositions (the secondary accumulator is connected to the laser bank), as a diagram (shown in Fig. 6.1), or implicitly as a series of steps to make the circuit work, such as "First flip switch 1, and if that does not work..." (Bibby and Payne 1996). Each of the representations has different strengths and weaknesses. The propositions may be easier to learn, the schematic allows some types of problem solving, and the rules require less knowledge to be learned or stored for later use.

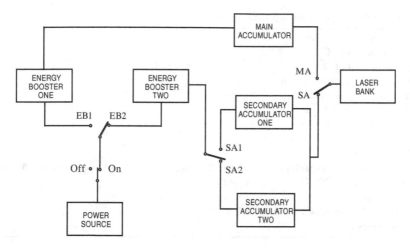

Fig. 6.1   A type of circuit schematic (based on Ritter and Bibby 2008)

6.2.1 Simple Representations

Representations can be classified in many ways. Two types of simple representations that occur repeatedly include semantic/propositional representations and visual/spatial representations.

Consider the information in Table 6.1, and attempt to memorize it. Then consider the information in Fig. 6.2. The information represented is the same in both places, but the representations give rise to different behavior and support different types of tasks.

The information about the sets of letters in Table 6.1 and Fig. 6.2 is probably better represented as a series rather than as a set of propositions—it is more succinct, easier to learn, and for most tasks it is easier to manipulate. The canonical series ABCD is particularly easy to memorize: it probably already exists as a series in your head. The other series is more difficult, but is probably easier to remember and use as a series than as a set of propositions.

The best representation for the workshop expenses will vary. For most tasks, users will be better off with the numbers themselves. The graphical representation on the left in Fig. 6.2 (created using the default settings of a common spreadsheet program) is less clear than the bespoke graph on the right in the same figure. The relative values can be quickly judged, but the absolute numbers will be more difficult to obtain. Both graphs are less useful than a table of numbers for many tasks.

Sometimes users will use propositional representations. Sometimes they will use a more visual representation. Interfaces should support the representation that users have, as well as be mindful of supporting the representation that will be most helpful for a task. It is the job of the designer to find the representations that best support the task, and those that users already have, and to balance the design to support these representations.

Table 6.1 Some propositional representations

Letters example—canonical
  A is to the left of C
  C is to the left of D
  B is to the immediate right of A
Letters example—non-canonical
  M is to the left of Y
  Y is to the left of S
  R is to the immediate right of M
Workshop expenses
  Gross income was $3,500. Expenses for coffee breaks were $1,218; copying was $400, and
  AV rental was $1,200. Net profit was $882
Puzzle sequence
  A series of numbers is 8 5 4 9 1 3 2 7 6
  What comes next?

Letters example—canonical: A B C D
Letters example—non-canonical: M R Y S

Workshop expenses:

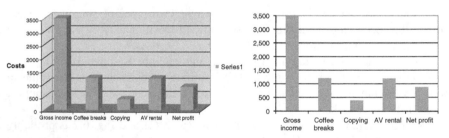

Fig. 6.2 Some graphical representations of the material in Table 6.1

6.2.2 User's Mental Models

The mental models that people use in performing tasks affect how they perceive
and interact with the world. There are several different meanings of the term
mental model, however, and the different ways in which it is used can be confusing
(e.g., Gentner and Stevens 1983; Johnson-Laird 1983; Moray 1996, 1999; Norman
1983; Wilson and Rutherford 1989). For our purposes we think of mental models
as a representation of some part of the world that can include the structures of the
world (the ontology of the relevant objects), how they interact, and how the user
can interact with them.

   As an example, work out how many windows there are in the place where you
live. The way that most people arrive at an answer is by referring to a structural
mental model of their home. They then imagine walking around their model of the

home and looking around the rooms at the walls to see where the windows are located.

If you had to come up with a mental model of a printer, though, it may be more of a functional model. So it would include the notion that you feed paper into it, that the paper gets images and text written onto it, and that the paper comes out of the printer into some sort of hopper. The mental model might not specify what the something is that produces the images and text, but could include further knowledge about the paper path. Figure 6.1 is another example of possible mental model, this time of a Klingon laser bank.

If the user's mental model accurately matches the device, the user can better use the mental model to perform their tasks, to troubleshoot the device, and to teach others about the task and device. If their mental model is inaccurate, however, the user will make poorer choices about what actions to take, may not be as happy, and may be less productive.

The complexity of the mental model will vary by user, by system, and by context. If the structure of the system is relatively simple, we can think of the model as an isometric model, in which every feature of the artifact is represented by a corresponding feature in the model. As the structure increases, however, people try to manage the complexity by grouping together related features from the real artifact and representing them using a single point in the model. This is what is called a homomorphic model. For more complex systems, and systems of systems (e.g., the Internet, the Space Shuttle, power grids, and so on), these mental models are also more likely to be functional, based on the way that the system behaves in particular circumstances, rather than structural.

Understanding users' mental models is important for system designers (Carroll and Olson 1987; Revell and Stanton 2012). The model the user brings to the task will influence how they use the system, what strategies they will most likely employ, and what errors they are likely to make. It is, therefore, important to design the system in such a way that the user can develop an accurate mental model of it.

While this is not a computer example, the design of Philadelphia airport's Concourse A violates most people's mental model and illustrates the role of mental models in using a system. A diagram of it is shown in Fig. 6.3. Users coming in on the left expect to see Gate A2 between A1 and A3. They might know that gates are sometimes numbered odd/even by side of concourse, but, in this case, the nearest gate on the other side is not even visible from most areas around A1. There are numerous informal signs taped up at A1 noting where A2 is that have been created by the airline ground staff, who clearly get asked where A2 is quite often. There are several ways to fix this. The numbers could run A1, A2 and wrap from A6 on the top to A7 and A8, or A2 and A4 could be A12 and A14.

Figure 6.4 shows another example of how mental models can lead to ambiguous and even misleading interfaces. The interface designer has created a default of 'Best', but it is not clear whether this is the faster $8\times$ speed or the more careful $1\times$ speed. Which is best? (One of us always selects a slow speed.)

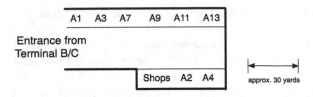

Fig. 6.3 Diagram of the Philadelphia airport concourse where the user's mental model does not support finding Gates A2 and A4

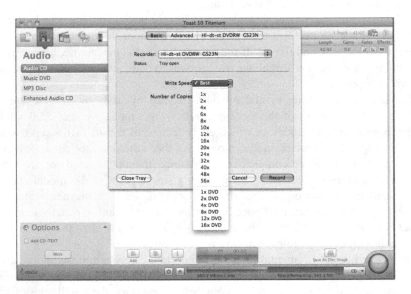

Fig. 6.4 Setting the speed for writing a CD. Which is best? Slow and careful, or faster but slightly more likely to throw an error? Taken from Toast 10 Titanium

Therefore, when you design a system you need to have an accurate mental model of how people will use it. This requires understanding how people will use it, the tasks they will perform using the system, and their normal working context. The developer's mental model of the system is often different from the user's mental model of the system (this book is intended to help designers build a better mental model of users in their own heads). Systems should describe things using conventions that are consonant with the users' mental models, for example, or be prepared to change either the users' mental models or the designer's. Making the system compliant with the user's mental model will almost certainly help reduce the time it takes to perform tasks, reduce learning time, and improve the acceptability of the system.

An important area of consideration for you and your users' mental model is processing speed and the complexity of the task. Computer programs and algorithms have a time to process an object that may be based on the number of objects (e.g., simply filing objects, or coloring them), or it may be based on their relationship to other objects (e.g., sorting them, or looking for relationships). When the process is based on the number of objects, the algorithm is linear. When the process for each item is based on the number of other objects as well, the algorithm is nonlinear (e.g., based on the square of the number of objects which represents the number of possible comparisons). Sometimes there are algorithms that are not too bad with increasing numbers of objects, and other times the costs quickly expand beyond the capabilities of even modern computers. This area is addressed by algorithm complexity, and your users will not understand it well.

Further illustrative examples of problems in interfaces caused by a mismatch from the designer's view of the task and the user's mental model (such as doors that open the wrong way, and buttons that are hard to find) can be found in books such as Norman (1988, 2013) and on web sites of interface bloopers.

6.2.3 Feeling of Knowing and Confidence Judgments

Users will vary in how confident they are in their representations. So they will ask themselves questions about objects such as "Is this a clickable region?," about processes such as "Is this the right way to do it?," and results such as "Is this the right answer?."

The way that confidence judgments are analyzed varies across contexts and research domains. Computer science and artificial intelligence (AI), for example, have tried to provide algorithms for computing a confidence level based on the available evidence. Psychology has studied feeling of knowing, about word retrieval, strategy selection, and how close you are to the answer. Business has studied confidence in decision making. In each of these cases, the measures of confidence form another part of a mental representation.

Users will base their feeling of knowing on a wide range of information. This includes having successfully used the answer before, being familiar with the domain, social expectations from the person asking (do you know the way to....?), and social comparison (others would know the answer, so I probably should also know it). Good interfaces will help users develop appropriate levels of confidence in their representations and decisions. Often, this means providing information to support learning, including feedback on task performance, and also providing information to build a mental model. If users do not get feedback, their calibration about how well they are doing will be poor to non-existent; this applies across many professions and businesses (Dawes 1994).

6.2.4 Stimulus–Response Compatibility for Mental Models

One aspect of mental models that can be applied to interface design is the idea of stimulus–response (S–R or SR) compatibility. This aspect of behavior is that the

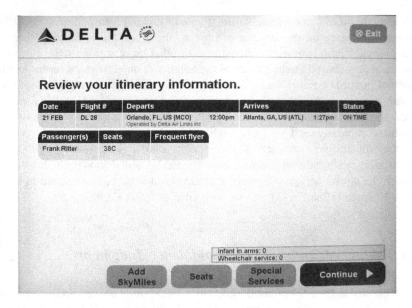

Fig. 6.5 An airport check-in kiosk. The phrase "Add SkyMiles," on the *bottom*, refers to their frequent flyer program account number which, if the interface is rarely used, can (and did) require the user to do extra work by asking an agent what SkyMiles is, and how to enter a frequent flyer number

stimulus and the response should be compatible. This is typically seen as having physical aspects of an interface (e.g., buttons) and displays (e.g., GUIs) match the world that they are representing. So the buttons to call an elevator to go up should be above the buttons that are used to call an elevator to go down. Systems where mappings like these are supported are faster to use and can lead to fewer errors.

Payne's (1995) work, reported in Chap. 1, provides several examples of how S-R can influence the usability of interfaces. The better designs (shown in Chap. 1 and explained further in the exercises) show that better S-R reduces errors by about 70% compared to a poor mapping, and that response times can be up to 30% higher with a poor mapping.

Another way to describe this aspect of behavior is making the task/action mappings appropriate. That is, the task the user is trying to perform should be easy to map to an action to perform. This is taken up in Chap. 12 as the Gulf of Execution.

The effect of S–R compatibility can also play out in computer interface menus and interfaces. If the user is searching for a widget, then an interface that explicitly labels something as a widget is a clearer interface than one that calls the widgets *thingamajigs*. Figure 6.5 shows an example where the phrase "Frequent flyer number" was replaced with "SkyMiles" (a type of frequent flyer number). Making improvements like this to interfaces requires knowing the terms that the users will be using, which may require substantial work when the users are distant, and creating designs that can support multiple terms when different types of users search using different terms. In Fig. 6.5 changing "SkyMiles" to "SkyMiles frequent flyer number" would be appropriate.

A related example of using multiple names for the same object leading to confusion happens with air travel from Dulles Airport. Its name is Dulles International Airport, and its code is IAD. It is located in the Washington, DC area about 25 miles west of Washington, DC; however, it is actually in Sterling, Virginia, near the town of Dulles, VA. In other words, there are several ways that you could search to find the airport. Some users may use all of these terms, but some will not recognize some of them. This variety of naming conventions in the real world can make interface design complex. One way of simplifying things is to use multiple levels of naming. LON, for example, is the city code used to represent all the London airports. This helps users who are trying to fly to any London airport when searching for tickets, although they will not be able to fly into an airport with the code LON, and will have to select the specific destination airport, such as Heathrow (LHR), Gatwick (LGW), or Stansted (STN).

6.2.5 *Implications for System Design*

When designing systems, you need to think about the users (what types of users, the range of skill levels and attributes they may have, and so on), how they will carry out work using the system, and the context in which they will use the system. If you can talk with and observe users, this may provide you with a chance to learn how they represent themselves, their tasks, and the system.

Mental models will often provide you with guidance about how to improve the usability of the system by matching the mental models the users have about themselves, their tasks, and the system (Krug 2005). Knowing about the users and their mental models will also help identify where you need to support them to develop an accurate mental model of the system. The areas where support is needed may not be obvious to you as a designer if you already understand—have a mental model appropriate to your purposes—the system, but your users are likely to have a different mental model of the system (based on beliefs, knowledge, capabilities, and attributes). Their models will differ between users and over time, so your design needs to take this into account.

For example, photo manipulation software will have to teach the novice user about the concepts used to describe photos and manipulations to them. Cell phones may have to disambiguate cleanly what method is being used to make a call (phone or voice over IP), and what network the phone is connecting to (a phone company or a local wireless).

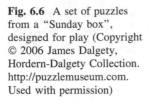

Fig. 6.6 A set of puzzles from a "Sunday box", designed for play (Copyright © 2006 James Dalgety, Hordern-Dalgety Collection. http://puzzlemuseum.com. Used with permission)

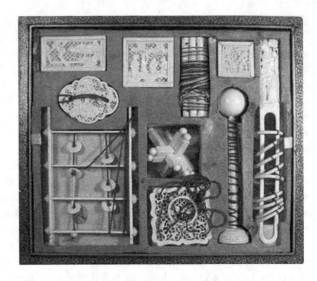

6.3 Problem Solving

Figure 6.6 shows a set of puzzles. Solving the problem of how to complete the puzzles can be great fun. This general notion of problem solving also applies when users try to perform tasks using systems in a particular context.

Problem solving essentially involves working out how to get from the current state of affairs to the goal that you are trying to achieve by taking appropriate actions. More formally, this can be described as applying operators to states to reach a goal. Problem solving is often studied by looking at how people solve puzzles, because the movement from one state to the next, and eventually to the goal, can be directly observed.

In the Tower of Hanoi, shown in Fig. 6.7, the goal is to move all the disks from the left hand post to the right hand post. There are several constraints. The disks can only be moved one at a time. The discs have to go on a post, and a disc cannot be placed on top of a smaller disk.

The first decision is therefore where to move the smallest disk? It can be moved to the middle or to the right post. The second decision is which disk to move, the smallest (probably not, but you could), and if you move the second smallest disk, there is only one post you can move it to. You continue in this way until all of the discs in the tower have been moved to another post. Although there are several ways to think about how to solve this puzzle, and several ways to solve it, there is only one correct minimal path.

The Tower of Hanoi has been used for a long time as a useful illustration of problem solving. Because it is a relatively simple, clear, but non-trivial problem, it has been used to study problem solving. There is a clear starting state and a clear goal state; the operations (operators) that can be applied are fairly evident and easy

Fig. 6.7 The Tower of Hanoi puzzle. In this picture, two towers of disks are shown here, but only one tower is normally used. The goal is to move a tower, disk-by-disk, to the far peg. The tower on the *left* would be easier to work with because the disks are easier to tell apart than the disks on the *right*, and because there are fewer disks (five vs. six). An example tower to play with is on the book's web site

to perform, and the constraints are relatively clear. It is easy to see the state of the disks, and it is basically easy to judge how close you are to the goal state. It takes effort to solve the puzzle, but people can generally solve it, particularly for three or four disks.

6.3.1 The Importance of Problem Solving

Problem solving occurs when users do not know what to do next. This happens when they are learning. Novice users will learn a lot, and expert users will learn in novel and unusual situations. When an expert sees a new type of fault or a novel combination of faults they will normally have to resort to problem solving. They have to function at Rasmussen's (1983) knowledge level, using knowledge in a problem solving manner, using strategies such as trial and error, for example. In the Tower of Hanoi, the user does not know the full sequence of moves, so they will have to do some problem solving. Some users will reason about the problem in their head, and consider what moves are possible and where this will take them. Other users will start by moving disks; it is a little easier to study how these users problem solve because their behavior is more visible. In both cases, their initial behavior will be slow and effortful. As they learn to do the task, however, their performance becomes faster.

6.3.2 Examples of Problem Solving

When you are installing software, you might know the goal state, and you might even think you know the starting state, but get into trouble because you don't have an accurate view of the actual starting state (you may have an old version installed) and you might not know the actual constraints on the installation process (e.g., you cannot install a new version correctly if the old version is still on the computer). Software can help with this, for example, noting the constraints for you.

In many hardware configurations for PCs there are hidden constraints: some disks require particular drives and graphics cards may require specific pieces of software as well. These constraints are often hidden, and sometimes can only be found through applying expensive operators, that is, configuring the hardware and then testing.

Problem solving is effortful and time consuming. In aviation they try to minimize the amount of problem solving that flight crews have to perform by providing a Quick Reference Handbook (QRH). This is essentially a set of procedures (checklists) that can be used to deal with known situations, both common and rare. In this way the pilots can operate at Rasmussen's rule-based level. In extreme situations, however, they may have to resort to problem solving. In the Sioux City air accident (NTSB 1990), for example, the aircraft lost all of its hydraulics systems whilst in the air, which basically meant that it could not be steered in the normal manner. The likelihood of such an event was so remote that there was no procedure to deal with it in the QRH, and even the aircraft manufacturer did not have a way to steer the aircraft. Fortunately there was another pilot on the aircraft who, together with the flight crew, worked out a way to steer the aircraft and get it down onto the ground.

6.3.3 Known Influences on Problem Solving

There are several known effects and influences on problem solving. These include ways that people like to problem solve and known ways that they are inefficient at problem solving. Knowing these effects can help build better interfaces and systems.

6.3.3.1 Based on Mental Models

Problem solving and decision making are thoroughly rooted in our world knowledge and world experiences. In trying to understand unfamiliar machines or unfamiliar behavior of common machines we try to construct a mental model (imagined world) in which we understand the device. This model enables us to operate the machine without having to recall what to do from memory. The correspondence between the imagined world and the real world is not important as long as the operations make sense in the imagined world, our mental model.

Mental models are thus used to perform Means-Ends Analysis (MEA) when problem solving. This approach to problem solving examines the current state of the device and notices differences between it and the solution. Systems that support this type of analysis can help users. If a disk is full, the user will want to create a less full disk. What are the large files that can be deleted, or what are the files that are rarely used or that were temporary? Displays of this information provide the way for users to understand and apply operators to solve their problem.

Metaphors for design exploit this process by prompting an appropriate mental model of the device. However, one needs to be careful. This type of problem solving fails when the mental model is wrong. Novice writers, for example, look at papers and notice that the paper is not long enough, and simply attempt to add more pages (this is not how good papers or textbooks are written).

6.3.3.2 Avoids Apparent Backtracking

Early work on problem solving found that problem solvers do not like to move away from the goal. This is sometimes called backtracking. This was found with problems like the Missionaries and Cannibals problem and the Goat, Cabbage, and Wolf problem, but occurs in many problems, and can include, for example, installing software that has to be then uninstalled to move on. These problems are shown in Table 6.2. In these problems you have to make some moves that appear to take you away from the goal. In each of these problems this means carrying something that you have already taken across the river back to the starting side.

Problem solvers have particular difficulty finding and doing this move, presumably because it looks like going away from the goal. These changes can be differentiated from simple undoing progress from a dead end.

So, if you are building a system, you should be careful how you represent the goal and the state of the system. If an action is required that might look like it's going away from the goal, you might support the user by providing a display that shows that the move is in the right direction, or you might emphasize it in other ways or with other instructional materials. Or, if you are trying to make a game more difficult, you might require backtracking.

6.3.3.3 Functional Fixedness, Einstellung, and Insight Problems

Sometimes the ways we view objects and problems is biased by previous experience. This leads to viewing objects and how to view problems not being done as well as they could be. Functional fixedness and Einstellung are two examples of this type of effect.

Functional fixedness is where a person becomes fixated on a particular use of an object. Figure 6.8 provides an example. In this task, solving it requires not fixating on a common usage of the objects, and using them in a very reasonable but harder to think of way.

Einstellung is related to Functional Fixedness but refers to the situation where a person gets fixated on a strategy to solve a problem. The most famous example is solving a puzzle using water jugs (Luchins 1942). In this task, people were given a

Table 6.2 Puzzles that require backtracking to solve

Goat, cabbage, and wolf

You have a goat, a cabbage, and a wolf that you have to carry across a river. Your boat can only hold you and one other object. If you leave the goat with cabbage, it will eat the cabbage. If you leave the wolf with the goat, it will eat the goat. How do you ferry them across the river without anything getting eaten?

Missionaries and cannibals

There are three missionaries and three cannibals that have to cross a river. Their boat can only hold two people. If there are more cannibals on a side of a river than missionaries, the cannibals will eat the missionaries. How do they ferry themselves across the river without anyone getting eaten?

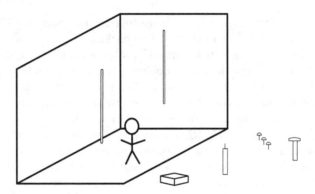

Fig. 6.8 You are in a room and have two strings to tie together (imagine you are MacGyver, a US TV personality who has to solve odd problems using odd things). You have a hammer, some tacks, a candle, and a box of matches. The two strings are too far apart for you to reach both of them when they are hanging down, but close enough to tie together if you have each in a hand. How do you tie them together?

series of problems using water jugs. In these problems, there were three jugs and a target amount of water to get. For example, one problem was to get 3 gallons using 1-, 4-, and 5-gallon buckets (fill the 4-gallon, empty into the 1-gallon, and be left with 3 gallons in the 4-gallon bucket). Over several trials they learned a strategy that worked (such as fill the first bucket, empty into the second bucket, fill the first bucket, empty into the third bucket, pour the second and third buckets together). When given a new problem that was solvable with a more efficient strategy (such as using 1-, 5-, and 7-gallon buckets, get 2 gallons by filling the 7-gallon, and emptying into the 5-gallon to get 2 gallons), they would continue to use the less efficient strategy (more pours), or if given a problem that required a different strategy, they would first try the old, unworkable strategy.

Functional fixedness and Einstellung both arise when people do not make full use of their knowledge, but are influenced too much by previous successes. As you design systems you should be mindful of what previous knowledge and mental

Fig. 6.9 Connect all the *dots* with four line segments without picking up your pencil

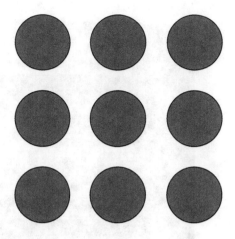

models they have encountered (functional fixedness) and what previous strategies they have used (Einstellung). Simply being aware that these effects can arise means that you can design systems that avoid them.

Insight problems are problems where novel behavior or understanding is required. Figure 6.9 shows a typical example. Most problem solvers have trouble solving this problem the first time. Solving it requires a singular insight, in this case, that you can and have to go outside the implied box the dots make up. Similarly, the problem in Fig. 6.8 is often presented as an insight problem because the way problem solving proceeds is that you are frustrated for a while until you 'see' the answer. While using Gimp to edit photos, for example, one of us has solved several insight problems.

Insight problem solving can be seen as having several stages (Sternberg and Davidson 1995):

Impasse: a point reached by an individual where they run out of ideas of operators or strategies to try that might solve the problem.

Fixation: an individual repeats the same type of solution again and again, even when they sees that it does not seem to lead to a solution; they become fixated on a solution.

Incubation: a pause or gap between attempts to solve a problem can sometimes appear to aid the finding of a solution, as if one is clearing one's mind of faulty ideas, or, as has been found, cues in the environment can help suggest solutions (Kaplan 1989).

The 'Aha' experience: the solutions to some insight problems can seem to appear from nowhere, like a Eureka moment.

Unless you are providing puzzles to your user as part of a game, you generally do not want to provide them with insight problems. Insight problems are hard to solve, are characterized by a relatively long solution time per number of steps, and

Fig. 6.10 An ATM machine that helps avoid the post-completion error because it does not retain the card. Another way is to return the card before giving money

unless you have an unusual set of users, they will not enjoy solving insight problems (although see the breakout box on "Need for cognition").

6.3.3.4 Post-completion Errors

The post-completion error (Byrne and Bovair 1997) is an interesting and important effect between memory and problem solving. This error arises when the goal for the task has been completed but the goals for the subtasks have not. For example, when you go to an old fashioned ATM machine, you will get your money before you get your card when making a withdrawal. You are there to get the money, not to get your card back. Once you have your money, you may walk away, leaving your card behind. Newer machines return your card before dispensing your money. Figure 6.10 shows another answer, a machine that does not retain the card.

Other examples of post-completion errors are available from email: when you write the email but do not send it, or when you mention an attachment but do not attach it. This error can also be seen in programming, where you allocate the memory for an array but do not release it when you have finished using it.

Post-completion errors provide a few suggestions for design. They suggest that the system should discourage the user from believing that they have completed the task until all the important subparts are done, and to put the most important goal last where technology and the situation permit.

6.3.3.5 Breakout Box: Need for Cognition

Many users do not want to do problem solving. They would prefer to perform the task directly. However, some users like to do problem solving; they like to think. These are people who do crosswords, solve Sudoku puzzles in meetings, like to build things, or debug systems. Cacioppo and Petty (1982), as well as previous researchers, describe this difference as a difference in the "need for cognition." Users with a great need for cognition agree with statements like:

I really enjoy a task that involves coming up with new solutions to problems.

I would prefer a task that is intellectual, difficult, and important to one that is somewhat important but does not require much thought.

I would prefer complex to simple problems.

Thus, users with a higher need for cognition will more likely find poor interfaces a challenge rather than impossible. As you develop your system, you might consider how interested your users are in problem solving with it. While the literature on individual differences suggest that the need for cognition varies by individuals, it might also vary by task: for games, you can encourage more problem solving; for entertainment and informal use, there may be some problem solving involved; for high stake interfaces, such as health, transportation, or financial systems, most users will not want to solve problems.

The need for cognition has also been used to study how people are persuaded and form opinions. Those with a high need for cognition focus on the arguments put forward. Those with a low need for cognition focus more on peripheral cues, such as body language, social status of the speaker, and fluency of the speaker. Your users may also be the judges of your system in the same way; and you may wish to make sure your system appeals to both types of users.

6.3.4 Ill-Structured Problems

Some problems appear harder than others. An important group of problems are more difficult because they are ill-structured. That is, they are not clearly defined. Writing, for example, is ill-structured. When you are writing the goal state is not clear—it is not clear when you are done. It is also less clear when writing what all the operators are (unless you examine everything on a character by character basis—then the problem is completely intractable!). Many aspects of design can also be seen as ill-structured problems. For example, when is the new phone or new interface finished being designed? These problems are also called *ill-defined* or *messy* problems. They often occur in the real world, and a major step forward is to make them more defined.

Ill-structured problems can be ill-structured in several ways. They can have poorly defined operators or the operators can be unknown to the problem solver.

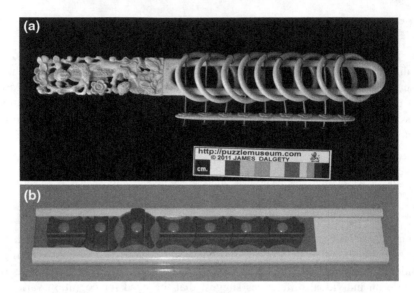

Fig. 6.11 The Chinese Ring puzzle. *Top*: classic version, provided by the Puzzle Museum (used with permission) of a classic version. *Bottom*: plastic version with the same search space, and slightly different state description and different operators (the knobs turn on a piece of plastic that slides in a track)

The Chinese Ring puzzles in Fig. 6.11 are like this. The puzzle on the top has the rings as actual rings, the puzzle on the bottom has a knob as a ring. The task is easy once you figure out what moves are possible and how close you are to the goal of removing the rings. A problem where you don't know or can't easily see the state of the system is also ill-defined. Most versions of the Chinese Ring puzzle also are difficult because you can't tell what the state is very easily; this is particularly true for the top puzzle in Fig. 6.11.

Ill-structured problems can be difficult because you do not know what the goal is or how close you are to the goal. Knowing how close you are to a solution is a problem for both of these Chinese puzzle versions. Tetris is pretty well structured; Rubik's cube is well structured, but users have trouble judging the state because it is so complex. Installing software can become very ill structured quickly if the error messages are not clear. Learning where you are in Rubik's cube or what software is not installed and is causing the error both improve problem solving.

Designers can help users with ill-structured problems in several ways. It is easier for users if the operators are clear. Thus, menus or lists of actions they can take help define the problem space. This list can also indicate what the constraints are on choosing operators. Having a clearly defined goal and good guidance towards the goal are also helpful. These distinctions can be modified or inverted for games and creative pursuits. Making problems less clear can make them more interesting and make the process of solving them a more creative experience.

Table 6.3 Problem solving requirements and several potential difficulties

Starting goal state	Can't tell if the system is at the starting state
Goal state	Can't tell directly what is a goal state
	Don't know the goal state
Intermediate states	Can't tell what state the system is in
	Can't tell distance to goal state
	Can't tell direction to goal state
Operators	Can't tell what are the operators
	Can't tell if operator had an effect
	Operators are difficult to perform (physically or mentally)
	Have to apply a lot of operators
	Can't tell which operators are safe/appropriate to use

6.3.5 Summary of Problem Solving with Implications for System Design

When you are creating systems, it is worth considering whether users will be problem solving and learning, or will they all be experts and be performing routine behavior all the time. In nearly every interface (although there are exceptions), some of the users some of the time will be problem solving. Small changes can often make it easier for them to problem solve.

Users will have to resort to problem solving with systems upon occasion. To help the users, you should support them in their problem solving (unless you are building games, when you may wish to make it more difficult deliberately) by making it obvious which operations can be performed in the current context, for example.

Making any aspect of problem solving more difficult will make an interface more difficult in several ways, as indicated by Table 6.3. You can make the user's life easier in several ways. These include making the state of the system visible, making the available operators known to the users (or enabling them to be learned easily), and having operators that can be applied physically or mentally. In some cases this may simply mean making the buttons bigger or the mouse-clickable regions easier to grab. The constraints on the application of operators should be consistent with the user's mental model, and the constraints should be visible or knowable. The results of applying the operators should be provided to the user.

6.4 Decision Making

Decision making is the result of problem solving. Where the amount of problem solving required is quite small, the problems solving and decision making may appear to blur together. Decisions can be small or quite large. They range from which button to push to which car to buy or where to land a failing airplane.

They can be quite simple and isolated, or they can occur within a string of decisions, perhaps while problem solving.

Decision making is studied by a wide range of disciplines, partly because there are many kinds of decisions, and partly because they affect all areas of human behavior. Interesting work on decisions are found in psychology (e.g., Gigerenzer et al. 1999; Kahneman et al. 1982; Evans 1990), business (e.g., Simon 1997), advertising (e.g., Ries and Trout 1986/2000), human factors (e.g., Cacciabue et al. 1992; Hoffman et al. 1998; Lehto 1997), HCI/marketing (e.g., Fogg 2003), and economics (e.g., Levitt and Dubner 2005). Here we focus on some of the generalities that are applicable to designing systems.

6.4.1 Decision Making is Often Not Rational

One of the fundamental truths in this area, and the first to note, is that often the most rational choices to an outside observer or experimenter are not chosen. People making decisions do not always take account of a lot of potentially relevant information when making decisions, and their decision making processes have general, knowable biases. That is, there are systematic ways that decisions are badly made.

Simon (1997) argues that, rather than trying to find the optimal answer, people typically satisfice. So, for example, if users were trying to find the cheapest price for something online they would choose a good enough price given the constraints of doing better which may involve looking at the price across 10 sites, rather than 500. In some sense, they are factoring in the price of further searching and the extra time needed to find a better price.

There are other problems with the way that people make decisions as compared to the way computers typically make decisions. These problems can often be related back to the cognitive processing capabilities introduced in earlier chapters. The rest of this chapter describes some of these systematic limitations, starting with simple decisions (Kahneman 2013).

6.4.2 Simple Decisions: Hicks Law and Speed–Accuracy Trade-Offs

As noted earlier, signal detection theory provides a simple way to categorize decisions in terms of their likelihood of being correct. It is also important, however, to know how long it takes to make a decision.

Pressing the corresponding button when a particular light illuminates involves a simple decision. It takes around 150–400 ms, depending on factors such as the strength of the light and the distance to the button. These numbers are useful in system design, because factors such as the time to press the brake pedal in a car determines the safe following distance in driving, and the time to press a button determines useful speeds for agents in video games.

The time to push a particular button also depends on the complexity of the decision. Adding more lights and buttons, for example, will make the task more difficult and will thus increase the time to perform the task.

Hick's Law (or sometimes the Hick–Hyman Law) describes the time to make the decision in relation to the number of choices. When there are many choices the time to make a decision may be very long (e.g., deciding which car to purchase), but for simple light sets the relationship is as shown in Eq. (6.1), where the time to make a choice is related to the product of the number of available choices and a constant, b, which represents the time to make the choice and accommodates changes related to the task details. So, increasing the number of choices increases the response time, but in a logarithmic way, which means the rate of increase is slower than it would be if the relationship was linear.

$$Time = b \log_2(n + 1) \tag{6.1}$$

The equation can be extended to take account of non-equally likely choices, such as menus which include items that are rarely selected. If the choices get too large, however, or the user has to look through every item in the menu, they may have to scroll down the menu, and the relationship will become more linear with a larger constant cost per item. Where the user is a consumer, in an eCommerce situation, for example, they may not make a choice at all (Schwartz 2004).

It has been argued that the law arises from a series of choices that subdivide the list in two with each decision. Having algorithmic explanations is useful because it helps apply this theory to other situations and to situate it in larger tasks.

Hick's Law and signal detection theory (from Chap. 4) both suggest that errors and time can be traded off against each other: the so-called speed–accuracy trade-off. For any given task, the user's performance will often range between very careful and slow, to very fast but less accurate. Psychology researchers study both relatively accurate and relatively fast behavior, trying to find the bend in the curve shown in Fig. 6.12.

When creating systems you may thus want to let users know how fast they are and how many errors they are making to let them adjust their performance (and hence change their position along the curve). For the purposes of design, though, you may want to know the time required to perform the task and what the acceptable error rates are so that you can help the user to meet these criteria.

6.4.3 Stimulus–Response Compatibility for Decisions

Stimulus-response compatibility, introduced earlier in this chapter, notes that responses that match stimuli are faster and more reliable. This is also true for mapping between a task and an action, and these two concepts are closely related. The classic example, perhaps, is that elevator buttons for the higher floors in a

Fig. 6.12 The speed
accuracy trade-off

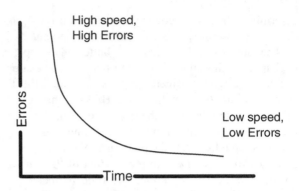

Fig. 6.13 An elevator that
has both good and bad SR
features. The open button is
closer to the doors (which are
to the *left*, not shown), but the
rooms do not map easily to
the buttons, 100-level rooms
are on floor 2, which does not
match many of the most
direct mental models, such as
100-numbered rooms being
on floor 1, or floor 3 being
above 2

building should be positioned above the buttons for the lower floors. Figure 6.13
shows another problem in an elevator control panel. It has good S-R compatibility
for the door opening and closing buttons (the open is near to the door, the close is
nearer the wall). The layout of the buttons for the floors are done in a British style
that may also be familiar in Canada (ground floor is where you enter, and the first
floor is the floor above that), but the rooms are numbered in such a way that labels
have to be attached to the panel to explain to users where they are (e.g., 200s are
on the 3rd floor). This might also be the result of a cultural mismatch between an
American company and a Canadian hotel, but, given the numbering scheme, one
can only wonder.

An old tale from Dick Pew (and documented in Norman's 1988 *POET* book) is that in a nuclear power plant the controls to raise and lower the rods were not clear, so the operators put beer taps on them to differentiate between them—with Loewenbrau on one (low) and Heineken on the other (high). This may be an urban myth, but it provides another clear illustration of what we mean by stimulus–response compatibility.

Probably the most powerful version of compatibility is the spatial compatibility that exists in the elevator example (and in Payne's example in Fig. 1.1). This effect can influence computer interfaces in many other places that use spatial and metaphorical content (e.g., that use relationships like up, down, left, right, higher, lower, more, less). Designs that violate this compatibility are likely to lead to a greater number of errors and take longer to use.

Two major operating systems have both included actions that violate this principle and rightly have been criticized for doing so. The Macintosh operating system originally had users drag the floppy disc icon onto the trash can icon in order to eject the disc: users just wanted their disc back, they did not want to throw it into the trash can. Also, both Windows and the Macintosh operating systems have users press the start button to shut down the operating system.

Finally, Fig. 6.14 gives an example of poor semantic mapping. OK normally means something is good. Cancel normally means stop doing something. In this example, OK means to cancel the email and cancel means do not cancel the email. A better design would be to have buttons that said 'cancel email' and 'continue with email'.

6.4.4 Known Influences on Decision Making

There are often differences between what people decide to do, and what an outside observer thinks that they rationally should decide to do. These differences are often predictable based on known biases and difficulties in reasoning. There are explanations for some of these effects showing how different assumptions by the user can lead to these effects. In other cases, these effects appear to be biases between otherwise equivalent choices, and sometimes they represent powerful tendencies that are not helpful most of the time.

Understanding people's biases—both your own and your users'—is important when designing software. It is important, albeit difficult, to counteract these biases when making decisions. Generally, these biases lead you to overestimate how good you are at something, and how much control you have over situations. You should design your system in such a way that it helps your users reason more accurately by highlighting information that they would otherwise naturally overlook or discount. The inherent biases described below are unique and have different causes, although in real-world settings several may apply at once, and even combine to make reasoning more complicated.

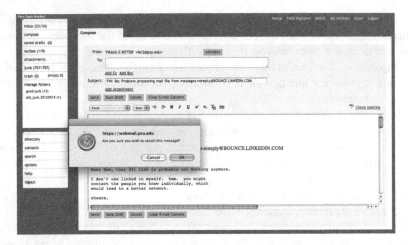

Fig. 6.14 A bad example of task-action mapping. Which button should you press to cancel the email, and which button to cancel the canceling of the email, or to OK the sending of the email?

6.4.4.1 Based on Mental Models

Problem solving and decision making are rooted in our world knowledge and world experiences. Users employ mental models in making decisions: if the mental model is wrong, the decision is also likely to be wrong. For example, if the user thinks that one cup of coffee helps thinking, they may reason that four cups might be four times better (which it patently is not). When you watch people use computer systems, you can often find examples of incorrect models such as the apocryphal tale of the novice user who looks for an "Any" key when asked to "Press any key to continue."

It is important to understand how mental models develop and evolve, and how they are used, so that you can support their development, evolution, and use. The system should provide the appropriate information needed to make a decision through displays, or help, or even in the surrounding context. If the information is difficult to retrieve from memory or to manipulate mentally, you should consider how you can either avoid or at least mitigate these effects. On solution would be to remove information that does not contribute to the decision, for example (Smallman and St. John 2005).

6.4.4.2 Confirmation Bias

Users tend to take the line of least effort. They want to find support in the world for their actions and reasoning steps that shows they were right. They therefore look for information that confirms their understanding of the situation. The corollary of this is that they have greater difficulty seeing things that conflict with their understanding of the world. This confirmation bias is pervasive.

Confirmation bias is related to noticing the lack of objects or stimuli. We all seem to have difficulty seeing negative instances. That is, we have trouble noticing when something is not there that should be there. In software testing, for example, this can happen when a file is not written, or in project management it can happen when an email does not come from a colleague about a project update.

6.4.4.3 Regression to the Mean/Sample Sizes

Users tend to over-generalize. Given a single instance of a concept, they will assume that all such instances will have the same characteristics. This leads them to make assumptions that are unsupportable and which may turn out to be false.

An argument can be presented as to why restaurants are not as good the second time round. On the first visit to what you perceive as a good restaurant, they may have been having a very good day, or you may have been very hungry, which made the food taste better. Thus, the results were a bit uncharacteristically good. On your second visit, they may be having an average day, or you were not as hungry. These factors will lead to more average ratings.

These regression effects can be found with music on iPods by a band you are trying; they will occur when users use an application to do a task where the task types may vary, and in other situations where are you repeatedly evaluating something.

6.4.4.4 Availability Bias (Representativeness)

Users have an easier time remembering the first few items and the last few items in a list, as we noted when discussing memory. The primacy and recency effects apply across users. People will also remember some items such as those that stand out for a particular reason, such as being particularly anomalous, like an elephant in a list of candy bars.

When users are asked to reason about and make decisions, they typically retrieve and use memories that are easy to retrieve. These memories are not necessarily representative nor do they cover the distribution of memories.

It is true that users judge people and things fairly quickly. This applies in interviews and when opening a new gadget. These judgments are based on relatively little information, and will take longer to reverse if they are unfavorable or incorrect. These are the first memories.

People also retrieve memories based on their experiences rather than the facts of the world. For example, if you ask people in America which of each of the following pairs of countries is larger by population: Ireland or Indonesia, Canada or Vietnam, Bangladesh or South Korea, and Iraq or Iran, you will often get

Table 6.4 Example problems illustrating the framing problem

Assume that you are preparing a new manufacturing process that will cost $600,000 to create.
 Two alternatives have been created to help save money implementing this system. Assume
 that the exact scientific estimates of the alternatives are as follows
 Program A: $200,000 will be saved
 Program B: there is a 1/3 chance to save $600,000 will be saved, and a 2/3 chance that no
 money will be saved
Imagine that the Programs A and B are not available, but only C and D are
 Program C: $400,000 will still have to be spent
 Program D: There is a one in three chance that no money will have to be spent, and a two in
 three chance that the original estimate will have to be spent

astounding answers. The actual population sizes differ by a factor of at least two in all of these pairs.

6.4.4.5 Framing Effects

The way that outcomes are presented (framed) has a powerful influence on how users choose between alternatives. The framing effect (Tverksy and Kahneman 1981, 1986) notes that decision makers are quite sensitive to the decision's frame of reference. Consider the choices shown in Table 6.4. Which would you choose? The most common answers are given in Exercise 6.2.

Where the outcomes are noted in positive terms, lives are saved, money gained, and so on—people making decisions are risk aversive. They appear to act as if they wish to lock in their savings, choosing an outcome with certainty.

Where the outcomes are noted in negative terms, lives are lost, money lost, and so on—people making decisions are risk seeking. They make decisions based on trying to avoid the loss.

The choices in Table 6.4 have the same expected statistical values, but how you and your users will choose solutions will depend in some part on how the information is presented.

For example, in an experiment, Kahneman gave students mugs in class. When they were asked to sell them back, they wanted $7.12 for them. When they just got to look at the mugs, and could either collect a mug or get paid, they valued the mug at $3.50. This process had the same outcomes, mug or money, but the people holding the mug valued it much higher than the people who could get the mug, showing that how information is presented and the order in which it is presented can influence cognition.

This effect of order on having and valuing also plays out for users and software and software features. Losing a feature is seen by users as much more costly than not adding a feature. When a subscription to an online service is dropped it is likely to be valued higher than when adding it. This is useful to know for marketing and for maintenance, although you are still likely to value the mug in hand more than the mug next to you.

6.4.4.6 Learning and Feedback

Dawes (1994) argues that decision making cannot improve without feedback. In his book, *House of cards*, he presents numerous examples of professionals some of whom do and some who do not get feedback about their decisions. Those that receive feedback have a chance of improving and usually do. Those that do not get feedback do not improve, although they do become more confident with practice, as they presumably get faster at it. He examines a wide range of tasks, but particularly takes psychotherapists to task, as very often in the past they provided treatment without receiving feedback on the outcomes of their treatments.

So, if you would like your users to improve their performance and to learn, you need to provide feedback. A failure to do so may only allow them to increase their confidence in their ability to do the task without increasing performance.

6.4.5 Larger Scale Decision Making Process: Expertise and RPDM

Decision making in the real world is also influenced by learning, mental models, and expertise. Work by Simon and his colleagues looked at how expertise influenced decision making. They showed that, in some cases, expertise led to faster decisions, but essentially the same decisions; for example, young business majors would make the same decisions for a business case, but would take longer (Simon 1997).

They also studied how people played chess as an analogue for other decision making tasks (Chase and Simon 1973; Gobet and Simon 1996b; Simon and Chase 1973). They found good chess players would consider more reorganization of the positions and better possible moves than would novices, who would have to do more problem solving. This expertise would also allow good players to remember positions more readily because they were not remembering all the pieces individually, but recognizing groups of pieces as patterns in a way similar to how ABC, 747, and HFE (and others noted in Table 5.1) might be considered as single objects instead of three separate characters (Gobet and Simon 1996a).

This approach has been implemented in computational models, including programs that solve problems (Ritter and Bibby 2008) and play chess (Gobet et al. 1997). These models start out with effortful problem solving or problem solving-like behavior that, with practice, becomes faster and uses recognition to drive its behavior. Sometimes the strategy does not change with improved learning (it is just faster), and sometimes the ability to recognize what to do changes how the models perform the task (Ritter et al. 1998), mirroring how behavior changes with expertise in the task (Larkin et al. 1980).

Within human factors a body of work has developed that looks at decision making in the wild—naturalistic decision making—like fire-fighting, and search and rescue. Work on recognition-primed decision making (RPDM, Klein 1997), argues that experts do not do problem solving, but that they recognize the situation which directly leads them to the correct actions to take. This approach is consistent with previous work in psychology, and with Rasmussen's work on levels of expertise (Rasmussen 1983).

The work on naturalistic decision making encourages designers to provide information to users to help them make decisions. They should also provide the information in a way that supports recognition of the correct decisions, and explicitly acknowledges that experts may move more quickly to a solution using cues that relate the current situation to previously encountered situations.

6.4.6 Summary of Decision Making with Implications for System Design

Many decision-support systems try to support the process of formalizing the information contributing to the solution/decision. However, human problem solving is not always based on logic and rationality in terms of using the information to the full. This makes good decision support systems helpful, but difficult to design because often the problem is not with the quality of the information being presented to users.

Users do not make decisions the way you might think they will in several ways. They will take more time the more choices they have. With good design, these choices can help them and the choices can be made relatively quickly. With more choices, or worse design, the time to choose might become large. Users will be able to make more accurate and rapid choices if the choices (as described) match their mental models and the names of the tasks they are attempting to perform. So, provide time, reduce choices where appropriate, and have the choices match the mental model and terms that the user has.

The decisions users make will be based on their mental models, and they will often have different mental models than you. The cognitive architecture they can bring to solve the problem will limit their ability to make rational choices. They will often make choices consistent with previous choices because these choices confirm their previous choices. They will base their decisions on what they can retrieve from memory, and what they can retrieve first and easiest from memory is not always the most useful information for making their decisions. So, if your users often have to modify their behavior, you might wish to make repetitive behavior less easy. If they choices are likely to be consistent, then options like "Apply to all?" are helpful.

How they will make their decision will be influenced by their context and how the choices are framed. Decisions based on gains will be slightly risk-aversive; decisions to avoid a loss will lead to choosing riskier options. So be careful how you frame the options, either as a gain or a loss.

If the users do not get feedback about their choices, their choice quality will remain the same, but they will become more confident in their choices. If they do get feedback, they can learn how to make decisions more accurately and quicker using a variety of knowledge sources including recognizing a situation as being like a previous situation, and also recalling a useful answer. So, provide feedback in your systems when you can.

Finally, their choices can be situated within a large context, including geography and social relationships. Good designers will learn about these factors in a variety of ways. Good designs will take these multiple factors into account, and attempt to minimize the biases that will hurt the users, and take advantage of biases that can help users. The breakout box on biases in reasoning provides a set of examples applied to a simple task, and the breakout box on incompetence provides both serious and humorous insights into limitations of human reasoning. So when you can get context, use it to frame your interface's interactions.

6.4.6.1 Breakout Box: Biases in Reasoning

We can illustrate how biases affect reasoning using the classic Wason (1960) selection task. This is an example of an abstract deductive reasoning task that should be solved using rules of logic:

> Every card (shown in Fig. 6.15) has a letter on one side and a number on the other. Given a set of four cards as shown below, which cards would you need to turn over in order to prove or disprove the rule that "If a card has a vowel on one side, then it has an even number on the other side."

Most people opt for the A card and the 4 card. Selecting only the A and the 4 card only gathers evidence to prove the rule, however, and is an example of confirmation bias. In other words, often people only look for evidence that supports (or confirms) their hypothesis. In this case, the hypothesis is the rule that they were given. The correct solution, however, is that the A card and the 7 card should be turned over. If the A card has an even number on the other side that is evidence to support the rule; if it has an odd number it disproves the rule. The 7 card has to be turned over because if it has a vowel on the other side, this also disproves the rule. The 4 card does not have to be turned over because if there is a vowel on the other side, the rule is satisfied and if there is a consonant then the rule would not apply.

The way this and many problems are framed, however, has a major influence on people's performance. If the problem is made less abstract by using real objects that people are more likely to encounter in their daily lives, more people give the correct answer. Johnson-Laird et al. (1972), for example, framed the problem in a

Fig. 6.15 Which cards do you need to turn over to verify that if a card has a vowel on one side then it has an even number on the other side? (Cards have a letter on one side and a number on the other)

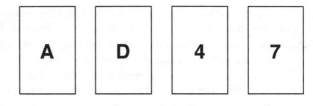

more concrete way, using sealed/unsealed envelopes (so the flap was open/closed) which had stamps of different denominations on the other side. They then asked participants to prove or disprove the rule: "if an envelope is sealed then it has a 5p stamp on the other side." With a more concrete representation, 22 out of 24 people gave the correct answer. Making problems more concrete generally makes them easier.

For a more detailed psychological description of the issues surrounding performance on various versions of the Wason reasoning task see, for example, Quinlan and Dyson (2008).

6.4.6.2 Breakout Box: Why Don't Users Do What They Should?

At this point in your reading you may have realized that users do not always do what they should, that they do not always act in their own interests. It is one thing to make mistakes, slips, and errors (covered in the chapter on errors, and which you can infer from the memory chapter); it is another to hold quite wrong beliefs continuously contradicted by the world, and to continue to perform poorly based on these beliefs. Why does this happen?

Academics use other phrases, such as why smart people can be so foolish (Sternberg 2004) and how people cannot recognize their own incompetence (Dunning et al. 2003). Generally, this area can be examined as a type of metacognition—do you know what you know and can you judge your performance in quantitative ways (how good is it?) and qualitative ways (how is it good and how can it be improved?).

Sternberg (2004) notes five factors that can lead to foolishness—poor decision making and problem solving in leaders. These are as follows: (a) Unrealistic optimism, assuming things will work out or strategies will work. (b) Egocentrism, focusing on your own goals rather than a broader set of goals. Sternberg notes cases where focusing on short-term goals hurts long-term goals, and where not looking after others leads to significant problems arising for the leader. (c) A sense of omniscience, assuming you know all you need to know to make the decision. (d) A sense of omnipotence, assuming that you are competent in one domain and thus in all, and that the plans you put into action will work. (e) A sense of

Fig. 6.16 Perceived percentile rankings for mastery of course material and test performance as a function of actual performance rank. Copied from Dunning et al. (2003) with permission

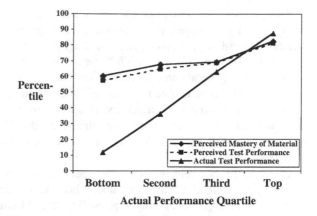

invulnerability, that plans cannot go badly wrong given the support you have. These biases in reasoning, however, are well known and occur in nearly everyone. They offer one set of reasons to explain why people are foolish at times.

When they study, students can be affected by these factors, and thus users who study manuals or are learning how to use software or systems would be equally vulnerable. Typically, students think they have learned more than they have through studying (Dunning et al. 2003; Winne and Jamieson-Noel 2002). This miscalibration can be based on judgments of the wrong measures. For example, some students measure the ease of reading the material. The real test is different, however. The real test is not how fast you can read the material, but how well can you recall it and apply it. Thus, students who stop studying when they can repeat the material or who write about the material will be better calibrated than students who make this judgment on factors not related to the test.

Figure 6.16 shows example results. Subjects who just took a sophomore psychology exam were asked how well they thought they had done. The subjects were grouped by quartiles by their exam score. The subjects who performed worst thought their scores were just above average (far left). The third quartile was relatively well calibrated in that their predictions matched their performance. The top quartile thought their performance would be a bit lower, showing modesty among the top performers.

Another problem is that the poor performers simply do not know any better. They lack the knowledge to judge that their performance is inadequate. Dunning et al. (2003) call it a double curse:

> The skills needed to produce correct responses are virtually identical to those needed to evaluate the accuracy of one's responses. The skills needed to produce logically sound arguments, for instance, are the same skills that are necessary to recognize when a logically sound argument has been made. Thus, if people lack the skills to produce correct answers, they are also cursed with an inability to know when their answers, or anyone else's, are right or wrong. They cannot recognize their responses as mistaken, or other people's responses as superior to their own. In short, incompetence means that people cannot successfully complete the task of metacognition, which, among its many meanings, refers to the ability to evaluate responses as correct or incorrect.

Thus, it is a rare and unhappy individual who knows that their answers are inadequate. For example, the knowledge to judge whether a sentence is grammatical, a word is correctly spelled, a diagram is well drawn, or program well written will be highly correlated with the ability to generate the correct behavior. So people who generate ungrammatical sentences or perform poorly on these other tasks are likely to be unable to know that they are ungrammatical.

What does this mean for users and designing for users? It means, on average, users will think that they know more than they do. They will be overconfident when performing tasks, and they will not always use the right cues to judge their knowledge.

Good design can help provide more feedback on performance, and could also provide education along the way about how to correct problems. Noting that "Error 23 occurred" does not help. Noting that "Removing disks without unmounting them can lead to disk errors" is a step in the right direction because it provides a way for users to learn from their errors through feedback.

6.5 Summary

This chapter has given you a broad understanding of how users think by providing high level descriptions of user behavior. Mental models, problem solving, and decision making all depend on the simple architectural mechanisms introduced in earlier chapters. When users interact with technology they depend on the high level cognition we have described. By understanding the capabilities and limitations of high level cognition you should be better equipped to understand some of the ways that users can represent systems and interfaces and how they interact with and use them.

Mental models are used to understand systems and to interact with systems. When the user's mental models are inaccurate, systems are hard to use. Designers can attempt to understand users' initial mental models. Designers can then either design to support users with those models, or they can help educate users to acquire more appropriate mental models.

Users problem solve when it is not clear what they should do next. Problem solving uses mental models, forms a basis for learning, and can be supported in a variety of ways. Systems that provide appropriate information to users can help with problem solving. When users are found to problem solve, it may be appropriate to modify the interface to support behavior to make it include less problem solving, to provide feedback to support problem solving such as distance to the goal, or to perform the task for the user.

Decision making is a more punctuated form of problem solving, made about and with systems. It is not always as accurate as outside observers would expect it to be. There are ways to support and improve decision making. Short-term, there are biases to avoid encouraging in the interface. Long term, providing feedback about past decisions and their accuracy can help users.

There are surprises for designers in each of these area, where folk psychology concepts and theories are inaccurate. The most general result and the one with the largest import is that, in each of these areas, users are likely to have different mental models, different problem solving strategies, and make decisions in different ways than system designers, so designers should study the users when these aspects of behavior are important. There is a rich literature on each of these areas in psychology and other areas. When you start to design interfaces that touch on other aspects of these areas, you should have enough background to go and learn more.

6.6 Other Resources

A classic text on human reasoning using mental models is Philip Johnson-Laird's book, *Mental Models*:

Johnson-Laird, P. N. (1989). *Mental models*. Cambridge, MA: The MIT Press.

You will find much material online that details some of the reasoning biases we have discussed in this chapter, but it is also worth reading some of the original texts, especially those by Kahneman and Tversky:

Kahneman, D. Slovic, P. and Tversky, A. eds. (1982). *Judgment under uncertainty: Heuristics and biases*. Cambridge, UK: Cambridge University Press.

A different approach to thinking about mental models is to think about the role of language in creating how we see the world. An interesting book to read for this approach is George Lakoff and Mark Johnson's 2008 book *Metaphors We Live By*.

Lakoff, G. and Johnson, M. (2008). *Metaphors we live by*. Chicago, IL: University of Chicago Press.

Hayes' (1981) book inspired parts of this book. It provides a good source for thinking about applied cognitive psychology and problem solving:

Hayes, J. R. (1981). *The complete problem solver*. Philadelphia, PA: The Franklin Institute Press.

Another classic text is the 1972 book by Allen Newell and Herb Simon, and is worth reading for historical context as well as for their ideas about human problem solving specifically:

Newell, A. and Simon, H. A. (1972). *Human problem solving*. Englewood Cliffs, NJ: Prentice-Hall.

The journal *Psychological Science in the Public Interest* publishes papers about how results in psychology have public policy implications. The series is worth reading because it examines important topics. It is available online, free, as PDF files. For example, a review paper by Dunning et al. (2004) summarizes why users are often poorly calibrated in their decision making and provides more examples and results. They have also published reviews on how to promote trust, how to improve learning in schools, and terrorism.

6.7 Exercises

6.1 Using a smartphone, explore it to find an ill-structured problem. This could be an application or function that has the features of an ill-structured problem. Discuss how you could improve this application, or note why the user would want it to be an ill-structured problem.

6.2 Find another "bias" in human problem solving or in decision making with particular attention paid to business problems. You might find implications in an earlier chapter, or you might find useful information in a book or journal on decision making in business. Compare this known bias in reasoning to the list shown here. Consider which are the more important biases.

6.3 Consider a web site that you know of medium complexity, such as your department's web site. Draw a map of it from memory (or, to be fairer, have some other people draw a map of it). Then, compare the maps with a map drawn from the web site. Compare the user's maps with the actual site, and draw conclusions about mental models.

6.4 Have some friends choose between the choices in Table 6.4. If your friends are like Tversky and Kahneman's subjects (Kahneman et al. 1982), they will prefer program A over program B (72–28%) and program C over program D (22–78%).

References

Bibby, P. A., & Payne, S. J. (1996). Instruction and practice in learning to use a device. *Cognitive Science, 20*(4), 539–578.

Byrne, M. D., & Bovair, S. (1997). A working memory model of a common procedural error. *Cognitive Science, 21*(1), 31–61.

Cacciabue, P. C., Decortis, F., Drozdowicz, B., Masson, M., & Nordvik, J. (1992). COSIMO: A cognitive simulation model of human decision making and behavior in accident management of complex plants. *IEEE Transactions on Systems, Man, and Cybernetics, 22*(5), 1058–1074.

Cacioppo, J. T., & Petty, R. E. (1982). The need for cognition. *Journal of Personality and Social Psychology, 42*(1), 116–131.

Carroll, J. M., & Olson, J. (Eds.). (1987). *Mental models in human-computer interaction: Research issues about what the user of software knows*. Washington, DC: National Academy Press.

Chase, W. G., & Simon, H. A. (1973). Perception in chess. *Cognitive Psychology, 4*, 55–81.

Dawes, R. M. (1994). *House of cards: Psychology and psychotherapy built on myth*. New York, NY: The Free Press.

Dunning, D., Heath, C., & Suls, J. M. (2004). Flawed self-assessment: Implications for health, education, and the workplace. *Psychological Science in the Public Interest, 5*(3), 69–106.

Dunning, D., Johnson, K., Ehrlinger, J., & Kruger, J. (2003). Why people fail to recognize their own incompetence. *Current Directions in Psychological Science, 12*(3), 83–87.

Evans, J. St. B. T. (1990). *Biases in human reasoning*. Hove, UK: Lawrence Erlbaum.

Fogg, B. J. (2003). *Persuasive technology: Using computers to change what we think and do*. San Francisco, CA: Morgan Kaufmann.

Gentner, D., & Stevens, A. L. (Eds.). (1983). *Mental models*. Hillsdale, NJ: Erlbaum.

Gigerenzer, G., Todd, P. M., & the ABC Research Group (1999). *Simple heuristics that make us smart*. New York, NY: Oxford University Press.

Gobet, F., Richman, H., Staszewski, J., & Simon, H. A. (1997). Goals, representations, and strategies in a concept attainment task: The EPAM model. *The Psychology of Learning and Motivation, 37*, 265–290.

Gobet, F., & Simon, H. A. (1996a). Templates in chess memory: A mechanism for recalling several boards. *Cognitive Psychology, 31*, 1–40.

Gobet, F., & Simon, H. A. (1996b). The roles of recognition processes and look-ahead search in time-constrained expert problem solving: Evidence from grandmaster level chess. *Psychological Science, 7*, 52–55.

Hayes, J. R. (1981). *The complete problem solver*. Philadelphia: The Franklin Institute Press.

Hoffman, R. R., Crandall, B., & Shadbolt, N. R. (1998). Use of the critical decision method to elicit expert knowledge: A case study in the methodology of cognitive task analysis. *Human Factors, 40*, 254–276.

Johnson-Laird, P. N. (1983). *Mental models*. Cambridge: Cambridge University Press.

Johnson-Laird, P. N., Legrenzi, P., & Sonio Legrenzi, M. (1972). Reasoning and a sense of reality. *British Journal of Psychology, 63*, 395–400.

Kahneman, D. (2013). *Thinking, fast and slow*. New York, NY: Farrar, Straus and Giroux.

Kahneman, D., Slovic, P., & Tversky, A. (Eds.). (1982). *Judgment under uncertainty: Heuristics and biases*. Cambridge: Cambridge, UK.

Kaplan, C. (1989). *Hatching a theory of incubation: Does putting a problem aside really help? If so, why?*, Carnegie-Mellon University, University Microfilms International, Catalog #9238813.

Klein, G. A. (1997). *Recognition-primed decision making: Looking back, looking forward*. Hillsdale, NJ: Erlbaum.

Krug, S. (2005). *Don't make me think: A common sense approach to web usability* (2nd ed.). Berkeley, CA: New Riders Press.

Larkin, J. H., McDermott, J., Simon, D. P., & Simon, H. A. (1980). Expert and novice performance in solving physics problems. *Science, 208*, 1335–1342.

Lehto, M. R. (1997). Decision making. In G. Salvendy (Ed.), *Handbook of human factors and ergonomics* (pp. 1201–1248). New York, NY: Wiley.

Levitt, S., & Dubner, S. J. (2005). *Freakonomics: A rogue economist explores the hidden side of everything*. New York, NY: William Morrow/HarperCollins.

Luchins, A. S. (1942). Mechanization in problem solving: The effect of Einstellung. *Psychological Monographs, 54*(6), 1–95.

Moray, N. (1996). A taxonomy and theory of mental models. In *Proceedings of the Human Factors and Ergonomics Society 40th Annual Meeting* (Vol. 1, pp. 164–168).

Moray, N. (1999). Mental models in theory and practice. In D. Gopher & A. Koriat (Eds.), *Attention and performance XVII: Cognitive regulation of performance: Interaction of theory and application* (pp. 223–258). Cambridge, MA: MIT Press.

Norman, D. A. (1983). Design rules based on analysis of human error. *Communications of the ACM, 26*(4), 254–258.

Norman, D. A. (1988). *The psychology of everyday things*. New York, NY: Basic Books.

Norman, D. A. (2013). *The design of everyday things*. New York, NY: Basic Books.

NTSB. (1990). *Aircraft accident report. United Airlines flight 232. Mc Donnell Douglas DC-10-10. Sioux Gateway airport. Sioux City, Iowa, July 19, 1989*. Washington DC: National Transportation Safety Board.

Payne, S. J. (1995). Naive judgments of stimulus-response compatibility. *Human Factors, 37*, 495–506.

Quinlan, P., & Dyson, B. (2008). *Cognitive psychology*. Harlow, UK: Pearson.

Rasmussen, J. (1983). Skills, rules, knowledge: Signals, signs and symbols and other distinctions in human performance models. *IEEE Transactions: Systems, Man, and Cybernetics, SMC-13*, 257–267.

Revell, K. M. A., & Stanton, N. A. (2012). Models of models: Filtering and bias rings in depiction of knowledge structures and their implications for design. *Ergonomics, 55*(9), 1073–1092.

Ries, A., & Trout, J. (1986/2000). *Positioning: The battle for your mind.* New York, NY: McGraw-Hill International.

Ritter, F. E., & Bibby, P. A. (2008). Modeling how, when, and what learning happens in a diagrammatic reasoning task. *Cognitive Science, 32*, 862–892.

Ritter, F. E., Jones, R. M., & Baxter, G. D. (1998). Reusable models and graphical interfaces: Realising the potential of a unified theory of cognition. In U. Schmid, J. Krems, & F. Wysotzki (Eds.), *Mind modeling—a cognitive science approach to reasoning, learning and discovery* (pp. 83–109). Lengerich, Germany: Pabst Scientific Publishing.

Schwartz, B. (2004). *The paradox of choice: Why more is less.* New York, NY: Harper Perennial.

Simon, H. A. (1997). *Administrative behavior* (4th ed.). New York, NY: The Free Press.

Simon, H. A., & Chase, W. G. (1973). Skill in chess. *American Scientist, 61*, 393–403.

Smallman, H. S., & St. John, M. (2005). Naïve realism: Misplaced faith in the utility of realistic displays. *Ergonomics in Design, 13*(Summer), 6–13.

Sternberg, R. J. (2004). Why smart people can be so foolish. *European Psychologist, 9*(3), 145–150.

Sternberg, R. J., & Davidson, J. E. (1995). *The nature of insight.* Cambridge, MA: MIT Press.

Tverksy, A., & Kahneman, D. (1981). The framing of decisions and the psychology of choice. *Science, 211*, 453–458.

Tverksy, A., & Kahneman, D. (1986). Rational choice and the framing of decisions. *Journal of Business, 59*, 251–278.

Wason, P. C. (1960). On the failure to eliminate hypotheses in a conceptual task. *Quarterly Journal of Experimental Psychology, 12*, 129–140.

Wilson, J. R., & Rutherford, A. (1989). Mental models: Theory and application in human factors. *Human Factors, 31*, 617–634.

Winne, P. H., & Jamieson-Noel, D. (2002). Exploring students' calibration of self reports about study tactics and achievement. *Contemporary Educational Psychology, 27*(4), 551–572.

Chapter 7
Cognition: Human–Computer Communication

Abstract This chapter addresses even higher level processes than the previous chapter. It discusses ways that users communicate with computers and other technological systems. The chapter starts by considering the role of language in communication and how the ideas can be applied to interface design. It then looks at factors that affect how users read both offline and online, and discusses the task of reading of menus. After considering the topic of information seeking behavior and the more general concept of how content is structured, this chapter looks at the broader implications for designing an interface that appropriately supports human–computer communication.

7.1 Introduction

Communication is a rich and complex area. When users communicate with each other and work together they need to coordinate their processes and manage the content that they are using. They rely on establishing a shared understanding or "common ground", (Clark and Brennan 1991), based on knowledge, beliefs, and assumptions shared between the two people in the conversation. To stay coordinated, both parties must make sure that they maintain their common ground in order to collaborate effectively.

In a similar way, when users work with computers, they also need to communicate with the computer to get the computer to do what they want it to do. This may be as simple as entering some data, then pressing a key or button, and waiting for a result. As they wait for the results, though, it is useful to know what the computer is doing (how much of the task it has completed, for example). Results should also be delivered in an appropriate and comprehensible format. When designing a system you need to be aware of this communication process, and the fact that it is important to keep the user aware of what the computer is doing, and this maintain common ground between the user and the computer. Although common ground may not be explicitly observable, it will still exist and evolve as communication happens.

F. E. Ritter et al., *Foundations for Designing User-Centered Systems,*   201
DOI: 10.1007/978-1-4471-5134-0_7, © Springer-Verlag London 2014

We focus here on the most important aspects of human–computer communication. First, we provide a very brief overview of language. After discussing how to organize information, we then address the topic of reading—one of the most common tasks for users—before discussing menu scanning, which is really a stylized form of reading. We next consider information searching, which can also be regarded as a type of communication. Information searching can also be seen as a high level type of problem solving, because it is normally highly dependent on language; this is why we have included it in this chapter. Finally, we consider how content is organized in a more general way.

7.2 Language

There is some debate over what constitutes language. Some people argue that animals use language to communicate. Others, however, argue that humans are the only species that have language. What makes human language unique is that speakers can generate an infinite set of utterances from a finite set of language elements. Language allows us to refer to other objects symbolically, and to communicate concrete and abstract ideas.

There are many sciences that study language, including psychology, linguistics, communication science, and computer science. We focus here on some of the results that are most directly related to providing and supporting human–computer communication. These results provide direct suggestions for how to construct interfaces, and will help ground further learning about language. First we introduce some basic concepts before describing Grice's maxims, which provide a way to view language.

7.2.1 Symbols, Syntax, and Semantics

Three high-level language concepts that are particularly useful are symbolism, syntax, and semantics. A symbol is a token or object that can be used to represent another object, token, or relationship. Words are symbolic in that they represent other things. Language uses symbols, as do nearly all interfaces. Keyboards use characters, dialogue boxes and menus use words. The Theremin, shown schematically in Fig. 7.1, is an early example of an electronic musical instrument. It is a relatively rare example of a system that does not use symbols because it plays continuous notes with continuous volume.[1] To generate notes the Theremin senses the positions of the user's hands and uses that information to create sounds. Mouse movements might also not involve symbols, but their clicks generate symbols.

---

[1] If you want to know what one sounds like, listen to "Good Vibrations" by the Beach Boys. You might also recognize its sound in sci-fi movies.

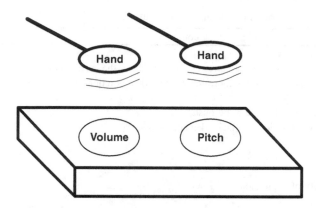

Fig. 7.1 A diagram of a Theremin. Users play it by moving one hand closer to or farther away from the volume control and the other hand closer to or farther away from the pitch control. The distance is measured through capacitance. There are no fixed volumes or pitches, unlike most other instruments. It is sometimes used to make eerie sounds in science fiction movies

Language relies on both syntax and semantics, as do interfaces. Syntax refers to how words are organized to create meaning. The order in which objects are chosen and the order of interaction are both questions of syntax. Is it better to select an object (a noun) and then an action to apply to it (a verb)? Or is it better to select an action and then the object? Some systems use the noun–verb syntax, whilst others use the verb–noun syntax. The Macintosh OS has you select a file and then choose to compress it or duplicate it. Eudora and Gmail, two commonly used email interfaces, have you select that you wish to attach a file to an email, and then choose the file.

Semantics refers to the meaning of words and symbols. How symbols are used in an interface is a question of semantics. The choice of type of symbols to use in an interface—usually words or icons—depends on their semantics. This is often a very difficult choice to make. The meaning that users ascribe to a particular word or the word that they first associate with an action is not uniform. Furnas et al. (1987), for example, found that there was a wide variability in the words users choose when asked to name actions: the users agreed on the same term for an action less than 20% of the time. The results suggest that designers should not just use the first word they think of, and that they should also support the use of aliases to help match the user's terms. (See Glushko 2013 and Kernighan and Plauger 1978 for more concrete suggestions.)

7.2.2 Grice's Maxims of Conversation

People routinely use language to converse and interact. Grice (1975) proposed that the way that they interact with one another can be described by the co-operative principle:

Table 7.1 Several of Grice's (1975) maxims of conversation

Consider saving some examples as they come up

Maxim of quantity
  Make your contribution as informative as is required (for the current purposes of the exchange)
  Do not make your contribution more informative than is required
Maxim of quality
  Do not say what you believe to be false
  Do not say that for which you lack adequate evidence
Maxim of relevance
  Be relevant
Maxim of manner
  Avoid obscurity of expression
  Avoid ambiguity
  Be brief (avoid unnecessary prolixity)
  Be orderly

> Make your conversational contribution such as is required, at the stage at which it occurs, by the accepted purpose or direction of the talk exchange in which you are engaged. (p. 45)

Although phrased prescriptively—it basically says try to say the right thing at the right time—the co-operative principle can also be seen as a description of the way that people normally converse. Grice suggested that there are four basic maxims underlying the co-operative principle as shown in Table 7.1. These maxims make strong suggestions about how people should communicate with other people. When these suggestions are followed, communication is more successful and more satisfying. When these maxims are not followed, you can often note humor, irony, mistakes, rudeness, and ill-feelings. As you read through these maxims, you should be able to think of examples (and counterexamples) of their use in interfaces.

Although these maxims refer to conversation, they can also be applied to facilitate better written communication as well. Help messages, manuals, and instructions should be informative, and avoid telling the user things that they do not need to know. The system should not report errors where errors do not exist. Help from automatic aids should be relevant to the task the user is doing, not to another task or to a task that has already been completed. One of the exercises at the end of this chapter encourages you to consider the application of these principles in more depth.

7.2.3 Implications for System Design

The use of language is an important topic for interface design, because interfaces often provide a language—possibly an informal, specialized language—for communication. This language provides a way to understand the interaction elements and their structure, how users interact with the system, and how interfaces can be related to other knowledge structures. By considering the interaction between the human and the computer as a sort of conversation, you can use Grice's maxims to help optimize the interaction.

7.3 How Users Read

One of the most common activities users do is reading. They read pre-printed matter such as manuals and the documents that they print out. Increasingly material is read on devices screens like monitors, laptops, tablets and smartphones. Understanding how users read will help you design interfaces that are better suited to the way people read and work.

We know enough about how people read (e.g., Just and Carpenter 1987; Rayner and Pollatsek 1989) to be able to develop computational models of the process (Just and Thibadeau 1984). The research in this area has identified several regularities of reading behavior that are useful for designing interfaces where written text is used. For example, we know that people typically read at a rate of about 150–230 words per minute when reading for comprehension, and that this rate varies with material and task. At this rate, it should take 2–3 min to read an A4 or $8.5'' \times 11''$ page of text.

Perhaps the three most important regularities of reading behavior, though, are the word length effect, the word frequency effect, and the difference in time between picture naming and reading. The word length effect arises out of the fact that longer words simply take longer to read (e.g., Rayner et al. 2011). Words like "mouse" and "polo" are faster to read (everything else being equal) than "keyboard" and "autocratic" because they are shorter.

The word frequency effect arises because words that are commonly used are faster to read than words that are less commonly used (e.g., Liversedge et al. 2011; Rayner 1998). This effect can be seen as being related to the learning curve. The word frequency effect and the word length effect are independent, so they both apply to the same word. So, for example, while the word "polo" is short, it is also relatively rarely used and hence will take longer to read than other more frequently used words of the same length. It will, however, be read more quickly than equally rare words that are longer.

Reading takes less time than picture naming (Chilton 1996). This explains why unfamiliar icons, which are accessed through picture naming, take longer to process than words that are used in the same place. Using icons instead of words for simple searching makes things slower. There is a trade-off, however, against generality and esthetics. An icon, once learned, is easier to recognize than a word irrespective of one's native language and literacy level. Icons are often created to be rectangular in shape, for example, and having consistent, regular shaped objects can make for a better, clearer design.

There are other effects as well that influence reading speed. Several known factors that make reading more difficult are noted in Table 7.2, and some of these effects are illustrated in Tables 7.3 and 7.4.

Table 7.2 Factors that make reading more difficult

Complex (such as Gothic fonts) or uncommon fonts, such as novelty fonts (wild west-like). They are harder to read if they are unfamiliar or perceptually complex

Fonts that have more detail than the display can provide, e.g., a small, serifed font on a mobile device. They are harder to read if necessary details are not visible

Long lines that make it difficult for the eye to jump back to the beginning of the next line. They are harder to read because the eye has trouble jumping that far that precisely

Small line spacing (spacing between lines). This also makes it more difficult for the reader's eye to find the beginning of the next line. They are harder to read because the target line to jump to is smaller

Smaller fonts. They are harder to read because they are harder to perceive, and often come with long lines and small line spacing

Poor spacing between words. This makes reading harder because the eye cannot see words as being distinct, and when it has to jump back the targets are not as clear

Incorrect spelling. This is harder to read because the reader may use the wrong word, or take longer to recognize the correct word

Fully justified text (that is, even on the right and left edges versus natural spacing, flush on the left but with a ragged right margin). This is harder to read because it causes uneven and too large spaces between words

The use of all upper case letters. These are harder to read because the reader will have less practice recognizing the letters and words, and it will also influence line spacing

Ambiguous and distal references, and pronouns (the use of 'it' and 'that', vs nouns and proper nouns). These are harder to read because the referent to the pronoun must be found and used correctly

Abstract words (vs concrete words). These are harder to read because the words are less common and require more processing to understand

Poor grammar. This is harder to read because the concepts' relations may not be well specified

Negative and double negative concepts (which can be particularly difficult to understand). These are harder to read because more processing is required to understand them

---

Table 7.3 Hard to read text. The following text contains examples of the factors that make reading more difficult as listed in Table 7.2

6 DOZEN, 12, AND SIX HALVES OF YEARS AGO OUR OWN PARENT'S GENETIC ORGINITORS PRODUCED HEREFORTH ON THIS COLLECTION OF TECTONIC PLATES A NOT OLD SOCIAL-POLITICAL ORGANIZATION, CO-NCEIVED IN LIBERTY AND AIMED TOWARD THE FACT TAHT ALL HUMANOIDS ARE CREATED EQUIVALENT. AT THIS POINT IN TIME WE ARE MORE THAN STARTED IN A PH-ENOMENAL CONFLAGRATION, TESTING AND VALIDATING WHETHER THE FACT THAT THAT OR-GANIZATION OR ANY ORGANIZATION SO CONCEIVED AND SEW DEDICATED CAN WILL NOT FAIL SOON. WE ARE MET ON A GREAT SPATIAL-TEMPORAL LOCATION OF THAT SPECIFIC LACK OF AMICABLE RELATIONS BETWEEN TO SOCIAL-CULTURAL-PO-LITICAL ENTITIES. WE HAVE COME IN ORDER TO DEDICATE A PROPER SUBSET OF THAT SPATIAL-TEMPORAL LOCATION AS A FINAL RESTING-LOCATION FOUR THOSE WHO HERE GAVE THAT, THAT IT MIGHT PROGRESS. IT IS ALTOGETHER APPROPRIATE AND PROPER THAT WE SHOULD DO SOMETHING LIKE THIS. BUT IN A LARGER DE-NOTATION, WE CAN NOT APPORTION, WE CANNOT MEMORIALISE, WE CANNOT HALLOW THIS.

THEY,   LIVING AND DEAD WHO STRUGGLED HERE HAVE BLESSED IT   FAR ABOVE OUR OWN IMPOVERISHED POWER FOR ADDITON OR SUBBSTRACTION FROM THEIR OUVRE.   THE   TEMPORAL REALM WILL LITTLE NOTE NOR LONG REM-EMBER WHAT   OUR OWN OPIONS PRESENTED HERE, BUT IT CAN NEVER FORGET WHAT THEY DIDIN THIS SPATIAL-TEMPORAL LOCATION. IT IS   FOR US THE NOT YET DEAD   RATHER TO BE DED-ICATED HERE TO THE   UNFINISHED WORK WHICH THEY WHO FOUGHT HERE HAVE THUS   SO NOBLY ADVANCED. IT IS RATHER FOR US TO BE HERE DE-DICATED TO THE NOT SMALL TASK REMAINING BEFORE US--THAT FROM THESE HONORED PEOPLE WE TAKE INCREASED CARE AND CONCERN TO THAT CAUSE FOR WHICH THEY GAVE THE LAST FULL MEASURE   OF DEVOTION--THAT WE HERE HIGHLY RESOLVE THAT THESE DEAD   MEN SHALL NOT HAVE DIED IN VAIN, THAT THIS AREA UNDER GOD SHALL HAVE A NEW BIRTH OF FREEDOM, AND THAT SOCIAL ORGANI ZATIONS RELATED TO POLITICAL STATES   OF, BY, AND FOR US ALL SHALL NOT SEASE TO EXIST ON THIS RO-TATING CELSTIAL ORB.

Table 7.4 Easier to read text. This is semantically the same text as in Table 7.3 but with most of the features that cause reading difficulties eliminated, and with the paragraphs indented

---

Fourscore and seven years ago our fathers brought forth on this continent a new nation, conceived in liberty and dedicated to the proposition that all men are created equal. Now we are engaged in a great civil war, testing whether that nation or any nation so conceived and so dedicated can long endure

We are met on a great battlefield of that war. We have come to dedicate a portion of that field as a final resting-place for those who here gave their lives that that nation might live. It is altogether fitting and proper that we should do this. But in a larger sense, we cannot dedicate, we cannot consecrate, we cannot hallow this ground. The brave men, living and dead who struggled here have consecrated it far above our poor power to add or detract

The world will little note nor long remember what we say here, but it can never forget what they did here. It is for us the living rather to be dedicated here to the unfinished work which they who fought here have thus far so nobly advanced. It is rather for us to be here dedicated to the great task remaining before us–that from these honored dead we take increased devotion to that cause for which they gave the last full measure of devotion–that we here highly resolve that these dead shall not have died in vain, that this nation under God shall have a new birth of freedom, and that government of the people, by the people, for the people shall not perish from the earth. —A. Lincoln, 1864

7.3.1 The Effects of Fonts

Reading also interacts with the choice of fonts. Figure 7.2 shows a menu from a web site (it is the links section on the left hand side of the page, a common design), where every item is in a different font, and one item even has different colors for each letter. While there may sometimes be good esthetic reasons for using several different fonts, that we do not think apply in this case, here it makes it harder to read the text in the interface. A good rule of is to use no more than three different fonts. If you are planning to use several different fonts, you should make sure that you have a very good reason for doing so.

As another example of the significant effect of the use of fonts, Fig. 7.3 shows the Clearview (also referred to as Clearview Hwy) font (www.clearviewhwy.com). This font was designed to aid readability and legibility for older drivers and has been evaluated (Garvey et al. 1998). The design addressed each attribute of letterforms including stroke width, letter shape, the resulting inside and outside of each letterform, and the proportional relationship of capital letter to lower case as well as letter spacing to optimize readability when viewed at a distance. It illustrates how the readability of fonts can differ. Research at Penn State has shown that the improved font is 20% easier to read, which means that drivers at 60 mph (miles per hour) can read the road signs 1–2 s earlier, which gives them more time to make decisions or to read more of the sign. Another major effect—not shown here—is that the font also works better at night, when the light used to read signs comes from reflected headlights, which changes the contrast between the letters and background (Garvey et al. 1998). Note, however, that the font works less well on negative contrast road signs (dark text on a light background).

Fig. 7.2 An example use of multiple fonts that makes the menu structure harder to read. (taken from www. woodburyskiarea.com/winter, February 2012)

7.3.2 Graphic Design to Help Reading and Scanning

The graphic design of textual material has evolved to support readers and the tasks they perform. Readers not only read—they also annotate, reread, search using the table of contents, headings, and the index, and refer to the references cited for further information. Specific graphic design elements have been created to support these activities, such as margins, headings, and citations. More information is available from graphic design books (Parker 2006; White 2002). If you are designing something for readers, like a book, or a brochure, or even technical reports, you should become a student of the tools, designs, and processes in this area as well as understanding how reading occurs in a variety of formats such as brochures and screens.

7.3.3 Paper-Based Versus Screen-Based Reading

Reading text on paper is not identical to reading the same text from a screen. There are some important differences that you need to be aware of because they can affect reading speeds and comprehension. Figure 7.4 shows an example of extensive material to read from the screen.

Fig. 7.3 The previous standard font, Highway Gothic (*left*) and in the ClearviewHwy font (*right*). These signs are on I-78, near Allentown, PA. The Clearview has larger holes in letters like e and o, and slightly more readable serifs on letters like l and t. The text is particularly more readable at night when illuminated by headlights. (Photos © Don Meeker and used with permission)

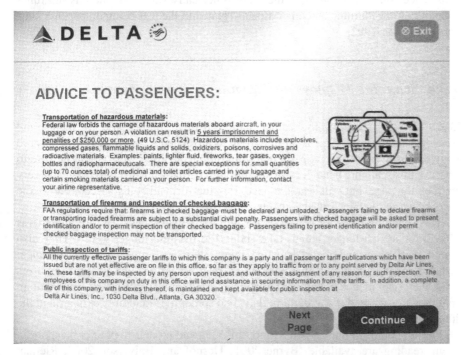

Fig. 7.4 A screen shot from Feb. 2008 that would be difficult to read because of font size and line width. Indeed, if passengers did read this screen, it would greatly slow the check-in process, which runs counter to the purpose of the kiosk, which is to make check-in faster (as opposed to safer or more pleasurable). This page also shows a change in the service as a system moves online. The original system, human check-in, did not pass as much information to users—but perhaps it did not need to

When reading text on paper, the print quality is usually quite high, often as high as 1,000 dpi (dots per inch) for a high-end or photo-quality printer, and usually at least 600 dpi for most laser and inkjet printers, with the light used to read it being reflected from the paper. When you read text from a screen, however, the resolution is typically much lower (at best, most laptops and display screens use not much more than 250 dpi), and the light to read comes from the display. Greater resolution of the text generally leads to faster, less fatiguing reading. Reflective light using printed inks generally provides greater contrast between light and dark than do luminance changes from a screen. So reflected light also tends to lead to faster, less fatiguing reading.

Reading from the screen is generally slower, more error prone, and more fatiguing than reading from hardcopies. Researchers have frequently found that reading from the screen is 10–30% slower, with similar results reported for errors and for fatigue (Dillon 1992; Gould et al. 1987; Kurniawan and Zaphiris 2001). It is hard to ascribe the difference between these factors solely to the resolution and luminance sources. Some think there are other causes as well, such as the functionality of page turning and other aspects related to the text being on paper or on a screen (Dillon 1992).

7.3.4 Scanning Displays and Menus

Users typically scan displays, rather than read them, particularly for menus and web pages with links. This is an important skill related to reading. If you observe someone using a web page, particularly a complicated one, you should be able to observe this scanning behavior. Most (although perhaps not all) will not read every item on the page, but will scan the page, looking for, and being susceptible to, the visual factors explained in the chapter on vision.

This scanning behavior is also seen when users read menus. Hornof and Kieras (1997) found that longer menus take about 120 ms/item longer to use. They also found that users read more than one menu item at a time. The physiological structure of the eye allows two items to be read within a single fixation. As users read, they scan menus in both systematic and random ways: they are systematic in that they mostly read top to bottom; they also sometimes randomly skip around the items on the menu.

Further details of human behavior in this area and models to predict behavior in menu reading are available (Byrne 2001; Hornof and Halverson 2003; Rieman et al. 1996). The models can help explain parts of behavior in this area that are predictable (e.g., walking through the menu items) although the reasons for the random skipping around menu items are not yet well explained. Figure 7.5 shows two menus for a VPN client. The first menu has many more items than the second. If the targets are ISPtoPSU and ITS Wireless at University Park, the first menu definitely makes the items take longer to find.

Fig. 7.5 The original menu for selecting a VPN client at Penn State, and a revised version created by Ritter for his own use. The version on the left encourages scanning; the version on the right is more easily read. Simon Robbie notes (personal communication) that hierarchical menus could be particularly useful here. (Screenshot taken June 2009)

7.3.5 Implications for System Design

When you design menus, you need to understand how vision works and how users scan menus, so that you can use this knowledge to help guide their vision to find the items they are looking for. When you create a menu, include items that are necessary, and be wary about creating menus that are too long. Submenus should be structured around how the user represents the world (their mental model) or how experts represent the world. You can find out how their world is structured by asking them or using a card sorting method (noted in Exercise 7.2). Menus structured in these ways are more likely to be useful than those which reflect the company's organization, for example. Long menus will be skimmed, but short menus with submenus will require the user to take more actions to find the same item. The final choice in these design cases requires understanding the social context and more detailed knowledge about how often the tasks are performed. You can favor more common tasks using a variety of designs including split menus (Sears and Shneiderman 1994).

When choosing menu items and button labels, or writing text to be displayed on a screen, it is important to consider the factors that influence readability and, hence, usability. These factors range from choices related to fonts (typeface, size, and so on) through to words (which words and how they should be laid out) and the context in which they will appear. There are inherent trade-offs between these different factors, and the results from research will tell you which is faster. They will not tell you, however, if the changes are worth the accompanying differences in estheticsor in the information, style, and tone.

7.4 Information Seeking Behavior

The other main area where human–computer communication has made significant contributions is where users are seeking information. This can be regarded as an information retrieval problem—finding the information—but we consider human information behavior to be slightly broader. Here we focus mostly on the ubiquitous task of searching for information on the web, but the concepts we discuss can be generalized to other tasks, such as searching for information on a hard drive (which routinely have capacities of over 1 TB nowadays) and in help systems and intranets.

7.4.1 Information

Information appears to many to be an elusive concept that is hard to define but, like the Supreme Court justice said, "…we know it when we see it." In general, though, information can be thought of as organized data. The extension of this is that knowledge and, ultimately, wisdom can be considered as organized information. It is also important to take into consideration the need for an entity to process the information, and the context, which can influence how the information is interpreted.

7.4.2 Human Information Behavior

Human information behavior is working with information. The ways that people work with information depends on several factors including the context in which they interact with information, which is sometime described as an information journey (Blandford and Attfield 2010).

Broadly defined, human information behavior includes problem solving, but a more typical task is searching for information. Human information behavior thus includes how users process, use, and produce information. How users interact to get information, and their strategies and tactics for handling information can therefore also be seen as human information behavior. So, for example, the content of this book could have been cast as a summary of human information behavior if it had been designed for a different target audience.

We know that users have inherent capabilities and limitations, and these constrain human information behavior. How users can process information is determined by their cognitive, perceptual, and motor capabilities, that is, their information processing architecture. There are other, external constraints too, such as the tools that they use to access and process the information: their databases, their interfaces, networks, and other forms of information delivery, presentation, and output capabilities. By some measures, the largest information processor in many buildings is a large photocopier/printer, which can produce literally reams[2] of information. The photocopier/printer's output is important because the results— the information—are processed more deeply by people than most computers will process the information passed through them.

7.4.3 Human Information Seeking Behavior

Human information seeking behavior can be viewed in several ways. One way to approach it is to ask "how do users search for information, particularly on the Internet?" Spink and her colleagues in information science have studied this area extensively (e.g., Spink and Cole 2001). They found that users seek information often, and from multiple sources. Different types of users search for different types of information, which is not so surprising, but they also seek it in different ways, look in different places, and trust the sources in different ways. Trends in what users search for can be identified, typically by studying user logs (Jansen and Spink 2006). Important trends have been found in this way, such as a shift towards more eCommerce queries and a rise in non-English queries over the period 1997–2001 (Spink et al. 2002). Work in this area has also examined how different types of groups use information (Barnes et al. 1996). The results have been used to make prescriptive statements about how to help groups.

Observational studies have examined how users search, including how many errors they make, how well they use the search tools (such as using the connectors 'and' and 'or'), and how many searches they do in parallel (Jansen and Spink 2006; Spink et al. 2002). Some researchers have argued that users do not search very deeply (Nielsen 1997), and others, with more detailed studies have found that some users will search quite deeply (Byrne et al. 1999). Byrne et al.'s research involved analyzing the tasks users were performing, and how web browsing fitted into those tasks. They found that the task influenced how long and how deeply users searched. In particular, medical information, work-related, and certain hobby searches can go quite deep over hours or days, and some searches are shallow. To support a wide range of users it is therefore important to understand them and the tasks they are performing, because different users will have different capabilities and needs when searching for information at different times.

7.4.4 Information Scent

The concept of information scent (Pirolli 1997, 2007) can also be exploited in helping users find the information they are looking for. Information scent is what

---

[2] A ream is 500 sheets of paper. Most photocopy and printing paper is sold in reams; thus the saying, reams of material.

leads a user to spend more time exploring a web page (or menu item) to find what they are looking for because the content, metaphorically, 'smells' like the thing they are looking for. The idea is to make sure that objects and links appear to smell like what they contain and to not smell like what they do not. In this way, the user should be able to detect more readily when they are looking in the right area.

This metaphor of information scent makes several suggestions for design. Thus, obtuse words or phrases on menus mask the scent; descriptions that are too general diffuse the scent; descriptions that mislead users have the wrong scent; content that is hard to find because, perhaps, it is at the bottom of a page, are hard to smell.

7.4.5 *Implications for System Design*

Understanding information and the ways that users search for and use information is important if you want to help users carry out their tasks. Research in this area has provided a perspective that focuses on the material that users are using and looking for, and gives us another way to think about users and to support design.

If you can understand what users are looking for, it should help you understand how you can support them in the task of finding it. This can be done through better interface design to display the information in a way that allows the users to understand it, which includes providing details about objects to help users find the information they are looking for directly or by providing information scent trails through increasingly more specific scents.

It is also worth briefly mentioning Search Engine Optimization (SEO) at this point. The algorithms that underpin the major Web search engines keep evolving, but the way that they generally work is quite well known. Web content writers should be aware of how they work, because they can construct their content in such a way that it promotes their page in the search results. The number of links into a page, and keywords, for example, are just two factors that have been used to increase the ranking of web pages.

7.5 Designing Content

As the web has grown and web pages have proliferated, designers have come to realize the full importance of content and the way it is structured and delivered. With so much information now available, users can be overwhelmed, and understandably are unwilling to expend significant time and energy trawling through hundreds of pages of content to find information. The way that content is written, structured, and delivered is therefore critical to the success of a system. The type of content you will have, and how it should be structured, will be determined by your content strategy and information architecture.

7.5.1 Content Strategy

A content strategy is a theory of what and how to create, update, and merge content in a system such as a web site. Halvorson (2010) suggests that there are several basic needs to take into account when developing a content strategy if you want it to be successful:

- The need to do less, not more. Content should support key objectives or help users complete the task they are trying to do, or both. It is also obviously cheaper and easier to write less content, which makes it easier to maintain and faster to use.
- The need to understand the existing content, and its provenance. You may need to do a content audit to address this.
- The need to be a good listener. Responsibility for content is not just down to the content creators, and customers are often the people who are best placed to understand what content they want or need.
- The need to have someone who is responsible for delivering content. A newspaper has an editorial executive who makes the final decisions about what goes into a particular edition of a newspaper; a web site should have someone in a similar role.
- The need to start asking questions. Always be prepared to ask "why?" when somebody says "we have to include this," "we need to do that," and so on.

These needs should be incorporated into—and help drive—the three steps (or phases) within your content strategy:

1. Auditing the existing content and documenting it.
2. Analyzing the different aspects within an organization that affect the content.
3. Creating the strategy for the creation, delivery, and governance of content.

The web and content are inextricably intertwined. If you want to deliver content that is both usable and useful, you should make use of the wide range of available processes, tools, and resources that have been designed to help make it easier to create content.

7.5.2 Information Architecture

The term Information Architecture (IA) is used to describe how online information is structured to support usability by both creators and users. As such, information architecture is one of the components that is included as part of user experience design. It is information architecture that occupies the intersection of content, context, and users (Morville and Rosenfeld 2007).

Developing an IA is not simply a matter of drawing container boxes around collections of related information and then moving them around. This process, sometimes called wire framing, is, however, often a large part of the development of an IA. Developing an IA does not just involve generating static content, but also includes developing the dynamic paths through a web site, for example.

When developing the IA, it is important to consider the information at several levels of abstraction. At the lowest level, this may be as simple as the way that items are ordered on a page. At the highest level it could involve how to organize the content appropriately to support the user's tasks. At a strategic level it could involve making decisions about how articles and metadata are placed into a content management system.

7.5.3 Creating Content

Getting the content strategy and information architecture correct are both important, but it is equally important to make sure that your content is usable too. Writing for printed material is a skill in itself, but creating content for web pages is also an important skill in its own right and one which often involves more than just writing text. The way that users read web pages is usually not the same as the way that they read printed pages (unless they are reading an online text article from start to finish).

In most cases, web content is written for a general-purpose audience, which means that it should be readable and understandable by a large proportion of the population. The usual guide rule is that you should try to write text that requires a reading age of around 12 years, and that can be understood by students in the eighth grade in the US (this equates to an age range of about 12–14 years). The readability of text can be assessed using the Flesch reading ease score (Flesch 1948): generally, you should be aiming for a score of 60–70. Comprehensibility is assessed using the Flesch–Kincaid grade level score (Kincaid et al. 1975), and here you should generally be aiming for a score of 7.0–8.0. Many word processors include tools that will let you calculate both of these scores, and there are several online calculators that can be used too.

These scores should be used as guidance, not as requirements that have to be pursued at all costs. The scores provide a relatively simple but useful assessment of the clarity and directness of the language that is used in the text.

7.5.4 Structuring Content

We know that users organize and associate concepts using something like a graph structure (e.g., Collins and Quillian 1969; Klahr, Chase, and Lovelace 1983; Woods 1975). This led to the suggestion that knowledge should therefore be presented to users as a hypergraph structure because if it goes into the eyes like a graph (like hypertext or the web) then it can simply be put into corresponding graph structure inside the user's head. This example of a homeopathic fallacy— that "like causes like"—may have arisen from a misinterpretation of Vannevar Bush's (1945, reprinted in numerous places) view of how information is organized by people and machines.

The fallacy has been debunked (McKendree et al. 1995). The user cannot simply lift material from the page and dump it straight into their memory without some processing. The material to be learned has to go through the serial processes of reading, understanding, and creating memories using the processes and capabilities noted in Chap. 6. The material that has to be read should be presented in a serial way so that it can be appropriately processed. Hypertext can be useful if the learner is expert enough to use self-directed learning, but, if the learner is a novice and does not fully understand what is supposed to be learned, it is better to provide them with appropriate guidance (Scheiter and Gerjets 2007; Swaak and de Jong 2007).

When preparing material to be read it is important to take into consideration the users' capabilities. These capabilities will differ, depending on the users' level of expertise, which will influence how they perceive things, and their mental model of the situation, for example. The material therefore needs to be structured to accommodate both users' capabilities and their previous knowledge.

7.5.5 Delivering Content

The medium that will be used to deliver content to users has to be carefully considered. The way the content of a message posted on Twitter (a "tweet") (which has a maximum length of 140 characters) is designed, for example, will be different from the way that the content for a podcast is designed, even if they are both presenting the same message. It is important to think about attributes such as the temperature of the medium, which relates to how actively the medium draws users in (McLuhan and Fiore 1967). Books, for example, are seen as cold, because they require lots of effort to use them; radio (and email), however, are hot.

Where and how content is read will influence how readers interpret the message. Material seen on a small screen on a mobile device, for example, may be received and understood differently from material on a larger screen or on paper prototypes and printouts. Advances in HTML and CSS have facilitated what is called responsive design of web pages where only one set of web-based content needs to created, rather than having to design separate content (and structure) for desktops, tablets, and mobile devices (e.g., see Kadlec 2013). The content is automatically re-displayed in the most appropriate format based on the size of the device that is being used to read it.

7.6 Implications for System Design

When you design a system you need to consider the context in which it will be used. You will need to understand the terminology and language that your users use to communicate and talk about their tasks. The language that describes how your users interact with your systems should be appropriate to the context and culture in which the system is used. This will make it easier for your users to carry out their tasks, and hence make the system more acceptable to them. More generally, you should try to use simple, direct, and clear language.

If your interface requires your users to read text, particularly large amounts of text, you need to take into consideration the factors that affect how users read. You should avoid using several fonts, for example, as this can adversely affect reading speed, and may also detract from the overall user experience. You should also lay out the text in a way that helps the user to comprehend it, making appropriate use of headings, subheadings, and white space between paragraphs, for example. If you are designing web pages, then you will need to be aware of how people scan web pages, rather than read them in depth, so that you can position your text so that they will see it.

Irrespective of whether your display shows only text, only graphics (including icons), or some combination of the two, it should be clear and apparent to your users what all of the items mean. This also applies to menu items where, once again, you should use terms and language that are relevant to your users, their tasks, and the context in which they are carrying out those tasks.

If your users need to seek information, you need to help them find the information they are looking for in an efficient and effective manner. Using information scent can help them to find out fairly quickly whether they are looking in the right area, so you should make similar information have the same sort of "smell" as the information they are looking for. When you return the information to them, you should present it in a way that makes it easy for them to interpret, understand, and learn. In other words, it needs to be appropriately structured, for example, using tables and charts to present numeric information.

For web sites in particular, the way that you write, structure, and deliver content are all major contributors to the success of a system. Managing content is an ongoing task, so you will need to maintain the content after you have written it, to make sure that it stays up to date and grows and evolves along with your users. It is therefore important to define a content strategy and information architecture up front to help you manage and deliver the content in a systematic way. You also need to think about how your users will access that content. If they will be using a range of devices (smartphones, tablets, desktops, and so on) you should seriously consider using a responsive web design approach which automatically resizes the content based on the size of the user's display screen. In this way you can help to ensure that your users get a similar experience when accessing your system from different devices.

7.7 Summary

This chapter covers some key issues regarding communication between users and systems. There is much more that could be said about the related topics of computer-mediated communication, non-verbal communication, and computer-supported cooperative work (CSCW). We have, however, provided some practical suggestions about how to support communication between users and systems.

The most common way that people communicate with each other and with technology is through language. By considering language, concepts such as Grices' maxims can be applied to help you optimize the way that users interact with your system.

Most systems require the user to do some reading from the screen. The reading process will be affected by factors such as the legibility of the text, which is influenced by the font size and the way the text is laid out. The quality of resolution of the text is also important: printed text usually has a much higher resolution than text displayed on a screen. In addition, users tend to scan rather than read text on a display screen, particularly if they are looking at menus or web pages containing hyperlinks.

One of the other main tasks that users do is seek information. The way they do this is based on their preliminary understanding of the information they are looking for, and how it is organized. How they will understand the information that they find depends on their previous knowledge and experience, and may be affected by the contexts in which the information is being sought and used.

When it comes to interacting with the web, the structure and delivery of content is critical. Content is an active element that has to be designed, developed, and maintained over time, which requires the setting up of a content strategy. The way the content is organized will be determined by your information architecture. When you create content you need to make sure that it will be intelligible (as well as legible) to your readers, and to structure it in such a way that the user can understand and learn what it means. Finally, the medium through which the content is delivered is increasingly important, as more and more people access the same content using a wide range of devices.

7.8 Other Resources

Users read material on the screen as part of systems, so learning how to write is a part of interface design. Strunk and White's very famous Elements of Style is well worth looking at for this topic. This book provides advice about how to present information to readers in a format that they can most easily digest:

Strunk, W., & White, E. B. (1979). *The elements of style*. NY, NY: Macmillan

Another skill worth picking up is how to structure documents. For this, Parker's Looking good in print is a good text. The advice is not specific to any word processor or page layout tool. It discusses the use of color, layout, white space, fonts, and other aspects of design. It is easy to read. It is a very gentle introduction to graphic design. While based on print, some of the guidance will apply to online materials:

Parker, R. C. (2006). *Looking good in print*. Scottsdale, AZ: Paraglyph Press

For further details on how to apply information foraging theory, see Nielsen's Alertbox on this: http://www.useit.com/alertbox/20030630.html

For more on information seeking more generally, a key figure is Carol Kuhlthau. A 2005 online article gives a nice overview and introduces some useful concepts:

Kuhlthau, C. C. (2005). Towards collaboration between information seeking and information retrieval. *Information Research* 10(2). 10–2.

Finally, a short magazine article by Churchill addresses some challenges in designing for human search behavior:

Churchill, E. F. (2008). Ps and Qs of candied herbs and happy babies: Seeking and searching on your own terms. *Interactions*. 15(6). 46–49.

7.9 Exercises

7.1. (a) Time how long it takes four people to read out loud (or silently) Tables 7.3 and 7.4. Time how long it takes four more people to read them on screen (a tablet, smartphone, computer, or all of them) vs on paper. (b) What are the differences? (There should be differences). Consider having the four people read the text in the tables in each of the four ways (two levels of font difficulty × two types of display, or 2 × 2). (c) Why would you want to have different people do each task, and how could you correct for having the same person do it each way?

7.2. Card sorting is a useful method for finding out how people organize the world. In this simple method, you give people a set of objects noted one per card. They can be words or pictures. The people then sort the cards into piles. The number and size of piles can either be left to the sorters or, if there is a design constraint that will have to be applied, into a restricted set of piles or sizes.

   As an application of this method, examine a large application like Word, Pages, GIMP, Excel, or Numbers. (a) Draw a graph or a table showing the complete menu structure. Ask two people to look at the menu items on cards (not on a menu) and organize the cards into groups. (b) What are average or typical groupings? (c) Do these groupings match the application, or are there differences between the personal groupings and menu structure? (d) What does this tell you about the mental models of the designers and of the users?

7.3. Create a web site or a document. Create five versions of it using different font types and sizes. Ask ten people to rate the documents on four different dimensions. You can choose dimensions, such as ease of use, trustworthiness, fun. Record how long they take to read several of the pages out loud (so you know they are reading them). You will need to present them in different orders to balance the effect of learning over multiple trials. Examine the time to read with respect to the measures to see if there are any correlations that predict readability as measured by reading time.

7.4. Find a source of interfaces and of jokes (cartoons or written jokes). Find an example joke or cartoon where one of Grice's maxims is violated. Find an interface where the same maxim is violated. You can also use interfaces noted in this book. Note how the interfaces could be repaired.

References

Barnes, D. M., Spink, A. H., & Yeatts, D. E. (1996). Effective information systems for high-performing self-managed teams. In *Information Seeking in Context: Proceedings of an International Conference on Research in Information Needs, Seeking and Use in Different Contexts* (pp.163–178). Taylor Graham: Tampere, Finland.

Blandford, A., & Attfield, S. (2010). *Interacting with information. Synthesis lectures on human-centered informatics*. San Rafael, CA: Morgan & Claypool.

Bush, V. (1945). As we may think. *The Atlantic Monthly, 176*(1), 101–108.

Byrne, M. D. (2001). ACT-R/PM and menu selection: Applying a cognitive architecture to HCI. *International Journal of Human-Computer Studies, 55*(1), 41–84.

Byrne, M. D., John, B. E., Wehrle, N. S., & Crow, D. C. (1999). The tangled web we wove: A taskonomy of WWW use. In *Proceedings of the CHI'99 Conference on Human Factors in Computer Systems* (pp. 544–551). ACM: New York, NY.

Chilton, E. (1996). What was the subject of Titchner's doctoral thesis? *SigCHI Bulletin, 28*(2), 96.

Clark, H. H., & Brennan, S. E. (1991). Grounding in communication. In L. B. Resnick, J. M. Levine, & S. D. Teasley (Eds.), *Perspectives on socially shared cognition* (pp. 127–149). Washington, DC: American Psychological Association.

Collins, A. M., & Quillian, M. R. (1969). Retrieval time from semantic memory. *Journal of Verbal Learning and Verbal Behavior, 8*, 240–247.

Dillon, A. (1992). Reading from paper versus screens: A critical review of the empirical literature. *Ergonomics, 35*(10), 1297–1326.

Flesch, R. (1948). A new readability yardstick. *Journal of Applied Psychology, 32*, 221–233.

Furnas, G. W., Landauer, T. K., Gomez, L. M., & Dumais, S. T. (1987). The vocabulary problem in human-system communication. Communications of the ACM, 30(Nov.) (pp. 964–971).

Garvey, P. M., Pietrucha, M. T., & Meeker., D. T. (1998). Development of a new road sign alphabet. *Ergonomics in Design, 6*(3), 7–11.

Glushko, R. J. (2013). *The discipline of organizing*. Cambridge, MA: MIT.

Grice, H. P. (1975). Logic and conversation. In P. Cole & J. L. Morgan (Eds.), *Syntax and semantics III: Speech acts*. New York, NY: Academic Press.

Gould, J. D., Alfaro, L., Barnes, V., Finn, R., Grischkowsky, N., & Minuto, A. (1987). Reading is slower from CRT displays than from paper: Attempts to isolate a single variable explanation. *Human Factors, 29*, 269–299.

Halvorson, K. (2010). *Content strategy for the Web*. Berkley, CA: New Riders.

Hornof, A. J., & Halverson, T. (2003). Cognitive strategies and eye movements for searching hierarchical computer displays. In *Proceedings of CHI 2003: Conference on Human Factors in Computing Systems* (pp. 249–256). ACM: New York, NY.

Hornof, A. J., & Kieras, D. E. (1997). Cognitive modeling reveals menu search is both random and systematic. In *Proceedings of the CHI'97 Conference on Human Factors in Computer Systems* (pp. 107–114). ACM: New York, NY.

Jansen, B. J., & Spink, A. H. (2006). How are we searching the World Wide Web? A comparison of nine large search engine transaction logs. *Information Processing and Management, 42*(4), 248–263.

Just, M. A., & Carpenter, P. A. (1987). *The psychology of reading and language comprehension.* Newton, MA: Allyn & Bacon.

Just, M. A., & Thibadeau, R. A. (1984). Developing a computer model of reading times. In D. E. Kieras & M. A. Just (Eds.), *New methods in reading comprehension research* (pp. 349–364). Hillsdale, NJ: Erlbaum.

Kadlec, T. (2013). *Implementing responsive design: Building sites for an anywhere, everywhere web.* Berkeley, CA: New Riders.

Kernighan, B. W., & Plauger, P. J. (1978). *The elements of programming style* (2nd ed.). New York, NY: McGraw-Hill.

Kincaid, J. P., Fishburne Jr, R. P., Rogers, R. L., & Chissom, B. S. (1975). Derivation of new readability formulas (Automated Readability Index, Fog Count and Flesch Reading Ease Formula) for Navy enlisted personnel. Research Branch Report 8–75, Millington, TN: Naval Technical Training, U. S. Naval Air Station, Memphis, TN.

Klahr, D., Chase, W. G., & Lovelace, E. A. (1983). Structure and process in alphabetic retrieval. *Journal of Experimental Psychology, 9*(3), 462–477.

Kurniawan, S. H., & Zaphiris, P. (2001). Reading online or on paper: Which is faster?. In *Abridged proceedings of HCI International 2001, Poster sessions* (pp. 220–222). Mahwah, NJ: Erlbaum

Liversedge, S. P., Gilchrist, I. D., & Everling, S. (2011). *The Oxford handbook of eye movements.* Oxford, UK: Oxford University Press.

McKendree, J., Reader, W., & Hammond, N. (1995). The "Homeopathic Fallacy" in learning from hypertext. *Communications of the ACM, 2*(3), 74–82.

McLuhan, M., & Fiore, Q. (1967). The medium is the massage: An inventory of effects: 1st Ed.: Bantam Books, Random House; reissued by Gingko Press, 2001.

Morville, P., & Rosenfeld, L. (2007). *Information architecture for the World Wide Web* (3rd ed.). Sebastopol, CA: O'Reilly.

Nielsen, J. (1997). *How users read on the Web.* http://www.useit.com/alertbox/9710a.html. Retrieved from 10 March 2014.

Parker, R. C. (2006). *Looking good in print.* Scottsdale, AZ: Paraglyph Press.

Pirolli, P. (1997). Computational models of information scent-following in a very large browsable text collection. In *Proceedings of the SIGCHI Conference on Human Factors in Computing Systems* (pp. 3–10). ACM: New York, NY.

Pirolli, P. L. T. (2007). *Information foraging theory: Adaptive interaction with information.* Oxford: New York, NY.

Rayner, K. (1998). Eye movements in reading and information processing: 20 years of research. *Psychological Bulletin, 124*(3), 372–422.

Rayner, K., & Pollatsek, A. (1989). *The psychology of reading.* Englewood Cliffs, NJ: Prentice Hall.

Rayner, K., Slattery, T. J., Drieghe, D., & Liversedge, S. P. (2011). Eye movements and word skipping during reading: Effects of word length and predictability. *Journal of Experimental Psychology: Human Perception and Performance, 37*(2), 514–528.

Rieman, J., Young, R. M., & Howes, A. (1996). A dual-space model of iteratively deepening exploratory learning. *International Journal of Human-Computer Studies, 44*, 743–775.

Scheiter, K., & Gerjets, K. (2007). Making your own order: Order effects in system- and user-controlled settings for learning and problem solving. In F. E. Ritter, J. Nerb, T. M. O'Shea, & E. Lehtinen (Eds.), *In order to learn: How the sequences of topics affect learning* (pp. 181–194). Oxford: New York, NY.

Sears, A., & Shneiderman, B. (1994). Split Menus: Effectively using selection frequency to organize menus. *ACM Transactions on Computer-Human Interaction, 1*(1), 27–51.

Spink, A., & Cole, C. (2001). Information and poverty: Information-seeking channels used by African American low-income households. *Library & Information Science Research, 23*, 45–65.

Spink, A., Ozmutlu, H. C., & Ozmutlu, S. (2002a). Multitasking information seeking and searching processes. *Journal of the American Society for Information Sciences and Technology, 53*(8), 639–652.

Spink, A. H., Jansen, B. J., Wolfram, D., & Saracevic, T. (2002b). From e-sex to e-commerce: Web search changes. *IEEE Computer,35*(3), 133–135.

Swaak, J., & de Jong, T. (2007). Order or no order: System versus learner control in sequencing simulation-based scientific discovery. In F. E. Ritter, J. Nerb, T. M. O'Shea, & E. Lehtinen (Eds.), *In order to learn: How the sequences of topics affect learning* (pp. 181–194). New York, NY: Oxford.

White, A. W. (2002). *The elements of graphic design: Space, unity, page architecture, and type.* New York, NY: Allworth Press.

Woods, W. (1975). What's in a Link: Foundations for Semantic Networks. In D. G. Bobrow & A. Collins (Eds.), *Representation and Understanding*. New York, NY: Academic Press. Reprinted in Brachman, R., & Levesque, H. (1985). *Readings in Knowledge Representation*. San Mateo: Morgan Kaufmann. Also reprinted in Collins, A., & Smith, E. E. (1988). *Readings in Cognitive Science*. San Mateo: Morgan Kaufmann.

Chapter 8
Social: Social Cognition and Teamwork

Abstract Most work is carried out by people working as part of a team. Even where work is carried out by one person it is likely to be in connection if not in collaboration with other people. This could be in a formal organization that has standard operating procedures or as part of a larger system, or it could be part of an informal group of loosely organized collaborators. Social processes—how people interact with each other—are important; they affect how systems interfaces are used. Any system that supports more than one person needs to take these phenomena into account along with the various factors that define the social context in which users especially user working in teams will make decisions take actions including extrinsic intrinsic motivation. In this chapter we introduce some concepts that have proven to be important for system adoption use.

8.1 Introduction

Much early work in HCI focused on single users because at that time most tasks were performed by individuals working on independent computers. However, even in the 1970s, as increased computer use came to the workplace, there was recognition that we need to consider social aspects of system use:

> We believe that the engineer who deals with human performance should avoid two faults that have made the "efficiency expert" one of the most hated in industry: (1) the neglect of personal and of social variables, and (2) the use of people as means to ends they do not share and do not determine. If a person is to design tasks for others, he has the responsibility to attempt to see the tasks and their implications in a wider context and to attempt to ensure that they are life-enhancing. This is not easy to do, nor are the criteria clear cut. It requires that the designer himself close feedback loops with reality at several levels, not only at the level of specific performance criteria of the given system or of the human task which are part of it, but also at the level of his own personal values (Sheridan and Ferrell 1974, pp. 18–19).

As distributed, networked computing systems have become the norm, team or group working has become routine, and the importance of social processes has risen (see, for example, Hinds and Kiesler 2002). We now have a much better

F. E. Ritter et al., *Foundations for Designing User-Centered Systems*,
DOI: 10.1007/978-1-4471-5134-0_8, © Springer-Verlag London 2014

understanding of how the context in which the technological system is used sig-
nificantly affects *how* it is used. Workplace systems are *socio-technical systems*
(see Chap. 2); that is, technical systems that are designed for and shaped by people
operating in social contexts. This means it is important to consider the interactions
and interdependencies between the social and technical aspects of any system that
is being developed or modified: How is it being used? How does it affect (transform, facilitate, impede) social processes?

Social psychology and other disciplines draw a distinction between individuals
acting alone, dyads (two people interacting), groups, teams, and communities. In
the context of work tasks, dyads, groups, and teams tend to share more clearly
defined goals. Here we use the term *team* to refer to a particular, formally defined
and workplace oriented type of group. Whilst what applies to groups generally
applies to teams, what applies to teams does not always apply to groups.

A team comprises two or more individuals who have to carry out work (a set of
related tasks) in pursuit of some common (specified) goal. Team performance, like
individual performance, is still based on the notion of particular people doing
particular tasks in a particular context. It is, however, complicated by the need to
communicate and co-ordinate actions and decision making, and by having to consider the effects of the way that the team may be distributed in both space and time.

When thinking about teams, it is important to remember that what counts as a
team depends on where you draw the boundaries when conducting your analysis
(Hollnagel 2007). In aviation, for example, if you draw your boundary at the
aircraft cockpit level you might consider the pilots to be a team. If, however, you
extend the boundary to cover the whole of the (interior of the) aircraft, then the
team would include the flight attendants. You can keep extending the boundary
outwards, which would bring more people into the team: ground crew; air traffic
control; and so on.

Social processes related to and mediated by technology also occur in other large
systems of systems such as medicine, entertainment, defense, and increasingly in
education. For example, in air transportation, many people—passengers, pilots,
ground crew, and so on—come together (see Fig. 8.1). Where a number of social
groups come together, as in this case, a large socio-technical system—a system of
systems—is formed smaller socio-technical systems each of which has their own
social rules and regulations, and often includes different technical systems. People
frequently end up as the points at which these systems overlap. For example, think
about the check-in agent at an airport who has to work with baggage handling
systems to ensure your luggage gets on to the right plane. Here, the agent who
prints and attaches the tag to your bag is the boundary point between the check-in
system and the baggage handling system, and the tag determines how the bag
moves into the baggage handling system.

Working as a team can bring problems of co-ordination and communication.
The aviation industry recognized this and developed the concept of cockpit
resource management (Wiener et al. 1993) as a way of dealing with the issues on

Fig. 8.1 The modern air transportation system includes many kinds of technology, including computer systems, and many types of users, ranging from passengers to pilots to support staff and including air traffic control

the flight deck. The concept was subsequently extended to cover the whole of the on-board flight crew, and was renamed crew resource management (Kanki et al. 2010). When teams are in the same location, or *co-located* a great advantage is overhearing what others are doing, even if they are not collaborating actively at that moment. This allows people to be aware of where others are in a task. There is a body of work looking at what happens in control rooms, for example, where teams of operators work together (e.g., Heath and Luff 2000).

Although teams may be co-located, teams nowadays are often distributed in space and time, even when working for the same organization. Teams may also be spread across different time zones and across different cultures. A lot of work has been done to understand the benefits and problems of distributed work and tele-commuting (see, for example, Hinds and Kiesler 2002; Ellison 2004). Research has also focused on the ways in which different technologies affect communication and coordination. Technologies that mediate communication between people in different locations are differentially suited to different kinds of tasks (Churchill and Bly 2000). Teams can also change dynamically, as they adapt to the situation at hand. In hospitals, for example, there is often a doctor that is on call. These doctors are usually only called up when the local team cannot resolve the case they are currently dealing with. This may result in the doctor acting as a remote team member to help diagnose and fix the situation, or it may result in the doctor physically attending in order to provide expertise and advice in situ.

In the rest of this chapter we look at the impact of social factors on performance. We begin by examining at the impact of the social context on decision making. We then go on to consider the factors that define the social context in which teams operate. It is worth noting at this juncture that team performance involves more than just the sum of the performances of the individual team members.

8.2 Social Effects on Decision Making

8.2.1 Introduction

Social psychology suggests that sometimes groups do not make better decisions than individuals. It is certainly true that groups often come to different decisions than individuals, and that groups are influenced by social factors. This section looks at some of the social influences on decision making, including the diffusion of social responsibility, the attribution of effects, and how groups make decisions differently.

8.2.2 Social Responsibility Effects

There are two effects related to decision making in social settings. The first of these is called *diffusion of social responsibility*. If a request for assistance is directed at a single person, that person must choose whether to respond or not. When many people are held jointly responsible for dealing with a situation, however, the responsibility diffuses across people: one person may choose not to do anything in the belief that someone else will. Figure 8.2 illustrates a version of this. It shows a fairly obvious typographical error in a local paper. While it can be argued that it is not the readers' responsibility to report typos to a newspaper, many readers take great delight in doing so. In this case, both the paper and the fans ignored this glaring mistake for weeks.

The second effect is *pluralistic ignorance*. When you are in a situation, you will often base your interpretation of the situation on how other people interpret it. Is that person ill or just acting strangely? Are they sleeping by the side of the road or have they had a heart attack? As Darley and Latané (reported in Abelson et al. 2004, p. 224) noted, "emergencies do not come with signs on them saying that they are emergencies." The observer has to interpret the event before responding. If others are ignoring the apparently anomalous behavior or interpreting it in one way, then it provides evidence to suggest that you should too.

Both of these effects apply in an early study designed to investigate how people choose to help. Darley and Batson (1973) had theological seminary (i.e., religious professional) students prepare a talk and then walk individually to the next building where they were supposed to give their talk to a panel. Some students prepared a talk on the tale of the Good Samaritan (a biblical story about a man who stopped and helped an injured man) and some prepared a talk on a topic that did not involve helping others. Some of the students were told to hurry to the next building because they were late, some were told they were somewhat late, and some had more time to make the trip. On the way to the next building each student passed a person slumped in a doorway. Unknown to the students, this person was a confederate of the experimenter. Data was collected on who stopped to help this person, and how much help they offered.

Fig. 8.2 This figure, which appeared in a pre-game (American football) newspaper program, ran for 3 weeks (with different opponents appropriately inserted), with the labels "When Penn State has the Ball" for its defensive team *and* for its offensive team

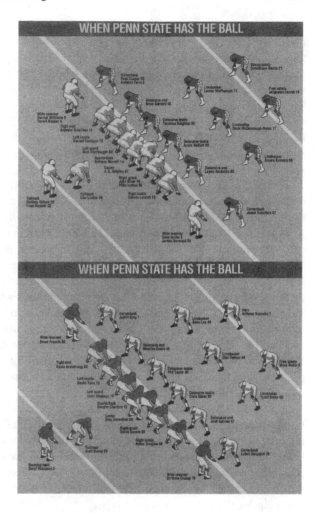

The students who had the most time to get to the next building helped the most (63%); those in the greatest hurry helped the least (10%). The students who were somewhat late helped 45% of the time. Ironically, the amount of help they gave was not influenced by whether the student was going to give a talk on the Good Samaritan or not. This work starts to examine who chooses to participate, and shows that it not only depends on the individual, but also on the context.

You can often see these effects in email. Some time ago we saw an email that was sent out about the potential closing down of an academic society. "Unless this vote [to amend the constitution] is successful, the committee will [have] no alternative [sic] to dismantling the Society, prior to closing it down." The email called upon the members of the society to vote for a new set of bylaws. It was targeted at the group (of society members) as a whole rather than individuals within the group. (The society continued, but it took several more emails.)

Remember that the diffusion of social responsibility requires that others are involved—a person is less likely to take responsibility for action or inaction when they think someone else will take the action. Size of the group is critical, and it must be the case that no one person is singled out as responsible. So, not all situations involving many participants will result in social responsibility diffusion. For such diffusion to occur, the relationship of the individuals in the group to the requestor—whether they are individually likely to be held accountable or not—is key. Your supervisor asking you to put information on a web site to help others is more compelling than a company president asking everyone to participate in a knowledge repository.

You do not always get diffusion of social responsibility. In a demo run as part of an HCI class we have repeatedly failed to achieve this effect. In this demo the class teaching assistant emails the students (some individually, and some in groups of 2, 4, 8, 16, or 32 students) asking them to bring along an example book to the next class. The numbers of students who bring in a book is about the same for those students who are emailed individually as it is for those who are emailed in groups. If there was diffusion of responsibility, there would be more books brought along by those who received the individual email than those who received a group email, Subsequent class discussions usually note that most of the students feel that this request is not individual, that the teaching assistant will know them individually, and that the lecturer will be able to tell whether or not they brought along a book. Sometimes students also report that the bland wording in the request is somewhat unusual, which leads them to suspect that there is an ulterior motive behind the request.

If you want to avoid diffusion of social responsibility, you should target particular individuals. It helps to use first names in emails, use individual communication, and to clearly note any possible consequences. In the case of bulletin boards and online forums, people asking for help have to be specific (which is possible with technical problems) and have to address individuals if possible. In the case of online forums this is difficult and thus it may be better in many cases to find help locally.

Note that diffusion of responsibility and pluralistic ignorance are not inevitable, and can be avoided or prevented. Keltner and Marsh (2006–2007) suggest making the need clear, so that there is no pluralistic ignorance about the need for help, and to direct the request at specific individuals, so that the responsibility does not get diffused.

8.2.3 Attributions and Attributional Style

Understanding why other people do things is called attribution. Attribution is central to how we understand social situations. When we examine how people make these attributions, we can start to identify some regularities:

- Self versus others: attributions about ourselves are usually different from our attributions about others behaving in exactly the same way. We give ourselves credit for success based on our internal capabilities, but blame the environment or others for our failures. On the other hand, when making attributions about others, we are more likely to attribute their success to their environment, and their failures to their personal deficiencies. Even university presidents do this (Birnbaum 1988, p. 215), attributing their own successes to hard work and their failures to outside events.
- If something bad occurs to someone else, we will seek explanations that attribute cause to a circumstance that creates the most distance from our own circumstances. The explanation is simple: we like to distance ourselves from the thought that the same thing could happen to us.

Attribution theory is an important area of research in social psychology. Jones et al. (1972) noted the tendency of people to attribute their actions to external situational causes, whilst external observers attributed the same actions to causes that were internal to the person carrying out the actions (the actor). They called this tendency the *actor-observer divergence*. The term *fundamental attribution error* was later introduced to describe how observers underestimate the impact of situational forces and overestimate the importance of internal dispositional factors (Ross et al. 1977).

One of the fundamental errors in design is for the designer to attribute their own feelings, needs, knowledge, goals, and so on, to users. In other words, for the designers to believe that other people, including their potential users, are exactly like them, and behave in exactly the same way. Good designers differentiate what they want, need, and can do from what their users want, need, and can do. From the user's perspective, the technology may not always behave as expected. In these situations, systems need to be designed to be transparent, to be effectively debugged, and thus to help the users make the appropriate attributions: *is this an issue with the system or the device or did I do something wrong?* Error messages should not be worded ambiguously, but should allow the user to attribute causes appropriately and learn from the error.

Related to the notion of attribution is the concept of *cognitivedissonance*. Cognitive dissonance occurs when a person holds two or more beliefs that are in conflict at one time as in when people do not get what they want. People will rationalize their choice by devaluing the one that is not chosen or that becomes unavailable. It is similar to the moral in Aesop's fable about the fox and the sour grapes. The fox reasoned that the grapes that he could not reach were sour, and hence not worth getting. People sometimes adopt a similar line of reasoning when they do not get the rewards they were expecting (such as a promotion to a new post) by convincing themselves that they are currently in the best position. Similarly, when people do things for little reward, when they explain why they did that activity, it can increase their perceived value of it. This explains why it can be better to give small rewards where the impact can last longer.

8.2.3.1 Breakout Box: Ways Email Has Gone Awry

How can we apply attribution theory to system design? Email is an example where most people are using the same type of system, but other people appear to behave differently from us and differently from how we would like them to.

Ritter has personally seen the following ways that email has been lost, misfiled, misdirected, or lost. Are these errors? In some ways they are. Are they the fault of the user or of the system or the system designer? It seems to vary. In all cases, the sender might want a response.

This list (selected from more) can also be explained with reference to attribution. Do the reasons you do not reply to email vary from why you think others do not reply (starting with whether they got the email!)? Many users assume that email is perfect, that the receiver received it, and that lack of response is due to the receiver not being willing to respond. This list illustrates that this is not always the case. Further discussion is available in the chapter on errors.

1. Date is off on the sending computer (by up to 5 years), so does not appear with today's email (mail to Ritter).
2. Simple typo in "To" address (mail to Saor-bugs, not Soar-bugs).
3. Extra letter(s) typed as an answer to another application, e.g., mail to "yesyen" instead of to "yen" (Ritter).
4. Complex typo, e.g., in "To" address, mail sent to research group's name, not to research group's email alias (Ritter).
5. "From" country (!) was on spam list (so not read by recipient) and not read by cc person (Ritter was cc).
6. Typo in domain (Ritter).
7. Local (university, government, hotel) mail server ate it and left no residue (Ritter, Spink).
8. No known reason, found months later where it should be (Ritter).
9. Reader meant to respond, but never got back to it or was waiting for 'the right time to send a really good and clear reply' (Ritter, too many times).
10. Admin assistant reading manager's email deleted it accidentally (multi-readers of account, anonymous).
11. Admin assistant reading manager's email deleted it, perhaps on purpose (multi-readers of account, anonymous).
12. Email came in batch of 500 messages after a break (Ritter, others).
13. Reader or mailer accidentally deleted incoming mailbox (anonymous!).
14. Filter misfiled it (Schooler, Ritter).
15. Email sent to Ritter (and from Ritter, more recently) where sender's machine filled in remainder as @<localhost>. Ritter replied with ritter@<localhost>. Both bounced.
16. RAID disk failure takes out department for 3 days (anonymous in UK).
17. "When I can't give someone the answer I want to give them, I don't give them an answer" (a publisher).

18. User was going through a life-changing event, such as moving, pneumonia, their own death, having a baby, losing a baby, loss of a relative, or several of these at the same time.
19. User wrote email and, instead of sending it, filed it as if it was the email being replied to. (Ritter, September 2006; to Ritter, 2009).
20. Print out of email was printed and deleted, and was then stapled to the back of another document printed before it. (Ritter, multiple times).
21. Auto expansion from first name (e.g., Jacob) instead of from last name (e.g., Jacob).
22. Email sent from local conference hotel run by major research university never arrived or bounced.
23. Emails included as attachments in the middle of the body of a message (rather than in the header or at the end of the body).
24. Email software and anything in between (e.g., router, ISP, recipient) changes security level. (Ritter, Feb. 2009, and earlier).
25. Students told/reminded to read their student email account (with clunky interface) by an email sent to that address.
26. User replied to questions by answering them on the same line, not a separate line as the quoted questions. The reader only saw their original questions.
27. Migration to MS Outlook server did not migrate all emails.

8.2.4 Majority and Minority Effects

The way that individuals behave when they are part of a group usually differs from how they would behave on their own. There is a strong tendency to be influenced by what the group says or does. If the majority of members of a group express a single opinion, it is much less likely that one individual will hold onto a different opinion, even if they know that they are correct. This effect derives from the desire in a group to maintain harmony or conformity, and minimizes conflict. This can result in incorrect or deviant decision making. This has been raised as a concern for juries, for example, where what is called *group think* can occur (McCauley 1989).

These issues have been studied with experiments using a group where some of the group members were confederates of the experimenter, that is, people who were not really subjects in the study. With a stooge majority (i.e., in a room full of experimenters pretending to be other subjects in the study), individuals readily capitulated to the majority view, even when they were fully aware of the right answer. With a stooge minority, where the group in the experiment had a minority of confederates who held an incorrect opinion, many individuals do capitulate occasionally to their view.

Another way in which this can play out is with what is called *choice shift*. Two good examples of this are the *risky shift*, where a group makes a riskier decision than an individual. Wallach et al. (1964) proposed that greater risk-taking results from diffusion of responsibility. Here, emotional bonds decrease anxiety and the risk is perceived as shared. Collins and Guetzkow (1964) suggested that high-risk-takers are more confident and hence may persuade others to take greater risks. This can result in those who tend toward less risky behavior becoming more risky; social pressure (I do not want to let my colleagues down) translates to moving to a riskier position. Familiarity and increased knowledge of a situation also leads people to feel that situations are less risky; more people may equate to more knowledge and deeper exploration of the issues, so perceived risk is diminished (Bateson 1966).

However, sometimes the opposite can occur; this is called *cautious shift* (Stoner 1968). Here the group moves to a more conservative, less risky position.

8.2.5 Summary

The effects of the social context on decisions are strong in situations that have social components. These effects arise when there are other parties to the decision and when there are other parties making the decision.

Social effects occur in individuals when they are part of a team but also occur in individuals in social situations where there are no organized teams such as chat rooms and forums. Some of these effects can be anticipated and can be marshaled to help systems, and some can be avoided with forethought.

There are further influences of decision making that arise from social effects. It is these social effects that keep life interesting. If you are interested, see the section on Other Resources.

8.3 Factors Affecting Team Performance

8.3.1 Introduction

It is important to understand the factors that underpin good teamwork so that you can facilitate and support teams with any system you design or develop. A team's performance, and whether it achieves its desired goals, will depend on collaboration and communication between the team members. Teamwork is based upon multiple components, including the team's set of competencies—that is, knowledge, skills, and attitudes (or KSAs). The relationship between the KSAs and teamwork is shown in Fig. 8.3.

Your system design should provide the appropriate levels and types of support to encourage team members to participate in team performance. Participation can range from simply making a comment on a bulletin board that can be seen by other members of a group, to interactively working with other people as part of a team to carry out a task. There are several situational factors that affect how users interact socially with others.

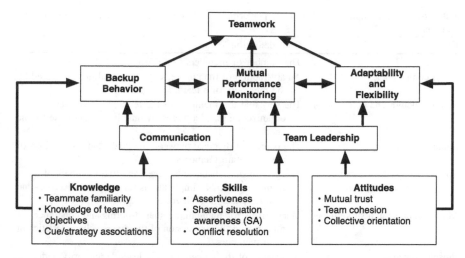

Fig. 8.3 A theory of the components of teamwork (based on a diagram by Salas et al. 2005)

Table 8.1 notes several factors that influence team performance based on a review of modeling teamwork (Morgan et al. 2010). The importance of each of the factors will depend on the task itself, and the context in which it is performed. Note that although we refer to team, these factors also apply to groups.

An example of a team is shown in Fig. 8.4. Much of the research in this area has been carried out in critical dynamic domains, such as aviation or defense, where good teamwork has high payoffs (and, more importantly, poor teamwork can lead to great losses). In addition to the way that teams are made up, and how the individual members work together, team performance is also affected by the availability of resources to carry out the task at hand. These includes physical resources like space, computers, networks, and databases, as well as intellectual and administrative support above and below the team in the organization (see Booher and Minninger 2003; Brooks 1975 for overviews of resourcing issues).

Achieving good teamwork is difficult. The situation is complicated because of the need to consider the interaction of multiple people, each with different backgrounds (knowledge, culture, and so on), which will influence their behavior. It is also important to take appropriate account of task-related factors, because the task structure, for example, may not readily map onto the team's structure. Here we draw on and extend Kozlowski and Ilgen's (2006) review to highlight areas of importance.

8.3.2 Team Size

The size of a team affects performance. If the team is small and its size is constant, it may be possible for communication and collaboration to take place directly between members. The group's size has a strong effect on intra-group interaction, as well as inter-group perceptions. Group size seems not only to influence the

Table 8.1 Factors that influence team performance by defining the social context of the members

Factor	Brief definition
Team size	The number of members in a team
Team competencies	An abstraction of the number of unique qualities possessed by the members of a team
Team structure and composition	The way that the members of the team are structurally organized, e.g., as a hierarchy, and how they relate to one another
Social distance	The perceived distance between the goals and motivations of any two team members
Spatial distance	The geophysical distance between any two members of a team; this also has implications for temporal distance–that is, differences in time zone
Mutual support and surveillance	Mechanisms for maintaining shared norms and coherence by minimizing the expression of the diverse characteristics of team members
Presence or absence of legitimate authority figures	A measure of the perception of a leader's authority and legitimacy by a team member; authority can be leaders or monitors
Task attractiveness	A measure of the alignment of the leader's task with the team members' internal motivations
Team processes and tasks	The relationship between the teams and the tasks that they have to perform

effectiveness of communication between group members (Cartwright 1968; Hare 1952) and its tendency towards hierarchy (Bales et al. 1951) but also the relationship dynamics existing within and between groups (Bales and Borgatta 1955; Benenson et al. 2000; Shalit 1988).

As the size of the team grows, it changes the dynamics of interaction between members, and may make it harder for individual members to participate in team working. In such a situation you need to consider other factors that can be used to facilitate member participation. If the team is too large for effective participation, you may wish to encourage (or even mandate) the use of smaller teams.

8.3.3 Team Competencies

Good teams are usually made up of good team members. If the team members have good levels of KSAs, this will usually be positively reflected in team performance. It also helps if the goals of the team members are aligned with those of the organization in general, and with the task goals in particular. A multidisciplinary team can benefit greatly from skill sharing between different team members, and a team can also be made stronger through appropriate education and training of the team and its members. It is worth noting that there are some tasks where team performance is determined by the performance of the worst team

Fig. 8.4 Teams are important for many processes. Here, two pilots are working together as a team to prepare a plane for flight, and, not shown, interacting with ground control and ATC

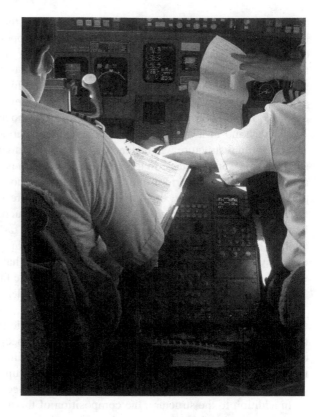

member, such as in an obstacle course, and there are other tasks where coordination is far more important than raw speed or talent (e.g., McNeese 2000), and yet other tasks where the best performances of individuals matter (e.g., gymnastics). Industrial and organizational psychology is an area that will provide more knowledge about how to improve teams through selection.

Olson and Olson (2000) suggest that collaboration readiness and technology readiness are also important factors for teams interacting using technology. The former relates to the willingness and ability of team members to collaborate. The latter relates the technological know-how about the tools that will be used, including tools that support synchronous (real-time) and asynchronous communication (and collaboration) such as Skype, Twitter, Instant Messaging, video chat, and text SMS—notably, the suitability of the tool itself, the match of its affordances to the communication needs of the group, and the tasks (Bly and Churchill 1999).

8.3.4 Team Structure and Composition

As the size of the team increases, some sort of structure will be needed to manage communication and collaboration between members. This often takes the form of a hierarchy. For larger teams (and where the size of the team can increase over time), it may become necessary to provide system support for communication and collaboration. This can be done through facilities for sharing information, or for allowing close grained collaboration with version histories to enable task awareness (e.g., Churchill et al. 2000) or by enabling team members to maintain a more general current awareness of what other team members are doing, as in the example of the control room operators mentioned above (Heath and Luff 2000). This latter kind of awareness is sometimes called shared situation awareness.

The optimal structure will depend on the team members, their relationships, the social context, and the task. In the ideal case, the team is balanced to the task, with appropriate KSAs to perform the task and the team coordination tasks. For complex, unpredictable tasks, or for situations where there is a broad range of tasks, flexible structures are better. For static tasks, static structures can help the teams to be more efficient. Thus in assembly line work, where tasks do not vary, structures tend to be more rigid. In academic research, and in creative pursuits such as design, where the tasks vary quite a bit, teams will have more varied and more variable structures. In Fig. 8.3 this would influence the factors of adaptability and, to a certain extent, the communication and team leadership.

Within the field of system design, Brooks (1975), has famously explored the issue of team structure. He argues that having a single system design architect is the best approach. He also notes that adding more people to a project can slow down development at certain times. There are two main reasons for this: first, you need to spend time and effort bringing the new people up to speed, and second, you often also increase the communication overhead (based on size and structure).

In addition to the structure, the composition of the team is also important: you need to have people who are capable of working together. Several researchers (Kozlowski and Ilgen 2006; Salas et al. 2002) note that teams work better when they leverage the knowledge of the team members, are cohesive and confident, allocate resources appropriately, coordinate well, and learn over time.

There is significant evidence that differences between group members negatively affect group performance (Byrne 1971; McGrath 1984; Newcomb 1961). This literature generally describes the level of group performance as a function of the organization's level of social integration, or the degree to which group members are psychologically linked or attracted towards interacting with one another in pursuit of common objectives (O'Reilly et al. 1989). Social integration constitutes a goal-driven process arising out of the daily interactions of team members, mediated by both the length of contact between members and their respective organizational roles.

Promoting interaction between team members also helps. Birnbaum (1988, p. 94) and others, have noted that people who interact with each other in groups tend to like each other. The interaction and liking are related, in that liking leads to more interaction, which leads to more liking.

The importance of diversity among team members is questioned by some, however. Mannix and Neale (2005), for example, have argued that the effect of diversity of team members is not as clear cut as some people say. They note that

Table 8.2   Social distance measures from Ethington (1997)

Distance	Bogardus (1925) "Would willingly admit members of each race..."	Bogardus (1933–1967)
1.	To close kinship by marriage	Would marry
2.	To my club as personal chums	Would have as regular friends
3.	To my street as neighbors	Would work beside in an office
4.	To employment in my occupation in my country	Would have several families in my neighborhood
5.	To citizenship in my country	Would have merely as speaking acquaintances
6.	As visitors only in my country	Would have live outside my neighborhood
7.	Would exclude from my country	Would have live outside my country

His work looked at race using scales developed by Bogardus (1933) and later works cited by Ethington, but it can also be applied to other social groups

"[s]imilarity on attributes such as attitudes, values, and beliefs will facilitate interpersonal attraction and liking." (p. 31), which will lead to more cohesion and integration within a team and hence to better teamwork performance. They note that diversity can help if it is task relevant, pointing out that "underlying differences, such as differences in functional background, education, or personality, are more often positively related to performance—for example by facilitating creativity or group problem solving—but only when the group process is carefully controlled."

The composition of a team will inevitably change over time as people change positions within the organization, change roles, or even move to other employment. Studies suggest that group performance and cohesiveness correlate more strongly with similarities in attitudes and values than with phenological characteristics (Terborg et al. 1976; Turban and Jones 1988), and that negative outcomes associated with surface-level diversity—ethnicity, social status, and so on—decrease the longer a team remains together (Milliken and Martins 1996).

These findings highlight how important organizational continuity is to organizational functioning. Large turnovers in personnel lead to a drop in overall group functioning as the members of the new team take time to acquire new deep knowledge about one another (Carley 1992; Carley and Hill 2001).

8.3.5   Social Distance

Social distance, a concept introduced by Park (1924), refers to the distance in social terms between two groups or between people. You may find it helpful to think of it in terms of a sense of belonging to a team. The scales for measuring social distance, such as Bogardus' (1933) social distance scale for race, and Westie and Westie's (1956) social distance pyramid for caste and class, are somewhat informal. Table 8.2 shows an example of social distance measures. The table shows that there are problems in these measures (i.e., units are unclear), that it is not an easy measure to create, and that even discussions about social distance can help us understand ourselves and users better.

More recently, social distance has come to be regarded as a continuum rather than discrete levels, stretching from an in-group bias—people just like me—to an out-group bias—people not at all like me (Eveland et al. 1999; Perloff 1993). Developments in network theory (see Chap. 9) also suggest that social distance is a function of the ties between group members rather than just their individual characteristics (Ethington 1997; Granovetter 1973; Wetherell et al. 1994). Nevertheless, the concept of a social distance continuum is a useful way of capturing the influence of culture, particularly as it relates to the development of out-group biases. It is worth noting that many people draw a distinction between social distance and psychological distance (Ginges and Eyal 2009), arguing that there are salient differences between the interactions of individuals who may belong to particular groups (psychological distance), and group-level interactions, where group identity is primary (social distance).

Smaller social distances are generally preferable because they make it easier for team members to both receive support from, and give support to each other, thereby making participation in the group more likely. Conversely, larger social distances increase the likelihood of team members acting against other team members or other groups.

8.3.6 Spatial Distance

Organizations are increasingly using teams that are distributed geographically and temporally. One part of the team can work on a task and, at the end of their day, pass it to a group in another time zone who are just starting their working day. Getting people to perform successfully in this way requires careful planning, because geographic distances between group members mediate the development of familiarity (Ethington 1997), and thus affect group cohesiveness. Notions of familiarity, in turn, act reciprocally to help create communities of practice (Seely Brown and Duguid 1991). Distortions to the perception of space, however, can also distort both the sense of accountability and attachment to others (Grossman 1996).

Spatial relationships influence decisions to participate. If group members are close to us this encourages participation in local activities. The scale of importance varies by task, but in collaboration by researchers, for example, 30 m is an important distance, above which much less collaboration happens (Kraut et al. 1990). Increasing distance will also decrease participation because increased distance weakens our relationship to others. There are both short distance (10–100 m) and large distance (time zone) effects. This may change as ways of connecting change and network bandwidth increases.

8.3.7 Mutual Support and Mutual Surveillance

In addition to issues of social and spatial distance, the nature of the relationships between team members influences team performance. In particular, peer-to-peer and subordinate–superior relationships, which we discuss here, are important (Harrison et al. 1998; Terborg et al. 1976; Turban and Jones 1988). If these relationships change, this can lead to significant and divergent outcomes in team performance (e.g., Grossman 1996).

Team membership offers several benefits. These include a sense of identity and belonging (group norms), guidelines for dealing with ambiguous situations, structuring of chaotic situations, and helping predict the actions of others (e.g., Chekroun and Brauer 2002; Cialdini et al. 1990; Smith and Mackie 1995). Furthermore, social support can help to moderate the effects of stress by buffering members from negative events (e.g., Caplan 1974; Cobb 1976; Epley 1974). The relationship between social support and stress reduction is complex: Sandler and Lakey (1982) found that the benefits of group support varied across individuals in relation to the coping mechanisms used to deal with adverse situations.

On a peer-to-peer level, teams can help regulate behavior. Viewed through the lens of appraisal theory (e.g., Cannon 1932; Festinger 1954; Lazarus and Folkman 1984), for example, group support facilitates participation. Appraisal theory proposes that you judge a task looking at what resources the task requires and what resources you have. If the task requires more than you have, it is a threatening task. If not, it is a challenging task. If you are part of a team, you have more resources, so being in a team will make the task more likely to be seen as challenging rather than threatening.

Where behavior is deviant, however, Chekroun and Brauer (2002) found that if the deviation could be clearly attributed to particular individuals, other team members offered larger and more rapid responses of disapproval of those acts. Contrary to expectations, larger deviations are typically met first with attempts to mediate actor behavior rather than expulsion (Festinger 1954; Liska 1997), as members try to eliminate the discrepancy. As the discrepancy narrows, the pressure for uniformity appears to increase and becomes even greater when either the relevance or the value of group membership increases (Festinger 1954). Simultaneously, however, the impulse to individuate oneself and, for many people, to increase one's relative status ensures a constant state of comparative surveillance, particularly for groups operating in risky situations for prolonged periods (Dinter 1985).

8.3.8 Authority Figures

Team leaders are often expected to exert authority as part of their role. Leadership, authority, and compliance have been extensively studied, most famously by Stanley Milgram (1963). In Milgram's study, participants gave increasingly powerful electrical shocks to volunteer learners, based on commands from the experimenter (an authority figure)—notably, shocks were not in fact delivered but study participants believed they were. The power wielded by the experimenter in this study was not physically coercive or economic, but rather symbolic, in that they were an authority figure in a study. Milgram noted that the goal (the advancement of knowledge) and the location (Yale) influenced participants to acquiesce more readily to the experimenter's demands (Milgram 1963, p. 377). In the Milgram study and subsequent obedience studies (e.g., Haney et al. 1973), belief in the legitimacy and power of the leader led to the leader being granted actual power over the participant.

The effects of authority are moderated by other factors, such as physical proximity. If the team leaders are physically located close to the team, they have more influence on team members. Distant leaders have less authority.

Authority can be expressed in several different ways online, for example, by an email address (e.g., president@psu.edu), by having someone send an email on your behalf (e.g., this is an email for a vice president sent by an admin assistant), by privileges or special tools in a game, and by login names (e.g., admin, webmaster, or root@company.com). How authority is implemented, used, and abused online is still not fully understood, however.

8.3.9 Task Attractiveness

The task that a team has to perform and, hence, its goals influence the behavior of the team. Frank's (1944) and Milgram's (1963) studies both note that obedience of authority depends on having legitimate goals that are related to the organization's mission. More legitimate goals lead to greater participation in systems. In addition, people often indicate in interviews and surveys that goals are a motivating factor in their behavior (Collins 2008; Frank 1944). Representing social goals poses a challenge, in that they emerge at the interface between cognitive and social activity, and hence tend to be more abstract. It can therefore be difficult to evaluate how successfully they have been achieved.

Over time, legitimate goals tend to make group members more compliant, whereas illegitimate goals erode the ability of leaders to influence their subordinates. Making the goals clear, and the payoff for achieving them direct and immediate, are just some ways to make tasks more appealing. Online systems, including computer games, can be designed to take advantage of this. Carma (http://www.car.ma), for example, is an online car ride sharing site where the goal is attractive to users for multiple reasons. The Carma app runs on a smartphone and connects to a server. When you want to travel somewhere, you note where you want to be picked up and how much you are willing to pay. As you drive, or before you drive, you check to see if anyone is looking for a ride.

The success of Carma's system appears to be more dependent on social factors than on technology. If there are not enough drivers and passengers, there will not be enough matches to make its use worthwhile for either driver or passenger. In the past, these rides were arranged informally (e.g., by word of mouth) and using bulletin boards. So the group size, location, and destination will all have an effect. Group size is likely to be a negative factor in rural areas where the group and the population density are both likely to be smaller. On the other hand, group cohesiveness may be greater, as the group members may know each other and be headed to the same destinations. The risks in developing this system do not appear to be technological, but more related to social engineering.

8.3.10   Team Processes and Tasks

It is important to understand the tasks the group is trying to perform. There may be different ways to do the task, and there may be different tasks that can be chosen. Within a volunteer organization, for example, some groups will perform better on activism tasks and some groups will perform better on outreach and education tasks.

The way that tasks are divided between the team members and how the team members communicate will affect team performance. Olson and Olson (2000, 2008) note the importance of the coupling of work, that is, how closely team members have to work together. For technical work and in discussions of risk, for example, the collaborators frequently need to be co-located so that they can communicate fully, whereas in other situations, such as open source software development, remote coupling may be possible.

It is therefore important to adapt the processes to the team and to the tasks. Common ground is a shared set of knowledge, expectations, and understanding about the people on the team and the task. Establishing common ground is an important factor in team performance (Clark and Wilkes-Gibbs 1986; Olson and Olson 2000) and should therefore be encouraged by systems and system designers.

You may also need to think about people's motivation for doing the task in the first place. Pink (2009) argues that boring and repetitive work still requires extrinsic motivation (Pink describes this as Motivation 2.0) to get people to do the tasks, and this was covered in Chap. 4. In those situations where people want to do the work, however, Pink argues that they are intrinsically motivated to do the tasks (he calls this Motivation 3.0). Pink suggests that Motivation 3.0 applies to creative work and leisure, most of design (including design of software, systems and interfaces), many engineering tasks, and most knowledge work.

8.3.11   Implications for System Design

These factors make numerous suggestions about how to design systems, and this section can only note a few for some common systems. For distributed users, like those on YouTube, these factors suggest that it is possible to encourage participation by helping the site seem smaller, perhaps by creating local regions like in Yelp where you search by a town or area. It is directly helpful to have friends identify each other on the site for mutual support; even to make moderate posts might need encouragement, and attempts to provide appropriate distance between people, both increasing it by calling someone Dr. Ritter, and decreasing it by calling him Frank. Allowing people to moderate interaction in online forums (moderators) as legitimate authority figures will help encourage pro-social behavior. Finally, making the goal attractive and noting the goal, payoffs, and value will help people choose to interact.

For collaboration at a distance, as an aspect of system design that will not go away, these factors remain very important too. Each of these factors will help such groups work together. Not directly mentioned, but influenced by all these factors, is trust, and space and time are important factors, being able to meet face to face, in the same place at the same time will, according to these theories, encourage participation, as does the trust across interactions.

8.3.12 Summary

Successful team performance depends on the social context in which the team will operate. This social context is defined by a wide range of factors. The relative weights of these factors and how they should be balanced will vary across systems and settings. Where differences exist between theories in this area they often arise from different assumptions about the teams, their contexts, and the things that can be changed. In general, teams (1) that are more cohesive, (2) who have worked together longer, and (3) who share more values, will perform better and be more likely to achieve their collective goals. When you design your system you should try to support the factors that enable cohesion and the sharing of values. You should also consider whether there are ways in which you can support new team members to bring them up to speed as quickly as possible.

8.4 Factors Affecting Performance in Community Settings

Having considered the factors that affect performance (and behavior) in team settings, it is also important to take a brief look at what happens in less structured settings. There are an increasing number of communities developing (more or less) organically online. Sites such as Yelp, lastminute.com, YouTube, Tripadvisor, and Epicurious now support self-reported consumer ratings, and some comprise only user-generated content. In addition, there is an increasing number of open source communities in a wide range of areas: for software development (e.g., Linux), for knowledge (e.g., Wikipedia), for stock photography (e.g., Open Stock Photography), and for music (e.g., Open Source Music).

Pink (2009) notes that many organizations still use extrinsic motivation theory, and argues that this approach frequently violates what psychological science is telling us. He suggests that what motivates people to participate without payment in these activities and communities is intrinsic motivation, noting that it is more important than extrinsic motivation for many tasks. It is not the perfect panacea, however, and he provides several counter examples of tasks where intrinsic motivation either fails or is not possible.

In community settings, many people get involved in their own time, and without any form of payment. In many ways, although they comprise a community, their motivation is invariably individualistic. These people are intrinsically motivated by the drives of autonomy, mastery, and purpose, as noted in Chap. 4. The tasks that they are doing are intrinsically rewarding, so people should not be given extrinsic rewards for doing them. The intrinsic drives need to be supported through providing feedback (positive and negative to help with mastery), and *now-that* rewards which only occasionally happen. These should not be monetary in order to minimize the likelihood of discouraging or discounting the user's intrinsic motivations to perform the task. The rewards might provide further autonomy, notes, and recognition about mastery, or emphasize the purpose that was served. Alternatively, make any extrinsic rewards a token: many $1 payments for patents get framed and saved, for example, in recognition of a job well done.

8.5 Implications for System Design

Teamwork is highly dependent on communication and collaboration. The team will often need to share information, for example, so that team members can use it to make individual and collective decisions. It is therefore important that your system supports both communication—of both information and outcomes—and collaboration. This may require the use of tools and technologies that are not an inherent part of your designed system, such as video communication. We used Skype as well as email during the writing of this book, for example, to allow the three authors in three different time zones to communicate and share ideas both synchronously and asynchronously.

Group decision making aids typically incorporate features to reduce bad effects and increase good effects of group decision making. These features often include a brain storming session, and anonymizing users counter the effects of hierarchy (organizational power) so that more ideas can be generated without the leader explicitly or implicitly affecting what people are willing to say.

As we have noted throughout the chapters in this book, most systems nowadays are socio-technical systems. In other words, there is a social system that needs to be considered because the technology and the social system will be interdependent and interact. If you do not spend time and effort understanding the existing social system, you run the risk of adversely affecting it. For example, if staff have to spend more time on maintaining and interacting directly with the new technology rather than on the tasks they need to perform, or on communicating plans and results, this will have a detrimental effect on the work processes and outcomes. Ultimately, staff may simply stop using the new technology because it gets in the way of them doing their job.

You should try to design your system in such a way that it minimizes the possibility of diffusion of social responsibility. Things that enable diffusion include getting aggregate rather than individual inputs, allowing people to be anonymous, and setting goals where no specific person is invited to contribute. Techniques that are widely used to help avoid diffusion of responsibility include providing representations of the people involved that can be seen by other users, by allowing reputations to be built according to system usage and expertise, and by making any requests for assistance appear more directed to individuals than to a group.

The attribution of causality suggests that responsibility can be moderated. Partly this has to be done by the user, but the breakout box on email suggests that email systems might be more apologetic and clear about what went wrong, and email systems are getting better about noting how and why mail was not delivered. This knowledge can help the sender understand why the receiver might or might not receive an email. Similar effects and results can be imagined for phone calls, text messages, and IMs.

If you are designing a very large system, of the scale of Yelp, for example, you may want to encourage participation by helping the users perceive the system as being smaller than it really is. To avoid overwhelming the user, Yelp does this by creating local regions where you search by town or area. It can also be helpful to have friendly faces available in the system to provide mutual support, and to provide moderators (in areas like online forums) as legitimate authority figures to help encourage pro-social behavior. You may also need to think about how you provide the appropriate social distance between people using the system (e.g., increasing it by using formal titles, such as Dr. Smith, or reducing it by using first names such as John, or even nicknames).

You will need to think about how and why people are motivated to use your system to carry out their particular tasks. Do they use it because they have to (are they paid to use it to do their job, for example)? Or do they use it because they want to use it (the classic example here being social networking systems)? Is their motivation *extrinsic* or *intrinsic*? That is, are they self-motivated because of their own interest, or because they will get a reward from an external source for doing it? Even in the case of developing a social networking system, there may be a need for extrinsic motivation to make sure that people keep the system active by providing new content, although the rewards for doing this may not be financial. You could highlight how the system increases their mastery, gives them autonomy, and increases the importance of doing the task. The balance between motivations may not always be clear cut. Some learning tasks, for example, will require a coach who sets tasks (which may be necessary, but are not necessarily intrinsically rewarding) for people to complete as part of their learning experience. Any reward structure for task performance needs to be appropriately aligned to teams and to individuals. If the rewards are targeted at individuals, and individual performance, for example, then the likelihood is that the team members will behave as individuals.

In addition to the team level issues, you may also need to think about organizational issues (sometimes referred to as the blunt end of a system, as noted in Chap. 10). If an organization has procedures in place for how a particular job has to be done, for example, then you will need to think about whether these procedures will have to be changed. If the procedures are imposed by a regulatory authority (as in nuclear power, for example) then you may not be able to change those procedures, so you will have to design your system to support those procedures. There can also be cultural effects (on several levels), so there may be a tradition for doing a task in a particular way, which is an effect of organizational culture; we cover this in Chap. 9.

8.6 Summary

Social factors are important. They affect the ways that teams operate, and hence affect system performance. If you are designing systems that will be operated by teams of people, you will need to understand that the ways that teams behave cannot simply be described by generalizing from individual behavior. Care needs to be exercised when generalizing from studies of different types of teams, or from teams doing different tasks in different contexts.

You need to use the results from studies of how teams work intelligently. Teams and their tasks will vary widely. The results probably rely on more factors than are reported, and the type of tasks and types of group members will influence the results but are often assumed to apply to all groups or all tasks. So we should be cautious when generalizing or overgeneralizing from existing results. The results about how teams work may only apply to that type of team with that type of task, rather than all teams (larger and smaller, with different types of people) competing or working in different environments and doing more or less similar tasks. This reflects Clark's (1973) concern about overgeneralization in language research. He noted that it was difficult, and even inappropriate to generalize from a few nouns and verbs to all nouns and verbs—they come from different languages, take different parts of speech as helpers, have different frequencies, and can be radically different in many dimensions—as well as for teams and tasks..

In addition to understanding how teams make decisions and take actions, the factors that influence team performance are important. In particular, the social context of the team your system will support needs to be understood. Often this context will not be static, but will change over time, so you need to understand how and when the various factors that define the social context can change.

There are many examples of how a failure to give appropriate consideration to the social aspects of systems has led to accidents. Casey (1998) notes several including disasters with the Space Shuttle program because they ignored social and political aspects (Starbuck and Farjoun 2005; Vaughan 1997).

8.7 Other Resources

There are a number of general texts about social factors in collaboration and teamwork that are worth reading if you wish to know more about this area. We have cited some in the main body of the chapter (e.g., Ellison 2004; Hinds and Kiesler 2002; Olson and Olson 2008) but there are many more. See, for example, *Intellectual teamwork: social and technological foundations of cooperative work* edited by Galegher, Kraut, and Egido (1990, Hillsdale, NJ: Erlbaum).

There is an extensive literature under the titles "computer-supported cooperative work" (CSCW) and "computer mediated communication" (CMC) where many of the topics we have covered are elaborated in more detail. Conference and journal publications in this area will provide more information and more current information. There are also a number of initiatives in trying to build systems that are smart about how people collaborate, employing computational agents to broker work task accomplishment in teams. See, for example, chapters in Ye and Churchill (eds.) (2003). *Agent supported cooperative work*. Boston, MA: Kluwer.

If you are interested in how to design teams, rather than just how to design systems to support team performance, Vicente (1999) presents a useful approach. He argues for laying out all the tasks that the team will do, effectively a task analysis writ large. Then you group the tasks so that there are natural breaks between sets of tasks, taking into account communication and how tasks interact. He argues that this leads to better team performance because the tasks are more naturally divided.

Work by Judy and Gary Olson are particularly relevant here. They have studied how computer-supported communication changes how teams work, and provide some design advice about how to support teams in such projects:

Olson, G. M., & Olson, J. S. (2007). Groupware and computer supported cooperative work. In J. J. Jacko & A. Sears (Eds.), *Handbook of human-computer interaction (2nd Ed.)*. Mahwah, NJ: Erlbaum.

Olson, G. M., & Olson, J. S. (2003). Mitigating the effects of distance on collaborative intellectual work. *Economics of Innovation and New Technologies, 12*, 27–42.

8.8 Exercises

8.1 Look through the list of the ways that email has gone awry, See how many examples you can find of (a) diffusion of social responsibility, (b) pluralistic ignorance, (c) attribution errors, and (d) majority/minority effects.

8.2 Imagine you are working on a project where the team is distributed across three locations, all in different time zones. You have been asked to identify videoconferencing tools that can be used to carry out monthly progress meetings and to select the best one for the job. List the factors that you would use to inform your decision, and explain why they are important.

8.3 You are managing a soccer team, where daily training routines are partly determined by the combination of the players' individual circumstances. The players are asked to record their weight, calorie intake, and exercises each morning using an app on their smartphone. Explain how you would motivate the players to provide this data every day before setting off for the training ground.

8.4 Choose an online, social web site, such as Facebook, YouTube, or Yelp. Sketch several tasks that can be done by users with the site. Describe the intrinsic and extrinsic motivation(s) for users to perform those tasks. Do the same for an online course site, and for an online game. Note at least four insights that arise from doing this analysis.

8.5 Consider the organization where you currently work (or are a student). Try to identify at least two people within that organization who are simultaneously members of several teams, and explain where the boundaries occur that delineate those teams.

8.6 Find a game that is designed to help someone learn a complex skill, such as World of Warcraft. Examine what components of that game are training individual skills and what are training social skills. Also, note if the game has collaborative or competitive or educational elements across learners.

8.7 Consider how forming, storming, norming, and performing can be done without technology and with technology for group class projects. Consider how these processes are done and could be done better in the workplace.

8.8 Generate a job description with at least eight activities for an office job where telecommuting occurs (e.g., sales, professor, management, software engineer, student). Discuss how technology might replace or support doing each task and note how many of these tasks can and cannot be performed remotely and what social activities are included. Using this analysis, provide suggestions for teleworkers.

References

Abelson, R. P., Frey, K. P., & Gregg, A. P. (2004). *Experiments with people: Revelations from social psychology*. Mahwah, NJ: Erlbaum.

Bales, R. F., & Borgatta, E. F. (1955). Size of group as a factor in the interaction profile. In A. P. Hare, E. F. Borgatta, & R. F. Bales (Eds.), *Small groups: Studies in social interaction* (pp. 495–512). Toronto: Random House.

Bales, R. F., Strodtbeck, F. L., Mills, T. M., & Roseborough, M. E. (1951). Channels of communication in small groups. *American Sociological Review, 16*, 461–468.

Bateson, N. (1966). Familiarization, group discussion and risk taking. *Journal of Experimental Social Psychology, 2*, 119–129.

Benenson, J. F., Gordon, A. J., & Roy, R. (2000). Children's evaluative appraisals of competition in tetrads versus dyads. *Small Group Research, 31*(6), 635–652.

Birnbaum, R. (1988). *How colleges work*. San Francisco: Jossey-Bass.

Bly, S., & Churchill, E. F. (1999). Design through matchmaking: Technology in search of users. *Interactions, 6*(2), 23–31.

Bogardus, E. S. (1933). A social distance scale. *Sociology and Social Research, 17*, 265–271.

Bogardus, E. S. (1967). *A forty year racial distance study*. Los Angeles: University of Southern California.

Booher, H. R., & Minninger, J. (2003). Human systems integration in army systems acquisition. In H. R. Booher (Ed.), *Handbook of human systems integration* (pp. 663–698). Hoboken, NJ: Wiley.

Brooks, F. P. (1975). *The mythical man-month: Essays on software engineering*. Reading, MA: Addison-Wesley.

Byrne, D. (1971). *The attraction paradigm*. New York, NY: Academic Press.

Cannon, W. B. (1932). *The wisdom of the body*. New York, NY: Norton.

Caplan, G. (1974). *Support systems and community mental health: Lectures on concept development*. New York: Behavioral Publications.

Carley, K. M. (1992). Organizational learning and personnel turnover. *Organizational Science, 3*(1), 20–46.

Carley, K. M., & Hill, V. (2001). Structural change and learning within organizations. In A. Lomi & E. R. Larsen (Eds.), *Dynamics of organizations: Computational modeling and organizational theories* (pp. Ch. 2. pp. 63–92). Live Oak: MIT Press/AAAI Press.

Cartwright, D. (1968). The nature of group cohesiveness. In D. Cartwright & A. Zander (Eds.), *Group dynamics: Research and theory* (pp. 91–118). New York, NY: Harper & Row.

Casey, S. M. (1998). *Set phasers on stun: And other true tales of design, technology, and human error*. Santa Barbara, CA: Aegean.

Chekroun, P., & Brauer, M. (2002). The bystander effect and social control behavior: The effect of the presence of others on people's reactions to norm violations. *European Journal of Social Psychology, 32*(6), 853–867.

Churchill, E. F., & Bly, S. (2000). Culture vultures: Considering culture and communication in virtual environments. *SIG Group Bulletin, 21*(1), 6–11.

Churchill, E. F., Trevor, J., Bly, S., Nelson, L., & Cubranic, D. (2000). Anchored conversations. Chatting in the context of a document. In *CHI 2000 Conference Proceedings* (pp. 454–461). New York, NY: ACM Press.

Cialdini, R. B., Reno, R. R., & Kallgren, C. A. (1990). Focus theory of normative conduct: Recycling the concept of norms to reduce littering in public places. *Journal of Personality and Social Psychology, 58*(6), 1015–1026.

Clark, H. H. (1973). The language-as-fixed-effect fallacy: A critique of language statistics in psychological research. *Journal of Verbal Learning and Verbal Behavior, 12*, 335–359.

Clark, H. H., & Wilkes-Gibbs, D. (1986). Referring as a collaborative process. *Cognition, 22*, 1–39.

Cobb, S. (1976). Social support as a moderator of life stress. *Psychosomatic Medicine,38*(5), 300–314.

Collins, B. E., & Guetzkow, H. (1964). *A social psychology of group processes for decision-making*. New York, NY: Wiley.

Collins, R. (2008). *Violence: A micro-sociological theory*. Princeton, NJ: Princeton University Press.

Darley, J. M., & Batson, C. D. (1973). "From Jerusalem to Jericho": A study of situational and dispositional variables in helping behavior. *Journal of Personality and Social Psychology, 27*, 100–108.

Dinter, E. (1985). *Hero or coward: Pressures facing the soldier in battle*. Totowa, NJ: Frank Cass and Company Limited.

Ellison, N. B. (2004). *Telework and social change: How technology is reshaping the boundaries between home and work*. Westport, CT: Praeger.

Epley, S. W. (1974). Reduction of the behavioral effects of aversive stimulation by the presence of companions. *Psychological Bulletin, 81*(5), 271–283.

Ethington, P. J. (1997). The intellectual construction of "social distance": Toward a recovery of Georg Simmel's social geometry. *Cybergeo: European Journal of Geography, 30*. http://cybergeo.revues.org/index227.html

Eveland, W, Jr, Nathanson, A. I., Detenber, B. H., & McLeod, D. M. (1999). Rethinking the social distance corollary: Perceived likelihood of exposure and the third-person perception. *Communication Research, 26*(3), 275–302.

Festinger, L. (1954). A theory of social comparison processes. *Human Relations, 7*(2), 117–140.

Frank, J. D. (1944). Experimental studies of personal pressure and resistance: I. Experimental production of resistance. *Journal of General Psychology, 30*, 23–41.

Ginges, J., & Eyal, S. (2009). Psychological distance, group size and intergroup relations. In *Proceedings of the 32nd International Society of Political Psychology* (pp. 51–65). Dublin, Ireland: ISSP.

Granovetter, M. (1973). The strength of weak ties. *American Journal of Sociology, 78*, 1360–1380.

Grossman, D. (1996). *On killing: The psychological cost of learning to kill in war and society.* New York: Back Bay Books, Little Brown and Company.

Haney, C., Banks, W. C., & Zimbardo, P. G. (1973). *Study of prisoners and guards in a simulated prison.* Washington, DC: Office of Naval Research (ONR).

Hare, A. P. (1952). A study of interaction and consensus in different sized groups. *American Sociological Review, 17*, 261–267.

Harrison, D. A., Price, K. H., & Bell, M. P. (1998). Beyond relational demography: Time and the effects of surface and deep level diversity on work group cohesion. *The Academy of Management Journal, 41*(1), 96–107.

Heath, C., & Luff, P. (2000). *Technology in action.* Cambridge, UK: Cambridge University Press.

Hinds, P., & Kiesler, S. (Eds.). (2002). *Distributed work.* Cambridge, MA: MIT Press.

Hollnagel, E. (2007). Flight decks and free flight: Where are the system boundaries? *Applied Ergonomics, 38*(4), 409–416.

Jones, E. E., Kanouse, D. E., Kelley, H. H., Nisbett, R. E., Valins, S., & Weiner, B. (1971/1972). *Attribution: Perceiving the causes of behavior.* New York: General Learning Press.

Kanki, B., Helmreich, R. L., & Arca, J. (Eds.). (2010). *Crew resource management* (2nd ed.). London, UK: Academic Press.

Keltner, D., & Marsh, J. (2006–2007). We are all bystanders. *Greater Good, 3*(2). http://greatergood.berkeley.edu/greatergood/archive/2006fallwinter/keltnermarsh.html

Kozlowski, S. W. J., & Ilgen, D. R. (2006). Enhancing the effectiveness of work groups and teams. *Psychological Science in the Public Interest, 7*(3), 77–124.

Kraut, R. E., Egido, C., & Galegher, J. (1990). Patterns of contact and communication in scientific research collaborations In J. Galegher, R. E. Kraut, & C. Egido (Eds.), *Intellectual teamwork: Social and technological foundations of cooperative work* (pp. 149–171). Hillsdale, NJ: Erlbaum.

Lazarus, R. S., & Folkman, S. (1984). *Stress, appraisal and coping.* New York: Springer Publishing.

Liska, A. E. (1997). Modeling the relationships between macro forms of social control. *Annual Review of Sociology, 23*(1), 39–61.

Mannix, E., & Neale, M. A. (2005). What differences make a difference? The promise and reality of diverse teams in organizations. *Psychological Science in the Public Interest, 6*(2), 31–55.

McCauley, C. (1989). The nature of social influence in groupthink: Compliance and internalization. *Journal of Personality and Social Psychology, 57*, 250–260.

McGrath, J. E. (1984). *Groups: Interaction and process.* Englewood Cliffs, NJ: Prentice-Hall.

McNeese, M. D. (2000). Socio-cognitive factors in the acquisition and transfer of knowledge. *Cognition, Technology and Work, 2*, 164–177.

Milgram, S. (1963). Behavioral study of obedience. *Journal of Abnormal and Social Psychology, 67*(4), 371–378.

Milliken, F. J., & Martins, L. L. (1996). Searching for common threads: Understanding the multiple effects of diversity in organizational groups. *Academy of Management Journal, 25*, 598–606.

Morgan, J. H., Morgan, G. P., & Ritter, F. E. (2010). A preliminary model of participation for small groups. *Computational and Mathematical Organization Science, 16*, 246–270.

Newcomb, T. M. (1961). *The acquaintance process.* New York: Holt, Rinehart, & Winston.

O'Reilly, C. A, I. I. I., Caldwell, D. F., & Barnett, W. P. (1989). Work group demography, social integration, and turnover. *Administrative Science Quarterly, 34*, 21–37.

Olson, G. M., & Olson, J. S. (2000). Distance matters. *Human–Computer Interaction, 15*, 139–179.

Olson, G. M., & Olson, J. S. (2008). *Computer-supported cooperative work.* New York: Wiley.

Park, R. E. (1924). The concept of social distance as applied to the study of racial attitudes and racial relations. *Journal of Applied Sociology, 8*, 339–344.

Perloff, R. M. (1993). Third-person effect research 1983–1992: A review and synthesis. *International Journal of Public Opinion Research, 5*, 167–184.

Pink, D. H. (2009). *Drive.* New York: Riverhead Books.

Ross, L., Amabile, T. M., & Steinmetz, J. L. (1977). Social roles, social control, and biases in social-perception processes. *Journal of Personality and Social Psychology, 35*, 485–494.

Salas, E., Priest, H. A., & Burke, C. S. (2005). Teamwork and team performance measurement. In J. Wilson & N. Corlett (Eds.), *Evaluation of human work* (3rd ed., pp. 793–808). Boca Raton, FL: CRC Press.

Salas, E., Wilson, K. A., Burke, C. S., & Bowers, C. A. (2002). Myths about crew resource training. *Ergonomics in Design, 10*(4), 21–24.

Sandler, I. R., & Lakey, B. (1982). Locus of control as a stress moderator: The role of control perceptions and social support. *American Community Journal of Psychology, 10*(1), 65–80.

Seely Brown, J., & Duguid, P. (1991). Organizational learning and communities-of-practice: Toward a unified view of working, learning and innovation. *Organization Science, 2*(1), 40–57.

Shalit, B. (1988). *The psychology of conflict and combat.* New York: Praeger Publishers.

Sheridan, T. B., & Ferrell, W. R. (1974). *Man–machine systems: Information, control, and decision models of human performance.* Cambridge, MA: MIT Press.

Smith, E. R., & Mackie, D. M. (1995). *Social psychology.* New York: Worth Publishers.

Starbuck, W. H., & Farjoun, M. (Eds.). (2005). *Organization at the limit: Lessons from the Columbia disaster.* Malden, MA: Blackwell Publishing.

Stoner, J. A. F. (1968). Risky and cautious shifts in group decisions: The influence of widely held values. *Journal of Experimental Social Psychology, 4*, 442–459.

Terborg, J. R., Castore, C., & DeNinno, J. A. (1976). A longitudinal field investigation of the impact of group composition on group performance and cohesion. *Journal of Personality and Social Psychology, 34*, 782–790.

Turban, D. B., & Jones, A. P. (1988). Supervisor-subordinate similarity: Types, effects, and mechanisms. *Journal of Applied Psychology, 73*, 228–234.

Vaughan, D. (1997). *The Challenger launch decision: Risky technology, culture, and deviance at NASAw.* Chicago: University of Chicago Press.

Vicente, K. (1999). *Cognitive work analysis.* Mahwah, NJ: Erlbaum.

Wallach, M. A., Kogan, N., & Bem, D. J. (1964). Diffusion of responsibility and level of risk taking in groups. *Journal of Abnormal and Social Psychology, 68*, 263–274.

Westie, F. R., & Westie, M. L. (1956). The social-distance pyramid: Relationships between caste and class. *American Journal of Sociology, 63*, 190–196.

Wetherell, C., Plakans, A., & Wellman, B. (1994). Networks, neighborhoods, and communities: Approaches to the study of the community question. *Urban Affairs Quarterly, 14*(3), 363–390.

Wiener, E., Kanki, B., & Helmreich, R. L. (Eds.). (1993). *Cockpit Resource Management.* London, UK: Academic Press.

Chapter 9
Social: Theories and Models

Abstract In the previous chapter we introduced concepts related to teams and teamwork. This chapter provides concepts for analyzing, interpreting, and modeling how teams work. We turn to models of social communication and coordination that have gained prominence as we think about people in technical and social networks and at higher levels of organization. This chapter introduces some of the many concepts, theories, and results related to social processes that can influence system design, and also notes how to model social processes for use as theories and for applications.

9.1 Introduction

As distributed, networked computing systems have become increasingly part of our everyday lives, new models for understanding group and team communication have arisen. Kang (2000, p. 1150) has noted that for the Internet, at least, the killer app is other people. It is certainly the case that our understanding of human–human interaction has evolved since the introduction of rich media connections. In part this is due to the fact that so many new forms of interaction have arisen since the development of the Internet. Thirty years ago, the idea that we would be able to videoconference in real time with colleagues and friends on the other side of the planet from a mobile phone was considered science fiction. Now it is a frequent if not commonplace occurrence.

In addition to making use of these innovations, we are also able to mine and analyze behavioral data at fine-grained levels of detail. All transactions online can be recorded and studied for interaction patterns at various levels of abstraction. Studies have combined observational and logged, transaction and activity data to look at email use in organizations (e.g., Desanctis and Monge 1998) and across national and cultural boundaries (Rutkowski et al. 2002), to study the use of text-based virtual environments for work coordination and collaboration (Churchill and Bly 1999), to consider how graphical virtual environments enable collaborative

F. E. Ritter et al., *Foundations for Designing User-Centered Systems*, 253
DOI: 10.1007/978-1-4471-5134-0_9, © Springer-Verlag London 2014

activity (Fig. 9.1; also see Churchill et al. 2001), to address how real-time rendering and manipulation of data visualizations affect mediated collaborations (Snowdon et al. 2003), and to understand more deeply the impact of networked mobile devices on ongoing work and recreational practices (e.g., Brown et al. 2001). Research is turning to consideration of how tools like LinkedIn, Facebook, and Twitter play into organizational information sharing (e.g., Zhao and Rosson 2009), and how enterprises are using their own internal bookmark sharing tools to foster deeper collaboration between their staff (e.g., Millen et al. 2006).

Figure 9.2 reminds us that social aspects of systems, like other aspects of interfaces noted earlier, do not guarantee success. They are just another factor to consider—another cause of risks, or another way to ameliorate risks in systems.

In this chapter we complement content in Chap. 8, introducing concepts, theory, and data related to social aspects of face-to-face and mediated communication and collaboration in our current world of pervasive, networked connectivity.

9.2 Analyzing How People Work Together

9.2.1 Introduction

As discussed in Chap. 8, people work together in different ways. Ideally you want them to collaborate and cooperate to carry out any shared tasks that they may have. When designing a system this means that you want to support collaboration and cooperation where it is appropriate, and avoid having people spend time interacting with the system when they should be more concerned with carrying out the task at hand. It is, therefore, important to understand how people collaborate and cooperate.

There are several ways in which social interactions can be analyzed. Here we consider three types of analysis that are quite widely used. The first type is fairly informal and is often used to analyze pairwise interactions, as happens in conversation, for example. The second analyzes interactions in terms of costs and benefits, and is sometimes described as a payoff approach. The third involves applying network theory to emphasize the inter-relationships between actors across interactions.

9.2.2 Informal, Pairwise Analyses

The simplest way of analyzing social interactions is fairly informal. It simply notes results and regularities that appear in social behavior. This is a type of framework in that it provides some common terms across analyses, and some basic assumptions, but does not provide or require that the results across analyses fit

Fig. 9.1 View of an author's avatar in second life watching another avatar give a talk to a live audience that was also broadcast into second life. This set-up, which was used to support remote viewing at a workshop on social modeling, shows how social interactions can occur simultaneously at multiple levels

Fig. 9.2 Including social aspects in your computer application (i.e., Zune), however, does not guarantee success compared to systems with less social aspects. (Photo taken at Circuit City in February 2009, as Circuit City was having a going-out-of-business sale)

together, and it is not organized on a higher level. This level of analysis is often used to look at how pairs of actors interact in a local manner, for example, during conversation and turn-taking in conversation. The framework varies widely between researchers, and is not extensively covered here because it varies so widely and is difficult to build a model from. However, it is often used, and provides some insights to help build systems.

When people work together on a one-to-one basis (in *dyads* or pairs), the way they communicate can be understood using techniques such as conversation analysis and linguistic analyses of the creation of a shared model or *common ground* (e.g., Clark and Brennan 1991a, b; Gottman et al. 2005; Sacks 1992; ten Have 1999). The notion of common ground also applies to communication among larger groups.

If you analyze how people talk to one another you will quickly see that it is rare for them to speak in full sentences and to always wait politely for the other person to finish before starting to speak themselves. The overall aim of this level of analysis is usually to generate a shared mutual understanding of the situation at hand. This can provide insights of how to support computer-supported communication (see, for example, Brennan 1998). For example, if the length of a pause in conversation is 1s, then if there are lags in the network approaching 1s, some users will start talking too soon (Ruhleder and Jordan 1999). If the task is computer-based (or at least requires information from the system), you will need to understand what sort of information is needed and used, and present it in such a way that it helps to facilitate a shared mental model of the situation between those communicating. Conversational analysis and the concept of common ground also are useful for analyzing larger groups.

9.2.3 Exchange Costs and Benefits

The second type of analysis involves looking at the costs and benefits of social interactions, a so-called payoff approach. In this approach, each interaction has associated with it a cost, a benefit (sometimes called a payoff), or both. Work in game theory will often lump costs and benefits together and call them payoffs. This approach has been used in many fields, but it is probably most closely associated with economics where it is extensively used (e.g., Levitt and Dubner 2005).

There are situations where people who are supposed to work together to achieve a particular goal, or perform a particular task, do not do so. Instead, they may pursue individual goals and decide what is best for themselves on the basis of the costs and benefits involved. In many cases, the payoffs are not financial rewards, but can be things like improved social status, for example, which is how companies entice people to provide useful content for their internal social networking applications.

The problems that can arise when people pursue individual goals (and payoffs) are highlighted by the classical Prisoner's Dilemma (PD) problem (Axelrod 1984). The central dilemma is whether to think about the costs and payoffs altruistically (as they affect the pair jointly), or as they affect each prisoner individually. You can see the costs and payoffs by drawing a matrix for all of the actors involved, like that shown in Table 9.1 for a Prisoner's Dilemma problem with two prisoners.

In the Prisoner's Dilemma, two prisoners have been caught doing something illegal, and can either plead not guilty or plead guilty giving state's evidence

Table 9.1 A typical prisoner's dilemma payoff matrix

Prisoner 1	Prisoner 2	
	Cooperate (with prisoner 1)	Defect (on prisoner 1)
Cooperate (with prisoner 2)	Both prisoners get 1 year in jail	10 years for prisoner 1 Prisoner 2 goes free
Defect (on prisoner 2)	10 years for prisoner 2 Prisoner 1 goes free	Both prisoners get 8 years in jail

against the other. These two decisions or strategies are usually called cooperate (with the other prisoner) or defect (on the other prisoner). The payoff if the two prisoners cooperate with each other and plead not-guilty is that they both go to prison for 1 year. If one prisoner defects and testifies against the other, they walk free but the other prisoner serves 10 years. If both prisoners defect, they share the full blame and get 8 years each.

Where there are costs and benefits involved in carrying out shared tasks, the costs should be kept as low as possible (not necessarily minimized), and the benefits should be kept as high as possible (not necessarily maximized). In any trade-off the benefits should be designed to outweigh the costs. If you think of online file sharing and email, for example, these have both radically reduced the costs of sharing information, sometimes with unanticipated effects, such as too much sharing.

Using a payoff matrix approach can be helpful in representing tasks where social interaction is involved, even if there is no dilemma involved. Thus a matrix can be used to show the payoff for asking questions in class, for responding to emails, and so on. The payoff matrix approach can be applied to situations that involved more than two strategies, more payoffs, and more players, although it becomes harder to draw the matrix as the numbers involved increase. You should also note that the players do not need to have equivalent payoffs: for example, the payoffs for teachers and for students in a class are different.

Note that some matrices do not have a single best choice (when there is a stable choice that maximizes the payoff for both parties, it is known as a Nash equilibrium point). If you have played Paper Rock Scissors, you know that paper covers rock, that rock breaks scissors, and that scissors cuts paper—there is not a choice that beats all the others. Similarly, if you play video games, you can create payoff matrices for different pieces playing against each other, for example, in Command and Conquer, for tanks vs tanks, tanks vs infantry, and tanks vs planes, etc. In each case, there may not be a dominant decision or choice that is better than all others.

Axelrod (1984) studied what happens when the PD game is played multiple times, also called an iterated Prisoner's Dilemma game. When the game is played repeatedly there is a chance for cooperation to emerge. If you defect early, your colleague may stop trusting you. If you cooperate longer, some opponents may not defect. If the game is ongoing, the promise of cooperation with a positive payoff

Table 9.2 Suggestions for how to do well in iterated PD games (Axelrod 1984)

1. Do not be envious: if you are envious in a situation where the payoffs are not symmetrical—the other player gains more when you both cooperate—you may be tempted to defect, but in doing so you may hurt yourself as well as the other player
2. Do not be the first to defect: this will allow you the chance to make a series of cooperative turns
3. Reciprocate both cooperation and defection: if the other person is choosing to defect and to cooperate, modifying your strategies reminds them of the potential payoff, and encourages them to choose a long-term strategy
4. Do not be too clever: you may be tempted to defect more often to take a little payoff now and then. This may be possible in some games against some players, but Axelrod showed that this strategy rarely ever works. In the real world, it appears to work sometimes, but often it does not

Table 9.3 Suggestions for how to promote cooperation between actors (Axelrod 1984)

1. Enlarge the shadow of the future
2. Change the payoffs
3. Teach people to care about each other
4. Teach reciprocity
5. Improve recognition abilities

for cooperation can lead to the best behavior for both participants. Overall, Axelrod found that a very good—and perhaps the best—strategy was to play tit-for-tat, which involves starting by cooperating, then if an opponent defects, you defect once, and then cooperate again.

There are several practical suggestions for improving social situations arising out of Axelrod's work. These suggestions, some of which are noted in Table 9.2, can be applied to system design, and you can see them play out on eBay, on YouTube, and in Second Life. These suggestions apply to teamwork across a wide range of domains. When they are applied across companies, however, they can give rise to cartels and price fixing.

One thing that you will need to consider when designing systems that support teamworking is that it will often take time for people to learn how to work together. In other words, the strategies that they start with may change over time as they learn how each other operates, and how they can work together to perform the task at hand. In repeated iterations of the Prisoner's Dilemma game, for example, Axelrod (1984) found that people can move towards a strategy of mutual cooperation over time. So you should try to support cooperation, and Axelrod suggested five ways in which this can be achieved, as shown in Table 9.3.

These suggestions apply to many situations, including classrooms, work environments (including knowledge sharing tools), web site maintenance, online auction sites, and public discussion forums.

To *enlarge the shadow of the future* you need to have people look beyond the current iteration of the task. They need to see that there is a bigger picture in that there may be higher level, longer term goals that need to be achieved, and that this task will be repeated, usually by the same people. This should help to change the perspective of the team members from one that may be initially oriented towards competition to one that supports cooperation.

The second suggestion, change the *payoffs*, is perhaps the easiest to influence. In the case of online communities this can be done by noting which people contribute the most. The form of the payoffs needs to be carefully worked out. They need not necessarily be financial. In social networks, prestige and recognition (which raise an individual's perceived status) are often valued more highly as rewards than monetary incentives.

To *teach people to care about each other* requires including other people's payoffs in your own matrix. This may be purely altruistic, when team members care about other team members. In some cases, such as the prisoner's dilemma, other people's payoffs may influence your own payoff (positively or negatively).

The fourth suggestion is to *teach reciprocity*. Participants should be taught to use tit-for-tat strategies. In social situations some people will always adopt a straight cooperation strategy, whilst others will adopt a defection strategy. Having some participants play tit-for-tat (reciprocity) and change strategy based on what others do helps to police the environment and protect those who cannot or will not follow a more aggressive strategy.

Finally, the need to *improve recognition abilities* relates to the issue of trust. Most web sites with forums require you to register to make comments. When you buy online you want to know who you are interacting with. Companies, both real and online, tell you how long they have existed, how to find and contact them, and what organizations they belong to (like chambers of commerce). By making themselves more recognizable (and establishing their credentials), others can tell who they are working with, and can expect to find them again if they return later to the same place.

Note that cooperation is not necessarily always a good thing. In regulation, rule enforcement, and auditing situations, for example, you do not want the inspectors to have a long-term relationship with the party being inspected. Long-term relationships in these cases lead to cooperation, not enforcement.

You should also be aware that supporting teamwork with team goals may lead to social loafing. This is where team members get a payoff based on the team's overall performance, rather than on their individual performance. Some team members may decide that this means that they can achieve their payoff without pulling their weight and contributing as much as the other members.

All these suggestions can be used to improve social interactions in large, complex systems where social factors are at play. Consider as an example eBay. On an individual level it implements many or all of these suggestions: eBay does not publish the profits of individuals (it cannot, but it would not). It does not defect; it cooperates and prosecutes (or drops sellers). It does not have a complex set of rules. On the level of its community, it encourages through its page design future sales. It takes steps to make the payoffs better with cooperation between buyer and seller and with eBay. We do not know whether it teaches about caring about one another, but eBay itself will help teach reciprocity—if you violate their rules they will remove you from the system. And, finally, it certainly cares about and works towards improving the ability to recognize buyers and sellers, serving as a type of recognition for sellers.

9.2.4 Networks

Another way to analyze social interactions is by using network theory (see, for example, Rainie et al. 2012; Watts 2003). This approach emphasizes how the actors are associated across multiple interactions, including how well connected they are, and who they are connected to.

People are linked to other people in many different ways. They can have family connections, or they may be work colleagues, for example. These relationships are a type of social capital. They can be represented using networks, which can be drawn graphically, showing people as nodes, and the relationships as links. An example of a network is shown in Fig. 9.3. Node 13 is the least well connected; node 14 has the most connections; nodes 6, 7, and 14 have the strongest connections. A more complex example is included as Sect. 9.2.5. The way that networks function can have some implications for the system that you are designing.

Leadership in networks. It is often useful to be aware of which nodes in a network are the most important, because all the nodes may not be equally important. If you know which nodes link groups within the network, you can make use of them to beneficial effect. This is what advertisers attempt to do when they plan campaigns. If they target the nodes (people, locations, etc.) which link groups together, this can lead to campaigns going viral, rather than just being of interest to a local group in a network. A more complex example is included in the breakout box explaining how connections influence work in an electronics firm.

The distance between two nodes can be calculated by identifying all the other nodes you need to pass through to get from the start node to the end node, and then adding up all the pairwise path lengths (between the adjacent nodes). If the two nodes are important (to the operation of the network, or the organization, and so on), then you may want to make sure there is more than one way to get from the start node to the end node, so that you can cope with failures of nodes or links. It turns out that the number of links that you need to get from one person to another can be quite small. This so-called *small world problem* is the basis for the film *The Six Degrees of Kevin Bacon*. Essentially, you know somebody who knows somebody who… who knows somebody who knows Kevin Bacon.

The small world phenomena. Perhaps the most common idea is based on connectivity between nodes, that is, what is the shortest path between two nodes? How many people would a letter from one person to another have to pass through, or how many introductions would you have to have to meet Brad Pitt? In a company or even the world, what is the longest path between any two people?

Fig. 9.3 An example small network. Nodes are agents. *Solid lines* are solid connections. *Dashed lines* are weaker connections

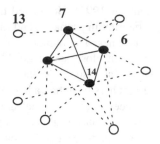

Mathematically, this problem is well defined. The answer is the maximum length of a path between every pair of nodes in a network. A more complete answer is the distribution of path lengths, that is, what are all the paths lengths for the network. Some networks, linearly connected, would have the longest average. These would be like telegraph stations in the old west. Networks that are completely connected, where every node knows every other node, like a grade school classroom, would have a maximum length of 1. Unconnected nodes would have either an undefined answer or infinity as their path length. If you were looking at this in a more applied context, you might also examine the cost of the links (e.g., the distance between people, and how much information can pass between them).

This question has been studied a few times, and the answers are less clear for people in more interesting situations. Milgram (1967) performed the first experiment. In this experiment he handed out a folder to be sent to someone the initiating agent did not know. He recorded how many people the folder passed through before it reached the target. The results were reported as between two and ten, with five as the median. The study, while intriguing, is deeply flawed. Most of the folders were not successfully returned, but we do not really know why. It could be that the world is large, or that the subjects were not motivated or the task was too hard. The minimum was not six, but ten, and it was a distribution. Numerous attempts have been made to duplicate this work. Later work with the real world (e.g., Travers and Milgram 1969) and with email (e.g., Dodds et al. 2003) has had the same problems, that of not having every package delivered (sometimes around 1%). On the other hand, work with closed worlds—for example, how well scientific authors are connected—does not find a minimum, because there are lots of unconnected nodes that only publish one paper. The averages, however, seem to suggest that those that are connected are not so far apart.

What does this mean for system design? It suggests that providing referrals can be worthwhile but not guaranteed. It suggests that most—but probably not all—people are well connected, that pairs of people who are long strings of connections apart are somewhat rare. It remains an interesting theory and empirical problem that is difficult to study completely because of the difficulty in obtaining complete data.

The Dunbar number. Some people may only have a single connection (they would have to have at least one connection to be part of a network), whilst others may have lots of connections. The maximum number of connections, or the largest degree that a node can have in a social network, is called the Dunbar number

(Dunbar 1992). He related the maximum productive group size to the size of the neocortex in primates, and in reference to strong social relationships, not distant or distal ones. The number is related to the question "how much time do you have to maintain close social ties"? Some of his ideas do not fully apply to the online world, and some of the data he presents seem anecdotal. Further writers and researchers have had a hard time coming to grips with the question; for example, it has been speculated that the scientific subspecialties can't be more than 150 scientists because of this effect (but this then implies that either the scientists have no other friends, or that they can handle exactly twice as many as other people!). How do you measure relationship strength? What counts as a strong relationship? Does improved communication media improve the ability to have a larger number of ties? Nevertheless, it remains a useful question, and has implications for system design, and limits are being applied in some systems.

What is perhaps most important from a system design point of view is the active connections. In other words, the connections that are used rather than dormant. If you think about Facebook, for example, some people will boast about having, say, 352 Facebook *friends*, but when you analyze how many people they really interact with, the number is much smaller, by a factor of between 10 and 100. If all of the Facebook friend connections were active, it would be a full time job for an individual just to monitor their friend's ongoing activity.

The concept of the Dunbar number provides suggestions of how many social connections systems should support. For example, how many email aliases should you support in an email program, or how many names can be on an email alias? What are optimal sized online groups? Can a classroom of 150 students (online or in a building) be a group, or can it only be a group of groups?

9.2.5 Good Personal Social Networks Lead to Better Work[1]

Burt (2004) examined how well the managers in an electronics company were connected to other parts of the company. This work serves as a good example of what implications there are for and from networks for designing teams and systems to support them, as well as how social networks influence systems. Burt computed how connectedness correlated with objective measures of job performance (i.e., salary and promotions) and how well connectedness correlated with subjective measures of performance (i.e., job evaluations and evaluations of their ideas by supervisors).

This is a type of network analysis, in that Burt examined how the managers were connected to groups in the company, and to whom. A summary is shown in Fig. 9.4. He also used the term *structural holes*, which occur when two groups that should be connected are not. For example, if two groups working on related,

---

[1] Umer Farooq brought this work to our attention as part of a talk by Peter Pirolli. We thank Umer and Peter for their help.

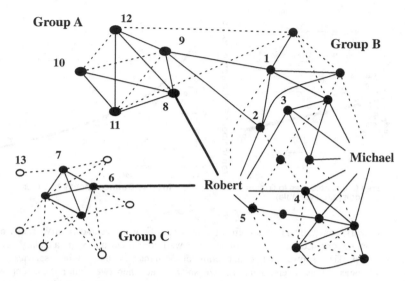

Fig. 9.4 A picture of a network of relationships. The people are the represented by the nodes, and the relationships by the links between nodes (based on data from Burt 2004, Fig. 1, simplified)

but different, topics should know about each other's work, but do not, then a structural hole is said to exist. Management works hard to avoid such a lack of connections, but there are often more holes than management can know about and fill. (Informal connections, family connections, and company sports teams are ways that such holes are sometimes filled). Figure 9.4 shows a structural hole between groups A and C—there is no direct connection between the two groups.

Burt's results showed the importance of social networks in work settings. Managers that were better connected (had less network constraints on having people to talk with) had greater compensation, better evaluations, more promotions, and better ideas as judged by their peers. Some of these results are shown in Fig. 9.5, which shows that being better connected (lower network constraints) led to higher salaries and better ratings of ideas by a neutral party. Overall, being better connected led to better performance in this type of job.

This work makes several suggestions. It shows the utility of social network analyses. It suggests that good workers will attempt to be well connected, and that managers should attempt to fill in the gaps between groups.

9.2.6 Summary

This section has laid out several ways to organize social behavior, several frameworks for organizing the information in this chapter and from later

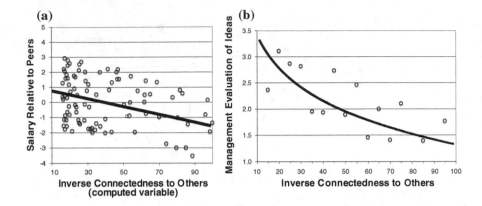

Fig. 9.5 Network constraint is a measure of how large, how close, and relative ranks of a manager's connections. Low constraint indicates a well-connected manager. **a** Salary versus inverse network size shows that better connected managers had higher salaries, and **b** Ratings of ideas versus inverse network size shows that when two senior managers were asked to rate ideas the better connected managers had more highly rated ideas (based on Burt 2004, Fig. 4 and 5, but drawn with a spreadsheet available on the book website to explore this topic)

readings. These frameworks use a high level of abstraction. They provide you with a way to organize what you learn. It is also worth noting that these frameworks need not be mutually exclusive. There are systems where multiple frameworks provide useful insights, and in any analysis of a large system both an exchange cost and a network view (or multiple network views) will be applicable.

One example of the application of these theoretical approaches to keep in mind regarding the network representation is that a network's value for communication is approximately equal to the square of the number of people in the network. A telephone system, or a social web site, with two people has only one connection. With 4 people there are 12 potential connections, and with 10 people, 90 potential connections. This is typically called a network effect, and applies when networks are used for communication or social interaction.

9.3 Higher Social Levels: Organizational and Cultural

There are higher social levels than small groups. These higher levels are focused less on the user and more on the user's context. They can influence what happens at the interface between the user and the technology, however, so we describe them, albeit briefly.

9.3.1 Organizational Effects

Users working in teams are often part of organizations. These organizations will influence the team climate and provide both resources and obligations to teams. There is a separate area of research that studies how organizations work, as opposed to teams (e.g., Simon 1997).

The network structures used to describe teams can be applied again to an organization, and indeed the figures of networks are typically scaled not for small teams but for organizations.

The comments about small teams also apply to organizations in many ways. Organizations are better if they are made up of better people and if these people have the knowledge, skills, and abilities to perform their tasks. They work better if their structure is adapted to the task, and so on.

As for teams, work is on going to provide computer support for organizations, perhaps even more so than for teams. It is clear that this computer support—if it is done mindlessly or without enough knowledge of the task, task distribution, and people—does not always help (e.g., see examples in Landauer 1995, or noted earlier in the book). However, there remain great possibilities for supporting teams with technology.

The way organizations work is usually heavily based on procedures that describe the way things should be done. This can be called a normative (or prescriptive) view. These procedures are invariably different from reality, which can be called a descriptive view. Many organizations have suffered disastrous effects from computerization of processes because the official procedures were computerized without recognizing that the reality was different. Often the users are not themselves fully aware of the differences, and these can be quite extensive, and even when they are aware they may be reluctant to tell a manager or a consultant who will be reporting back to management about the shortcuts and common procedure violations. The breach of procedures may only be that procedures are written as though they are performed by one person when they are, in fact, shared amongst a number of team members—or they may be written down as though they occur at one time without interruption when, in fact, they are always interleaved with numerous other similar tasks and problem solving. It might also be the case, and you can see this for yourself, that the forms and procedures ask for extensive information, and this is routinely not requested, not used, or does not have to be provided.

9.3.2 Cultural Effects

System behavior is the result of people interacting with technology in a context. That context includes the physical environment, as well as aspects such as the organizational structure, the culture of that organization, and possibly even national cultural factors. When you are designing systems you need to study the environment in which the system will be deployed to make sure that it will be acceptable to the users and to reduce the risk that any assumptions or misunderstandings will lead to an unusable or unsafe system. There are numerous examples of lessons learned in this area (e.g., Olson and Olson 2003–2004).

There is no magic bullet for avoiding these risks. There are several steps you can take. You can study the culture and laws by visiting the environment the system will be in, something that is advocated by techniques such as contextual design (Beyer and Holtzblatt 1999). You can read about the culture or have your own team members visit and work in the culture. You can include members of the culture in your design team. These members will not be perfect representatives, but will help avoid some problems and decrease the risk of system problems. You can also include time to pilot test and get feedback from users in that culture using a spiral design process (Boehm and Hansen 2001; Pew and Mavor 2007).

9.3.3 Summary

This section reminds us that, in addition to the users and their teams, there are higher social levels that will influence system design. These levels are important, but vary much more than users and even teams. As you start to design systems you should also consider that differences between your understanding and the actual levels can pose a risk to the success of your system.

You should study these levels for a system to the point where you understand whether they pose risks and, if they do, reduce the risks through appropriate actions. Some of these may be done by changing the organization (difficult, but worthwhile where appropriate), or by changing the system to reflect the organization, laws, and cultural reality.

9.4 Models of Social Processes

9.4.1 Introduction

Models of social processes can serve as more concrete theories and they also "have enormous potential to resolve the problem of system-team design" (Kozlowski and Ilgen 2006). There is a range of models of social processes that can be created using existing tools and methods. These range from less formal representations that are not computer-supported that can help system design on the ground to computer-supported models of social processes that help provide policy guidance for governments (Fan and Yen 2004). This section introduces the range of these models by providing examples at several levels.

As theories, these models provide a way to summarize behavior. That is, they provide a way to organize the results we have obtained about how people behave in groups into a single representation. The results can be used in system design and also as agents in video games and simulations. As theories they also provide suggestions about what we do not know and what we would like to know. As a simple example, some of these models work with small groups, but not with large groups. This difference suggests questions about how small and large groups work in different ways.

We start here with descriptive theories that describe in declarative terms the structures and relationships of groups. A more complex model is a model that describes not only the structures but also how the structures are created and how they interact. We also describe two approaches to creating these models, the Soft Systems Methodology and Rich Pictures.

9.4.2 Descriptive Social Models

Descriptive models provide a description of the components of interest. These can be grouped into static and dynamic models. Both of these have been seen earlier in this chapter in the descriptions of networks.

9.4.2.1 Ethnographic Descriptions of Social Processes

Ethnography is studying the users in their environments, including the physical location and objects, who and what they interact with and how, why, and when, and what they think their interactions mean. Ethnography provides a way to summarize and discover how social factors interact with systems. This approach thus provides a way to reduce risks to systems because it helps the designer understand the context of how the system will be used. It is also really important to conduct observations of people in their normal settings because it reminds us that not all users are like us. Notably, many Internet companies have experienced failures in developing social experiences because they have not taken their users' perspectives into account (Churchill 2010). Ethnographic studies can be started by reading about the culture of your users (e.g., military biographies if your users are in the military, about astronauts if they are astronauts, and about insurance claim adjusters if they are insurance claim adjusters). This work can also involve watching users do their work, or even participating in it (e.g., Coleman 1974 studied ditch digging, restaurants, and garbage men; Suchman 1983 studied office work; see also Crabtree 2003; Plowman et al. 1995; Viller and Sommerville 2000). The take-away message here is that you need to study the social situation more the further it is from your own background.

9.4.2.2 Communities of Practice

Another way is to view a set of people working with the same topic or task and their social connections as a community of practice (e.g., Wenger 1998). These communities can be seen in informal, recreational situations, such as party fishing boats (personal observation), to formal work situations such as in Japanese industry (Nonaka and Takeuchi 1995), and the wide range in between. Work on knowledge management and knowledge management systems has similar lessons on how groups work to help each other.

This view of a community of practice encourages viewing the users as a community rather than as a set of individuals. Thus, individual users might have a problem, but the community may, as a group, have solved the problem.

This view suggests that it is important to encourage users to communicate and to provide them with ways for them to interact over time, and to provide ways to acknowledge contributions and expertise. This approach is increasingly being used to help users help each other to solve a wide range of needs (e.g., Carroll et al. 2006; El Helou et al. 2008). Further comments and suggestions on how to apply this approach are in the references and in the literature on communities of practice and on knowledge management systems.

9.4.2.3 Static Models of Social Processes

Some of the most influential, interesting, and easily approachable models appear to be network models of social processes. The earliest work in this area noted how everyone was "connected to everyone else by only six degrees" (Travers and Milgram 1969). That is, for every pair of people in the world, only five friendships were necessary to connect them. This work has been perhaps discredited now (with the answer that we do not actually know how well connected people are, but it might be that close for most but not all people), but the idea of how people are connected into a network remains a useful concept. It has been used to explain, for example, why Silicon Valley is successful, because there are multiple connections between people (Castilla et al. 2000). It has also been used to analyze the connectivity within groups (Carley 1996).

These models are useful for system design in that they encourage you to keep in mind the connections between people, and to support connections and appropriate connections.

9.4.2.4 Dynamic Models of Social Processes

A more complex view of groups examines how the connections are formed and used, and the processes within the groups. These descriptive theories provide insights into how groups work and how to support them.

A view of the stages that groups go through by Tuckman (1965) and then picked up by everyone (partly because it is useful and we think partly because the stages have fun names) notes that groups go through forming (orientation/testing/dependence), storming (conflict), norming (group cohesion), and performing (functional role-relatedness). This type of stage theory of group formation helps with defining group behavior, but more importantly makes predictions about how to help groups work better together. For example, it would be useful for teachers, managers, and group members to encourage activities that help groups transition through the early stages more productively and quickly. There are multiple ways to help groups form, from helping people meet to helping the groups know their tasks. Norming, for example, can be assisted by providing standards and behavior to compare.

9.4.3 Soft Systems Methodology

Soft Systems Methodology (SSM, Checkland 1981; Checkland and Scholes, 1999) has its roots in systems engineering, and builds on ideas from action research. It was developed as a move away from thinking about systems in hard engineering terms. So, instead of talking about social systems and technical systems, SSM treats purposeful action as a system: logically linked activities are connected together as a whole, and the emergent property of the whole is its purposefulness.

SSM is based around a cycle of four activities:

1. The problematic situation that requires action to improve it is identified
2. Models of purposeful activity that are judged to be relevant to the identified situation are developed. Each of these models is built on the particular worldview of the different stakeholders
3. The models are used for structuring discussions about the problematic situation. The goal is to find changes that are desirable and culturally feasible in that situation
4. The actions that are needed to improve the situation are defined and, perhaps, implemented.

Systems development usually starts with activity 1, although the other activities will often be carried out in parallel, and these can feed back into the other activities in the process. The discussions in activity 3, for example, may lead to an improved understanding of some of the more subtle aspects of the problematic situation (activity 1), which may lead to changes in the set of models developed in activity 2.

One of the key features of SSM is its focus on developing an understanding of the problem (SSM uses the term problematic situation, which is more general). This understanding takes into account the roles, responsibilities, and concerns of the stakeholders that are associated with the particular problem. The understanding of the problem provides the basis for the solution, which again takes into account stakeholders' differing viewpoints. SSM explicitly acknowledges that the final solution is based on attempting to accommodate the views (and needs) of the various stakeholders.

SSM is essentially an analytical approach, mostly focusing on organizational aspects of the system. It does not purport to support systems design. Although SSM does not deal explicitly with the technical system, it is possible to transform an activity model into an information model, by considering the sorts of information that are: (1) required to perform the activity and (2) generated by the activity. In this way an information system can be developed that supports the purposeful activity. SSM has also been used in the evaluation of existing information systems (Checkland and Poulter 2006).

9.4.4 Rich Pictures

Before designing any system, it is important to understand the environment (or context) in which that system will be embedded. There are several aspects to the environment that are critical to the system being acceptable to the end users. Some of these may seem trivial, such as the need for an available power supply to operate the system, and the need for space to house the required technology. Just walking around the working context can help you to identify the physical aspects of the environment that need to be considered.

In addition to the physical aspects, there are social aspects too, which are often more subtle, and much harder to identify. Most work nowadays is a social activity, carried out by teams of people with a range of skills, who have to communicate and collaborate to make systems work, and to deliver services. There are some methods available to help you understand and take appropriate account of the work context when designing a system. One of the best known of these is Checkland's (1981) Rich Pictures, which are part of the Soft Systems Methodology described above. An example Rich Picture for the work context in a hospital neonatal intensive care unit is shown in Fig. 9.6 (Baxter et al. 2005). Rich pictures have been used to help analyze pubs, a web design consulting firm, and a cold storage warehouse (Monk and Howard 1998).

The rich pictures are generated from semi-structured interviews that are carried out with representatives of each of the groups of system stakeholders. Interviewees are asked about their roles, responsibilities, and concerns. One typical way of identifying these is to ask the interviewee to talk you through what they would do in a typical day (or shift). That way, they tell you about the sort of jobs that they do and the people they have to work with, so you can go on to probe the issues further. The roles, responsibilities, and concerns are typically represented in simple pictures that show how the groups of stakeholders are linked.

The rich pictures are annotated with text as appropriate, and supplemented by extended textual descriptions of how work is carried out. When you have created a draft of the rich pictures, you take them back to each of the interviewees to make sure that you have correctly captured what they told you.

Fig. 9.6 A Rich picture for the work context in a hospital neonatal intensive care unit (adapted from Baxter et al. 2005)

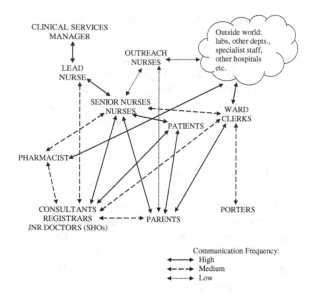

The problem with many design methods, however, including Rich Pictures, is that they require a lot of time and effort to carry them out properly. Nielsen (1993), Monk (1998), and Lewis and his colleagues (Blackmon et al. 2002; Lewis and Reiman 1998) have all proposed a range of lightweight or discounted methods that can inform design in a timely manner, without a massive investment in time, effort, and other resources. These lightweight methods are simplified versions of the larger methods.

Lightweight rich pictures provide a useful way of showing the roles and responsibilities of the various system stakeholders along with any concerns they may have about the work system. To get a complete picture of the social and work contexts, it is useful to supplement rich pictures with background reading and, where possible, informal visits and meetings to the place where the system will be deployed; this is sometimes referred to as bootstrapping into the domain.

As befits most pragmatic methods, lightweight rich pictures should be thought of as a framework rather than as a set of rules that have to be rigidly followed and applied. When carrying out a case study of a neonatal intensive care unit, for example, Baxter and his colleagues (Baxter et al. 2005) found that staff did not report any concerns. The rich pictures for the work context were drawn as two separate diagrams, highlighting the two most important aspects of the work context: communication and the use of written records. Both of these are social activities, and carrying out a rich picture analysis made it much quicker to see the importance of communication. Because communication is very much a social activity, and was central to the operation of the unit, it was important that the proposed new system did not detract from the existing levels of communication or block any communication channels.

9.4.5 Computational Models of Social Behavior

As social models get more complex, it becomes necessary to use computers to implement them and their predictions. Analytic models simulate the social processes but without modeling the individual transactions in detail. Process models model the information processing that is performed and they will typically also model the interactions between agents.

9.4.5.1 Analytic Models

Analytic models provide a description of a social process. They may include equations for how often people meet, or how often and what they communicate. These equations are used to simulate how the social process unfolds.

As an example, a group of researchers modeled the transmission of a possible influenza pandemic (Halloran et al. 2008). It can be viewed as a social model (as well as a epidemiological model) because it primarily models social interactions between people at schools, work, home, and neighborhoods. It uses equations to model how often people interact, how often a disease would be transmitted, and the impact of medical interventions to stop the transmission of the disease. Importantly, these simulations explore how well public health interventions would be followed and what would be the impact of these interventions on the spread of the disease. The authors argue that the results are not accurate enough to be predictions, but are useful for framing the discussion of how to handle pandemics, and which interventions to consider. For example, closing schools is one that is both easy to follow and greatly helps reduce the spread of disease. These simulations do not cover the details, but they present a broad description of a large social system. The Halloran et al. (2008) work modeled the population of greater Chicago of 8.6 million people. This is one of the largest social simulation models we know.

9.4.5.2 Process Models

As social processes are being better formulated, there has been an increase in modeling them using information processing models. These models simulate smaller groups, ranging from 2 to 100 people.

Current examples include work on optimizing the structures of groups to increase performance (e.g., Levchuk et al. 2002), creating models for use as colleagues and adversaries (Jones et al. 1999; Tambe et al. 1995; Zachary et al. 2001), and fundamental work on understanding how changes in group processes and individual behavior lead to changes in group performance (e.g., Carley 1996). This is an exciting emerging field, and further examples are available from conferences in AI and in organizational process, and in the *Journal of Mathematical Sociology* and *Computational and Mathematical Organization Theory*. Search engines can provide further references.

9.4.6 Summary

These approaches to modeling social processes offer different advantages and disadvantages. The analytic models can represent large systems, over millions of entities. They can be used to provide useful suggestions for public policy. On the other hand, their details get applied millions of times and their assumptions can become very important but at the same time hard to know.

The process models work harder to get the details right on a more fine-grained level but have difficulty scaling. Process models can be used to provide useful suggestions on smaller scale systems, but they cannot provide as many suggestions on large scale systems because they cannot simulate very large systems because they require so much computational power. They are useful, however, in simulations and games because they can live in an environment.

9.5 General Implications for System Design

Whenever you design a new system, it will almost invariably be a socio-technical system (the main exceptions are some deeply embedded systems that speak only to other pieces of technology). In other words, there will be a social system involved. You will need to take account of that social system, because the technology and the social system will be interdependent and interact. If you do not spend time and effort understanding the existing social system, you run the risk of adversely affecting it—if staff have to spend more time on interacting with the new technology that takes away time from communication or learning, for example—and can end up in the situation where staff will simply stop using the new technology because it gets in the way of them doing their job.

Many of the implications for system design require you to think about the impact of the system that you are designing. In some cases there will be aspects of interaction that you can build into your system, but in others it will be a case of making sure that what you have designed does not take anything away from what already exists (or if it does, it improves the overall socio-technical system). The modeling tools and techniques described in Sect. 9.8 should help.

The first thing you need to consider is how people work together in the environment where your system will be deployed. If you are putting a global system in place, along the lines of YouTube for example, which has distributed users, you may want to create local regions within the system that will help to encourage use and participation. You will also need to think about creating the most appropriate social distances between people, either increasing it, through the use of formal titles (e.g., Dr. Ritter), or reducing it by just using first names (e.g., Frank) or nicknames (Killer-ace).

The way that people interact will be affected by the goals, costs, and payoffs (benefits) involved, so you should make them clear and attractive. If goals are shared, then you need to think about how people make decisions about those goals, and the actions that need to be taken to achieve those goals. If the decisions are shared, then you have to think about how you will share information between the people involved. Although the team may self-support and self-regulate, you should consider the need for an authority figure to moderate behavior, where appropriate. Remember that the make-up of the team is likely to change over time, so you need to consider how to deal with experienced people leaving the team and new people joining the team, which will affect overall system performance.

You will need to think about how and why people are motivated to use your system. Do they use it because they have to (are they paid to use it to do their job, for example)? Or do they use it because they want to use it (the classic example here being social networking systems). Even in the case of developing a social networking system, there may be a need for extrinsic motivation to make sure that people keep the system active by providing new content, although the rewards for doing this may not be financial. You could highlight how the system increases their mastery, gives them autonomy, and increases the importance of doing the task. The balance between motivations may not always be clear cut, so some learning tasks, for example, will require a coach who sets tasks (which may be necessary, but are not necessarily intrinsically rewarding) for people to complete as part of their learning experience.

If your system will support many users working together as a team, you will need to be aware of the potential diffusion of responsibility and how you can guard against this. One way of doing so is to make sure that any requests are directed at specific people rather than general groups. You can also make the requester appear more human by associating personal images or details with their request, because people are more likely to respond to real requests from real people!

The factors that influence team performance may be relatively well known, but it may not always be possible to ensure that all the factors are optimal. As noted above, teams that are (1) more cohesive, (2) who have worked together longer, and (3) who share more values will perform better. You need to be able to support teams with these attributes, but also help teams that do not have all of the attributes to achieve them. Reducing social distance may help to make the team more cohesive, and sharing information can lead to the sharing of values.

In addition to the team level issues, you will also need to think about organizational issues. If an organization has procedures in place for how a particular job has to be done, for example, then you will need to think about whether these procedures will have to be changed. If the procedures are imposed by a regulatory authority (as in nuclear power, for example) then you may not be able to change those procedures, so you will have to design your system to support those procedures.

There can also be cultural effects (on several levels), so there may be a tradition for doing a task in a particular way, which is an effect of organizational culture.

The main message to take away is that all systems are deployed in an environment that includes social elements that you need to take into account. If you ignore them, you increase the risk of your system being unacceptable, because it is less likely that it will fit in with their way of working. The other important thing to remember is that the social environment is likely to change, so you should at least be aware of this, and design your system to take account of this, where possible.

9.6 Summary

We hope that this chapter has convinced you that social aspects of users are important. We and many designers certainly did not think so 20 years ago when a lot of systems were created. Increasingly, the individual aspects are either well supported or in some cases less important, so social aspects are becoming more important, or at least can be paid attention to.

Social factors appear to be complex, and currently it appears to be difficult to combine them a priori. Social factors include the group members (which are complex), their organization (which can be complex), their mutual and individual tasks (which can be complex), and the task distributions (how often each task has to be performed). This makes the social factors not reducible to a single number or summary because the construct is a group, a set of individuals and their relationships to each other, and their ability to perform a range of tasks that might not be equivalent. These factors are also moderated by the task environment, including other groups and other members of the team's family, culture, and nation.

Designers will need to keep in mind during design the social aspects of the system, sometimes on a par with the technical system. There are more examples where ignoring social aspects of systems lead to risks that can cause systems to fail. Casey (1998) notes several, and Goolsby (2005) starts her paper with an example of a system that failed immediately because it ignored social and political aspects.

9.7 Other Resources

Cheyne and Ritter (2001) argue that there are right ways and wrong ways to contact people on the Internet. Their position has been upheld by most responsible organizations, but is consistently being violated by less responsible organizations (e.g., spammers). They offer an application of some of the theories in this area to how to make announcements using email, bulletin boards, and through search engines, rather than unsolicited direct email, which pushes the cost on the receiver.

For more on networked sociality see Rainie et al. (2012). *Networked. The new social operating system*. Cambridge, MA: MIT Press.

A short article by Churchill cautions us to remember as designers we may not be like the users we are designing for, and to think carefully when designing social systems. This is of course a general point, but when it comes to social communication tools, it is particularly important.

Churchill (2010). The (anti) social net. *interactions. 17*(5). 22–25.

Generally, the question of how to support teams using technology is considered by human factors and computer-supported cooperative work (CSCW). Conferences and journals in this area will provide more information and more current information. An early collection of readings is still useful: Baecker (1993).

For more on collaborative virtual environments, Churchill, Snowdon, and Munro's book contains articles on the topic:

E. F. Churchill, D. Snowdon and A. Munro (Eds). (2001). *Collaborative virtual environments. Digital places and spaces for interaction*. London, UK: Springer Verlag.

There are several places where work on computational models of social behavior can be found. In addition to the *Journal of Mathematical Sociology*, there is a society focused on this, NAACSOS—The North American Association for Computational Social and Organizational Science (www.dis.anl.gov/naacsos). Their conference is associated with the Computational and Mathematical Organization Theory Conference (CASOS) (www.casos.ece.cmu.edu). The National Research Council, an independent agency that gives independent scientific advice to the government, has written a report that lays out a summary of work that can and should be done: (Committee on Organizational Modeling from Individuals to Societies 2007).

9.8 Exercises

9.1 Spam regularly appears in our email and now battles for our attention and our resources alongside legitimate emails. In some cases the spam is non-trivial in that the author is serious, genuine, and locatable. The rest are often removed automatically using spam filters.

    (a) Use the frameworks from informal groups, transaction costs, and networks, to explain the incentives and impact of spam. Generate an equation to compute the transaction costs of spam. Generate an equation to compute how many email addresses are visible on the Internet.

    (b) Discuss, using costs and benefits, how much it would cost to ask people to donate to charity on your campus using email, and the wisdom and practical matters of this approach. (You might be able to use information from Cheyne and Ritter 2001).

9.2 Second Life is a web site/application that puts you into a virtual world. It has a set of commands for moving around the environment and manipulating objects in it. It has an interface for following yourself and for recording orally as well as textually. If you have read any of Gibson's (1988) or Vinge's (2006) books, it may seem familiar in that it realizes some of the important aspects of these virtual worlds including social interaction, and Second Life may even have been inspired by these books.

Discuss Second Life with respect to the ABCS, particularly the social aspects. Note where it is better than (first) life and where it is worse. Try to summarize when and where it will be important.

9.3 Examine eBay or another online site with social aspects using the representations and frameworks in this chapter. Choose a framework from this chapter, e.g., network analysis. Map the concepts onto the social web site. Note whether there are any concepts missing on the web site, and also whether there are any concepts in the web site that are missing in the theory.

References

Axelrod, R. (1984). *The evolution of cooperation*. New York, NY: Basic Books.

Baxter, G. D., Monk, A. F., Tan, K., Dear, P. R. F., & Newell, S. J. (2005). Using cognitive task analysis to facilitate the integration of decision support systems into the neonatal intensive care unit. *Artificial Intelligence in Medicine, 35*, 243–257.

Baecker, R. M. (Ed.). (1993). *Readings in groupware and computer-supported cooperative work: Assisting human–human collaboration*. San Mateo, CA: Morgan Kaufmann.

Beyer, H., & Holtzblatt, K. (1999). *Contextual design. interactions, 6*(1), 32–42.

Blackmon, M. H., Polson, P. G., Kitajima, M., & Lewis, C. (2002). Cognitive walk through for the Web. In Proceedings of *CHI'02 Conference on Human Factors in Computing Systems*, 463-470. ACM: New York, NY.

Boehm, B., & Hansen, W. (2001). The spiral model as a tool for evolutionary acquisition. *Crosstalk: The Journal of Defense Software Engineering, 14*(5), 4–11.

Brennan, S. E. (1998). The grounding problem in conversations with and through computers. In S. R. Fussell & R. J. Kreuz (Eds.), *Social and cognitive psychological approaches to interpersonal communication* (pp. 201–225). Hillsdale, NJ: Erlbaum.

Brown, B., Green, N., & Harper, R. (2001). *Wireless world: Social and interactional aspects of wireless technology*. London, UK: Springer-Verlag.

Burt, R. S. (2004). Structural holes and good ideas. *American Journal of Sociology, 110*(2), 349–399.

Carley, K. M. (1996). A comparison of artificial and human organizations. *Journal of Economic Behavior & Organization, 31*, 175–191.

Carroll, J. M., Rosson, M. B., Convertino, G., & Ganoe, C. H. (2006). Awareness and teamwork in computer-supported collaborations. *Interacting with Computers, 18*(1), 21–46.

Casey, S. M. (1998). *Set phasers on stun: And other true tales of design, technology, and human error*. Santa Barbara, CA: Aegean.

Castilla, E. J., Hwang, H., Granovetter, E., & Granovetter, M. (2000). Social networks in Silicon Valley. In C.-M. Lee, W. F. Miller, M. G. Hancock & H. S. Rowen (Eds.), *The Silicon Valley edge* (pp. 218–247). Stanford, CA: Stanford University Press.

Checkland, P. (1981). *Systems thinking, systems practice*. Chichester, UK: Wiley.

Checkland, P., & Scholes, J. (1999). *Soft systems in action* (2nd ed.). Chichester, UK: Wiley.

Checkland, P., & Poulter, J. (2006). Learning for action: *A short definitive account of soft systems methodology and its use for practitioners, teachers and students*. Chichester, UK: Wiley.

Cheyne, T., & Ritter, F. E. (2001). Targeting respondents on the Internet successfully and responsibly. *Communications of the ACM, 44*(4), 94–98.

Churchill, E. F. (2010). The (Anti) Social Net. *interactions, 17*(5), 22–25.

Churchill, E. F., & Bly, S. (1999). Virtual environments at work: Ongoing use of MUDs in the workplace. In *Proceedings of the International Joint Conference on Work Activities Coordination and Collaboration*, 99–108. ACM: New York, NY.

Churchill, E. F., Snowdon, D., & Munro, A. (Eds.). (2001). *Collaborative virtual environments. Digital places and spaces for interaction*. London, UK: Springer Verlag.

Clark, H. H., & Brennan, S. E. (1991a). Grounding in communication. In L. B. Resnick, J. M. Levine, & S. D. Teasley (Eds.), *Perspectives on socially shared cognition* (pp. 127–149). Washington, DC: American Psychological Association.

Clark, H. H., & Brennan, S. E. (1991b). Perspectives on socially shared cognition. In L. B. Resnick & J. M. Levine (Eds.), *Washington*. DC: American Psychological Association.

Coleman, J. R. (1974). *Blue-Collar journal: A college president's sabbatical*. Philadelphia, PA: Lippincott Williams & Wilkins.

Committee on Organizational Modeling from Individuals to Societies, & G. L. Zacharias, J. MacMillan, and Susan B. Van Hemel (Eds). (2007). *Behavioral modeling and simulation: From individuals to societies*. Washington, DC: National Academies Press. http://www.nap.edu/catalog/12169.html.

Crabtree, A. (2003). *Designing collaborative systems: A practical guide to ethnography*. London, UK: Springer.

Desanctis, G., & Monge, P. (1998). Communication processes for virtual organizations. *Journal of Computer-Mediated Communication, 3*(4), [online file].

Dodds, P. S., Muhamad, R., & Watts, D. J. (2003). An experimental study of search in global social networks. *Science, 301*(5634), 827–829.

Dunbar, R. I. M. (1992). Neocortex size as a constraint on group size in primates. *Journal of Human Evolution, 22*(6), 469–493.

El Helou, S., Tzagarakis, M., Gillet, D., Karacapilidis, N., & Yu Man, C. (2008). Participatory design for awareness features: Enhancing interaction in communities of practice. In *Proceedings of the 6th International Conference on Networked Learning*, 523–530. Networked Learning Conference Office, Lancaster University: Lancaster, LANCS.

Fan, X., & Yen, J. (2004). Modeling and simulating human teamwork behaviors using intelligent agents. *Physics of Life Reviews, 1*(3), 173–201.

Gibson, W. (1988). *Mona Lisa overdrive*. New York, NY: Bantam Books.

Goolsby, R. (2005). Ethics and defense agency funding: Some considerations. *Social Networks, 27*, 95–106.

Gottman, J. M., Murray, J. D., Swanson, C., Tyson, R., & Swanson, K. R. (2005). *The mathematics of marriage: Dynamic nonlinear models*. Cambridge, MA: MIT Press.

Halloran, M. E., Ferguson, N. M., Eubank, S., Longini, I. M. J., Cummings, D. A., Lewis, B., et al. (2008). Modeling targeted layered containment of an influenza pandemic in the United States. *Proceedings of the National Academy of Sciences, 105*(12), 4639–4644.

Jones, R. M., Laird, J. E., Nielsen, P. E., Coulter, K. J., Kenny, P., & Koss, F. V. (1999). Automated intelligent pilots for combat flight simulation. *AI Magazine, 20*(1), 27–41.

Kang, J. (2000). Cyber-race. *Harvard Law Review, 113*, 1130–1208.

Kozlowski, S. W. J., & Ilgen, D. R. (2006). Enhancing the effectiveness of work groups and teams. *Psychological Science in the Public Interest, 7*(3), 77–124.

Landauer, T. K. (1995). *The trouble with computers: Usefulness, usability and productivity*. Cambridge, MA: MIT Press.

Levchuk, G. M., Levchuk, Y. N., Luo, J., Pattipati, K. R., & Kleinman, D. L. (2002). Normative design of organizations—Part I: Mission planning. *IEEE Transactions on Systems, Man, and Cybernetics—Part A: Systems and Humans, 32*(3), 346–359.

Levitt, S., & Dubner, S. J. (2005). *Freakonomics: A rogue economist explores the hidden side of everything New York*. NY: William Morrow/HarperCollins.

Lewis, C., & Reiman, J. (1998). *Task-centered user interface design*. hcibib.org/tcuid/.

Milgram, S. (1967). *The Small-World Problem. Psychology Today, 1*, 61–67.

Millen, D. R., Feinberg, J., & Kerr, B. (2006). Dogear: Social bookmarking in the enterprise. In *Proceedings of the SIGCHI Conference on Human Factors in Computing Systems*, 111–120. ACM: New York, NY.

Monk, A., & Howard, S. (1998). The rich picture: A tool for reasoning about work context. *interactions [sic], 5*(2), 21–30.

Monk, A. F. (1998). Lightweight techniques to encourage innovative user interface design. In L. Wood (Ed.), *User interface design: Bridging the gap between user requirements and design* (pp. 109–129). Boca Raton, FL: CRC Press.

Nielsen, J. (1993). *Usability engineering*. Chestnut Hill, MA: AP Professional Press.

Nonaka, I., & Takeuchi, H. (1995). *The knowledge creating company: How Japanese companies create the dynamics of innovation*. New York, NY: Oxford University Press.

Olson, J. S., & Olson, G. M. (2003–2004). Culture surprises in remote software development teams. *ACM. Queue, 1*(9), 52–59.

Pew, R. W., & Mavor, A. S. (Eds.). (2007). *Human-system integration in the system development process: A new look*. Washington, DC: National Academies Press. http://books.nap.edu/catalog.php?record_id=11893. Accessed 10 March 2014.

Plowman, L., Rogers, Y., & Ramage, M. (1995). What are workplace studies for? In *Proceedings of the Fourth European Conference on Computer-Supported Cooperative Work ECSCW'95*, 309–324. Kluwer: Dordrecht, The Netherlands.

Rainie, H., Rainie, L., & Wellman, B. (2012). *Networked. The new social operating system*. Cambridge, MA: MIT Press.

Ruhleder, K., & Jordan, B. (1999). Meaning-making across remote sites: How delays in transmission affect interaction. In *Proceedings of the Sixth European Conference on Computer Supported Cooperative Work (ECSCW'99)*, 411–429. Kluwer: Norwell, MA.

Rutkowski, A. F., Vogel, D. R., Van Genuchten, M., Bemelmans, T. M., & Favier, M. (2002). E-collaboration: The reality of virtuality. *IEEE Transactions on Professional Communication, 45*(4), 219–230.

Sacks, H. (1992). *Lectures on Conversation, Volumes I and II*. Edited by G. Jefferson with Introduction by E.A. Schegloff. Oxford, UK: Blackwell.

Simon, H. A. (1997). *Administrative behavior* (4th ed.). New York, NY: The Free Press.

Snowdon, D., Churchill, E. F., & Frecon, E. (Eds.). (2003). *Inhabited information spaces: Living with your data*. London, UK: Springer Verlag.

Suchman, L. (1983). Office procedures as practical action: Models of work and system design. *ACM Transactions on Office Information Systems, 1*(4), 320–328.

Tambe, M., Johnson, W. L., Jones, R. M., Koss, F., Laird, J. E., Rosenbloom, P. S., et al. (1995). Intelligent agents for interactive simulation environments. *AI Magazine, 16*(1), 15–40.

ten Have, P. (1999). *Doing conversation analysis*. London: Sage Publications.

Travers, J., & Milgram, S. (1969). An experimental study of the small world problem. *Sociometry, 32*(4), 425–443.

Tuckman, B. W. (1965). Developmental sequence in small groups. *Psychological Bulletin, 63*, 384–399.

Viller, S., & Sommerville, I. (2000). Ethnographically informed analysis for software engineers. *International Journal of Human-Computer Studies, 53*(1), 169–196.

Vinge, V. (2006). *Rainbows End*. New York, NY: Tor Books.

Watts, D. (2003). *Six degrees: The science of a connected age*. New York, NY: W. W. Norton.

Wenger, E. (1998). *Communities of Practice: Learning, meaning, and identity*. Cambridge, UK: Cambridge University Press.

Zachary, W., Santarelli, T., Lyons, D., Bergondy, M., & Johnston, J. (2001). Using a community of intelligent synthetic entities to support operational team training. In *Proceedings of the*

Tenth Conference on Computer Generated Forces and Behavioral Representation, 215–224. Institute for Simulation and Training, University of Central Florida: Orlando, FL.

Zhao, D., & Rosson, M. B. (2009). How and why people Twitter: The role that micro-blogging plays in informal communication at work. In *Proceedings of the ACM 2009 International Conference on Supporting Group Work*, 243–252. ACM: New York, NY.

Chapter 10
Errors: An Inherent Part
of Human-System Performance

Abstract In this chapter we consider how errors contribute to accidents, large and small, and what we can do about them. We discuss the problem of post-hoc analyses, the types of human error that can occur, and how to design systems in such a way that the errors can be appropriately managed. The examples illustrate how user's characteristics in terms of psycho-physiology, fatigue, cognitive processing, and social situations can all contribute to failures. We especially note the importance of Norman's (and others') main guideline about needing to design for error.

10.1 Introduction to Errors

In this chapter we provide an introduction to the topic of what is often called *human error*. As Reason (1990) notes, "human error is a very large subject, quite as extensive as that covered by the term human performance," so we can only really provide a selective overview of some of the major issues.

We have deliberately separated the discussion of errors into a separate chapter. This is because errors are an inherent part of system performance. In other words, they often arise as a combination of factors at the anthropomorphic, behavioral, cognitive, and social levels in the ABCS framework. If you look again at the example of the Kegworth air accident (see the Appendix), you should be able to appreciate this more fully at this point in the book.

Our purpose here is to highlight the need to think about your users in context, and to determine what kinds of factors can give rise to erroneous performance. By highlighting the relationship between system performance and error, we hope to show you why it is important to think about designing for error (Norman 1988, 2013). One way of designing for error is to identify the situations that can lead to erroneous performance, and then put in place appropriate mechanisms to either prevent the errors, or at least mitigate the adverse consequences arising from those errors.

F. E. Ritter et al., *Foundations for Designing User-Centered Systems*,
DOI: 10.1007/978-1-4471-5134-0_10, © Springer-Verlag London 2014

We will illustrate our points using examples taken from a range of incidents and accidents, large and small. In doing so, we hope to show how errors do not just arise because of any inherent error-proneness or maliciousness of the users. Instead, errors are usually the result of an interaction of several contributing factors (people, technological, and contextual). Once we accept this state of affairs we can begin to move away from the need to find someone to blame, and start to learn from erroneous performance as a way of improving future system performance.

10.1.1 What is Error?

Errors are generally regarded as precursors to accidents. The error triggers a set of events—often referred to as a chain or sequence, although it is not always a linear set of events—ultimately leading to an outcome that has serious consequences involving significant loss of life, money, or machinery. Causal analyses of accidents usually highlight the fact that there were many contributory factors. There are obviously exceptions, where a single catastrophic failure leads directly to an accident, but generally accidents involve a series of several individually minor events. This process is sometimes described as a domino effect, or represented by the Reason's (1990) Swiss cheese model in which there are holes in the various layers of the system, and an accident only occurs when the holes line up across all the layers.

A similar idea is encapsulated in Randell's (2000) *fault-error-failure* model that comes from the field of dependability. A failure is defined as something that occurs when the service that is delivered is judged to have deviated from its specification. An error is taken to be the part of the system state that may lead to a subsequent failure, and the adjudged cause of the error is defined as a fault.

It is very important to note that identifying whether something is a fault, error, or failure involves making judgments. The fault-error-failure triples can link up so that you effectively end up with a chain of triples. This is possible because a failure at one level in the system may constitute a fault at another level. This does not mean that errors inevitably lead to failures, however. The link between an error and a failure can be broken either by chance or by taking appropriate design steps to contain the errors and their effects.

Those errors that have immediate (or near-immediate) effects on system performance are sometimes called active errors (Reason 1990). This is to distinguish them from latent errors, which can lie dormant within a system for some considerable time without having any adverse effect on system performance. The commission that investigated the nuclear accident at Three Mile Island, for example, found that an error that had occurred during maintenance (and hence was latent in the system) led to the emergency feed water system being unavailable (Kemeny (chairman) 1979). Similarly, the vulnerability of the O-ring seals on the Challenger Space Shuttle was known about beforehand and hence latent in the system (Vaughan 1997). The vulnerability was only exploited after the decision was made to launch the shuttle in very cold weather.

The general approach used to study errors focuses on how to understand errors so that we can take appropriate steps to manage them before things get out of hand. When, rather than if, things go wrong, the aim is to learn from what happened to help prevent a repeat performance.

Immediately after a major accident of any kind the press coverage almost invariably attributes the cause of the accident to human error. The problem is that the term *human error* is ambiguous and has three subtly different meanings (Hollnagel 1998), which are often confused by the press. It is therefore worth spelling out these different meanings, using examples from the field of aviation:

1. Human error is the cause of the event or action. An example of this would be if an aircraft deviated from its assigned flight altitude to a different flight altitude (either higher or lower than the one that the flight crew had been given by Air Traffic Control) due to the actions of the flight crew.
2. Human error is the event or action itself. An example of this would be if an aircraft pilot did not change the altimeter setting when they were supposed to. Note that in this case the action is really a deliberate non-action.
3. Human error is the consequence of the event or action. An example of this would be if an aircraft collided with another aircraft because the pilot started to taxi before receiving clearance to taxi by air traffic control.

The differences between the meanings are quite subtle, but it is important to ensure that you understand them. In most cases the press combines the first two meanings, even though they may not intend that the primary attribution of blame should fall on the human.

The interpretation of human error is further complicated by the fact that an action can only be judged as erroneous in hindsight (Woods et al. 1994). People will generally do what they think is the right thing in that particular context at the right time. So an action can only be judged as being erroneous after the fact, based on:

- A comparison with some expected level of performance
- A degradation in performance
- The person who performed the act having been unable to choose to act in a way that would not have been considered as erroneous.

There is one exception to this notion of erroneous actions being judgments made in hindsight: violations. If a person deliberately decides to do the wrong thing—to sabotage the system, for example—then this can be determined at the point when the action occurs, rather than afterwards. In some cases, however, it may be necessary to violate the established rules or procedures to keep a system in a safe state, or to get it out of an unsafe one. The Federal Aviation Authority (FAA) in the US acknowledges this type of violation—sometimes called safe violations—and explicitly allows them under its regulations in certain situations.

Erroneous actions, then, can be seen generally as the result of one of two things:

1. Performing the right action in the wrong circumstances. This is what Reason (1990) calls a mistake, or a failure in planning.
2. Performing the wrong action in the right circumstances. This is often referred to as a slip (Norman 1981; Reason 1990), or failure in action execution.

In either case the action could have been deemed correct if the circumstances had been slightly different. This helps to explain Rasmussen's (1988) description of erroneous actions as being the results of carrying unsuccessful experiments in unfriendly environments.

It is also important to take into account different perceptions when trying to interpret what people mean by error. Rasmussen et al. (1994) suggest that the following perspectives can be identified:

• Common sense: to explain an unusual event
• The lawyer: to find somebody to blame and/or punish
• The therapist: to improve human performance
• The scientist: to understand human behavior
• The reliability analyst: to evaluate human performance
• The designer: to improve system configuration.

As interactive system designers, our perspective tends to be mostly a combination of the scientist's and the designer's perspectives. The two are somewhat related, because by understanding the human behavior, we can provide appropriate support to prevent errors happening or to mitigate the consequences of any errors that may not be preventable. In most cases this will be by changing the design of the system.

10.1.2   The Fine Line Between Success and Failure

As long as there have been people, there have been errors. Getting things right is not always easy, and often requires knowledge and skills that have to be acquired over an extended period of time: you cannot become an expert overnight. One of the ways in which people learn is through practice, by reflecting on their performance, using feedback, and then trying to do it better next time. This approach is nicely illustrated in the works of Henry Petroski (e.g., Petroski 1985/1992, 1994, 2006), who has shown how the development of engineering has progressed over the centuries by learning from past errors.

The study of errors has fascinated psychologists for over a century. It received renewed impetus from the end of the 1970s with major events like the Three Mile Island disaster in 1979, the runway collision at Tenerife in 1977, and a range of catastrophes in medical care (e.g., Bogner 2004), when the gauntlet was picked up by the human factors and ergonomics community. The focus of study has changed somewhat, however, and there is now recognition that it is important to think about success as much as failure because there is often only a fine line dividing the two, and there are many more instances of success than of failure (e.g., Hollnagel et al. 2006). This changed emphasis is a reflection of Ernst Mach's (1905) prescient view that "Knowledge and error flow from the same mental sources, only success can tell one from the other......the same mental functions, operating under the same rules, in one case lead to knowledge, and in another, to error....". Although couched in slightly different terms, it is a view that others have concurred with and reiterated, such as Reason (1990, p.1):

> Not only must more effective methods of predicting and reducing dangerous errors emerge from a better understanding of mental processes, it has also become increasingly apparent that such theorizing, if it is to provide an adequate picture of cognitive control processes, must explain not only correct performance but also the more predictable varieties of human fallibility. Far from being rooted in irrational or maladaptive tendencies, these recurrent error forms have their origins in fundamentally useful psychological processes.

The consequences of errors have also increased over the years. Or perhaps that should be the consequences are *perceived* to have increased. The mass media these days are often very quick to report on air accidents, for example, where a single accident may give rise to hundreds of casualties. The fact that more people get killed on the roads, however, goes largely unreported, mostly because each fatal road accident often only involves a few deaths (Gigerenzer 2004).

10.1.3   The Accident was Caused by Human Error, Right?

Most accidents could naively be attributed to human error because the systems that fail, leading to the accident, are designed by humans. This is an over-simplistic view, however, and would lead to an equally simplistic solution, i.e., that removing the human would remove a major source of failures, and hence eliminate many accidents. The idea of humans being accident prone in a volitional way (i.e., of their own free will) dominated early thinking in human error research.

The cause of an accident is often attributed to human error (pilot error, driver error, operator error, and so on). This is a judgment that is built on several underlying assumptions that, at best, usually only represent a partial view of the true situation. There are many examples of such a view. Arnstein (1997), for example, found that the number of problems that could be attributed to human error in anesthetics ranged from 64 to 83%, whilst in aviation the range was 40–88%. Johnson and Holloway (2007) also noted the tendency to over-emphasize human error as the reported cause in transportation accidents for the years 1996–2003. Whilst it was still found to be the main attributed cause, the levels were somewhat lower at 37% for the US National Transportation Safety Board (NTSB), and 50% for the Canadian TSB.

One of the main reasons that accidents end up being attributed to human error is because of the limitations of causal analysis. It is difficult to continue the analysis through the human when we do not have direct access to what was going on in the operators' heads when the accident happened. So once the human is reached in the sequence of attributable causes, the analysis frequently gets terminated, and we are left with human error as the result.

As we have noted several times, system performance is the result of people interacting with technology in a particular context (organizational and physical environment). The importance of context should never be underestimated. Very often, when we look at accidents we find that the users were working in a context constrained by time pressures and limited resources.

Nowadays, there is a greater awareness of the influence of the context in which work takes place, and the fact that human attentional resources are limited (see Chap. 5). Many events that previously were typically attributed to humans being accident prone would now be analyzed and categorized differently.

In aviation, for example, where multitasking is an inherent part of flying a plane, distractions are recognized as being a particular problem. Dismukes et al. (1998) noted that nearly half the reported NTSB accidents attributed to crew error involved lapses of attention associated with interruptions, distractions, or an excessive preoccupation with one task to the exclusion of another that had to be performed within a similar time frame. The vast majority (90%) of competing activities that distracted or preoccupied pilots fell into four categories: communication; head-down work; searching for other traffic in good weather (visual meteorological conditions or VMC); or responding to abnormal situations. Flight crews have to work as a team, but this has to be done in such a way that it does not detract from the individual tasks that have to be performed as the following excerpt from incident report #360761 from NASA's Aviation Safety Reporting System (ASRS) illustrates:

> Copilot was a new hire and new in type: first line flight out of training IOE. Copilot was hand-flying the aircraft on CIVET arrival to LAX. I was talking to him about the arrival and overloaded him. As we approached 12,000 feet (our next assigned altitude) he did not level off even under direction from me. We descended 400 feet before he could recover. I did not realize that the speed brakes were extended, which contributed to the slow altitude recovery.

Here the Pilot Not Flying (PNF) was trying to help the co-pilot (the Pilot Flying or PF), which led to problems on two levels. First, the combination of flying the plane and trying to heed the PNF's advice simply overloaded the PF. Second, the fact that the PNF was focused on making sure that he gave the PF appropriate assistance meant that he was distracted from his task of monitoring the ongoing status of the plane. Both flight crew members were trying to do the right thing, but they did not have enough resources to accomplish everything they needed to do. The distractions in this case were at least partly self-created; such distractions often lead to incidents in many domains (Baxter 2000). This incident would traditionally have been attributed to pilot error, but a closer examination of the context suggests that this is an over-simplification.

We noted earlier that there is a fine line between success and failure. In the aviation incident described above, where the plane descended too far, it seems obvious that there were time pressures involved. The PF knew that he had to respond relatively quickly whilst still listening to the PNF's advice. Perhaps if the PF had been more experienced, and the PNF had not felt the need to talk the PF through the arrival route, neither of them would have been distracted from the task at hand: the PF would have been more likely to level off at the appropriate altitude, and the PNF more likely to detect any anomalies in the plane's status.

The air accident at Kegworth in the UK (Air Accidents Investigation Branch 1989), described in the Appendix offers another example of a failure that was officially attributed to pilot (human) error. One of the problems was the fact that when the crew shut down the good engine, this coincided with a reduction in vibration, and a cessation of the smoke and fumes from the faulty engine. This led the crew to believe that they had taken the correct action, which can be at least partly attributed to the use of a flawed mental model (Besnard et al. 2004).

It is also important to ensure that appropriate account is taken of the physiological limitations of users as well as their psychological limitations. A simple example is the original design of packaging for medication tablets (and some other potentially hazardous household items such as domestic bleach). It used to be quite easy for a young child to unscrew the cap from a medicine bottle and then eat the contents because they looked like sweets. The solution was the child-proof safety cap. Although children could not open them in tests, older people also found it difficult to open the cap, particularly if they suffered from arthritis. In complex situations, such as flying an airplane (and particularly smaller ones), the issues involved may be more subtle. Here it is important that the pilot is not asked to do things like move their head in one direction whilst the aircraft is moving in another, because this can lead to severe disorientation.

The design limitations of the system also need to be taken into account. What often happens is that there is a general expectation that the human operator should compensate for any inadequacies in system design. Usually training is used to bridge the gap, but sometimes users are simply left to work it out for themselves.

The technique of Crew—originally *Cockpit*—Resource Management (CRM) was developed (Wiener et al. 1993) to anticipate some potential problems that can arise from the interactions between people, technology, and context within aviation. CRM aims to minimize the potential for failures in interpersonal communications at crucial times during a flight, for example, which can lead to real accidents such as:

- A plane crashing on take-off because the distracted crew failed to complete a safety checklist that would have confirmed that the aircraft's flaps had not been extended.
- A plane crashing into a river when the co-pilot failed to get the attention of the Captain about concerns that the take-off thrust had not been properly set. The co-pilot felt that he could not tell his superior what to do.
- A plane crashing when it ran out of fuel due to a communications breakdown between the Captain, the co-pilot, and air traffic control about the amount of fuel onboard.

Fig. 10.1 The influence of the blunt end on the sharp end of an incident

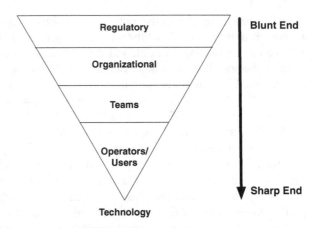

It is only when you start to give deeper consideration to the circumstances in which the error occurred that you really appreciate how hard it is to decide who (or what) is *really* to blame. If a doctor makes a medication error after having worked for 24 h continuously, for example, can we *really* blame the doctor? We know that fatigue adversely affects cognitive performance, yet the system still put the doctor in a situation where they were likely to suffer from fatigue. Similarly, we know that the way that system controls are laid out can either help or hinder performance. If a design is inappropriate, can we really blame the users?

In fact, the actions that are performed at the lowest level (usually where the user interacts with the technology) are only a small part of the picture. This level of interaction is often referred to as *the sharp end* of the system. Actions at the sharp end are often influenced by what happens at the so-called *blunt end* of the system, as shown in Fig. 10.1. The idea of a sharp end and a blunt end comes from Woods et al. (1994). This figure illustrates that final users are often seen as causes at where users meet the task, but that there is a lot of structure behind them that influences the situation as well; structure that is harder to change but that has a large amount of influence.

Decisions and actions taken at the regulatory level can affect what the operators do. In the USA, for example, the FAA's regulations state that pilots must not perform deliberate violations, unless the violation is needed to put the aircraft into a safe state. Similarly, standard operational procedures (which are generally defined at the organizational level) usually define what the operators can (or cannot) do.

10.2 Studying Error

The issue of data collection is fundamental to the study of human error. If we could reliably predict exactly when an error was going to occur, it would be a simple matter to warn the person or people involved so that they could avoid it.

Alternatively, we could design the system so that it would prevent the error occurring, or at least mitigate the consequences of the error.

There is a standard set of questions that applies to the collection of human performance data:

- Why gather data?
- What sort of data to gather?
- Where (and when) to gather data?
- How much data to gather?
- How to gather data?

These questions provide a basic framework for the discussion of the various issues involved. The issues interact and overlap, so it is not possible to answer each of the questions in isolation.

It is worth re-emphasizing at this point that erroneous behavior is an inherent part of human performance, i.e., there is a close link between knowledge and error (Mach 1905). The corollary of this is that knowledge or data relating to correct performance are also needed to make an informed judgment regarding each potential instance of state misinterpretation.

Here we only address the question of how to gather data, focusing on complex domains where the system can change dynamically without human intervention (such as aircraft, cars, and power plants). There are three basic data collection methods that can be used: laboratory-based experiments; field-based observation; and archive data. Each has its own set of strengths and weaknesses, as discussed below. The final choice of method depends on the particular situation at hand.

10.2.1 Laboratory-Based Experiments

The first method is the standard behavioral science method of using laboratory-based experiments. The main advantage of this method is that it allows for the independent variables associated with a particular phenomenon to be experimentally controlled. By varying one (or more) independent variables, the effect on the dependent variable can be observed.

The main drawback is the lack of face validity between laboratory-based experiments and the real world situation. This lack of validity makes it inappropriate at best, and impossible at worst, to generalize from the results obtained in the laboratory to the situation in the real world. The use of laboratory-based experiments largely ignores the current consensus of opinion on the importance of context in shaping human performance (Hollnagel 1993a; Hutchins 1995; Nardi 1996).

It is a long and difficult task to develop and conduct laboratory experiments that would meet all the requirements of a situation that would definitely lead to a human error. This is partly because of the problems of availability and selection of appropriate experimental subjects. The subjects would need lengthy experience of operating the system being used. Whilst it might be possible to use operators from the relevant domain, their experience is liable to be biased towards the particular system they normally work with (as opposed to your new system). The practicality of getting access to operators for the length of time needed to conduct the experiments also mitigates against using this approach. In addition, if subjects can identify the purpose of the experiment they may behave more cautiously, to guard against performing erroneous actions.

It can also be difficult to choose an appropriate experimental task and setting. Complex systems often require operators to perform multiple tasks, sometimes simultaneously. The difficulty is to find a complex system (or an appropriate simulation) that can be readily deployed under laboratory conditions. The system would also need to be familiar to the subjects to fulfill the criterion regarding expertise. Unfortunately, laboratories that have their own high fidelity simulations, such as Halden's nuclear power plant simulator (Hollnagel et al. 1996) are still the exception rather than the rule.

10.2.2 Field-Based Observation

The second method is to carry out longitudinal observation of experienced operators. The main advantage of this method is that it guarantees the ecological validity of the data. In general, observation is a valid technique, particularly if the aim is to investigate human reliability per se. In light of Mach's (1905) observation about the relationship between knowledge and error, there is a lot to be learned about operator performance under abnormal system operating conditions from observing performance under normal operating conditions.

Observational research tends to focus on one specific aspect of operator behavior, however, rather than on operator behavior per se. The observational method, therefore, has a number of drawbacks. The first is the relatively low frequency of occurrence of human error. Although there may be a deterministic element to the occurrence of human error, it is very difficult to predict precisely when a set of events or actions giving rise to an observable error will occur. So there is no guarantee that human error will occur, even during extended periods of observation.

The second drawback is the high costs associated with extended observation and the subsequent data analysis. Even if it could be guaranteed that human error would occur once in every 24 h period, for example, then gathering enough data for 100 errors would require 2,400 h of recordings. Because analysis of recorded data takes an order (or two) of magnitude longer than the recording, the time to gather and to analyze such a large amount of data quickly becomes prohibitive.

The third drawback is the inherent adaptability of human behavior. One of the characteristics of experienced operators is their ability to detect and recover from potential erroneous actions. In other words, recovery is performed before unwanted consequences arise. Unless verbal reports are also recorded, which can be used to try and identify these recoveries, it can be difficult to detect where a recovery has taken place.

The fourth drawback is that the presence of an outside observer may affect the operator's behavior. In particular, operators may be more careful than usual if they know their performance will be recorded for subsequent analysis. This may reduce the frequency of occurrence of human error, thereby requiring even longer periods of observation to gather enough data.

10.2.3 Archive Data

The third method is to use existing available data. Archive accident and incident reports, for example, have been successfully used within human error research (e.g., Pew et al. 1981; Rasmussen 1980; Wagenaar and Groeneweg 1987; Woods 1984). As with the other data collection methods, there are several pros and cons to using archive data (Chappell 1994).

The first advantage of archive data is that the data are real in that they are typically provided by participants in the incident. The second is that there are large numbers of observations available (in contrast to accident data). The third is that the data have high ecological validity because it relates to real incidents that occurred under normal operating conditions. Finally, the cost of collecting the data is generally low, because the data already exist.

The main disadvantage of using archive data is that they usually have not been gathered for the specific purpose of the investigation at hand. The data therefore often have to be re-ordered and possibly re-represented before it can be appropriately analyzed. The second disadvantage is that the detail in the reports may not have been validated. The third is that the data may be subject to reporter biases, in terms of who reports, and the information that gets reported which may be biased by selective retrieval and rational reconstruction (Ericsson and Simon 1993).

10.2.4 Selecting the Most Appropriate Data Collection Method

The aim of each of the methods described above is to generate data that can be used to develop theories and models of human performance. Over the last 20 years, since the earliest work there has been a shift towards an increased use of real world data (e.g., Hutchins 1995), especially when studying expert performance in dynamic environments. The ideal method, however, would combine the contextual richness of real world situations with some of the experimental control of laboratory conditions. The work on the HEAP (Hollnagel et al. 1996) comes close to this ideal. The HEAP involved observing teams of operators running a high fidelity nuclear power plant simulator. Even with the HEAP work, however, there were problems. The operators either knew or could guess the purpose of the study. As a result they had a higher than normal expectation that an abnormal situation would arise during a simulator session. The sessions were also usually limited to 1 h rather than the duration of a normal shift.

If you are designing an interface for a nuclear power plant control system, for example, you may regard ecological validity as being of paramount importance, and therefore decide against the use of laboratory experiments. Similarly, the hit and miss nature of using field observation for relatively infrequent events mitigates against its use, except perhaps in longitudinal studies or where unusual resources are available. Archive data, on the other hand, naturally have high ecological validity—a judicious choice of data source should make it possible to gain access to the hundreds of instances of human error required for analysis (Baxter 2000).

Ultimately your choice of method will depend on the weights you give to the pros and cons of the individual methods. In addition, however, you should make sure that you take into account the availability and access to the resources you will need to carry out your study.

10.3 Error Taxonomies

Most scientific study is underpinned by a well-defined classification system or taxonomy of the relevant phenomena. The taxonomy provides a frame of reference for the study, and enables other researchers to evaluate the results of that study. Although several human error taxonomies have been developed, there is no universal taxonomy that serves all the various purposes of error research (Senders and Moray 1991). Below we consider three well known examples.

The critical factor in generating a taxonomy of erroneous behavior is the choice of level of abstraction to use for categorization. Determining an appropriate level of abstraction requires that the purpose of the research be clearly defined. A useful rule of thumb is to model behavior at a level that allows remedies to be generated to facilitate the avoidance of a repetition of the same type of error in similar circumstances in the future.

10.3.1 The Technique for Human Error Rate Prediction

The taxonomy used in the Technique for Human Error Rate Prediction (THERP, Swain and Guttman 1983) is based around the commonly used notions of errors of omission and commission. In this taxonomy, actions can either be:

- Correct.
- Errors of omission: actions that are omitted. It may be difficult, however, to determine whether an action has been omitted or has just been delayed for a long time.

Table 10.1 GEMS	Planning	Knowledge-based mistakes
taxonomy		Rule-based mistakes
	Storage	Skill-based lapses
	Execution	Skill-based slips

- Errors of commission: actions that are performed inadequately, out of sequence, or at the wrong time (too early/late); or are qualitatively incorrect (too much/too little/wrong direction).
- Extraneous actions: actions that would not normally be expected at that particular time and place.

In THERP the probabilities of the different errors occurring are conditioned by performance shaping factors (PSFs). The PSFs are intended to take some account of the context in which the error occurs, to improve the accuracy of the individual error probability estimates. They are usually divided into external PSFs (such as situational characteristics), stressor PSFs (such as psychological stressors), and internal PSFs (such as organismic factors like previous training).

10.3.2 Generic Error Modeling System

Rasmussen's (1976) SRK model of behavior (see Chap. 5) has been used as the basis for several taxonomies that describe human performance in the operation of complex control systems, including Reason's (1990) Generic Error Modelling System (GEMS). Reason distinguishes between three types of errors: slips, lapses, and mistakes (see also Norman 1981). Slips (execution failures) occur when the person has the right intention but performs the wrong action. Lapses (memory storage failures) occur between the formulation of an intention and the execution of some action. Mistakes (intention failures) occur when the person initiates the wrong plan of action for the task at hand. Within the GEMS taxonomy, errors can be associated with planning, with storage, or with execution of actions (see Table 10.1).

Skill-based errors (slips and lapses) are normally attributable to monitoring failures. In particular, they are often linked to a lack of attention, whether deliberate or unintentional.

The rule- and knowledge-based errors (mistakes) are usually associated with problem solving activities. At the rule-based level, mistakes can arise when good rules are misapplied, or bad rules are applied. At the knowledge-based level, mistakes usually arise due to a lack of expertise, because people do not have all the knowledge required to perform the task at hand. Figure 10.2 shows the relationship between the different types of errors in GEMS and a typical stage model of human information processing.

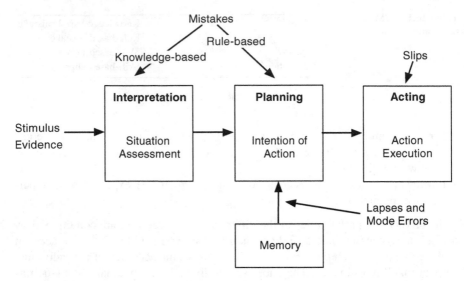

Fig. 10.2 Reason's Generic Error Modelling System (GEMS) error types related to a simple stage model of human information processing (adapted from Wickens and Holland 2000)

10.3.3 The Cognitive Reliability and Error Analysis Method

Hollnagel's (1998) Cognitive Reliability and Error Analysis Method (CREAM) tacitly acknowledges the fact that there is no single ideal taxonomy. Instead, the CREAM provides a generic framework for developing a domain specific taxonomy of causes and effects of erroneous actions.

In the CREAM, performance takes place in a context that is defined by the interaction between three high level factors:

1. The human operator
2. The technology (usually the system being operated by the human)
3. The wider organization (including the environment in which the system is located).

Each of these factors is explicitly accounted for in the CREAM that includes a scheme for classifying actions and events. The CREAM also takes account of the current consensus view that there is not a separate uniquely identifiable part of the human physiology that can be conveniently labeled *error generator*. As noted earlier, in many cases erroneous behavior occurs when the user takes what appears to be the appropriate action in conditions that are similar to, but not quite the same as what the operator believes them to be.

Any erroneous actions that can be detected can be categorized as belonging to one or more of eight possible error modes or effects—Hollnagel (1993b) also

Table 10.2 The CREAM genotypes of human error	Person-related	Observation
		Interpretation
		Planning
		Temporary
		Permanent
	Organization-related	Communication
		Training
		Ambient conditions
		Working conditions
	Technology-related	Equipment failure
		Procedures
		Temporary interface problems
		Permanent interface problems

refers to these as the logical phenotypes of human error—each of which can manifest itself in several ways (shown in italics):

- Timing: the action is *too early/too late/omitted*.
- Duration: the action is *too long/too short*.
- Force: the action uses *too much/too little force*.
- Distance: the action is carried on *too far/too short*.
- Speed: the action is *too fast/too slow*.
- Direction: the action is performed in the *wrong direction* or involves the *wrong type of movement*.
- Object: the action was carried out on a *proximal object/similar object/unrelated object* rather than the required object.
- Sequence: in a sequence of actions there was an *omission/skip forward/skip backward/repetition/reversal* or the *wrong action* was performed.

In addition, the CREAM makes provision for the inclusion of correct actions. Hollnagel (1998) suggests that a category labeled *no erroneous action* should be incorporated, either by adding it to each of the classification groups or by keeping it as a separate group.

The category of error mode to which a particular instance of an erroneous action belongs may not always be immediately obvious. In such cases, the particular situation at hand has to be carefully considered before any judgment can be made. This need for considered judgments is critical to the field of human error research, because the labeling of a particular action as being erroneous is invariably a judgment made in hindsight (Woods et al. 1994).

The other part of the CREAM taxonomy is made up of the possible causes, or genotypes. These are divided into three main categories as shown in Table 10.2. There is one category for each of the main factors that contribute to system performance: people, technology, and context (described as organization-related in the CREAM).

10.4 Analyzing Errors

There are many techniques available for analyzing errors, and any of them will usually provide some useful insights to help you understand what happened. Here we briefly discuss four techniques. Two have been widely used for several years in the safety systems engineering community. The others are more recent, and are less widely used, but offer interesting (and useful) perspectives for analyzing errors. Irrespective of which technique you choose (including those not covered here), you should make sure that it can be applied systematically.

10.4.1 Event Trees

Event trees are a bottom-up (inductive) technique for analyzing errors. They show the sequences of events that lead to all the possible outcomes. The trees are based on simple binary logic: at each node in the tree there are two possible branches based on whether an event does or does not happen (or whether a component failed or did not fail). The trees start with an initiating event, and are generated by thinking of all the possible consequences at each node in the tree. Each of the events can be assigned a probability (the sum of the probabilities for each of the two branches for a single node must add up to 1). The probability of all the identified outcomes can be calculated by multiplying together (ANDing) all the event probabilities along the path that leads from the initiating event to the outcome.

Figure 10.3 shows a quantified event tree for the case where a fire breaks out in an office block. The initiating event (shown at the left of the tree) is the fact that the fire starts, and the estimated frequency of this occurrence is one per year. The likelihood of the various resultant events (outcomes) is calculated by multiplying the appropriate probabilities together. The probability of multiple fatalities for this scenario, for example, is 0.015 (i.e., $0.1 \times 0.3 \times 0.5$).

10.4.2 Fault Trees

Fault trees are similar to event trees, although they are generated in a top down (deductive) manner, starting with the outcome and working backwards in time to try to find all the things that could have caused that particular outcome. Fault trees do not have to be binary trees, and an outcome can be determined by ANDing and ORing together a set of causal factors, as appropriate. Fault trees are normally only concerned with immediate effects, rather than the creation of latent conditions that can lie dormant within a system until some particular trigger activates them.

Fault trees can be either qualitative or quantified. To quantify a fault tree, a probability of occurrence is allocated to each of the lowest level leaf nodes in the

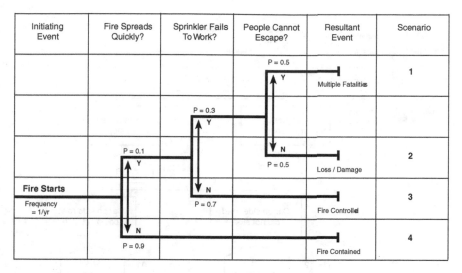

Fig. 10.3 Example quantification of event tree for a building protected by a sprinkler system (reproduced with permission from the Institution for Engineering and Technology)

tree. Fault trees can also be modified to include recovery actions; the resultant trees are usually called recovery trees (van der Schaaf 1991).

Figure 10.4 shows an example of a quantified fault tree for accidents at a particular road junction. The legend at the left of the figure describes the probabilities used in the figure. Cars driving too fast at this road junction, for example, occur frequently, so it is given a probability of 0.1.

10.4.3 CREAM

The CREAM can be used both for the retrospective analysis of accidents and the prospective analysis of possible errors in a system that is being designed. In both cases, the method that is followed is essentially the same.

Here we will only focus on the simple retrospective use of the CREAM (as shown in Fig. 10.5). The process starts with the description of the initiating event (which could be an accident or incident). This description needs to provide enough detail to form the basis for the analysis. From this description it should be possible to identify the error mode(s) (or phenotypes) associated with the event. The next step is to try and identify the possible antecedents for that error mode, using the set of tables of antecedents and consequents that lie at the heart of the CREAM method. If a specific antecedent is found, or there are no general antecedents for the error mode, then the analysis is complete. If a general antecedent is found then the next step is to find the general consequent associated with that antecedent. If none can be found, the analysis terminates, otherwise we use the general consequent as a specific consequent, and go through the loop again, this time trying to find a matching

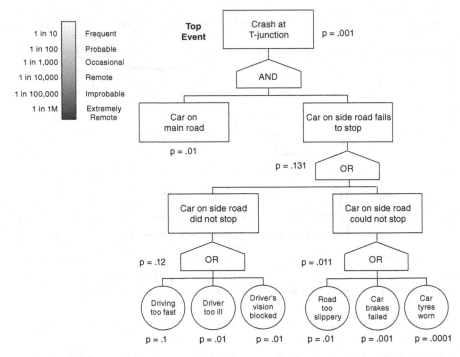

Fig. 10.4 A quantified fault tree showing the likelihood of a crash occurring at a given road junction (reproduced with permission from the Institution for Engineering and Technology)

antecedent for the specific consequent (rather than the error mode). As the process continues, a structure that looks like a tree of antecedents and consequents is built up. Note that these are really the *possible* antecedents and *possible* consequents. Some of them may be ruled out by what really happened during the event.

Using the CREAM to analyze errors can become quite involved, and is beyond the scope of this book. Hollnagel's (1998) book includes a good example of an analysis of a railway accident that occurred in New York in 1995 which is worth looking at, for those who are interested. Although the CREAM has not been widely adopted—partly because of a lack of tool support[1]—it does offer a nice illustration of how taking a different view of errors can generate new insights.

10.4.4 THEA

The Technique for Human Error Assessment (Pocock et al. 2001) assumes, like the CREAM, that the context in which actions are performed is one of the major influences on human performance. Like the CREAM, THEA is an iterative

---

[1] Although there is a browser based tool at http://www.ews.uiuc.edu/∼serwy/cream/.

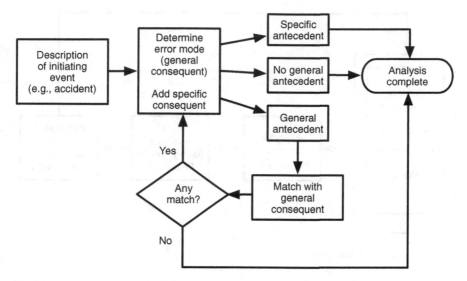

Fig. 10.5 CREAM. The basic CREAM analysis process (redrawn by the authors)

process, although the iterations take place at a higher level, i.e., the level of the design of the system or device.

The THEA process (see Fig. 10.6) starts with a description of the system in terms of its functional behavior, its interface, and how it communicates with other systems. This description is accompanied by a corresponding description of the work performed by the system. This comprises one (or more) descriptive scenarios, particularly focusing on the potential vulnerabilities of the system, and a description of the sorts of tasks that will be performed in terms of goals, actions, and plans.

The system description and work descriptions are used to structure the scenario. Any appropriate method that can be used to decompose goals, such as hierarchical task analysis (described in Chap. 11), can be used.

Once you have a structured scenario, you can do the error analysis. The analysis is based on a set of questions and a model of human information processing. Although the THEA reference guide uses Norman's (1988/2013) cyclic model of interaction, the process is model independent.

The final step is to consider the probability of the occurrence of the identified errors, and then make suggestions about changes to the design to deal with them. The process then iterates until some stopping point is determined, which will usually be down to the judgment of the designer.

As with the CREAM, THEA's uptake has been somewhat limited but, like the CREAM, it also shows how a systematic approach to analyzing errors can be used to inform design. Those who want more information should consult the THEA reference guide. THEA was originally designed to analyze situations involving a single person using a single artifact, whereas nowadays most work is performed by

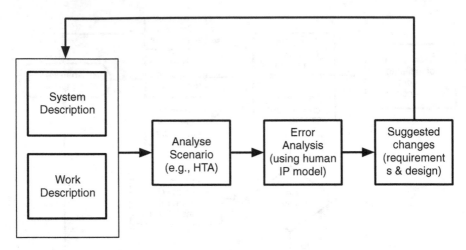

Fig. 10.6 The THEA process

teams of people. THEA was therefore adapted and extended to create a new method, CHLOE. CHLOE takes into account how people collaborate to get work done, and has been used to analyze errors in Air Traffic Control (Miguel and Wright 2003).

10.5 Implications for System Design

We need to consider how people interact with technology in a particular context when designing systems. Each of the components (people, technology, and context) can give rise to errors, so we need to design systems to take account of this, and try either to prevent the errors or at least to mitigate their consequences. It is also vital that we consider the interdependencies between people, technology, and context, because these can also give rise to errors.

We know that most systems can be described as socio-technical systems, in that they have social (people-related) components and technological components. Unfortunately, however, many designers think this means that the system can be decomposed into a social subsystem and a technical subsystem. In reality, such an atomistic decomposition is inappropriate, because of the interactions and interdependencies between the system's social and technical components. If these interactions and interdependencies are ignored, the emergent system behaviors (including errors) that they give rise to may be overlooked. Many system developers who claim that they use a socio-technical approach often decompose the system into social and technical subsystems, and focus most of their attention on the technical subsystem.

Allied to the decomposition into human and technical components is a technique called function allocation. When designing a system, you will need to identify the list of functions that the system has to perform. These functions are then allocated to either the human or the machine using a static approach that is often based on Fitts' (1951) list, which is also referred to as the MABA-MABA (Men Are Better At–Machines Are Better At) approach. The problem with this approach is that designers often allocate all the tasks that they know how to automate to the technology, and then leave the human to carry out all the others. If we want to allocate functions effectively we need to consider the processing characteristics of both the humans and the technology so that we can reduce the chances of errors whilst performing a particular function.

If your system requires a lot of functions to be carried out in the same time frame, you may overload the operator (and the technology), thereby increasing the chances of an error occurring. In this case you may want to consider whether you can allocate functions dynamically, allowing tasks to be shed, and reallocated as workloads change. So, if operators get really busy, it should be possible for them to hand off tasks to the automation to reduce their workload, thereby improving overall system performance, and vice versa.

One of the ironies of automation (Bainbridge 1987) is that the more complex socio-technical systems become, the more we rely on people to intervene to fix them when errors occur. You will therefore often hear people talking about the need to keep people in the loop. It is important that the users are kept aware of what the system is doing, by providing them with feedback about the system's state. They can use this to detect errors, and to update their own mental model of how the system is working. It is also important that users are given the opportunity to practice their skills, so they do not forget how to carry out particular tasks, especially those that they perform infrequently. This is one of the reasons why aircraft pilots have to undergo recurrent training, and are expected to hand fly their aircraft on a fairly regular basis.

10.6 Summary

Human error is a complex subject, for several reasons:

- Confusion over the term itself, which gets used to describe the action, the cause of that action, and the consequence of that action too.
- The same factors govern the expression of both expertise and error.
- Some of the contributors are latent, and lie hidden, waiting for other triggering or potentiating factors.
- Errors are judgments made in hindsight and require some measure of expected human performance for comparison.
- Human performance involves a distributed system of people interacting with technology at the sharp end and organizational elements at the blunt end.
- Decisions made at the blunt end of the system can constrain the way that work is carried out at the sharp end.

- The way technology is deployed shapes human performance, creating the potential for new forms of error and failure.

Errors will happen. You may be able to get some idea of the sorts of errors that may occur with your system by looking at archive data, where it exists. Alternatively, you may be able to collect data by running experiments using your system or an appropriate simulator.

You can take appropriate account of potential errors by carefully considering the type of system that you are designing, the people who will use it, and the context in which they will operate it. There are several methods that will help you analyze your system for potential errors, including Event Trees, Fault Trees, the CREAM, and THEA, even at design time.

10.7 Other Resources

It is worth looking at Sidney Dekker's books to get a fuller understanding of the new (some would say more enlightened) view of human error. *Ten Questions About Human Error* (Dekker 2005) is an easy and entertaining read, whilst also being thought provoking. In it he addresses the issue of human error by posing the following questions, and then going on to explain and to answer them at length:

1. Was it mechanical failure or human error?
2. Why do safe systems fail?
3. Why are doctors more dangerous than gun owners?
4. Don't errors exist?
5. If you lose situation awareness, what replaces it?
6. Why do operators become complacent?
7. Why don't they follow procedures?
8. Can we automate error out of the system?
9. Will the system be safe?
10. Should we hold people accountable for their mistakes?

You should be able to start to answer at least some of these questions for yourself at this point.

The problems of dealing with blame, and how to establish a just (i.e., fair) culture, form the content of Dekker's book, *Just Culture* (Dekker 2007). In it he gives several examples of the sorts of problems that can occur when trying to make sure that justice (in the widest sense of the word, rather than just the legalistic view) is served. The main focus of the book is on trying to balance safety and accountability so that people who make honest mistakes are not necessarily held to be culpable. He dispels the simplistic idea about needing to punish those that cross the line, by showing that who gets to draw the line, and where they get to draw it, are major determinants in deciding whether someone will be regarded as culpable or not.

10.8 Exercises

10.1 Redraw Fig. 10.3, the event tree, for errors when entering a purchase on a smartphone or other mobile device. You can make (and may need to make) assumptions about the application and about people. Note these assumptions, and note briefly what studies or references you would need to read to find out more accurate answers.

10.2 Interact through several transactions with an online commerce site, such as abebooks.com, or an online library, or other online service that delivers information. Keep a log of errors you make using a keystroke logger, an observer, or video. Analyze these errors for frequency and type using two different taxonomies.

10.3 What are the error rates while typing? When you read a finished document, it looks like there are none. In this exercise, gather some data on error rates while typing. You can do this in several ways. You could ask people to type without looking at what they are typing. This would give an uncorrected error rate. You could show them a paper to type, and check how many letters are different between the source and their typing (using the Unix 'diff' tool, or using Word's compare documents). You could also set up a web page and see how many times a user clicks on the correct link when asked. In your analyses you should consider what errors are more common, and what may lead to increased errors.

10.4 In 2009 a man drove his $1 million Bugatti Veyron car into a lake. He blamed it on dropping his cell phone. Extend the fault tree in Fig. 10.4 to include the effect of cell phones on accidents. To do this, you will have to note where cell phones will interact with driving, and you will have to attempt to provide quantitative measures of how often events happen with a cell phone.

References

Air Accidents Investigation Branch. (1989). Report on the accident to Boeing 737-400- G-OBME near Kegworth, Leicestershire. Retrieved 8 March 2014, from http://www.aaib.gov.uk/publications/formal_reports/4_1990_g_obme.cfm

Arnstein, F. (1997). Catalogue of human error. *British Journal of Anaesthesia, 79*, 645–656.

Bainbridge, L. (1987). Ironies of automation. In J. Rasmussen, K. Duncan, & J. Leplat (Eds.), *New technology and human error* (pp. 271–283). Chicester: John Wiley.

Baxter, G. D. (2000). *State misinterpretation in flight crew behaviour: An incident-based analysis*. Unpublished PhD Thesis, University of Nottingham.

Besnard, D., Greathead, D., & Baxter, G. (2004). When mental models go wrong. Co-occurrences in dynamic, critical systems. *International Journal of Human-Computer Studies, 60*(60), 117–128.

Bogner, M. S. (Ed.). (2004). *Misadventures in health care*. Mahwah, NJ: Erlbaum.

Chappell, S. L. (1994). Using voluntary incident reports for human factors evaluations. In N. Johnston, N. McDonald, & R. Fuller (Eds.), *Aviation psychology in practice* (pp. 149–169). Aldershot, UK: Avebury.

Dekker, S. (2005). *Ten questions about human error: A new view of human factors and system safety*. Mahwah, NJ: Erlbaum.

Dekker, S. (2007). *Just culture: Balancing safety and accountability*. Aldershot, Hampshire, England: Ashgate Publishing.

Dismukes, K., Young, G., & Sumwalt, R. (1998). Cockpit interruptions and distractions: Effective management requires a careful balancing act. *ASRS Directline, 10*, 4–9.

Ericsson, K. A., & Simon, H. A. (1993). *Protocol analysis: Verbal reports as data* (2nd ed.). Cambridge, MA: MIT Press.

Fitts, P. M. (1951). *Human engineering for an effective air navigation and traffic control system*. Washington, DC: National Research Council.

Gigerenzer, G. (2004). Dread risk, September 11, and fatal traffic accidents. *Psychological Science, 15*(4), 286–287.

Hollnagel, E. (1993a). *Human reliability analysis: Context and control*. London: Academic Press.

Hollnagel, E. (1993b). The phenotypes of erroneous actions. *International Journal of Man-Machine Studies, 39*, 1–32.

Hollnagel, E. (1998). *Cognitive reliability and error assessment method*. Oxford, UK: Elsevier Science.

Hollnagel, E., Drøivoldsmo, A., & Kirwan, B. (1996). Practical insights from studies of operator diagnosis. In *Proceedings of ECCE-8. Eighth European Conference on Cognitive Ergonomics* (pp. 133–137). Granada, 8–12 Sept, 1996. Rocquencourt, France: European Association of Cognitive Ergonomics.

Hollnagel, E., Woods, D. D., & Leveson, N. (Eds.). (2006). *Resilience engineering: Concepts and precepts*. Aldershot, UK: Ashton Press.

Hutchins, E. (1995). *Cognition in the wild*. Cambridge, MA: MIT Press.

Johnson, C. W., & Holloway, C. M. (2007). A longitudinal analysis of the causal factors in major maritime accidents in the USA and Canada (1996–2006). In *The Safety of Systems: Proceedings of the 15th Safety-Critical Systems Symposium* (pp. 85–104). London, UK: Springer.

Kemeny (chairman), J. G. (1979). *The need for change: The Legacy of TMI*. Washington, DC: The President's Commission on the accident at TMI.

Mach, E. (1905). *Knowledge and error* (English Trans., D. Reidel, 1976). Dordrecht, Netherlands: Reidel.

Miguel, A., & Wright, P. (2003). CHLOE: A technique for analysing collaborative systems. In *Proceedings of 9th Conference on Cognitive Science Approaches to Process Control* (pp. 53–60). New York, NY: ACM Press.

Nardi, B. A. (1996). *Context and consciousness: Activity theory and human-computer interaction*. Cambridge, MA: MIT Press.

Norman, D. A. (1981). Categorization of action slips. *Psychological Review, 88*, 1–15.

Norman, D. A. (1988). *The psychology of everyday things*. New York, NY: Basic Books.

Norman, D. A. (2013). *The design of everyday things*. New York, NY: Basic Books.

Petroski, H. (1985/1992). *To engineer is human: The role of failure in successful design*. New York, NY: Vintage Books.

Petroski, H. (1994). *Design paradigms: Case histories of error and judgment in engineering*. Cambridge, UK: Cambridge University Press.

Petroski, H. (2006). *Success through failure: The paradox of design*. Princeton, NJ: Princeton University Press.

Pew, R. W., Miller, D. C., & Feeher, C. E. (1981). *Evaluation of proposed control room improvements through analysis of critical operator decisions (EPRI-NP-1982)*. Cambridge, MA: Bolt, Beranek & Newman.

Pocock, S., Harrison, M., Wright, P., & Johnson, P. (2001). THEA: A technique for human error assessment early in design. In *Proceedings of Human-Computer Interaction: INTERACT'01* (pp. 247–254). Amsterdam, The Netherlands: IOS Press.

Randell, B. (2000). Facing up to faults. *The Computer Journal, 43*, 95–106.

Rasmussen, J. (1976). Outlines of a hybrid model of the process operator. In T. G. Sheridan & G. Johannsen (Eds.), *Monitoring behavior and supervisory control* (pp. 371–383). New York, NY: Plenum.

Rasmussen, J. (1980). What can be learned from human error reports? In K. Duncan, M. Gruneberg, & D. Wallis (Eds.), *Changes in working life* (pp. 97–113). Chichester, UK: Wiley.

Rasmussen, J. (1988). Human error mechanisms in complex work environments. *Reliability Engineering and System Safety, 22*, 155–167.

Rasmussen, J., Pejtersen, A.-M., & Goodstein, L. P. (1994). *Cognitive systems engineering.* Chichester, UK: Wiley.

Reason, J. (1990). *Human error.* Cambridge, UK: Cambridge University Press.

Senders, J. W., & Moray, N. P. (1991). *Human error: Cause, prediction, and reduction.* Hillsdale, NJ: Erlbaum.

Swain, A. D., & Guttman, H. E. (1983). *A handbook of human reliability analysis with emphasis on nuclear power applications.* Washington, DC: US Nuclear Regulatory Commission.

van der Schaaf, T. W. (1991). A framework for designing near miss management systems. In T. W. v. d. Schaaf, D. A. Lucas & A. Hale (Eds.), *Near miss reporting as a safety tool* (pp. 27–35). Oxford, UK: Butterworth-Heinemann.

Vaughan, D. (1997). *The Challenger launch decision.* Chicago, IL: University of Chicago Press.

Wagenaar, W. A., & Groeneweg, J. (1987). Accidents at sea: Multiple causes and impossible consequences. *International Journal of Man-Machine Studies, 27*, 587–598.

Wickens, C. D., & Hollands, J. G. (2000). Engineering psychology and human performance (3rd ed.). Upper Saddle River, NJ: Prentice-Hall.

Wiener, E., Kanki, B., & Helmreich, R. L. (Eds.). (1993). *Cockpit resource management.* London, UK: Academic Press.

Woods, D. D. (1984). Some results on operator performance in emergency events. *Institution of Chemical Engineers Symposium Series* (Vol. 90, pp. 21–31).

Woods, D. D., Johannesen, L. J., Cook, R. I., & Sarter, N. B. (1994). *Behind human error: Cognitive systems, computers, and hindsight.* Wright-Patterson Air Force Base, OH: CSERIAC.

Part III
Methods

Chapter 11
Methodology I: Task Analysis

Abstract Task analysis (TA) is a useful tool for describing and understanding how people perform particular tasks. Task analyses can be used for several purposes ranging from describing behavior to helping decide how to allocate tasks to a team. There are several methods of TA that can be used to describe the user's tasks at different levels of abstraction. We describe some of the most commonly used methods and illustrate the use of TA with some example applications of TA. TA is widely used but when using TA there are considerations to keep in mind such as the fact that many approaches require an initial interface or specification, and that many do not include context multiple users or ranges of users. These considerations help describe where and when TA can be successfully applied and where TA will be extended in the future.

11.1 Introduction

You should by now be familiar with the idea that when we are designing user-centered systems we are thinking about particular people doing particular tasks in a particular context. So far in this book we have looked in some detail at people-related aspects, and at some of the context-related aspects. In this chapter we focus more on task-related issues.

To understand what people do when they perform a task we use a technique called task analysis (TA). TA provides a way to describe the users' tasks and subtasks, the structure and hierarchy of these tasks, and the knowledge they already have or need to acquire to perform the tasks. Using these descriptions it becomes possible to predict how long users will take to learn a task, and how long they will take to perform a task. In this chapter we will mostly focus on the sorts of tasks that are nowadays carried out using some form of computer-based system.

TA can be used in most stages of system development. Before carrying out a TA, however, Diaper (2004) suggests that you first identify the stages of

F. E. Ritter et al., *Foundations for Designing User-Centered Systems*,
DOI: 10.1007/978-1-4471-5134-0_11, © Springer-Verlag London 2014

development when TA will be used, and then ask four interrelated questions for each of the identified stages:

1. What knowledge do you want the TA to provide? Frequently this is not an easy question to answer and your answer may need to be refined as you start to learn more and uncover interesting issues.
2. What format should the output of the TA take? The output from a TA may not map directly onto software engineering representations, so the contribution of a TA may sometimes be indirect, e.g., building models of the world through TA can improve the models that are used in software engineering.
3. What data can be collected? Data can be collected using several methods such as observing performance, interviews, document analysis, training program analysis, and analysis of existing systems.
4. Which method should be used? The choice should be based on knowledge about the input data and the desired output data, rather than familiarity with a particular method.

The results of a TA can be prescriptive or descriptive, depending on the aims of the analyst. Prescriptive analyses show how the user should carry out the task, and hence are associated with normative behavior. Prescriptive analyses can be used to help create safety procedures, and standard operating procedures, which prescribe how the user should carry out particular tasks. In contrast, descriptive analyses show how users really carry out the task, and are hence associated with actual behavior. Descriptive analyses are usually more situation specific than prescriptive analyses. It is important to be able to distinguish between the two, however. A prescriptive analysis of car driving, for example, would not include anything about driving above the speed limit; a descriptive analysis would be more likely to include details about people driving faster than the speed limit (perhaps only for particular sections of the road network).

When thinking about the different types of TA that are available, it is important to remember that there may be some slight differences in the way they use terms such as *goals*, *tasks*, and *actions*. In general, goals are achieved by carrying out tasks. These tasks are usually performed as a series of actions on some object.

In the rest of the chapter we first provide some examples of how task analysis can be used before describing four approaches to TA. The different approaches should be seen as complementary, as each has its own particular strengths and weaknesses. Although the approaches are similar in several respects, such as the need to apply them systematically, they also differ in many respects, such as the types of development activities they can support, and the level of detail that they can provide. For each of the different TA approaches we provide examples of how they can be used, and note some of their strengths and weaknesses. We finish by noting some of the limitations of TA.

Table 11.1 Areas where TA can be applied, adapted from Kirwan and Ainsworth (1992)

1. Person specification
2. Staffing and job organization
3. Skills and knowledge acquisition
4. Allocation of function
5. Performance assurance
6. Task and interface design

11.2   The Uses of Task Analysis

TA can be used for many different purposes. Kirwan and Ainsworth (1992), for example, identify six areas where TA can be applied, which are noted in Table 11.1.

It should be noted that these areas are not all independent and sometimes overlap. Here we focus our discussions on the last three items, because these are the ones that are most closely associated with the process of designing user-centered systems.

11.2.1 Allocation of Function

The traditional way of allocating functions to users has been to use a Fitts' (1951) list approach, based on whether the associated tasks are better carried out by people or by computers. In the original formulation there was often only one person, and one machine to think about. Nowadays, however, there may be several people, working together as a team, and several computer-based systems to consider. A task analysis helps you identify the knowledge that is needed to carry out the functions, and so can be used to inform how the functions are allocated. At the highest level it also lets you lay out a list of all the tasks that will need to be allocated. As part of Cognitive Work Analysis, Vicente (1999) has developed an approach to take large descriptions of tasks and use the complete set of tasks across a team of users to allocate sets of tasks to users that make sense to the users based on the large set rather than traditional job descriptions or existing interfaces.

11.2.2 Performance Assurance

The way that systems are used often changes over time. This is due partly to the way the system evolves, partly to the way people learn to use the system over time, and partly to changes in the context in which the system is deployed. The net effect is that there will often be a change in the tasks that the user carries out. It is

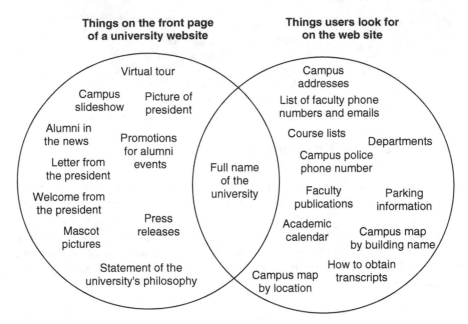

Fig. 11.1   The potential mismatch between university department web sites built without a thoughtful task analysis and what users want from university department web sites. Inspired by a cartoon from xkcd.com

therefore important to continually check that the system still supports the user in carrying out those tasks that have changed. When there are large numbers of tasks, this can be both particularly daunting and important.

For example, university department web sites have a large number of tasks or information content types that users look for. Figure 11.1 notes the mismatch that has happened on some sites. The list for a department or college consists of over 100 types of information (Ritter et al. 2002). Sites can use that list to investigate whether a site supports all the anticipated information needs of their users. Ritter and colleagues' list has been used to make specific suggestions about how these sites should be updated, including putting up more information, and distributing the updating across members of the college because it is too much for a single person to update.

Another use of TA is to find out more about how a task is done. When you compare the way that people are supposed to perform tasks, and the way they actually carry them out, there are often several noticeable differences. Creating a TA can help you to understand what the user is doing because you have a better understanding of the task, and often discussion based on a TA with users to update the TA provides further insights into why they are behaving in a particular way, for example, because of their particular knowledge or the context in which they perform the task.

11.2.3 Task and Interface Design

TA can be used in several ways to guide task and interface design as listed below.

1. To predict user task performance. These predictions of time, errors, or work-load can be used to compute whether an interface can be used to perform a time-sensitive task (e.g., interact with a video game), or how many copies of an interface are needed to support a number of users (e.g., the minimum and the optimal number of ATMs or ticket machines in an airport), or when a system needs to be speeded up to keep pace with the user. This approach has been and is being used to guide the requirements of how many sailors are needed to run a ship (Chipman and Kieras 2004).
2. To suggest where users will make mistakes. Furthermore, we can take two types of task analysis and look at their relationship—for example, is the rela-tionship between goals/subgoals and the chronology of actions simple or complex? Are similar tasks similar? Are common safe tasks easy to do and expensive or dangerous tasks harder to do? Where there is a complex rela-tionship between the users' goal structure and the interface's action structure, then an interface may be hard to use and may lead to more errors than it should or could. This approach has been applied to tasks in aviation. Models are built of how ATC interacts with pilots (Freed and Remington 1998) or how ground control navigates planes (Byrne and Kirlik 2005). The results suggest ways to avoid errors and ways to mitigate the effects of errors.
3. To understand the relationship between old and new versions of a system. Given a task analysis of how people currently do a task, or would conceive of doing the task, we can ask how much that process and knowledge overlaps with the formal analysis of how it should be done in the new system. Increased similarity of how to use both systems can help with efficiency of learning, use, and comfort, and can lead to greater acceptance of the new system. The original work in this area (Bovair et al. 1990; Kieras and Polson 1985) noted the knowledge to use an initial editor, and then compared that to the knowledge to use a new editor. The results provide several suggestions, including: that ignoring old knowledge is easy; that modifying existing knowledge is, of course, slower; and that learning new knowledge slows the user down the most.
4. To compare different designs. A task analysis of two interfaces can predict which interface will be faster and easier to use, as long as the two designs are reasonably distinctive. In most cases, however, the comparisons are accurate and useful. Gray et al. (1992), for example, used TA to compare the interface for a new system that was to be used by telephone toll operators—the people who used to respond when you dialed 0—against the old system's interface. The new interface was predicted to be slower, and an empirical test confirmed this. It also showed that the effect of the difference in performance would cost the telephone company about $2 million per year.
   TA has been used to investigate the design of menus using real and simulated cell phones (St. Amant et al. 2004, 2007). In this project a user model was

created to perform a set of five tasks using a particular cell phone. The tasks were to adjust the ringer volume, access the tip calculator, view all contacts, view the date, and access the web browser. The resulting model was used to predict how long it would take to perform the five tasks with a cell phone and its initial menu structure. When compared with data from five practiced users the predictions turned out to be fairly accurate, but also showed where there was room for improvement in the design of the menus. The model suggested that reordering the menus to put the most often used menu items first would save about 30% of the total interaction time.

5. To create user manuals. The results of the TA show in detail the steps that are involved in carrying out a task. User manuals can be created by translating this into text and elaborating, where appropriate. Basing the manual on a task analysis helps to make the manual more accurate, and more acceptable to the users, particularly if the TA was used to analyze how users really did the tasks.

Closely related to the idea of user manuals is the notion of training people to do the task. In safety critical systems, for example, you want all the users to do the same task in (more or less) the same way. A TA can be used as the basis for developing standard operating procedures (which are used in domains other than safety critical systems too). In addition, because the TA shows the knowledge that is required to carry out particular tasks, it becomes possible to compare what the users know with what they need to know. Where any gaps are identified, this suggests where training could be useful to increase the users' knowledge to the appropriate levels.

11.3 Hierarchical Task Analysis

Hierarchical Task Analysis (HTA) is probably the most widely used method in human factors and ergonomics. An initial HTA is often a precursor to the use of other methods, largely because it provides details about task activity. The precise level of detail depends on the depth of the analysis, which is determined by the original purpose of the analysis. Like most methods of task analysis, HTA takes a decompositional approach.

11.3.1 HTA Components

HTA involves decomposing goals into subgoals (Annett 2005), although it is often described in terms of decomposing tasks into subtasks. The order and structure of these goals and subgoals is represented visually. The analysis is usually presented either as a hierarchical graph structure, or in a tabular textual format. Each goal (and subsequent subgoals) will be accompanied by a plan. These plans, which describe how goals and subgoals are achieved, cover aspects such as the (possibly conditional) sequencing of subgoals, the need for concurrency, and how cued actions can direct performance.

11.3.2 Example Application of HTA

Table 11.2 shows a simple HTA for making an online purchase. It is not complete, but illustrates the major steps, and would be useful when talking about how to perform the task, and how to help users perform the task. It is complete enough that it could be used to start a design. The plan at the bottom of the table is an example, high-level plan. The plan—plans are usually numbered, with plan 0 being the plan associated with the top level goal—suggests that 1 must be completed before 2. There would also be plans for the subgoals, and sub-subgoals as necessary. There might also be other plans for different users and uses.

Examining the HTA in Table 11.2, we can start to identify some suggestions for design. If you wanted to provide your users with the option of browsing the listing before logging in, for example, you would have to change the plan to allow task 2 to happen before task 1, as well as afterwards, so the revised plan would look something like:

Plan 0: 1 or 2, then 2 as needed, then 1 if needed, then 3.

Figure 11.2 shows the HTA (this time drawn as a graph) for getting a file from a web-based email system. A plan for downloading the first file would include all the sub-tasks (1.1–1.4). A plan to download a second file could skip sub-tasks 1.1 and 1.2.

The analysis in Fig. 11.2 can also suggest changes to the design of the way that the task is performed. Sub-task 1.2.2, for example, could be made more general, allowing that users might move and click, and that CR might be accepted as a way to move between fields. Further, it may be possible to skip some sub-tasks in particular circumstances. If the browser remembers the user's details then sub-task 1.2 could be skipped. Similarly, if the mail client downloads the files automatically (like many mail clients), sub-task 1.4 can be skipped. The details about skipping sub-tasks would normally be described in the associated plans.

Performing an HTA can be a time-consuming process involving many choices. Although it yields a useful representational description, the technique does not specify how to go about gathering the task information that you wish to represent.

There is no hard and fast rule about the lowest level at which you should terminate the analysis. In general you should consider stopping at a natural level, where further analysis would not contribute any more to your understanding of the situation. Usually it is fairly obvious when to do this. More formally, you can consider using the so-called stopping rule. For this you need to assess the probability, P, of inadequate performance and the cost, C, of inadequate performance if

Table 11.2 An example hierarchical task analysis for making an online purchase

0 Perform online purchase
1. Login
  1.1. Select login screen
  1.2. Enter ID
  1.3. Enter password
2. Choose object
  2.1. Browse listing
  2.2. Select item
3. Pay
  3.1. Choose pay screen
  3.2. Select payment method
  3.3. Enter payment method details
Plan 0: 1, then 2 as many times as needed, then 3

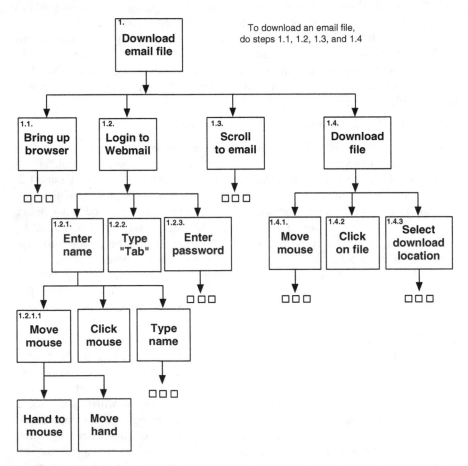

Fig. 11.2 Hierarchical task analysis of downloading an email attachment. (Further subtasks shown as three *small boxes*.)

you did not expand the hierarchy down a level. You then multiply these together to get the stopping value: if this is acceptable, then you terminate the analysis (Kirwan and Ainsworth 1992).

11.3.3 Summary

The main advantage of HTA is that, when carried out correctly by a skilled analyst, it can provide useful information to inform design relatively quickly. It does not require the interface or the interface details to be fully specified, so it can be used during the early stages of system development. Once created, the analysis can be extended, using appropriate methods to provide further details on the cognitive aspects of the task. HTA's main disadvantage is that the way in which its results are usually presented do not map readily onto the representations used by software engineers. Either the task analyst or the system developer will probably have to carry out further work to translate the results of the HTA into something that can be used during development.

11.4 Cognitive Task Analysis

As the nature of work in many domains moved from mostly manual control to mostly monitoring and supervisory control—sometimes described as a change from doing to thinking—it became increasingly important to take account of the cognitive aspects of work. Rather than pulling levers, opening and closing valves, the users now spent most of their time tracking the behaviour of a computer-based system on a display screen, making decisions and interacting with the system using the relevant input devices (e.g., in aviation many aircraft now employ a joystick device rather than a control yoke to help fly it).

Cognitive Task Analysis (CTA; e.g., see Schraagen et al. 2000 for an overview) extends more traditional task analysis techniques to facilitate the collection of information about the mental processes that underpin observable task performance. It should be noted that this does not mean that CTA and HTA are mutually exclusive: normally they should be used to complement one another.

11.4.1 CTA Components

A CTA will usually comprise the application of a set of methods (e.g., Seamster et al. 1997 discuss a range of methods that can be used in the aviation domain). One of the first steps in carrying out a CTA is therefore to choose the methods and tools that are appropriate to the particular situation that is being studied. The methods that can be used include:

1. Interviews
2. Concept (or card) sorting
3. Verbal reports
4. Cognitive walkthroughs
5. GOMS (described in more detail below).

The choice of methods is influenced by factors such as the objectives of the CTA, the available resources, the types of tasks involved, and the skills of the person doing the CTA.

Once the data for a CTA has been collected, the results from the various methods have to be compiled and interpreted. The results of the CTA should provide details about the cognitive aspects of how tasks are performed, as well as details of the information and knowledge needed to perform those tasks and how that information and knowledge are used.

11.4.2 Example Application of CTA

Baxter et al. (2005) carried out a case study of work in a neonatal intensive care unit where a new decision support system (Fuzzy Logic Respiratory Neonatal Care Expert, FLORENCE) was being developed. FLORENCE was intended to help clinical staff make decisions about changes to the mechanical ventilator that is used to treat respiratory distress syndrome (RDS) in premature babies. It was important that the introduction of FLORENCE did not adversely affect the dependability of the delivery of care in the unit, and that it was acceptable to users. A CTA was therefore carried out using lightweight rich pictures analysis (Monk 1998), the critical decision method (CDM; Klein et al. 1989), and observation.

Task analysis methods, in general, pay little attention to the context in which the tasks are carried out; rich pictures analysis provides a way to take account of that context, although it is quite novel for it to be included as part of a CTA. In this case study, a rich pictures analysis was carried out to capture details about the context in which FLORENCE was to be deployed. Data was collected using semi-structured interviews to identify the roles, responsibilities, and concerns of eight members of staff working in the unit, including the staff that provide administrative support in the unit. The analysis also showed how staff communicate and interact with members of staff who work in other parts of the hospital, such as the test laboratories. The importance of communication within the unit was also identified, since it forms the basis for clinical care of the babies. Furthermore, the central role of the various patient records was highlighted: FLORENCE would have to find some way to produce appropriate records.

The CDM was used to analyze how clinical staff make decisions about any changes that need to be made to the settings of the mechanical ventilators used to treat the babies. It is critical that these decisions are correct and timely, otherwise they can seriously adversely affect the babies' health. The basic steps of the CDM were followed for the incidents selected by each of the eight participants, and a critical cue inventory—highlighting the cues that clinical staff paid attention to—and situation assessment records—which describe how the incident unfolded in terms of cues, goals, expectations, and decisions—were developed for each incident. These highlighted aspects such as the importance of having a distinctive alarm for FLORENCE because the unit already has several alarms sounding on a fairly regular basis, and the hierarchy of decision making which flattens when dealing with acute incidents.

Finally, observation was used to capture details of how clinical staff work in situ to treat babies with RDS. RDS is self-regulating, and usually lasts around 72 h. The treatment of two babies was recorded using timed note taking—the unit is a high stress situation, so video recording was not a viable option—over a 2-h period. The first baby was moved off the unit after 1 day; the second baby was observed on three consecutive days all at the same time of day. The results showed how often staff interacted with the equipment around the babies' cots under normal conditions and when an alarm sounded.

The results of the CTA were analyzed and used to inform the development of FLORENCE. These included decisions about the interface (e.g., the need for instructions about changes to ventilator settings to be precise and unambiguous, such as "increase PIP by 2–16"), as well as training (e.g., staff need to learn how to prioritize their response to FLORENCE's alarm) and more general physical ergonomics concerns (e.g., space is needed around the baby's cot to accommodate the PC running FLORENCE).

11.4.3 Summary

As its name suggests, CTA is particularly suited to analyzing the cognitive processes and products that people use when performing tasks. It is not so good at dealing with the work context in which performance takes place (although using rich pictures analysis does provide at least a partial solution, e.g., see Baxter et al. 2005). Carrying out a CTA can be quite time consuming, particularly when the selected methods require access to experts. CTA also requires that the analyst(s) are competent in carrying out a range of methods. Furthermore, it requires a high level of skill to be able to interpret the results of several methods in a holistic way so that they can be presented to the system developers.

11.5 GOMS

GOMS is an acronym for Goals, Operations, Methods, and Selection rules (Card et al. 1980, 1983). It is a method that can be used as part of a CTA, but we include it in its own right because of its close relationship with the field of HCI.

The focus of GOMS is on specifying the details of error-free, expert behavior, and using the resulting specification to predict learnability, usability, and task execution times, allowing that there may be multiple strategies available for similar tasks. GOMS tends to be used when designing interactive technology like phones and GPS systems, where milliseconds can matter, where consistency in the users' knowledge and in the interface matters, and where operators may be expert but not trained to do things in a single way.

The four GOMS techniques:

- GOMS: sometimes referred to as CMN-GOMS, using its authors' initials to distinguish it from the generic name
- NGOMSL: Natural GOMS Language
- CPM-GOMS: Cognitive Perceptual Motor GOMS, which supports concurrent actions
- The Keystroke Level Model (KLM) which is described in more detail below

are sometimes described as a family (John and Kieras 1996a). They vary in how easy they are to apply and use.

11.5.1 GOMS Components

The components of GOMS are listed in Table 11.3. With GOMS models, the cognitive structure is represented in the concept of starting from Goals, and also from the explicit use of Selection rules to indicate how Methods—comprising sub-goals and Operators—are chosen to accomplish those Goals.

11.5.2 Example Application of GOMS

Table 11.4 provides an example GOMS model for editing text. This model consists of two parts. The main task (which comes second in the table) is to perform all the edits. This is a cyclical task, and represents starting with a marked up manuscript and then performing the edits marked on the paper (or highlighted in the electronic file). Each of the edits are *unit tasks* which define a single edit. A full model would have multiple types of unit tasks for editing. The first part of the model notes a declarative memory chunk about the Cut command, a unit task, including how to find it and what the keystroke accelerator is. A more complete model would have further unit tasks defined.

The method for editing a document is shown as a looping algorithm of working through a set of tasks to edit a document. This algorithm represents how people work through editing a document with changes to be made in the document, stopping when there are no more edits. This remains a relatively common task, for

Table 11.3 The components of GOMS

Goals are the desired states of affairs. They are brought about by the application of methods and operators

Operators are elementary perceptual, motor, or cognitive actions. Intended either to change the world (a normal key-press) or to change our knowledge about the world (e.g., reading). In practice, operators are really those subgoals whose methods of solution we have decided not to analyze any further. The choice of appropriate operators is critical to a GOMS analysis. Some critics note that there are no clear guidelines for doing so, although it is often a fairly straightforward decision

Methods describe procedures for achieving goals. They contain a sequence of subgoals and/or operators, with conditions potentially attached to each part of the method. These conditions relate to the current task environment (e.g., repeat until no tasks left)

Selection rules augment the basic control structure of the model. Where multiple methods are available the selection rules indicate how to choose between the methods. These include, for example, when scrolling a document: if you want to scroll a long distance, use the search function; if you want to scroll a short distance, use the scroll bar; and if you want to scroll a very short distance, use the arrow keys

Table 11.4 Example GOMS model for text editing (reprinted from St. Amant et al. 2005). This model is written using NGOMSL notation

LTM [long term memory] item: Cut Command [a unit task]
    Name is Cut.
    Containing Menu is Edit.
    Menu Item Label is Cut.
    Accelerator Key is "Control-X".
[[There would be more types of commands here in a complete model.]]

Method for goal: Edit Document
    Step. Store First under <current task name>.
    Step. Check for done.
    Decide: If <current task name> is None, Then
        Delete <current task>;
        Delete <current task name>;
        Return with goal accomplished.
    Step. Get task item whose
        Name is <current task name>
        and store under <current task>.
    Step. Accomplish goal: Perform Unit task.
    Step. Store Next of <current task>
        under <current task name>;
        Goto Check for done.

example, how an author right now is working through this chapter making changes to improve the text and how students revise lab reports.

The loop has several types of substeps. These steps can store state (e.g., what the current task is); they can perform conditionals (if); and they can subgoal (Perform unit task). Within the unit tasks (not fully shown), information can be obtained from the display and mental and physical actions performed. GOMS manuals provide a full list of the actions (e.g., Kieras 1999) and when to include mental operators to retrieve task structure, but in practice these lists can be extended to include unusual devices such as joysticks or different types of manual controls (such as different knobs or toggle switches). The analysis in Table 11.4 does not include all the details of all the subtasks that can be performed, and not all the details of how to do a unit task.

Table 11.5 shows a model for dialing a cell phone. In this example the tasks are slightly smaller and the interaction and memory aspects are more prominent.

11.5.3 Summary

GOMS models sometimes appear structurally quite similar to other hierarchical task analyses of goals/subgoals. The main difference is that GOMS has formalized its components to a greater level of detail. It is assumed that the methods are known before the GOMS analysis is carried out, and that they are not developed during task performance. The particular strengths of GOMS lie in assessing how to make interfaces easier to use by comparing alternative models, or methods, for a particular task.

Many people question the utility of GOMS analyses, arguing that there is no such thing as error-free, expert performance. This limitation can be somewhat ameliorated by incorporating the error correction strategies in the analysis. Probably the biggest limitation of GOMS, however, is that the interface has to be implemented or at least described in enough detail to be able to identify the actions for a particular task. There is also a lack of a clear specification of what can be used in Selection rules—there is an implication that it should be the current task context, but real behavior, for example, undoubtedly allows choices to be based on previous selections. It is also difficult to do a vanilla GOMS analysis when multitasking or task interleaving is involved. CPM-GOMS was developed to address this, but at the expense of making it more difficult to create models.

11.6 The Keystroke Level Model

A simplified version of GOMS is the keystroke level model (KLM) of Card et al. (1983). Like GOMS, it is a method that can be used as part of a CTA, but we include it here in its own right because of its close relationship with the field of HCI.

Table 11.5 Example GOMS model, written using NGOMSL notation, for telephone dialing taken from St. Amant et al. (2005)

Task item: T1   [[tasks will go from T1 to T11 to dial (814) 865-3528]]
          Name is T1.
          Digit is "8".
          Next is T2.
Visual object: first digit
          Content is "8".
Task item: T2
          Name is T2.
          Digit is "1".
          Next is T3.
Visual object: second digit
          Content is "8".
. . .
Task item: T11
          Name is T11.
          Digit is "8".
          Next is NONE.

Visual object: second digit
          Content is "1".

Method for goal: Dial Number
          Step. Store T1 under <current task name>.
          Step Check for done.
                    Decide: If <current task name> is T11, Then
                    Delete <current task>;
                    Delete <current task name>;
                    Return with goal accomplished.
          Step. Get task item whose Name is <current task name>
                    and store under <current task>.
          Step. Accomplish goal: Dial Digit.
          Step. Store Next of <current task> under <current task name>.
          Goto Check for done.

Method for goal: Dial Digit
          Step. Look for object whose Content is Digit of <current task>
                    and store under <target>.
          Step. Point to <target>; Delete <target>.
          Step. Click mouse button.
          Step. Verify "Correct digit pressed".
          Step. Return with goal accomplished.

The KLM is usually applied where there is just one person interacting with a computer-based system. It is a fast and approximate way to compute how long users will take to perform a unit task. A unit task is essentially a small cognitively manageable task. Large tasks can be decomposed into several unit tasks, although not all tasks will have a unit task substructure. The time to do the whole task is calculated by simply adding up the calculated times for all the component unit tasks. It should be noted that you also need to include the time it takes to acquire the task, i.e., the time it takes for the user to work out what to do. The KLM does not provide a way of calculating this but Card et al. (1980) suggest that the time needed for each unit task when manipulating a manuscript is 2–3 s if the instructions are written down, 5–30 s if it is a routine design situation, and even longer for creative composition situations.

To calculate the time for a unit action involves analyzing the operations into their elemental perceptual, motor, and cognitive actions (e.g., keystrokes). Then by adding together the times for these individual actions it can be possible to make time predictions for expert, error-free performance of that task.

11.6.1 Description of KLM Components

The execution of a unit-task requires operators of (basically) four types:

1. Keystrokes (K): unit time based on typing speeds (0.08–1.2 s/keystroke, mouse click, or button press)
2. Pointing (P): moving mouse to target (clicking is a keystroke) (approximately 1.1 s, but Fitts' law can also be used)
3. Homing (H(mouse) or H(keyboard)): moving hand to/from mouse and keyboard (approximately 0.4 s)
4. Drawing (D): dragging mouse in straight-line segments (0.9 n + 0.16 l where n = number of segments and l = length of segments).

To these should be added some number of mental operators (M or Mop, 1.35 s). Well practiced tasks with a simpler structure will require less mental operators. Getting the number of mental operators correct is a difficulty in using this method, but if it is done consistently across applications it is less of a problem. Finally, the system's response time (Sys), if it limits the user's task performance, also has to be included. This can be estimated, or, again, if the estimate can be assumed to be consistent across interfaces, is less important than you might fear.

The number of mental operators is computed using a set of rules—basically between all operators, except those linked through knowledge or skill (e.g., the keystrokes in a single word, or a set such as point and click a mouse).

Where there are selection rules governing the choice of methods then it is up to the analyst to decide whether to go for best or worst case time predictions.

The time to perform these operators as noted above can be done in an approximate style. There are several ways to improve the predictions of KLM models.

(1) Keystroke times vary. Card et al. (1983) include tables that provide different times for different keystrokes. These tables do not differentiate different typist speeds, but do show that different keys take different times. This suggests that

Table 11.6 Example application of the KLM to a simple editing task

Method
1. Delete 3rd clause. H[mouse] K[mouse down] P K[mouse up] M K[D]
2. Insert it in front of 1st clause. P M K[l] K[ESC]
3. Replace ": o" with "O". P M 2 K[SHIFT R] H[keyboard] 2 K[O ESC]
4. Replace "T" by ": t". H[mouse] K[mouse down] M K[R] H[keyboard] 4 K[: SPACE t ESC]
5. Delete 3rd clause. H[mouse] P K[mouse] M K[D]
6. Insert it in front of 2nd clause. K M K[l] K[ESC]
7. Find next task. M K[F]
Time Predictions
Texecute = $[23\ t_K + 4\ t_P + 5\ t_H] + 7\ t_M$
$= 22\ (0.15) + 4\ (1.1) + 5\ (0.4)] + 7(1.35)$
$= 19.15$ s

Note that in this example the same average time is used for each keystroke

interfaces should choose keys that are fast (and presumably easy to type). This suggestion includes choosing words that use both hands for touch typists and avoiding punctuation characters (which are slower to press).

(2) The gross predictions of mouse moves and drags can be made more accurate by using Fitts' law to make predictions based on the target size and distance. When the initial location of the mouse is not known, it can be approximated.

(3) The system response time can be computed using tools to analyze key press times. The response times are still important in devices such as ATMs, and in systems which may be required to present the same data simultaneously on different continents, within a multinational company, for example.

11.6.2 Example Application of the KLM

Table 11.6 shows an example KLM analysis worked out for a simple text editing task of cutting a phrase (Step 1), inserting it (Step 2), changing the case of two letters (Steps 3 and 4), and taking up the next task (Step 5). The analysis suggests that the time to perform this task is not so long (24 s). Thus, if this edit takes longer, it is not the interface that is restraining the user's progress, it is the cognition to come up with the letters or to think about other changes. It is the writing, essentially, to come up with the changes that takes so long!

11.6.3 Summary

Although closely related to GOMS, note how keystroke-level analysis is closer to time-and-motion (chronological) analysis than goal/subgoal analysis. It assumes a simple world: concentration on one task at a time, a fully specified interface, no interleaving of goals, no interruptions, a single method, error-free, expert performance, and so on. Indeed, KLMs can be developed without worrying about goals and selection rules. These limitations make the KLM easier to use, but they also highlight the types of tasks that cannot easily be modeled using the KLM and where it will not give accurate results.

Quite a considerable effort has gone into trying to make KLMs more usable—particularly by building computer tools to apply them (Beard et al. 1996; Nichols and Ritter 1995; Williams 2000) and to extend them to new types of interfaces such as mobile GPS systems (Pettitt et al. 2007). These tools provide a language for defining KLM and GOMS models and computing the task time based on the analyses, although sometimes it may be just as easy to use a spreadsheet.

11.7   Considerations When Choosing a TA Method

There are some general issues that you need to be aware of when deciding whether to carry out a TA to inform system design, as they will influence how successful the TA is. Superficially it appears quite an easy technique to use, but to carry out a TA that produces useful results that can inform system design is an acquired skill. It requires skills in collecting the appropriate data or task specifications, analyzing that material, and then interpreting it.

It may seem obvious, but to perform a TA, you need to have access to a detailed enough task description. This can either be written (documentation) or captured through interviews and observation. If you are using interviews and observation, you need to make sure that you can get access to the appropriate people in a timely manner. For new or unimplemented interfaces you can often base your analyses on existing interfaces and extrapolations. If you are analyzing an unbuilt interface you should note your assumptions very clearly.

Different types of TA place emphasis on different aspects of task performance. You need to be aware of this. If you are interested in the work context, for example, then HTA will help; if you are more interested in the cognitive aspects of the task, you will be better off using some form of CTA. The different methods are not mutually exclusive.

In general, TA cannot easily simultaneously represent users with different levels of knowledge, skills, and abilities. Novice users and the way a task is learned, for example, are not well represented by most of these techniques. TA techniques, when applied sympathetically, can help support novice users, but this has to be done by the analyst. Most methods can deal with some aspects of task learning, such as how much knowledge has to be learned in order to do the task. To model the time course of learning you may need to develop a more detailed cognitive model (e.g., see Paik et al. 2010; Ritter and Bibby 2008).

Most methods of TA are strongly goal-oriented. These methods cannot generally be applied to situations that have little structure or only very abstract goals, such as play, conversation, and team building. All TA should be done with an understanding of the general context in relation to work and activities. Methods like activity theory address these issues (e.g., see Bertelsen and Bødker 2003 for an introductory review). Activity theory is a very high level method that analyses the types of user activities, generally using a very informal representation. It uses these descriptions to suggest how to design the context in which the activities take place. For example, identifying children's activities (play activities, painting, block stacking, and doll-house play, for example), would inform the design of a kindergarten room. Similar analyses make strong suggestions about the design of research labs (collaboration spaces, mailing rooms, teaching rooms) and interfaces where goals are less important than activities such as drawing, designing, interacting, team-building, exploring, or enjoying.

Most TA methods do not note and are not sensitive to context, including physical context such as lighting and heating, social norms such as doing what helps others in the environment, and not using others space or resources. It is especially common in work places to discover that the physical or social context produces changes in the way people do tasks from how they would ideally do them, or from the way they are supposed to do them. Casey (1998, 2006) provides numerous examples where not understanding the context on task analyses and on design led to problems, such as where other people are when the user is doing a task (not in the path of the rocket!), or the effect of weather on how to do tasks and which tasks to do on a ship.

11.8 Summary

Task analysis in all its various guises is a very useful technique, and usually fairly easy to perform when designing systems, which may help explain why it is so widely used. The results of a task analysis can be used to help designers create easier to use interfaces by highlighting the structure of tasks, and the time it takes to perform tasks, as well as making it easier to compare alternative methods for carrying out those tasks. Task analysis can also be used to represent the trade-offs in designs, helping designers to make informed decisions. TA can also be used directly to improve interfaces, and Table 11.7 notes a few common ways in which TA can help improve interfaces.

There are many different uses for task analysis, and the method that you choose will depend to some extent on how you intend to use the results. Choosing any one is better than none, that you should choose one that is easy for you to use because you are a user as well. The choice will also be affected by the context in which you will use the method, the limitations, and possibly the experience of the analyst(s) (several of the methods work at similar levels of abstraction, so they can be used somewhat interchangeably).

Using task analyses to guide system design has a good return on investment (RoI), ranging from 7 to 20 to 100 in one survey (Booher and Minninger 2003) to 1,000 in another more focused HCI study (Nielsen and Phillips 1993). Given the

Table 11.7 Ways to use TA to improve interfaces

1. Modify the interface to support all the tasks in the TA
2. Modify the interface to not support tasks not required by the task analysis
3. Modify the interface to do steps for the user where choices are not required
4. Modify the interface to use fewer actions
5. Modify the interface to use a simpler task structure
6. Modify the interface to provide more regular knowledge/interactions to perform related tasks
7. Modify the interface to not require holding state variables in the task analysis or user's head
8. Modify the interface to make common tasks faster
9. Modify the interface to make expensive tasks slower/harder to initiate
10. Teach any alternative methods through and in the interface

multiple ways that task analyses can be used and the savings they suggest, these numbers are quite plausible.

The various forms of task analysis can be ordered by how much detail they include. A preliminary classification can be into declarative and procedural representations. The declarative representations merely denote the actions or tasks the users will perform. The simplest of these are HTA and CTA. The KLM is a slightly more complex example of this because it attributes time to each action.

Procedural task descriptions, such as advanced versions of GOMS (John and Kieras 1996b) and models in cognitive architectures (noted in the final chapter), can include enough procedural knowledge of how to perform the task such that they can also perform the task in some way, perhaps with a simplified version of the interface. Declarative representations of behavior, like the KLM, for example, will note that the result of a mathematical task is "a number," whereas a fully procedural task analysis will be able to compute the actual number. This chapter discusses several examples of each type. There is a wide range of approaches, and descriptions of them are available in surveys (Adams et al. 2012; Beevis 1999; Schraagen et al. 2000), as well as in manuals and tutorials on these other TA approaches.

As you use TA in a wider range of situations, you should become more skilled in applying it. For specific situations you may want to look at some of the more specialized forms of task analysis. For example, if you have many novice users, you might create a situation where the user has to read the documentation to find the commands, which means that your design should ensure that the knowledge of how to use the interface is findable or transmitted to the novice through instructions, conventions, and other design elements. When you need to do more complex analyses, for example, where error recovery or multi-tasking is important, you may need to consult further material to find the most appropriate technique, as well as investigate supplementary techniques such as knowledge elicitation (e.g., Ericsson and Simon 1993; Kirwan and Ainsworth 1992; Schraagen et al. 2000; Shadbolt 2005; Shadbolt and Burton 1995).

The results of a task analysis on their own will not tell you whether a particular system or interface is acceptable or not. It just shows how well the system or interface will work for particular tasks for particular people (in a particular context). Decisions about modifications to the system or interface will often require consideration of other factors, such as the resources that are available for further development, other systems or interfaces (to cater for consistency and interoperability, for example), and assumptions about the target users. Task analysis cannot suggest whether novices should be served preferentially by the system, or whether experts should be supported in an interface design, but TA can help compute the costs and represent the trade-offs involved in making such decisions.

11.9 Other Resources

The Handbook of task analysis for human-computer interaction, edited by Dan Diaper and Neville Stanton (2003), although 10 years old, still provides a fairly comprehensive overview of TA. It makes a useful reference book, rather than being something that you should read from cover to cover. A more general, but still useful overview of the many types of TA and their application is Kirwan and Ainsworth's *A Guide to Task Analysis* (1992) even though it is now over 20 years old.

Clayton Lewis and John Rieman's shareware book, *Task-Centered User Interface Design* (1994), www.hcibib.org/tcuid/ provides a useful expansion of the material in this chapter, particularly on the role of task analysis in system design.

Shepherd's book, *Hierarchical Task Analysis* (2004), provides a detailed discussion of HTA. It illustrates how it can be applied to a wide range of tasks, and how the results can generate a wide range of benefits.

For a practical guide to using CTA it is worth looking at *Working Minds: A practitioner's guide to Cognitive Task Analysis* by Crandall et al. (2006). For details about the sorts of methods that can be used in a CTA, it is worth consulting *Applied Cognitive Task Analysis in aviation* by Thomas Seamster et al. (1997), and *Human factors methods* by Neville Stanton et al. (2005).

David Kieras has papers, manuals, and tools covering the KLM, GOMS, and task analyses available via his web site: www.ai.eecs.umich.edu/people/kieras/kieras.html. You can also find several KLM calculators online. With these you simply enter the KLM operators that are used to do the task, and the total time is automatically calculated for you.

Kim Vicente's book *Cognitive Work Analysis* (1999) describes a broader, integrated framework which includes models of the work domain, control tasks, strategies social-organizational factors, and worker competencies. This framework builds on the body of work called cognitive (systems) engineering which focuses on the analysis, design, and evaluation of complex socio-technical systems.

The book's web site has additional information on task analysis including some tools.

11.10 Exercises

11.1 Create a table showing each type of task analysis. Note (a) the focus of the approach (work, the task, what the user knows, etc.); (b) what they are typically used for, for example, what predictions they can provide; (c) an example snippet of analysis; (d) how time intensive you believe they will be (easy to do, hard to do); and (e) the advantages and disadvantages of each type.

11.2 Choose an existing interface and list the tasks it can or should be used for. Perform a task analysis. From this task analysis make five suggestions how it could be improved. Interfaces to consider include word processors, spreadsheets, online libraries, and email clients.

11.3 Write a short report on tasks you or a study partner do at your desk, and the quality of the desk and work area to support those tasks. Compare it with the non-work related tasks that you do indulge in (e.g., play with a pencil, line up your toy cars, doodle, drink coffee) at your desk. Make suggestions for improving the workspace in question. Then, do the same thing for your computer display.

11.4 List ten ways that the KLM or GOMS methods could be made more accurate. You should be able to do this using this book. For example, the section on reading makes several suggestions for making these models more accurate with respect to adjusting for users' reading speed and the material being read.

11.5 Consider a smartphone or tablet computer, either a specific one or a composite one. Devise a trade-off function between a set of features (which you specify) and weight. Describe how to choose a reasonable point on that curve. Use a task analysis that provides estimates of task time to represent this design trade-off.

11.6 Use a task analysis methodology to examine two related online systems, such as bookstores. You should choose three to five important tasks, and explain why these are important tasks for this analysis. How do their assumptions differ as represented in the task analysis? For example, does one assume that you log in before browsing, or does one assume that you read recommendations before purchasing?

11.7 Use a task analysis methodology that you choose to calculate how long it takes to perform the following tasks using a spreadsheet program, using a calculator, and using your cell phone: (a) a tip on a \$13.28 restaurant bill; (b) your salary raise as a percentage from \$8.50 to \$8.85/h (c) your hourly rate if you work 40 h per week and 48 weeks per year and make \$45,000 per year, and (d) your hourly rate from the previous problem, but starting from scratch, if you had a 3% raise. Comment on at what point in time you should switch between these three tools.

11.8 Use a task analysis methodology to calculate how long it takes to select and to delete an automatic signature to your email, using your signature rather than the one in Sect. 11.8. Is it faster to insert the signature manually when you need it, or to included it automatically and delete it when you do not need it?

Draw a curve representing the time to use both strategies as the frequency of need to sign an email changes from 0 to 100% in 10% increments.

11.9 In 2003 the University of Denver (noted in the Chronicle of Higher Education, 19 December, p. A35) decided to require all applicants to be interviewed by college officials. The question on the interviewers' minds, according to the assistant vice chancellor for enrollment management, is "Will the kid graduate?" The retention rate has gone from 82 to 86% because (or despite) the college starting using the system 2 years ago.

(a) Based on your experience as a college student, come up with a task analysis of what you have to do to be (i) successful in college and (ii) graduate. Include multiple strategies and allow tasks you need to terminate or avoid. (This integrates results from several chapters.) Do keep in mind that GPA is an important but surely not the only measure of success in college, and you might note other successes besides graduation.

(b) Discuss how you would interview someone to find out whether they can do these tasks.

(c) Can you provide any alternative hypotheses about why retention might have gone up besides the interview process?

References

Adams, A. E., Rogers, W. A., & Fisk, A. D. (2012). Choosing the right task analysis tool. *Ergonomics in Design: The Quarterly of Human Factors Applications, 20*(4), 4–10.

Annett, J. (2005). Hierarchical task analysis (HTA). In N. Stanton, A. Hedge, K. Brookhuis, E. Salas & H. Hendrick (Eds.), *Handbook of human factors and ergonomics methods* (pp. 33-31–33-37). Boca Raton, FL: CRC Press.

Baxter, G. D., Monk, A. F., Tan, K., Dear, P. R. F., & Newell, S. J. (2005). Using cognitive task analysis to facilitate the integration of decision support systems into the neonatal intensive care unit. *Artificial Intelligence in Medicine, 35,* 243–257.

Beard, D. V., Smith, D. K., & Denelsbeck, K. M. (1996). Quick and dirty GOMS: A case study of computed tomography interpretation. *Human-Computer Interaction, 11,* 157–180.

Beevis, D. (Ed.). (1999). *Analysis techniques for human-machine systems design: A report produced under the auspices of NATO Defence Research Group Panel 8.* Wright-Patterson Air Force Base, OH: Crew Systems Ergonomics/Human Systems Technology Information Analysis Center.

Bertelsen, O. W., & Bødker, S. (2003). Activity theory. In J. M. Carroll (Ed.), *HCI models, theories and frameworks: Toward a multi-disciplinary science.* San Francisco, CA: Morgan Kaufmann.

Booher, H. R., & Minninger, J. (2003). Human systems integration in Army systems acquisition. In H. R. Booher (Ed.), *Handbook of human systems integration* (pp. 663–698). Hoboken, NJ: Wiley.

Bovair, S., Kieras, D. E., & Polson, P. G. (1990). The acquisition and performance of text-editing skill: A cognitive complexity analysis. *Human-Computer Interaction, 5,* 1–48.

Byrne, M. D., & Kirlik, A. (2005). Using computational cognitive modeling to diagnose possible sources of aviation error. *International Journal of Aviation Psychology, 15*(2), 135–155.

Card, S. K., Moran, T. P., & Newell, A. (1980). The keystroke-level model for user performance time with interactive systems. *Communications of the ACM, 23*(7), 396–410.

Card, S. K., Moran, T. P., & Newell, A. (1983). *The psychology of human-computer interaction.* Hillsdale, NJ: Erlbaum.

Casey, S. M. (1998). *Set phasers on stun: And other true tales of design, technology, and human error.* Santa Barbara, CA: Aegean.

Casey, S. M. (2006). *The Atomic Chef: And other true tales of design, technology, and human error.* Santa Barbara, CA: Aegean.

Chipman, S. F., & Kieras, D. E. (2004). Operator centered design of ship systems. In *Engineering the Total Ship Symposium.* NIST, Gaithersburg, MD. American Society of Naval Engineers. Retrieved March 10, 2014, from http://handle.dtic.mil/100.2/ADA422107

Crandall, B., Klein, G., & Hoffman, R. R. (2006). *Working minds: A practitioner's guide to cognitive task analysis.* Cambridge, MA: MIT Press.

Diaper, D. (2004). Understanding task analysis. In D. Diaper & N. Stanton (Eds.), *The handbook of task analysis for human-computer interaction* (pp. 5–47). Mahwah, NJ: LEA.

Ericsson, K. A., & Simon, H. A. (1993). *Protocol analysis: Verbal reports as data* (2nd ed.). Cambridge, MA: MIT Press.

Fitts, P. M. (1951). *Human engineering for an effective air navigation and traffic control system.* Washington, DC: National Research Council.

Freed, M., & Remington, R. (1998). A conceptual framework for predicting error in complex human-machine environments. In *Proceedings of the 20th Annual Conference of the Cognitive Science Society* (pp. 356–361). Mahwah, NJ: Erlbaum.

Gray, W. D., John, B. E., & Atwood, M. E. (1992). The precis of project ernestine or an overview of a validation of GOMS. In *Proceedings of the CHI'92 Conference on Human Factors in Computer Systems.* New York, NY: ACM Press.

John, B. E., & Kieras, D. E. (1996a). The GOMS family of user interface analysis techniques: Comparison and contrast. *ACM Transactions on Computer-Human Interaction, 3*(4), 320–351.

John, B. E., & Kieras, D. E. (1996b). Using GOMS for user interface design and evaluation: Which technique? *ACM Transactions on Computer-Human Interaction, 3*(4), 287–319.

Kieras, D. E. (1999). A guide to GOMS model usability evaluation using GOMSL and GLEAN3: AI Lab, University of Michigan. Available from www.ftp.eecs.umich.edu/people/kieras

Kieras, D. E., & Polson, P. G. (1985). An approach to the formal analysis of user complexity. *International Journal of Man-Machine Studies, 22*, 365–394.

Kirwan, B., & Ainsworth, L. K. (1992). *A guide to task analysis.* London, UK: Taylor & Francis.

Klein, G., Calderwood, R., & MacGregor, D. (1989). Critical decision method for eliciting knowledge. *IEEE Transactions on Systems, Man, and Cybernetics, 19*, 462–472.

Monk, A. F. (1998). Lightweight techniques to encourage innovative user interface design. In L. Wood (Ed.), *User interface design: Bridging the gap between user requirements and design* (pp. 109–129). Boca Raton, FL: CRC Press.

Nichols, S., & Ritter, F. E. (1995). A theoretically motivated tool for automatically generating command aliases. In *Proceedings of the CHI'95 Conference on Human Factors in Computer Systems* (pp. 393–400). New York, NY: ACM.

Nielsen, J., & Phillips, V. L. (1993). Estimating the relative usability of two interfaces: Heuristic, formal, and empirical methods compared. In *Proceedings of InterCHI '93* (pp. 214–221). New York, NY: ACM.

Paik, J., Kim, J. W., Ritter, F. E., Morgan, J. H., Haynes, S. R., & Cohen, M. A. (2010). Building large learning models with Herbal. In D. D. Salvucci & G. Gunzelmann (Eds.), *Proceedings of ICCM: 2010- Tenth International Conference on Cognitive Modeling* (pp. 187–191).

Pettitt, M., Burnett, G., & Stevens, A. (2007). An extended keystroke level model (KLM) for predicting the visual demand of in-vehicle information systems. In *Proceedings of the SIGCHI Conference on Human Factors in Computing Systems* (pp. 1515–1524). ACM.

Ritter, F. E., & Bibby, P. A. (2008). Modeling how, when, and what learning happens in a diagrammatic reasoning task. *Cognitive Science, 32*, 862–892.

Ritter, F. E., Freed, A. R., & Haskett, O. L. (2002). *Discovering user information needs: The case of university department websites* (Tech. Report No. 2002-3): Applied Cognitive Science Lab, School of Information Sciences and Technology, Penn State. www.acs.ist.psu.edu/acs-lab/reports/ritterFH02.pdf

Schraagen, J. M., Chipman, S. F., & Shalin, V. L. (Eds.). (2000). *Cognitive task analysis.* Mahwah, NJ: Erlbaum.

Seamster, T. L., Redding, R. E., & Kaempf, G. L. (1997). *Applied cognitive task analysis in aviation.* Aldershot, UK: Avebury Aviation.

Shadbolt, N. R. (2005). Eliciting expertise. In J. R. Wilson & E. Corlett (Eds.), *Evaluation of human work* (3rd Edition, pp. 185–218). London: Taylor and Francis.

Shadbolt, N. R., & Burton, A. M. (1995). Knowledge elicitation: A systematic approach. In J. R. Wilson & E. N. Corlett (Eds.), *Evaluation of human work: A practical ergonomics methodology* (pp. 406–440). London: Taylor and Francis.

St. Amant, R., Freed, A. R., & Ritter, F. E. (2005). Specifying ACT-R models of user interaction with a GOMS language. *Cognitive Systems Research, 6*(1), 71–88.

St. Amant, R., Horton, T. E., & Ritter, F. E. (2004). Model-based evaluation of cell phone menu interaction. In *Proceedings of the CHI'04 Conference on Human Factors in Computer Systems* (pp. 343–350). New York, NY: ACM.

St. Amant, R., Horton, T. E., & Ritter, F. E. (2007). Model-based evaluation of expert cell phone menu interaction. *ACM Transactions on Computer-Human Interaction, 14*(1), 24.

Vicente, K. (1999). *Cognitive work analysis.* Mahwah, NJ: Erlbaum.

Chapter 12
Methodology II: Cognitive Dimensions and the Gulfs

Abstract This chapter introduces two useful high-level approaches that summarize a wide range of aspects of users: how users interact with artifacts and how users perform tasks. A type of analysis, Cognitive Dimension/dimensions, provides a way to represent common and important aspects of interface design. The dimensions are used to describe and then evaluate interfaces. Norman has a similar description of user behavior based on how hard it is to understand the state of the interface (the Gulf of Understanding) and how hard it is to perform an action in an interface (the Gulf of Execution). Both approaches are useful techniques for thinking about, planning, and performing interface design.

12.1 Introduction

So far we have presented several methods and techniques for analyzing Human-System Interaction, including task analysis as a general tool, and GOMS and the KLM as more detailed formal approaches for use prior to user testing. Most of the methods we have presented are applied at a low level of abstraction. In contrast, the Cognitive Dimensions (of Notations), usually just referred to as Cognitive Dimensions or CDs (e.g., Blackwell and Green 2003; Green 1989), was developed as a mechanism for discussing and analyzing systems at a higher level of abstraction.

The CDs are based on the assumption that it is useful to have a language for discussing design. One way of trying to understand design is to describe the object that is being designed, and the trade-offs that the designer faces using a small number of fundamental dimensions. These dimensions can then provide a common language (sometimes called an ontology) for discussing usability problems, as well as a means of comparing aspects of interface and system design, and for comparing whole designs. Thus, the CDs can be seen as a way of providing a common ontology for naming aspects of design as well as for naming design trade-offs.

F. E. Ritter et al., *Foundations for Designing User-Centered Systems*,
DOI: 10.1007/978-1-4471-5134-0_12, © Springer-Verlag London 2014

The goal of the CDs is to provide a fairly small, representative set of labeled dimensions that describe critical ways in which interfaces, systems, and environments can vary from the perspective of usability. Once the dimensions have been labeled the designers can more easily discuss alternative designs.

In this chapter we will outline some of the dimensions and illustrate them with examples. The complete set of dimensions, however, does not yet exist—this is still a research issue and the set of dimensions for a given design is probably tied to the context of the design. Research in this area is proceeding in two directions: trying to find ways of formalizing and measuring the dimensions currently proposed, and trying to explore the completeness and redundancy of the current set of dimensions.

We will also describe an alternative viewpoint on dimensions, based on the work of Norman (1988, 2013). Norman's dimensions describe how users interact with devices, focusing on the relationship between actions and intentions, and between the results of actions and the way they are interpreted.

12.2 The Cognitive Dimensions

Table 12.1 notes the (current) set of 14 Cognitive Dimensions. Research into the CDs is ongoing, so the list should not be regarded as finalized or complete. The CDs can be extended to make them more appropriate to your own situation.

Below we describe the first five CDs in more detail. Our main purpose here is to illustrate what the CDs are, and how they can be used.

12.2.1 Hidden Dependencies

Dependencies are the number and direction of relationships between objects. For example, spreadsheets show you formulae in one direction only, that is, which cells are used to compute the value in a cell, but not which cells use a given cell's value; similarly, variable declarations in programming languages like Java or Pascal show you which variable type a structure is made from, but not the other way around; and the Microsoft Word Styles dialogue box (Fig. 12.1) shows you the parent of a style but not its children.

In all of these examples there are two hidden (or invisible) types of dependency: ancestors and children. Only the parents are visible, and finding the ancestors involves following a chain of parents. Working in the opposite direction, finding the children involves checking every entity for its parent, which creates a high memory and work load. Another example of the problem of hidden dependencies occurs in variable initialization and use: in many procedural and production system languages you need to use a combination of tools and deep knowledge to find out what the dependencies are.

Table 12.1 The Cognitive Dimensions

1. Hidden dependencies: how visible the relationships between components are
2. Viscosity: how easy it is to change objects in the interface
3. Role-expressiveness: how clear the mapping of the objects are to their functions
4. Premature commitment: how soon the user has to decide something
5. Hard mental operations: how hard are the mental operations to use the interface
6. Secondary notation: the ability to add extra semantics
7. Abstraction: how abstract the operations and system are
8. Error-proneness susceptibility: how easy it is to err
9. Consistency: how uniform the system is (in various ways, including action mapping)
10. Visibility: whether required information is accessible without work by the user
11. Progressive evaluation: whether you can stop in the middle of creating some notation and check what you have done so far
12. Provisionality: whether you can sketch out ideas without being too exact
13. Diffuseness: how verbose the language is
14. Closeness of mapping: how close the representation in the interface (also called notation) is to the end results being described

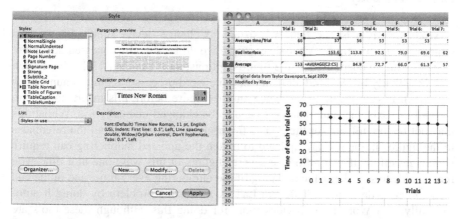

Fig. 12.1 The Word Style editor (*left*) shows the parent of the ref style, but cannot show the children of the Normal style. The spreadsheet (*right*) shows what cells the formula is dependent on (and can show those that appear as the line on the graph), but does not show where a given cell is used

The implications of considering hidden dependencies are that all dependencies that may be relevant to the user's tasks should be represented. Or, as a minimum, tools should be provided which enable them to be represented. This is consistent with the notion we saw earlier in the book of recognition being easier than recall. For example, spreadsheets would be easier to use (for certain tasks anyway) if they could show forward relationships (e.g., this cell's value is used in all these other places). Recognizing this fact (the need for visibility) is quite separate from designing a solution to the problem—one option would be to use color coding (e.g., child cells could be shown in the same color; ancestor cells could be shown in ever paler shades of the same color). Some spreadsheets now provide the capability to show child cells, thus making the dependencies less hidden.

A much richer form of hidden dependency occurs in many modern operating systems, where several files are both generated and used. Applications other than those that created them may be dependent upon these files, such as a pictorial figure in a spreadsheet file, a graphics file used in a report, or a preferences file stored somewhere away from its application and labeled with the name of the company or user rather than the application. These dependencies are not visible—deleting files from system and user preferences directories therefore becomes a hazardous task. The corollary is that people's file stores get filled up with old, unused files and you cannot easily tell whether or not they are used. The normal solution, albeit one that strictly ignores the problem rather than solves it, is to never delete any files from these directories. The reason this works as a solution is that storage space is so cheap!

12.2.2 Viscosity

A *viscous* system is one that is resistant to change—even small changes can require substantial effort. A classic example would be a word-processed document in which the numbers used in the figure captions, such as "Fig. 12.1," have been typed explicitly by hand (rather than using the word processor's built in numbering facilities). If you decide to introduce another figure before this in the document, then all the existing figure numbers need to be changed manually too. Whilst this may not be too difficult for the figures themselves, ensuring that all the references to the figures in the text are updated to match the updated numbering can require significant effort. If you introduce several figures in this way, one at a time, you may decide to skip doing the updating of the numbering every time, and in the end may forget to do it at all. TeX and LaTeX avoid this problem by doing it automatically, and Word also provides tools for doing this, although these tools are somewhat viscous and error prone.

In some circumstances viscosity can be beneficial for users. If things are hard to change this encourages reflective action and explicit learning. Learning in some puzzles (noted in Chap. 6) is more explicit if the user has to work harder to make moves in the puzzle. Deleting files is also made somewhat more viscous by many operating system interfaces ("Are you sure you want to delete this file?"). In contrast, if things are easy to change this encourages tinkering, which leads to implicit learning. When it is very easy to make small changes this can often lead to many small, unnecessary changes being made.

On the other hand, visualprogramming languages, one of the original analyses that led to the CD approach, can have changes that are difficult to implement and change. For example, it is most productive in most cases to vary fonts uniformly and to have them vary by several points. It is not as productive to have them vary by only one point. If you want to modify the fonts in a PowerPoint presentation by one point, then you have to use more detailed tools and it takes longer. You can do it, but it is more viscous. As another example, iTunes makes it relatively easy to add a new playlist or to modify a playlist. It makes it more difficult (viscous) to erase songs.

Two types of viscosity can be differentiated:

- Repetitive viscosity—where what appears to be a single goal has to be carried out as lots of small, repetitive actions. For example, if you want to change in a document every number followed by a tab into the same numbers followed by a space, this has to be done by hand in Word because, while the number can be found, it cannot be included in the replace, thus increasing the viscosity of editing Word documents. Similar effects can be found in many systems when renaming files within a graphical user interface.
- Knock-on viscosity—where what appears to be a single goal requires several more small changes to restore consistency (e.g., adding a sentence at the beginning of a document and having to redo all the work involved in ensuring that appropriate page breaks occur).

Solutions to the problems of inappropriate amounts of viscosity can involve either redesigning the system or providing tools to help manage the difficulties. The latter is more likely to be useful where viscosity may be desirable, as a way of promoting reflective action and encouraging learning. In some cases there may be a trade-off, however, and making some actions less viscous may lead to others becoming more viscous. It is also worth noting that it can be useful to deliberately make some actions viscous, e.g., if there are safety critical elements, or an action may be dangerous if carried out incorrectly, or they are expensive in time or money. On the other hand, simple, routine actions should normally be made as non-viscous as possible.

12.2.3 Role-Expressiveness

Role-expressiveness describes the extent to which a system reveals the goals of the system's author/designer to the reader/user. It should be easy, for example, for a reader to see what each component in a program does, and how each component relates to the whole. This need to infer the other agent's goals and plans is important, as we noted earlier in Chap. 7, with particular reference to how Grice's maxims describe successful communication.

One obvious example of role-expressiveness is that the buttons on an interface should be clearly recognizable as buttons that the user can press. In some interfaces, however, role-expressiveness is poor because interface objects that are clickable are not easily recognizable as being clickable—"But how was I meant to know that it would do something if I clicked there?" This effect is particularly found on those web pages where banners and logos are designed as clickable images, but users more commonly (and more naturally based on their experience) perceive them as just being graphical images.

A piece of program code with well-chosen variable names can be very role-expressive. The goals of the programmer in each statement can be made readily apparent to the reader if the functions and variables are given names that clearly indicate their purpose.[1]

The Microsoft Excel spreadsheet application also supports role expressiveness. When you add a formula to a particular cell, for example, it color codes the cells that are referenced by that formula. Note that the color coding only happens as the formula is created, and disappears when you calculate the result of evaluating that formula.

Classic problems of role-expressiveness occur where two similar looking features achieve different functions or where two different looking functions achieve similar effects. That is, where the role-expressiveness for two similar looking objects is different, or where the function of two different looking objects appears the same. For example, the *Border and shadings* functions in some older versions of Microsoft Word can be accessed using the top level menu but also appear in three other places in the interface, with different sets of functions available to the user in each place with differing effects. This can confuse users who fail to distinguish between paragraph borders and table cell borders because Word displays them in apparently unpredictable ways.

There may sometimes be a conflict between role-expressiveness and consistency. Designing a system to be role-expressive will usually mean using a richer vocabulary with less (apparent) uniformity. A good way to resolve this conflict is to carry out a clear and effective analysis of the users' tasks and the importance of learning versus other measures of usability rather than focusing solely on consistency (Grudin 1989). Role expressiveness might also be poor on purpose to encourage exploration. This may occur in games or educational software and hardware (Yeh et al. 2010).

12.2.4 Premature Commitment

The point at which users have to commit to taking a particular action varies across environments and systems. For example, when you go into a café you sometimes find that you have to select which cutlery you need before you have seen what food is on offer that day. Until you know this you will not know whether you will need a

---

[1] Jonah Gregory (personal communication, 2008) notes that programmer's comments can be helpful in these situations, and we agree. However, comments can also be a nightmare because they often do not get updated when the code changes. So, there are design decisions about when to update and how to update such documentation.

soup spoon or a dessert spoon (or both). Similarly, many database systems require that you plan and commit to particular record structures and size limits before entering any data or actually using the system. Until you know how the system will be used, however, it is often difficult to finalize these decisions.

These limitations are examples of *Premature Commitment*. Computer programming environments often require premature commitment such as declaration of variables before working out how they will be used, and developing the system in sequential order. Like many of the CDs, premature commitment will interact with other dimensions. Premature commitment can contribute to viscosity, for example, because the effect of the commitment is to make future changes very hard to make.

The solution to the problem of premature commitment is usually to allow (and provide support for) users to perform tasks in many orders (e.g., outlining tools in many word processors allow the user to develop the outline and write the text in any order). This support comes at a cost, however. Allowing users more freedom often makes the system more complex to design and to build, and may contribute to errors in program code. Paying attention to this trade-off, however, is completely consistent with the Risk-Driven Incremental Commitment Model that we will discuss in Chap. 14.

12.2.5 Hard Mental Operations

The final CD that we will examine here is the number of *hard mental operations* involved, which will vary across systems. In GOMS, KLM modeling, and several other task analysis methods, the mental operations are all assumed to be equivalent, for convenience's sake. Psychology and human factors work show us that some kinds of problems (and operations) are substantially harder for users to perform, and that users thus prefer easier mental operations (although harder does not necessarily mean slower).

The issue of hard mental operations can be illustrated by the isomorph of the Towers of Hanoi problem, in which monsters manipulate balls according to a formal monster protocol for swapping balls. The subjects in Kotovsky and Simon's (1990) study had monsters either follow a complex protocol to swap balls around based on which size monster could hold which size ball, or a protocol that required monsters to change size to swap balls around. Subjects found the latter protocol to be much more difficult, possibly because we tend to think of size as a relatively constant aspect of an object, so having to mentally change the size of an object is more strenuous and error prone than applying simple rules to behavior. Similar effects have also been found in mentally rotating objects, with larger objects being rotated more slowly.

As another example, multiple negative facts can be very hard to disentangle (e.g., the packet that was not lost, was not put out on the Ethernet). The concepts of pointers and indirection in C and other programming languages also prove very difficult—most people can usually handle one level of indirection, but multiple levels of pointers tend to be more difficult to follow. Another type of hard mental operation is boundary problems, for example, counting fence posts—If you have a ten-foot fence to put up, and fence pieces are one foot long, how many posts do you require? In this situation, the boundaries of an object have to be explicitly and carefully represented and manipulated. If you thought there should be 10 posts, you have left out the first post, because there needs to be 11 (you can see this much more easily if you actually draw the fence).

An important thing to remember about these kinds of hard mental operations is that they can be easy to implement computationally, but can be especially troublesome for users. Again, these problems can be solved at several levels, including either by avoiding the problem by understanding the relative difficulty of operations, or by providing tools to assist in these operations (e.g., graphic displays of indirection in C programs) and providing representations designed to be shared between types of system implementers.

12.3 Turning Cognitive Dimensions into a Methodology

The CDs can be used as a method for informing design during the early or middle stages of development (e.g., Cohen et al. 2012). The designer can ask questions based on the appropriate dimensions for the system, such as:

1. Are there hidden dependencies and one-way links in the structure?
2. Is the system viscous, or can users and designers reconstruct structures easily and fluidly?
3. Is the order of generation and action the same as the order in which users will want to do things and have the appropriate information? Are there multiple, appropriate orders of behavior and strategies supported?
4. Is the system role-expressive? Are the functions of the components obvious and discriminable?
5. Does the system require any hard mental operations?
6. Are there conceptual gaps between the user and the system? (Blandford et al. 2008)

The answers to these questions are shared among the design team. They can then be used to moderate the design of the system, or may lead to other design activities such as studying the relative costs of mental operations or other tasks that help reduce the risks associated with the design.

Designers might wish to order the dimensions they use, and they may also wish to add other dimensions. A new dimension could be added, for example, to consider the role of cognitive load (Sweller 1988) describing how much the user has to know, do, and learn at any given point in a task.

The CDs have been used to develop extensions to the Microsoft Excel spreadsheet that integrate user defined functions into the worksheet grid (Peyton

Jones et al. 2003). This was done by initially focusing on the cognitive requirements of the user, using the CDs and the Attention Investment model of abstraction use (Blackwell 2002). The Cognitive Dimensions approach has also been used to understand issues that arise for programmers when solving complex systems integration problems and with contemporary, *mash-up* programming practices with APIs (application programming interfaces) (see Jones et al. 2010 for an example).

12.4 What is Omitted by the Cognitive Dimensions?

The CDs do have some limitations. This approach does not offer a complete way to create an interface design, and it may not always be applicable. Those aspects of a system that are of particular interest may not be covered by the dimensions noted, for example.

Even for the existing CDs, there are areas where they could be expanded. The current list includes error proneness, for example, but does not directly address the quality of feedback and support for error recovery. The CDs also focus on usability issues, and do not currently address issues related to user acceptability—does the system fit in with the way users do the task or want to do the task, and so on.

The CDs are an attempt to provide a way for designers to discuss issues related to usability. If we had a rich enough vocabulary to adequately describe the sources of poor usability, then the problems could be solved simply by reducing or eliminating each of these sources. The real benefit of the CDs is as a tool that can highlight the trade-offs inherent in interface design in a way that can be easily understood by designers.

As their name suggests, the CDs focus on the cognitive aspects of interfaces. They do not address design trade-offs related to the other aspects of users that we have introduced—anthropometric, behavioral, and social aspects—in any great depth. The CDs approach, however, suggests that a similar approach to understanding design trade-offs could be used for these other aspects of usability. The physical dimensions of a device will typically be related to the features that can be provided, for example, iPods versus iPads. Similarly, other aspects can be put into this framework. For example, social aspects could be included such as how the size of a social network will influence the usability of devices designed for communicating with others.

12.5 Norman's Seven Stages of Action

In his book *The Design of Everyday Things*, Norman (1988, 2013) describes the process of how users interact with systems to achieve their goals as a series of activities (see Table 12.2). This process is an approximate theory of action: all of

Table 12.2 Stages of user activities

- Establish the goal
- Form the intention to take some action
- Specify the action sequence
- Execute the action
- Perceive the system state
- Interpret the system state
- Evaluate the system state with respect to the goals and intentions

the stages may not always be used, and they may not always be applied in the same order. The stages are done in a cycle (thus, the last stage, *Evaluate*, also occurs before the first stage, *Establish the goal*). The process does, however, capture the essential aspects of how users perform tasks, and is therefore useful for analyzing and guiding the design of systems. The process should be seen as cyclic rather than a single shot linear sequence of activities. Activities may also overlap, and there can be feedback loops between activities.

There may be not be a direct correspondence between the user's psychologically expressed goals and the physical controls and variables that have to be used to carry out the task to achieve those goals. In many cases the goals and intentions are highly context dependent, and often opportunistic rather than planned. The goals and intentions may also be rather vague or ill-defined. Generally the user will set up some goal that they want to accomplish, and then formulate an intention to carry out some actions to ensure that the goal is achieved. Goals and intentions are psychological concepts—they exist in the mind of the user and relate directly to the user's needs and concerns. In most cases, however, the actions have to be performed on a physical artifact or system, manipulating some physical mechanisms to produce changes in the physical variables and the state of the system or environment. The user must, therefore, turn psychological intentions into actions that can be physically carried out upon the system or environment. The user then has to look for the effects of those actions, and interpret those effects in terms of the psychological goals to decide what to do next.

You do not want your users to have to resort to effortful problem solving just to interpret the effects of any actions. If they do, this usually means that they have not found the interface easy to use. This situation should normally only occur when something goes wrong with the system, or where the purpose of the interface is to deliberately force the user to resort to problem solving, such as in a game. Providing some level of built in redundancy will help users when they have to perform problem solving. You could provide them with multiple email accounts, for example, in case one is down, or provide multiple ways to get email, e.g., POP and webmail; similarly, you could provide multiple ways to print with multiple printers. These are usefully redundant rather than just duplicates.

When you design systems you should think about how to support users in ways that help them to achieve their goals, and reduce the need for them to resort to problem solving. You can provide users with some means to access commands, for example, using keystrokes, menus, buttons, and so on, as a way of helping them perform their tasks to achieve their goals. You should also try to anticipate potential problems, and understand how your users will use problem solving to resolve them. By doing so you should be able to identify redundancies that you can build into the system to allow (and help) users to work around the problem until it can be fixed.

12.5.1 The Gulfs of Evaluation and Execution

In Norman's seven stages of action he explicitly talks about the need to map between psychological and physical concepts. Often there is not a direct correspondence between the two. If we think about behavior in terms of Neisser's (1976) perceive-decide-act cycle we can identify two areas where the mapping occurs.

When the user perceives the state of the system (or more generally, the environment) this will be in terms of physical concepts (usually variables and values) that the user will have to translate into a form that is compatible with their mental model of how the system operates. Norman describes the gap between the physical concepts and the psychological concepts as the *Gulf of Evaluation* (see Fig. 12.2). The user will normally have to do some (cognitive) work to bridge this Gulf. If the user cannot interpret the effects in terms of the original goals and intentions, this may mean that they have to resort to problem solving to determine whether the effects of their actions indicate that the goal has been achieved.

When the user formulates a goal, this usually leads to the intention to perform some actions to attain that goal. The user then has to translate these psychological concepts into physical concepts, which are usually actions that can be executed on the system (or, more generally, the environment). Norman describes the gap between the (psychological) goals and intentions and the physical actions as the *Gulf of Execution* (see Fig. 12.2). If the user cannot readily work out how to translate the goals and intentions into the available actions that can be performed on the system, they may end up not knowing what to do, or how to do it. In such cases they will often have to resort to problem solving to determine what actions to take and how to execute them.

When designing systems you should normally try to minimize the size of the Gulfs of execution and evaluation. Often it may not be possible to eliminate them completely, but you should try to make it obvious what the user needs to do to bridge the Gulfs.

12.5.2 The Gulfs in Practice

A couple of examples should help to illustrate the two Gulfs more clearly, and show how serious the effect of large Gulfs can be. In the Kegworth air crash (see Appendix) and in many other air disasters a large Gulf of Evaluation can be identified. The true state of the aircraft was not very clear from the instruments in the cockpit, and there

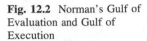

Fig. 12.2 Norman's Gulf of
Evaluation and Gulf of
Execution

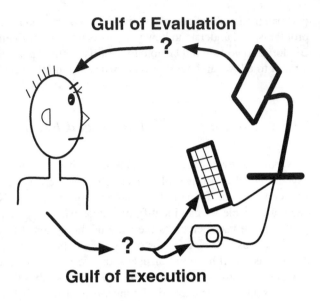

Gulf of Evaluation

Gulf of Execution

was little directly observable feedback about the effects of the pilots' actions. There
were also some apparent discrepancies between the pilots' mental model of the state
of the aircraft and the state of the physical aircraft, and the instrumentation in the
cockpit did not make it easy to identify and rectify these discrepancies. In the
Kegworth disaster the air traffic control operatorsasked a lot of questions. These
questions may also have contributed to the Gulf of Evaluation for the pilots because
they would have taken time away from understanding their situation.

The situation in the Kegworth disaster was further exacerbated by coincidental
effects that led the pilots to falsely believe that they had attained some goals
(Besnard et al. 2004). There was an identifiable Gulf of Execution in that the
actions that the pilots took did not have the effects they thought they would. While
they had removed the vibration by shutting down one of the engines, they had not
shut down the failing engine.

As you look at other interfaces, you will encounter further examples where
details and feedback on the state of the system can be difficult to interpret, and
where it can be difficult to work out what actions are available and how to execute
them. These sorts of problems provide an indication of where the usability of the
system can be increased by improving the interface.

12.6 Implications of the Gulfs for Design

Norman uses the Gulfs to highlight the central importance of visibility in design.
Good design involves making sure that information that is crucial to task evaluation and performance are made clearly visible to the user. In this way you can

reduce the size of the Gulf of Execution and the Gulf of Evaluation. Table 12.3 provides some general guidance on how you can try to narrow the Gulfs during design.

Visibility is not an adequate guideline on its own, however, and making too much information visible can be a bad thing. Norman uses the example of a washer/drier that had multiple controls and several symbols displayed on the front of it. There was no easy way to discern what each control did and what all the symbols meant without looking at the instructions or undergoing extensive training. (This example assumes that the designer was not trying to drive the user to the manual to learn these symbols, a type of controlled viscosity.)

There is often a design trade-off between presenting too much information and overloading controls to allow them to perform several different actions using modes. In moded systems, the way that you interpret the displays and feedback depends on which mode the system is currently in. This can be problematic, particularly if it is not immediately obvious which mode the system is in.

The visibility guideline, like most guidelines, needs to be adapted to the user's particular situation. You should think of it in terms of:

"Visibility of the appropriate information for carrying out relevant tasks," or

"So viel wie nötig, so wenig wie möglich." → "as much as necessary, as little as possible," is a neat way of phrasing it, taken from a German aphorism.

What counts as appropriate information will vary across tasks, and sometimes across users, and even across contexts of use (e.g., same driver, same task, different road conditions).

When you think about visibility you should make sure that you give appropriate consideration to feedback, consistency, and the user's mental model of the system. These factors can all be used to help reduce the size of the Gulfs. Feedback is obviously important in helping to reduce the Gulf of Evaluation, because it shows the effect of performing a particular action.

Users often rely on consistency within and across systems and applications. They expect interface layouts to be consistent, for example, with particular controls always being located in the same place and always behaving in the same way. This can be particularly important when it comes to new systems, because users will often try to apply their knowledge of other interfaces to the new interface. Consistency is important because it will help the users to help themselves.

We know that users rely on mental models to help them perform tasks. These mental models develop over time, so your design should facilitate the development of appropriate mental models, and support the use of those mental models by making the appropriate information visible to users at the right time and in the right place.

In many cases you want it to be easy to use the system you are designing, so that you can get to the point where people can use it with little or no conscious control. In other words, they will be operating at a point close to Rasmussen's (1983) skill-based level of behavior.In critical systems, however, you often want people to pay close attention to the actions that they are taking, and for behavior to

Table 12.3 Design principles derived from Norman's analysis to make the Gulfs narrower where appropriate

---

1. Use both the knowledge in the world and the knowledge in the head. Provide information in the environment to help the user determine the system state and to perform actions, such as explicit displays of system state, and affordances on the system controls
2. Simplify the structure of tasks. Require less of the user by automating subtasks, or using displays to describe information without being asked, or provide common actions more directly. However, do not reduce this below their natural level of abstraction
3. Make the relevant objects and feedback on actions visible. Bridge the Gulf of Evaluation. Make the state of the system easier to interpret
4. Make the available actions visible. Bridge the Gulf of Execution. Make the actions the user can (and should) perform easier to see and to do
5. Get the mappings correct from objects to actions. Make the actions that the user can apply natural
6. Exploit the power of constraints, both natural and artificial, to support bridging each Gulf. Make interpretations of the state and of possible actions easier by removing actions that are not possible in the current state and reducing the complexity of the display for objects that are not active or available
7. Design for error. Users will make errors, so you should expect them and be aware of their effects. Where errors cannot be prevented, try to mitigate their effects. Help the user see errors and provide support for correcting them
8. When all else fails, standardize. If the user does not know what to do, allow them to apply their knowledge of existing standards and interfaces

---

be more deliberate (closer to Rasmussen's rule-based level of behavior). Making interaction harder can be useful for safety critical systems (e.g., nuclear power, aviation, and so on), security critical systems, and more generally as a way of preventing inappropriate, costly, and illegal actions in any interface. If you want to make the Gulfs wider, you should apply the inverse of these principles; some are noted in Table 12.4. Figure 12.3, for example, shows a picture of an electrical outlet designed, one can only presume, to be difficult for travelers to use.

At this point it should be clear to you that you are not simply designing to make the system fit the user in isolation. At the same time, you need to consider how to mold the task environment to fit the user. In other words, you need to fit the environment to the tasks, goals, knowledge, and expectations of the user.

12.7 Limitations of the Gulfs

While Norman's approach has been very useful as a metaphor and approach for improving interface design over the years, it has some limitations that should be noted. The most obvious limitation is that it is intentionally simplistic. The suggestions that it makes are context independent. The sizes of the Gulfs are not measurable, and this makes it difficult to apply this approach to choose between alternative designs.

Table 12.4 Design principles derived from Norman's analysis to make the Gulfs wider where appropriate

1. Hide components: Make things invisible to help make the visible easier to see, and what should be hard to find (because it is uncommon or unhelpful or dangerous), is hard to find
2. Avoid natural mappings for the execution side of the action cycle, so that the relationship of the controls to the things being controlled are inappropriate
3. Make the unavailable action physically impossible or difficult to do
4. Require precise timing and difficult physical manipulation
5. Do not give any feedback
6. Use unnatural mappings for the evaluation side of the action cycle, so that the system state is difficult to interpret

Fig. 12.3 An electrical outlet (*circled*) on a column designed to be difficult to use?

To fully understand the Gulfs, designers need to understand perceptual and cognitive psychology fairly well (which is partly why we have included lots of information on cognition and perception in this book). To apply this approach the designer has to be able to accurately judge the Gulf of Evaluation, which implies understanding how the user perceives and interacts with the display. It also assumes that the designer either understands motor output fairly well, or that the details of motor output do not matter. When the interface is either simple, or has been poorly designed, it will be relatively easy to make judgments about where it can be improved. For more complex interfaces, where there are realistic design trade-offs that need to be made, it will be more difficult to make these judgments accurately and for a wide range of users.

12.8 Summary

The Cognitive Dimensions and the Gulfs of Evaluation and Execution both provide a less formal and much lighter weight approach than task analyses and user modeling techniques. They provide useful heuristics about interface design, and a way to describe interface trade-offs, but they cannot always be used to compute the quality of alternative designs.

The Cognitive Dimensions provide a way to discuss particular aspects of interface design. They are not a complete method, but do provide a useful way to carry out an early sanity check on a particular interface design. It is useful to have such techniques that can be used early on and with little effort.

The Gulfs of Evaluation and Execution remind us how users interact with a system. Nearly all users have some common tasks related to interaction, including evaluating the system state and executing actions. Bridging these gaps (Gulfs) will mean creating the system to support these two fundamental aspects of task performance. Thinking about the Gulfs can yield practical suggestions for improving designs, such as making things more visible but avoiding clutter.

12.9 Other Resources

There are many resources related to Blackwell and Green's Cognitive Dimensions available at their web site. These include papers, reports, and tools.

http://www.cl.cam.ac.uk/~afb21/CognitiveDimensions/

Don Norman's book *The Design of Everyday Things* (originally published as *ThePsychologyof Everyday Things*) includes several examples of the Gulfs of Evaluation and Execution arising out of poor design. These include a fridge freezer, doors on buildings, and a slide projector where how to evaluate or how to use the devices were not clear. He also discusses how the designs could be improved to reduce or eliminate the Gulfs:

Norman, D. A. (1988). *The psychology of everyday things.* NY: Basic Books. (2013 ed., *The design of everyday things*).

Norman's (2009) text is also worth reading. This book covers technologies like self driving cars, and applies the basic philosophy laid out in the earlier *Design of Everyday Things*:

Norman, Donald A. *The design of future things*. Basic Books, 2009.

12.10 Exercises

12.1 Consider a smartphone, either a specific one or a composite one. Attempt to come up with a set of trade-offs based on Cognitive Dimensions. Describe how to choose a reasonable point in these trade-offs.

12.2 Choose an existing interface, find five similar interfaces, and note how they are related as different positions on Cognitive Dimensions. For example, there are puzzle interfaces where you directly manipulate pieces and others where you type in the piece number. These differ in viscosity and hard mental operations. The more viscous interface encourages more hard mental operations and learning. Find similar trade-offs within a single type of interface.

12.3 Look at your work desk, and consider where you can note three trade-offs or effects in its design with respect to the Cognitive Dimensions. For example, some desks have printouts pasted to walls near the desk. These can be seen to reduce the viscosity of the information on them.

12.3 Discuss how an online training system and a safety critical system can encourage different behaviors (e.g., learning, avoiding errors) by using Cognitive Dimensions.

12.5 Consider ways that the Word, PowerPoint, or other help system can help reduce the Gulf of Evaluation, and the Gulf of Execution. For example, try to create multiple lines in an Excel file, or to create a string (like "1 2" or "p < .05") where the 1 and 2 and the "p" and "5" always stay on the same line.

12.6 Create six design dimensions related to anthropometric, behavioral, and social trade-offs. Provide an argument in each case as to why these are fundamental dimensions. The dimensions should cross the areas (i.e., note how they are related), or you should note why you think they are not relatable onto a single dimension

References

Besnard, D., Greathead, D., & Baxter, G. (2004). When mental models go wrong. Co-occurrences in dynamic, critical systems. *International Journal of Human-Computer Studies, 60*, 117–128.

Blackwell, A. (2002). First steps in programming: A rationale for attention investment models. In *Proceedings of the IEEE Symposium on Human-Centric Computing Languages and Environments*, 2–10. Arlington, VA: IEEE Press.

Blackwell, A., & Green, T. (2003). Notational systems—The cognitive dimensions of notations framework. In J. M. Carroll (Ed.), *HCI models, theories, and frameworks* (pp. 103–133). San Francisco: Morgan Kaufmann.

Blandford, A., Green, T. R. G., Furniss, D., & Makri, S. (2008). Evaluating system utility and conceptual fit using CASSM. *International Journal of Human-Computer Studies, 66,* 393–409.

Cohen, M. A., Ritter, F. E., & Haynes, S. R. (2012). Discovering and analyzing usability dimensions of concern. *ACM Transactions on CHI, 19*(2), Article 9. 18 pages.

Green, T. R. G. (1989). Cognitive dimensions of notations. In *People and Computers V* (pp. 443–460). Cambridge, UK: Cambridge University Press.

Grudin, J. (1989). The case against user interface consistency. *Communications of the ACM, 32*(10), 1164–1173.

Jones, M. C., Churchill, E. F., & Nelson, L. (2010). Mashed layers and muddled models: Debugging mashup applications. In A. Cypher, M. Dontcheva, T. Lau & J. Nichols (Eds.), *No Code Required: Giving Users Tools to Transform the Web*: Burlington, MA: Morgan Kaufman.

Kotovsky, K., & Simon, H. A. (1990). What makes some problems really hard: Explorations in the problem space of difficulty. *Cognitive Psychology, 22,* 143–183.

Neisser, U. (1976). *Cognition and reality*. San Francisco, CA: W. H. Freeman.

Norman, D. A. (1988). *The psychology of everyday things*. NY: Basic Books.

Norman, D. A. (2009). *The design of future things*. NY: Basic Books

Norman, D. A. (2013). *The design of everyday things*. NY: Basic Books.

Peyton Jones, S., Blackwell, A., & Burnett, M. (2003). A user-centred approach to functions in Excel. In *ICFP'03: Proceedings of the eighth ACM SIGPLAN International Conference on Functional Programming* (pp. 165–176). ACM Press: New York, NY.

Rasmussen, J. (1983). Skills, rules, knowledge: Signals, signs and symbols and other distinctions in human performance models. *IEEE Transactions: Systems, Man, and Cybernetics, SMC-13,* 257–267.

Sweller, J. (1988). Cognitive load during problem solving: Effects on learning. *Cognitive Science, 12,* 257–285.

Yeh, K.-C., Gregory, J. P., & Ritter, F. E. (2010). One laptop per child: Polishing up the XO laptop user experience. *Ergonomics in Design, 18*(3), 8–13.

Chapter 13
Methodology III: Empirical Evaluation

Abstract Evaluation is an essential part of development. There are several good reasons for carrying out user testing in particular. A successful evaluation requires careful planning. Here we describe the issues that you need to take into account and discuss several effective methods that can be used to collect data. User testing reduces the risk that you will deliver a system to your users that is unusable and is therefore ineffective. We also touch briefly on the need make sure that any evaluation that you carry out is conducted according to appropriate ethical guidelines.

13.1 Introduction

Evaluation should be a routine and regular part of system development. Attitudes to evaluation continue to vary widely, however, with many people still mistakenly believing that testing only happens at the end of development. The main problem with such an approach is that if development overruns while the delivery deadline remains fixed, it is usually testing that gets cut (because it is the last thing to happen). The net result is that the delivered system ends up being tested inadequately and, as a result, does not work as expected.

There are two statements that are worth remembering when it comes to evaluation. The first is "Test early, test often." The second is "Quick and dirty is better than nothing." Any evaluation program should deliver something informative for the system design and development. Testing can be expensive, but need not be. Lightweight methods that offer a proportionately larger return on investment are also available (Monk 1998; Nielsen 1993).

It is also worth remembering that when software engineers, in particular, talk about evaluation they will often refer to V & V, or verification and validation. Verification is about making sure that you are building the product right, and it is a process that is often carried out within the developer company. In contrast, validation is about making sure that you are building the right product, and usually

F. E. Ritter et al., *Foundations for Designing User-Centered Systems*,
DOI: 10.1007/978-1-4471-5134-0_13, © Springer-Verlag London 2014

involves some sort of acceptance test with the customer to make sure that the requirements have been met. You should make sure that you have the distinction between these two clear in your own head.

In this chapter we provide an introduction to the topic of evaluation and the methods that can be used to collect data. For a much fuller discussion about which analytical methods to use, you should consult an appropriate textbook such as Lazar et al.'s (2010) book *Research methods in human–computer interaction*. We do not go into the details of the methods you need to use to analyze your data. The way that you analyze the data is important, but is highly dependent on the type of data that you collect, and the overall purpose of the evaluation. More information about how to analyze your data can be found in statistics books, such as Howell (2010) or, for qualitative data Miles et al. (2013) and Todd (2004).

13.1.1 Why Do We Need User Testing?

If we could always guarantee that systems would be built correctly, based on a complete and accurate analysis of user requirements, then there would not (theoretically, at least) be a need for user testing. There are several reasons why we cannot give such guarantees, however. Perhaps the most pertinent one here is what has been called the *envisioned world problem* (Carroll and Rosson 1992; Woods and Dekker 2000), which is based on the fact that the world will inevitably change between the time when the user requirements are analyzed and the time when the final system is delivered. Often the changes are in ways that cannot be (fully) controlled by the users. So, when the requirements analysis is carried out, the users are effectively being asked to define what the system will need to do to work acceptably in some future context which they cannot fully predict or envision.

There are still some system developers who believe that as long as a system does what they consider to be the right thing, then that is enough. Their attitude is that if the users cannot make the system work, it is due to the users' lack of knowledge or ability, rather than being due to some fault of the developers. The fundamental problem with this view is that if the delivered system does not fit with the way that users normally carry out their work, there is a risk that it may not be accepted (e.g., see Berg 1997). The acid test of acceptability often comes when the users have to try to use the new system in their normal working environment.

The purpose of user testing is not to understand users but to evaluate how particular users can carry out particular tasks (using your system) in a particular context. There are still some designers who mistakenly believe that they know exactly how users carry out their work. In practice, however, when you observe users you see that they are often very creative, and use systems in ways that were never conceived of by their designers. The use of spreadsheets to format text or to make art, the use of thumbs to press cell phone buttons, and the use of social media broadcast tools like Twitter to organize political activities are just a few examples of creative use that were never imagined by their designers.

We know a lot about users, and their capabilities and limitations. We have covered much of this in the first part of this book and considered the implications for system design. Given what we know about the human visual system (Chap. 4), we can deduce that a 3-point font is likely to be too small to read. User testing is not necessary here; the decision can be derived from first principles. User testing may still be essential, however, for other system related questions—for example, to provide evidence that the right design choices and assumptions have been made when theories and assumptions make different suggestions, and that the system will work in its intended context.

Comprehensive user testing can be expensive and time consuming, but that does not mean that user testing should be ignored. As noted above, there are several discount or lightweight methods that can be used (Monk 1998; Nielsen 1993) to identify potential problems more cheaply, and at an earlier stage of development.

13.1.2 When Do We Carry Out User Testing?

Everybody makes mistakes—in the most general sense of the term—from time to time. This includes developers who may base their design decisions on insufficient or incorrect information at any stage of the development process—for example during analysis, design, and/or implementation. The consequences of these mistakes may not always be immediately apparent, but may surface much later. Carrying out evaluations helps to identify potential problems so that they can be appropriately rectified before the system gets delivered.

The ultimate goal of user testing is to make sure that the users can get the delivered system to do what they want it to do. In addition to helping to show that a system meets its requirements and is acceptable to the users, testing can also help to identify flaws in the development process. User testing is therefore often an effective way of providing designers with timely feedback at a relatively early stage during ongoing iterative development. Evaluating cheap, simple prototypes early in the development cycle can help to avoid potentially costly mistakes at a later stage in the lifecycle.

It is worth noting one of the practicalities of design that has implications for evaluation. It may not always be possible for designers to consult users during all stages of development. Instead, they work with a customer representative to come up with a system that will be acceptable to the users. Sometimes, however, the customer representative is not one of the target users, so they may not fully understand the subtleties of how the users really carry out their work using the system. It is therefore better to try to make sure that you can involve real users during evaluation.

Many developers still neither really understand what their users do, nor why they do what they do. Design and development are often carried out in isolation from the end users—agile methods can help address this limitation—with the result that the delivered system is not acceptable, because it does not fit in with the way that the users work. User testing during the early stages of development can highlight potential problems: making developers watch users wrestle with their product in an effort to make it do what they want is often a real eye-opener.

At least some part of systems development is based on the use of guidelines and principles. There are many guidelines and principles available, and they are mostly generic, which can make selecting the relevant ones for a specific project a major task. If you do use guidelines and principles, user testing can help to highlight the more subtle aspects of the system's context that need to be taken into account during development, thereby providing evidence to support your particular choice.

13.2 Planning Your Evaluation Study

Collecting data is not difficult. Collecting the *right* data—data that is pertinent to the questions that are being posed—is not so straightforward. Collecting the appropriate data to answer strategically relevant questions requires careful planning. Here we identify some of the main issues that can help to improve the chances of your evaluation study being a success. Many of the issues that we highlight are central to good experimental design.

13.2.1 What Type of Data: Qualitative or Quantitative?

One of the first things you will need to consider is the type of data that you will collect. The general rule of thumb is that you should think about collecting data to help you understand the thing (system, product, application, and so on) before you collect data to more precisely measure it. Typically the first type of data to collect is qualitative data, in other words, statements or general behavior, rather than precise numbers. Quantitative measures (e.g., times, number of clicks) can be used to verify assumptions with some degree of confidence over the intended population of users.

13.2.2 Selecting a Hypothesis

Creating hypotheses for your evaluation study helps to frame the study but also to keep it focused and grounded. A hypothesis is a proposition of what you believe to be the case (e.g., that a change you have made will cause a change in user behavior in some way) and will check with data. The null hypothesis (H_0) normally states that there is no difference between the things you are testing, e.g., there is no difference between the usability of application A and of application B. The alternative hypothesis (H_1) and the null hypothesis are mutually exclusive, so in our case it would be that there *is* a difference between the usability of application A and of application B. The multi-dimensional nature of usability means that experiments are often set up with several pairs of hypotheses, one for each dimension of usability. Some user studies might have multiple hypotheses to be tested.

13.2.3 Identifying the Dependent and Independent Variables

An independent variable is a factor that is independent of user behavior, and which can be varied by the person carrying out the evaluation (or the experiment, more generally). The dependent variable is the thing that depends on the user's behavior, or on the changes in the independent variable(s). Within user centered design, the sorts of things that would often be considered as independent variables include the type of input device (e.g., touch screen or keyboard), or different web page designs. The dependent variables are often more limited, however, to those things that are generally taken to measure the usability of a system (e.g., efficiency, effectiveness, satisfaction, ease of learning, and workload).

13.2.4 What Type of Evaluation: Formative or Summative?

There are two basic types of user-based evaluation: formative and summative. Each of these has a different purpose, and takes place at a different stage of development, as described below. They each help to remove different types of uncertainty, and to reduce the risk that the system will not be usable, or will be unacceptable to the end users.

Formative evaluation can take place at any point during development. It is used to help designers refine and form their designs. The focus of formative evaluation is to identify problems and potential solutions. In this type of evaluation the desired result is an indication of any problems that there may be in using the system, possibly with some indication of their frequency of occurrence. The designers can then use these frequencies to help rate the severity of the problems so a decision can be made about which problems should be fixed first.

Summative evaluation is concerned with assessing the success of the finished system or product, summarizing its overall impact and effectiveness. It is often used to test for any fixes that may be needed before the system is released, and to assess future releases. The end result may be some sort of usability score, and individual organizations may have their own particular threshold values for acceptability. One useful metric is to require that novice users of a new system are able to demonstrate performance levels that are some predetermined percentage of expert levels on the same system. The performance levels are measured using a set of predefined benchmark tasks. Defining a set of appropriate summative measures remains a difficult problem to solve, however, because systems, unlike many manufactured goods, cannot be assessed against tight specifications and tolerances.

13.2.5 Validity, Reliability, and Sensitivity

When it comes to designing an evaluation study, you want to make sure that you are evaluating the right thing, that you can measure the effects that you are looking for, and that the results can be generalized to other situations. To achieve these goals, you will need to think about the issues of validity, reliability, and sensitivity. This is true irrespective of whether you are collecting qualitative or quantitative data.

13.2.5.1 Validity

Validity refers to whether the measure that you are using is really measuring what it is supposed to be measuring. Reliability, on the other hand, refers to the consistency of a measure across different conditions. Note that it is possible to use a measure that has validity, but is not reliable, and vice versa. You should be aiming for high degrees of validity *and* reliability.

In addition to validity and reliability, you will also need to consider the sensitivity of the measure that you are using: does it react sufficiently well to changes to the independent variable. Validity, reliability, and sensitivity will all differ, depending on the context in which you are doing the evaluation.

There are several types of validity that you will need to think about. Here they are classified into two basic types:

- Instrument validity which relates to the instruments or measures that you will use in your evaluation. There are three subtypes: construct validity, content validity, and face validity.
- Experimental validity which relates the generalizability of the results. There are three subtypes: internal validity, external validity, and ecological validity.

We discuss each of these in more detail below as well as explaining the trade-offs that you may need to make when deciding on which type of experimental validity is important to your evaluation study.

Construct validity refers to the extent that your instrument or measure really does measure what you think it does. Probably the simplest example is to think about an IQ test as a whole, and how much it actually measures intelligence. Supporting evidence usually comes from both theory and testing, and can include statistical analysis of how responses and test items are related. If you think about usability, and how you measure that, things start to get a bit trickier because there are several different dimensions to the concept of usability. In other words, you cannot directly assess the usability of an artifact using a single measure. In this case you first have to operationalize the concept of usability, and then measure the different dimensions separately to assess efficiency, effectiveness, satisfaction, and so on. So although you are not measuring usability directly, by measuring the separate dimensions you are improving your construct validity. At this stage you will also need to think about the *content validity*.

Content validity refers to whether the content of a measure or instrument corresponds to the content of the construct that the test was designed to cover. Again, if we think about an IQ test, its content validity is determined by whether the items in the test cover all the different areas of intelligence that are discussed in the literature. For a usability survey, you would systematically examine the items in the survey to make sure that you had covered all of the relevant aspects of usability for the artifact that you are evaluating. So you might have items about the display layouts, the content, and so on. Often the way that content validity is evaluated is by having domain experts compare the test items against the specification for the thing that is being tested.

Face validity (also called surface validity) refers to whether a test *appears* to measure a certain criterion. It is closely related to content validity. The main difference is that you assess content validity by using a systematic review, whereas you assess face validity by having people make judgments about the test simply based on the surface appearance of the test. You could assess face validity, for example, by asking somebody (it does not have to be an expert) what they think the test is measuring. Sometimes you may get more honest answers if you have lower face validity, because the people doing the test are focused more on the task than what they think is being tested. It is also worth noting that you should not rely on face validity alone, because even so-called experts can get it wrong (consider, for example, the way they used to test whether someone was a witch or not in the Middle Ages).

Note that a test may have poor face validity but good construct validity. A game in which you shoot a gun at letters might not appear to measure spelling ability, for example, unless the letters pop up in a pattern that is based on correct spelling. Similarly, a tank simulation game might have poor surface validity for a naval task. However, both of these situations might have good construct validity in that the mental representations or the perceptual goals and cues are accurately represented (Smallman and St. John 2005). So you may have to consider how to trade off face validity against construct validity (and content validity) when designing your evaluation study.

Internal validity refers to how well conclusions can be drawn about cause-effect (causal) relationships based on the study design, including the measures used, and the situation in which the study was carried out. Internal validity is generally highest for tightly controlled studies which investigate the effect of an independent variable on a dependent variable, often run in a laboratory setting. To get good internal validity you need to make sure you control for other effects that could have an impact on the results you obtain. These include:

- Maturation of the participants: if their condition changes over the duration of the study, e.g., they become more tired.
- The types of participants: it is often impossible to use randomly selected participants, so you need to make sure that you do not end up with unbalanced groups of participants (e.g., all males, or all people aged over 50 in one of the groups).
- Testing effects: if you give participants in the study the same test at two different times, they may find it easier the second time because they already know the questions.

These potential confounding effects are well known. In many cases there are well documented solutions too which can be found in books on experimental psychology methods such as those by Calfe (1985), Ray (2008), and Campbell and Stanley (1963).

External validity relates to how far the results of the study can be generalized to other populations (such as different user groups), other places, and other times. One of the main factors that needs to be considered is the choice of participants used in the study. If all your participants are university students, for example, how can you be sure that the findings will apply to people who are aged over 60? To get good external validity you need to be aware of other effects that could have an impact on the results that you obtain, and provide some way of alleviating them. These effects include:

- Awareness of anticipated results: if participants can guess what they think the outcome of the study should be, they may adapt their behavior to what they think you expect them to do.
- The Hawthorne effect: people's performance can change simply as a function of being watched or recorded.
- Order effects: if you test people on artifact A first and then artifact B, there may be some carryover effect which means that their results with artifact B are better than they would otherwise have been.
- Treatment interaction effects: it may be the case that the participants in your study are motivated differently, and the way they are allocated to groups for testing means that you have one group that is more highly motivated than the other, which hence performs at a higher level.

Again, these potential confounding effects and solutions to the problems caused by them can be found in the literature mentioned above.

One way to increase external validity is to make sure that you use a wide range of users, stimuli, and contexts. The downside is that this will increase costs (time and money) and make it more difficult to detect real differences. Care is also needed to make sure that you do not reduce reliability (which is discussed below).

Ecological validity refers to the extent to which your results can be applied to real world settings. You should be able to see that it is closely related to external validity. For an evaluation study to have high ecological validity, the methods, materials, and setting of the study must approximate the real-life situation that is being investigated. If you wanted to conduct an evaluation of the usability of an application that is used in an office environment, for example, you would need to make sure that your setting resembled that of a normal office, where telephone calls and conversations (work and non-work related) are both constant sources of interruptions to task performance. The downside of having high ecological validity is that you cannot control all the possible independent variables that may affect the thing you are trying to measure.

At first glance there appears to be a conflict between internal and external (and ecological) validity. The main reason for carrying out evaluations in a laboratory setting is so that you can control for all interfering variables. Although this will increase your internal validity you lose external and ecological validity because you are using an artificial context for collecting data, and your results may not generalize to the real world—you may lose external and/or ecological validity. If you are carrying out an evaluation in a real world setting, however—using observation, for example—you will have high external (and ecological) validity but your internal validity will be reduced. Whether this is a problem or not depends on your research strategy. If you are following an inductive research strategy, then it is a problem because you will be concerned with the generalization of results; if you are following a deductive strategy, to test a theory, for example, then it is not a problem, because you are only concerned with threats to internal validity.

13.2.5.2 Reliability

Reliability refers to the ability of a measure to produce consistent results when the same things are measured under different conditions. Usually this is used in the context of *test–retest reliability*. In other words, if you conducted the same test again under the same conditions, but on a different day or with a similar set of participants, for example, you should get the same results if the measure is reliable. Reliability is also used in the context of assessing coding schemes, particularly when you need to encode the responses that you collect from users. If a coding scheme is reliable, then when you give the scheme and the data to another person, they should code the same data items in the same way. The level of agreement between the people who do the coding is what is called the *inter-rater reliability*, and you can measure this statistically (Cohen's Kappa test is often used to calculate the results).

13.2.5.3 Sensitivity

Even if the selected measure is both valid and reliable, it may not be sensitive enough to produce discernible effects that can easily be measured. The chosen measure may not change very much when you change the independent variables, for example. In this case it may be necessary to use a large number of participants. To achieve results that are statistically significant, however, you will still need to make sure that the measure has high reliability; otherwise your results will still be open to question.

Fig. 13.1 A user working with a system being tested (*left*) and the observation room where designers and analysts can watch the study going on (*right*). (Copyright © Fluent Interaction Ltd, www.fluent-interaction.co.uk, reproduced with permission)

13.3 Evaluation Methods

Evaluation methods are generally divided into four categories: usability testing, field studies, expert (heuristic) evaluation, and A/B testing. One of the fundamental notions behind expert evaluation is that a small number of experts can be used to quickly identify a large number of the problems with the system. You should think carefully before using these methods because they are not ideally suited to all types of system. Each of the evaluation methods has its own strengths and weaknesses, and they are often used in combination with each other.

13.3.1 Usability Testing

The term usability testing is usually restricted to describing the evaluation of the usability of a system under controlled (laboratory) conditions. Quite often usability testing is carried out in dedicated laboratories that have been specially designed for the purpose. Fluent Studios, for example, is a usability laboratory based in central London. It consists of two purpose-built usability rooms, equipped with high definition audio-visual technology. These rooms are shown in Fig. 13.1.

Different organizations will set up their usability testing facility in different ways. Generally, one room is set up for testing whilst the other is configured as an observation room, which allows the developers, testers, and other interested stakeholders to see what the users are doing without disturbing them through their presence in the same room. The rooms are physically separated rather than being connected by a one-way mirror. Any action that takes place in the testing room is projected into the observation room. There are several advantages to using projection rather than a one-way mirror:

- Observers feel less intrusive
- Observers can talk in the observation room
- Observers can move around, allowing brainstorming activities
- Participants are less aware of being watched (because there is no large mirror in the room, and sound contamination is reduced)
- A visual area larger than the participant's screen can be used to observe what they are doing
- There is greater flexibility in the way the observation room can be configured
- Costs are reduced
- It is easier to use
- The volume of what the participant is saying can be controlled within the observation room.

Fluent Studios' laboratory is used to conduct usability tests in a creative environment. Whilst one-to-one testing is carried out with users in the testing room, it is regarded as very important to get the observers involved as well. So, often when a new design or prototype is being tested, the tests will be designed to try and identify usability issues early on in the testing, so that they can be resolved at the earliest opportunity.

Usually the first step in testing is to develop a set of task scenarios that capture the critical characteristics of the tasks that are likely to be carried out using the system (Carroll 2000). These scenarios are usually descriptions of real-world tasks that users can be expected to understand, but the scenario does not describe *how* the task is done using this system. They are typically expressed as problems that the user would normally be expected to solve using the system as part of their work.

For example, consider the following scenario:

> You are a system administrator for a software system that schedules and allocates resources ranging from company pool cars to meeting rooms. Unfortunately one of the meeting rooms has unexpectedly been designated to be refurbished, which will take 2 months beginning in July. Your task is to notify those people who have booked the room for July and August and to provide alternative resources.

You should be able to see that this scenario contains a goal, information about that goal, and information about the context in which the task takes place. It does not, however, contain instructions about how to use the system to achieve the desired goal.

The focus of the scenarios determines the shape of the evaluation: everyday usage scenarios, for example, will capture information about everyday usage of the system. Similarly, for critical systems (safety critical, mission critical, business critical, and so on) the scenarios would be designed to focus on critical (but unusual) incidents. Ideally a more comprehensive evaluation could be carried out using both types of scenarios.

An illustration of the benefits of usability testing occurred when new designs for a national educational site were being tested in Fluent Studios. Some usability problems were quickly observed with the method of global navigation: the first four users who were tested all struggled to find the site's home page. Between testing sessions a new page header was developed, and tests with the next four participants demonstrated that the introduction of the new design had resolved the problem. This rapid development methodology is used to test designs in an agile way, which makes the most effective use of the testing time allocated to a project.

13.3.2 Field Studies and Field Experiments

Field studies, as the name implies, are evaluations that are carried out in the field, that is, in real world settings. Field studies are often carried out to discover more about the context of use of a technology that is to be designed or is being designed. Studying activities in the "real" world can be challenging. If you just think about the things that happen every day in an office environment you should start to get the picture. In an office, users may be carrying out some task using the computer. They can break off from their work at any point, though, such as when they are interrupted by the telephone ringing, if a colleague stops by to discuss something (work or otherwise), or if their boss calls them into a meeting. So carrying out the task is not simply a matter of planning what to do, then just getting on and doing it step by step in sequence, from start to finish: people will often have to juggle several, possibly unrelated, and often unscheduled, activities at once. The big advantage of field studies is that they show you how people really work. One obvious design implication of the fractured nature of work is that you should make it relatively easy for people to pick up where they left off after an interruption. The main disadvantage of field studies is that it is often very difficult to exercise experimental control over what happens, so it is harder to focus on the relationships between some of the task variables, and to have results that are both general and applicable to other settings or times.

Field experiments are trials of technologies in real world settings. This is often when a fully functional prototype can be deployed into a real world setting and, as designers and developers, we want to see how users will interact with the technology. Such field experiments tend to be for non-safety–critical systems, such as recreational and social Internet sites. Often there is some latitude for changing the technology, but most of the functionality is set. In this instance, the evaluation will likely involve many different methods: collecting usage data, conducting observations of the technology in use, interviewing and surveying users, small controlled experiments, and so on (for an example of a technology that was fielded and evaluated see Churchill et al. 2003).

13.3.3 (Expert) Heuristic Evaluation

Heuristic evaluation (Nielsen and Molich 1990) is a relatively informal way of analyzing the usability of an interface design. A small select number of people— ideally interface design experts, and preferably domain experts too—are asked to

Table 13.1   Heuristic basis for user interface evaluation (adapted from http://www.nngroup.com/articles/ten-usability-heuristics)

1. The current system status should always be readily visible to the user
2. There should be a match between the system and the user's world: the system should speak the user's language
3. The user should have the control and freedom to undo and redo functions that they mistakenly perform
4. The interface should exhibit consistency and standards so that the same terms always mean the same thing
5. Errors should be prevented where possible
6. Use recognition rather than recall in order to minimize the mental workload of the users
7. The system should have flexibility and efficiency of use across a range of users, e.g., through keyboard short-cuts for advanced users
8. The system should be esthetic and follow a minimalist design, i.e., do not clutter up the interface with irrelevant information
9. Users should be helped to manage errors: not all errors can be prevented so make it easier for the users to recognize, diagnose, and recover
10. Help and documentation should be readily available and structured for ease of use

make judgments, based on a set of guidelines or principles together with their own knowledge, about a particular design. The individual results are then aggregated together. In this way it is possible to overcome the inherent inaccuracy of individual evaluations.

In the ideal world all of the evaluators would use the same (standard) set of criteria for judging what is good or bad. In reality, most people tend to rely on intuition and common sense, partly because most usability guidelines tend to be excessively large, often having many tens or even hundreds of rules (e.g., Brown 1988; Mosier and Smith 1986). Molich and Nielsen (1990), however, suggested that a relatively simple set of guidelines can be used as the basis for evaluation. Initially they used nine guidelines, but over the years, these have been refined and the number increased to ten, as shown in Table 13.1.

Each expert works their way through the user interface design individually noting compliance with the heuristics. Note that the user interface may just be a paper-based prototype, because the experts are not being asked to carry out tasks using the system. Problems that are detected can either be written down or recorded verbally (e.g., by taking verbal protocols). The individual results are then aggregated to highlight the detected problems.

Typically, only three to five experts are required to carry out a heuristic evaluation and generate useful results. Many people have taken this to be a hard and fast rule for all types of evaluation, however, which can be a serious mistake. The requisite number, to a large extent, depends on the diversity of the eventual user population. So, for example, if you were designing an on-line population census, then it would not make sense to just use three to five users, since such a small sample is very unlikely to be truly representative of the diversity inherent in a nation's general population.

It should be noted that many of the problems that are identified by heuristic evaluation may not affect the usability of the system. In addition, the results are often only presented in negative terms, focusing on what is bad about the design, instead of also highlighting the things that are good.

13.3.4 Co-operative Evaluation

Co-operative evaluation is another type of expert evaluation method. It was developed at the University of York (UK), and is related to Scandinavian design practices (Monk et al. 1993; Müller et al. 1997). As the name suggests, the evaluation is carried out co-operatively, with the user effectively becoming part of the evaluation team. The method is based on the notion that any user difficulties can be highlighted by two simple tactics:

1. Identifying the use of inefficient strategies by the user (e.g., copy-paste-delete, rather than cut and paste).
2. Identifying occasions when the user talks about the interface, rather than their tasks. These are called breakdowns, based on the notion that good tools should be transparent, so the user should be talking about the task rather than the technology.

The user is asked to talk aloud as they carry out a series of tasks, and can be prompted with questions. It is a formative evaluation technique, in that it is used to gather information about the design as it is being formed. The method can therefore be used with a working prototype or with the real system.

13.3.5 A/B Testing

A recent trend is to do live testing of multiple interfaces. This is called A/B testing or bucket testing. In this approach a web service exposes different users to different interfaces and/or interactions. This can be seen at Google, for example, who was one of the first Internet sites to use this method extensively to guide their interface and interaction design decisions. In bucket tests, interfaces can vary in subtle ways, such as color changes, or may differ substantially, including manipulations of key functionality. User actions such as clicks (measured as CTR or click through rates) are studied to see the impact on user behavior, if any, of the changes.

There are many advantages to these kinds of studies—not least that a test can be run at scale and while maintaining ongoing business, and that feedback is fast. Of course, this approach requires building the test interfaces, and having the platform on which to partition users into conditions and deliver the experiences.

13.4 What to Evaluate?

In general, the sooner evaluation is done during development, the sooner you will get feedback, and the more likely it is that the delivered product will be both usable and acceptable to users. There is a trade-off here between the need for evaluation and how closely related the current version is to the final version. If an iterative development life cycle approach is used, this means that evaluation should be carried out as part of each iteration. Obviously, the earlier in development that evaluation takes place, the less developed the system that is being evaluated will be. The way that evaluation is often carried out during development is using some sort of prototype, until eventually the full system can be evaluated. The prototype usually starts out as something with low fidelity (possibly just one or more sketches), and increases in fidelity as the project progresses.

13.4.1 Pencil and Paper Prototypes

At the earliest stages of development, pencil and paper mockups of the interface can be shown to the users, who are then asked how they would carry out particular tasks. This technique, which is often described as storyboarding should ideally be carried out with real users, although other designers, and even hostile users, could be employed.

Using pencil and paper sketches is cheap, and can be used very early in design. At this stage, ideas are usually still being explored, so the evaluations are usually formative. The data collected are normally qualitative rather than quantitative, with the results being used to inform the design of the artifact.

13.4.2 Computer-Based Prototypes

The next level of sophistication involves building a computer-based prototype. There are now several tools around that can be used for prototyping at several levels, from pencil and paper style sketches to interactive working prototypes.

At the earliest stages of computer-based prototyping you can employ *Wizard of Oz* techniques, where the user will interact with a prototype (computer-based) interface. The full functionality of the rest of the system is usually not available at this point, so a human acts behind the scenes to process user input and actions and provide the required responses (like the Wizard of Oz did in the film!). This technique has been used very effectively for evaluating the potential of speech-based systems.

The level of sophistication of the prototype should naturally increase as development progresses, and the prototype becomes closer to the finished product. How it develops will depend mostly on which basic method of prototyping you use: evolutionary or revolutionary. In evolutionary prototyping, the original prototype is refined after each iteration of the development cycle: the prototype evolves towards the deliverable version. This is the sort of approach that is used in developing web sites, where they use wireframes to lay out the basic initial design, which then gets filled in and refined as the design evolves. In revolutionary prototyping, the current prototype is thrown away at the end of each iteration of the development cycle, and a new prototype is developed.

In addition to helping identify design issues, prototypes can also be used to help users to articulate requirements. People often find it much easier to talk about something concrete, referring to the prototype, than to talk about something abstract, where they have to imagine what the application or product should do.

Prototypes vary in cost, depending upon the sophistication of the prototype and the length of the evaluation period (laboratory-based user testing vs field studies). They do tend to give good results and are suitable for many stages of the design process, for both formative and summative evaluations.

13.4.3 The Final System

Evaluations of the final system will often be performed in house first, possibly using laboratory-based testing. If there is latitude for some redesign, systems may be deployed and field experiments conducted, but this only tends to be the case for systems that are not safety–critical, as noted above. For enterprise, and safety- and security-critical systems, it is more usually the case that the system is evaluated in full before it gets delivered to the customer. The final system will usually be subjected to a formal acceptance test, normally on the customer's premises, where the customer will sign to say that the system has successfully passed the agreed tests. You should note that web sites are very rarely tested at the customer's site (largely because they will normally be used from elsewhere).

Once a system is delivered and has been accepted by the customer, it is unlikely that any further formal evaluation will take place. The picture is slightly different for web sites, however, where the delivered system will normally reside in a dynamic environment, so the iterative development may continue, albeit with iterations that have a longer duration. In both cases, data on patterns of usage may be collected, along with information about problems logged with customer support, as noted above, and this can be used to inform future development projects and refinements to existing systems and products.

13.5 Measuring Usability

There are several dimensions to usability, so there are several measures, both qualitative and quantitative, that can be used to indicate how usable a particular artifact is. Most people will be familiar with task time as the de facto standard for measuring efficiency and productivity, and hence giving an indication of usability. There are several others too, though, and they are usually concerned with either performance (quantitative measures) or process (qualitative measures). There is also the concept of user experience, related to how much satisfaction the user obtains from the system. Here we briefly describe the measures that you are most likely to encounter. Often you will use several complementary methods to measure usability, such as a combination of task performance times, and a usability survey.

13.5.1 Task Time

Task performance time is widely used as a measure of efficiency within the fields of HCI and human factors and ergonomics. The task is usually one of three: a small cognitively manageable task, often referred to as a *unit task* (Card et al. 1983); a standard, predefined benchmark task (that you use to assess efficiency for similar artifacts); or a task scenario (as described above).

It is easy to determine task time using a stop watch, for example, or using time stamps if you are recording task performance. Time is a measure that is widely understood, and is easy to analyze statistically. Time is generally used as a measure in summative evaluations of the final system. Where the performance time is relatively insensitive, however, it can be costly to carry out evaluations, because you will have to run the test many times to be able to draw solid statistical conclusions from the results.

Remember that usability is not only concerned with how easy something is to use, but also how easy it is to learn to use. Task times can also be used to determine how long it takes to learn to use a system. Normally some threshold level of performance is defined in advance, and the length of time it takes to reach that threshold is measured. Alternatively, the length of time it takes to recover from observable errors can be measured: you would expect to see this time reduce as people learn how to do the task and how to manage the errors.

One of the main problems of using time measures is that they are not easily compared unless all the contextual elements (tasks, level of expertise, lighting conditions, and so on) are kept constant. The corollary of this is that if you want to compare times when you cannot fully control the contextual effects, you have to convert the data into a more stable metric, i.e., one that is not so easily affected by changes in these elements. One way of doing this, which was proposed by Whiteside et al. (1985), is to calculate a score in the range 1–100 as shown in Eq. (13.1):

$$\text{Score} = (1/T) \times P \times C \qquad (13.1)$$

where T = time, C = constant based on fastest expert time, and P = percentage of task completed.

13.5.2 Errors

Errors can be measured quantitatively (by simply counting them) or qualitatively (by noting the different types of error). Whilst time is best suited to summative evaluations, error measures can be used in both summative and formative evaluations.

As we have already seen in Chap. 10, however, errors are not easy to define, and they can be hard to count too. This is particularly true when observing expert behavior. One of the key aspects of expert performance is that they often detect and recover their own errors before the effects of the error become apparent to outside observers. So if you watch an expert perform a task, you may not even realize that they have made an error.

We can distinguish many types of errors—slips, mistakes, violations, mode errors (e.g., problems with grayed out menu items), discrimination errors (e.g., selecting the wrong menu item because of ambiguous labels), and so on. The types of errors will vary depending on which taxonomy of errors you use (see Chap. 10 for examples).

13.5.3 Verbal Protocols

Verbal protocols can be a useful way of understanding the issues that confront users as they try to tackle particular problems using some artifact. Some care is needed when reading about verbal protocols, because many people use the terms *talk aloud* and *think aloud* interchangeably. Strictly speaking you usually want people to produce *talk aloud* reports, reflecting the things that are in their short term memory as they do the task; if they generate *think aloud* reports, this suggests that they are processing things more deeply and (possibly) rationalizing their decisions and actions before they verbalize them.

The two main types of verbal protocols are concurrent, which are taken whilst the person performs the task, and retrospective, where the person describes what they did after completing the task. In concurrent verbal protocols, the user is asked to talk about information as it comes to mind, to "say out loud everything that you say to yourself" (Ericsson and Simon 1980, 1993). The user should not be reflecting upon their own behavior and providing explanations of causality. While this kind of reflective behavior (referred to as introspection) may provide some useful insights, these insights are not considered valid data because they are easily influenced by other aspects, such as expected task performance, social pressure, and the user's (often incorrect) theories of how their own mind works. Talking aloud about content is generally regarded as being more objective than thinking aloud, which usually involves introspecting about the process.

Providing concurrent protocols can be hard for users, but they are more reliable than other types of verbal protocol. When you take concurrent verbal protocols, you should ask the user to practice providing a concurrent verbal protocol whilst carrying out a simple task, such as an arithmetic addition or counting the windows in their childhood home (Ericsson and Simon 1993, appendix).

You may find it easier to collect concurrent protocols by having two users work together on a task. The natural dialogue that takes place (assuming that dialogue occurs or is required for the task) will encapsulate the information they are using to do the task. Another possible variation is to use expert commentary. Here one expert describes what the user is doing as they perform the task.

Retrospective protocols can also be used, and these are taken after the task has been performed. They tend to be more useful when people can watch a video or pictorial record—we discuss visual protocols in the next section—of their performance to help them remember what they did. This helps them to recognize their actions, rather than just having to recall them from memory. Although subjects may find it easier to provide retrospective verbal protocols, they can lead people to provide post hoc rationalizations of actions that they now perceive to be incorrect or that they performed instinctively.

Another way that you can interrogate what users are doing is by using pop-up menus (Feurzeig and Ritter 1988). This idea has not been fully tested, however, and does not have the same level of theoretical support as concurrent verbal protocols. The obvious criticism is that the pop-up menu interrupts the task, and may break the user's flow of activity because it draws their attention away from the task. A similar but more intrusive approach is to freeze the task and ask users about what they are doing at that particular point in time. This latter technique has been used in measuring situation awareness (Endsley 1995).

13.5.4 Video Protocols

Video protocols (also called visual protocols) involve making a video recording of users as they carry out some prescribed task. The recording is often made using multiple cameras positioned to capture different aspects of performance, such as what is currently shown on the screen, the position of the user's hands, and a more general view that shows both the user and the system together. Sometimes the recordings are made directly from the monitor. Although video protocols provide very rich data, the fact that they are being video recorded does make some users feel under pressure, and can lead to unnatural behavior.

The main problem with video protocols is that analyzing them can be very hard and is very time-consuming. Typically, analysis can take anywhere between 10 and 100 times as long as the duration of the recording.

As noted above, video protocols can be shown to users to help in the collection of retrospective verbal protocols. This technique is sometimes called auto-confrontation, because the users are shown the video recording and asked to explain their behavior.

Video protocols can be shown to developers to let them see the sorts of problems that real users encounter with their system. It is arguably better, though, to let the developers watch users try to use their product in a usability laboratory in real time. Both of these methods are generally much more effective than simply providing the developers with a written report of qualitative and quantitative performance data. They can also be used when the developers are remote from the site where the evaluation is taking place, as long as suitable network connections are available to transmit the recordings.

13.5.5 Eye Movement Tracking

In the last 10 years an increasing number of people have begun to collect data on eye movements to analyze how people use web pages (e.g., Nielsen and Pernice 2010; and see Navalpakkam and Churchill in press, for a more general review of eye-tracking). The current eye-tracking equipment is much easier to use, much cheaper, and much less invasive than earlier generations of eye-trackers which required you to have your head clamped in place, and required frequent re-calibration. They also generated large amounts of data that required significant effort to analyze and interpret, whereas there are now several good software packages available that will help you make sense of the data. You should recall that we discussed eye-tracking in Chap. 4.

Eye movement data is particularly useful as a way of generating heat maps which show the hot spots on a web page. These are the parts of a web page that users spend most of their time looking at, either by gazing at it for a long period of time, or visiting it for several shorter periods of time. In general, users have predetermined expectations about where they expect certain items such as menus, navigation bars, back/next buttons, and so on to appear on a web page. This leads them to automatically look for those items in the expected places first. If they are not where they are expected to be, you start to see scan patterns in the eye movements as the eyes jump around trying to find the required element.

There are some drawbacks to using eye movement data, which mean that you often need to complement it by using an additional method. The two main drawbacks are that the data do not tell you *why* users fixated on a particular point on the page and that the data do not tell you *what* items on the page the participant missed or did not notice.

13.5.6 Questionnaires and Surveys

If you want to discover opinions about something, often the best way is to ask people. Subjective measures are frequently used to assess attitudes towards a new piece of technology—feelings of control, frustration, etc. Sometimes just asking people for their opinions is the only way of gathering this data. Note, however, that sometimes surveys can measure opinions but not actions; early work has shown that what people do and what they say they will do can vary up to 100% (LaPiere 1934). Surveys are more valid when the attitudes are more stable, relevant, and salient to the behavior, and there are less situational pressures on the behavior (Hock 2002, pp 281–288). Questionnaires and surveys allow you to gather large amounts of data in a relatively short period of time, as long as you distribute them appropriately.

Designing questionnaires and surveys is an art in itself, as great care needs to be exercised to make sure that any potential biases are avoided. It is also important to make sure that the questionnaires are well structured and tested, as this helps to ensure the validity of the resulting data. For this reason, it is almost invariably a good idea to carry out a pilot study on a small sample of users, and then refine the questionnaires appropriately. Having a pilot study is also very useful for determining how long it will take to complete the survey. As a rule of thumb, most people are relatively happy with filling in surveys that take 10–15 min to complete, without any reward.

The questions need to be carefully designed, because you will not have a chance to explain them to respondents. So they need to be clear, unambiguous, and easy to understand. It is also important that you do not ask leading questions that reflect any biases that you may have. You also need to think about the answers that you require. In some cases it may be a simple "Yes/No/Don't Know," or it may be "select one (or more) options" from a possible list. In other cases (and quite often in usability surveys) you will be trying to gauge people's opinions about something, in which case you are more likely to use rating scales, such as a five-point Likert scale, where you will ask respondents how much they agree with a particular statement, such as "I found it easy to locate the home page button." In this case the response scale would normally be from *Strongly Disagree* to *Strongly Agree*.

Distribution of questionnaires and surveys requires careful thought. Usability surveys are frequently handed out on paper to participants as part of a usability study (often at the end). There are some standard usability rating scales that you could use or adapt for your own purposes, such as the System Usability Scale (SUS, Brooke 1996). More generally, however, you may want to use electronic surveys, in which case you need to think about how you will attract people from your target audience to complete the survey.

Note that if you intend to use follow-up surveys at the end of a test, you need to be aware of what is called *the media equation* (Reeves and Nass 1996). This refers to the fact that if you give people the survey on the same machine as the one on which you give them the test, they rate things more highly than if they complete the survey on a different machine! They treat the machine they used as an agent that needs to be treated socially.

13.5.7 Interviews and Focus Groups

Interviews can take three different forms: structured, unstructured, and semi-structured. Whichever type you decide to use, it is often a good idea to record them, with the written consent of the interviewees. It is also a good idea to make some written notes. These will help add extra context to help interpret the content that has been recorded, and will also act as a back-up in case recording fails for some reason.

Structured interviews are based around a fixed set of questions that the interviewees must answer. These questions are often closed, i.e., the user is expected to answer the question and no more. Typically these questions have "Yes/No" type answers.

Unstructured interviews are generally more informal, and are a bit more like a chat with the users. So you may start off with a small number of issues (perhaps as few as one or two) that you want to discuss with the users, and then the direction you take for the rest of the interview is determined by what they say.

Semi-structured interviews fall somewhere between structured and unstructured interviews. Usually you will have a short standard list of questions, which may be open, and then you direct the interview based on what the users say in response to the questions you ask. Unstructured and semi-structured interviews tend to be slightly harder to carry out because they will often require the interviewer to think on their feet during the interview. Their big advantage, however, is that they can uncover issues that may not previously have been thought of.

Whilst interviews tend to be carried out on a one-to-one basis, it can be useful to have group discussions, which are often carried out as focus groups. Usually a focus group is carried out with a small group of up to about ten users or stakeholders. The basic aim is to get the focus group members to express their opinions in a relatively friendly environment. To conduct a focus group successfully you need to have a list of issues or questions for discussion, and to have an experienced facilitator who can make sure that everybody gets a chance to air their opinions. The sessions can produce lots of useful data, so it is often best to record them as well as making notes (it may help to have separate people taking notes and facilitating the discussions).

13.5.8 Workload Measures

Workload measures attempt to describe how much mental effort the user expends in performing a particular task. They are generally used more often to evaluate critical systems rather than web sites per se. The measures are hard to devise, but can be useful in many contexts. The most common approach is to periodically ask users to state (or rate) what they think their current workload is, although this can be quite disruptive of performance and hence affect their perceived workload.

The NASA-TLX (Task Load indeX) workload measurement instrument (Hart and Staveland 1988) is probably the most commonly used method. NASA-TLX can be administered on paper or on-line. The NASA TLX is a multi-dimensional rating procedure that provides an overall workload score based on a weighted average of ratings on six workload dimensions: mental demands, physical demands, temporal demands, own performance, effort, and frustration (NASA, 1987).

During the standard NASA-TLX procedure users carry out pairwise comparisons of the six dimensions. In each of the 15 (5 + 4 + 3 + 2 + 1) comparisons, users select the dimension that contributed more to workload. Each dimension receives one point for each comparison where it was greater. The relative weight for each dimension is then given by the sum of those points, divided by 15 to normalize it.

Probably the most accurate approach for measuring workload is to use a secondary task that the user must perform as and when they can (e.g., responding to visual or auditory signals). For example, at random intervals the user has to push an 'A' when the number that pops up on the screen is odd and a 'B' when the number is even. The time and correctness of the response is a measure of how hard the user is working.

We sometimes find that while two systems give comparable performance results on the primary task, performance on the secondary task may be very different., This suggests that one interface is more demanding than the other, i.e., where performance on the secondary task is worse, this indicates that the user is expending more mental effort on the primary task.

13.5.9 Patterns of Usage

Rather than looking at performance on unit or benchmark tasks in a laboratory setting, you can place prototype versions of your system in real work settings and observe actual patterns of use, either directly or through videotape. Often you will find that certain features, including those that have been requested by users, are very rarely used, e.g., style sheets in Word.

You could also consider instrumenting the user interface or using a general keystroke logger (e.g., Kukreja et al. 2006) to collect (timed) logs of the keystrokes, and other interactions that the user performs. This data gets logged in what are sometimes called dribble files. These files can quickly become excessively large, however, and thus be hard to analyze. They can be used as a way to identify errors, error recovery, and patterns of use. Note that if you will be collecting data in this way, you will need ethical approval, which we talk about below.

If you are evaluating a system that has been released into the marketplace, you can also get some information on patterns of usage by looking at the logs of calls to customer/technical support services. Note that this data only measures problems that have been reported, rather than all of the problems. Users are often very flexible and adaptable and will develop ways of making the system do what they want it to do, such as workarounds, rather than spend extra time and effort on the end of a phone line trying to contact technical support to report the problem.

Customer support activity data can be both politically and commercially sensitive—it may allow competitors to see where the problems are with a particular product. Such data can be very valuable, however, because it does give a good indication of where the real problems may lie.

13.5.10 User Experience

Finally, there is the concept of user experience (Tullis and Albert 2008). In addition to these mostly quantitative measures, there is the qualitative experience of using the system that is being tested. This is an important concept, and is related to several concepts that can sometimes be hard to define, and even harder to measure. Many organizations now rate a high level of user experience (explained in Chap. 2) as being a major determinant in the success of a system or product.

One of the factors that will influence user experience is task importance. If the task is important to the user and the system gets the task done, then, it will be a successful system. Early systems, e.g., TVs, phones, portable phones, PDAs, Blackberries, were all hard to use and the times taken to use them were relatively high compared to today's standards. However, they were successful because they provided a better experience or supported a task that was not supported before. Over time and extended use, other measures and aspects became important.

13.6 The Ethics of Evaluation

Studies that involve users interacting with technological products now routinely need to be vetted to ensure that participants are treated appropriately. This means that ethical clearance (or approval) is required from the appropriate authoritative body. In most countries this will normally be done by an ethics committee, whilst in the US it will be carried out by an institutional review board (IRB). They will review the study to determine that the relevant guidelines are being followed. The main things they check are whether vulnerable people will be involved, whether participants are aware of what they are committing to in the study, and that any collected data is stored appropriately. Usually the latter involves anonymizing data so that they cannot be linked to the participant. These requirements vary based on funding, use, publication, and teaching, so take advice if you have not done this before.

As a matter of routine you should produce information sheets for participants, describing the study and explaining that they can withdraw from the study at any point. You should also take informed written consent, having them sign a consent form that says that they have read and understood the information sheet, that they are willing to take part, and that they understand that they can withdraw at any point. You should also think about how you will debrief at the end of a testing session: you could either give them a debrief sheet, explaining the purpose of the study in more detail, or simply verbally debrief them. You may also want to ask them not to discuss the study with others, because it could influence their behavior if they were subsequently in the study. Further details on this process are available (Ritter et al. 2013; Ritter et al. 2009).

13.7 Summary

There is a lot more to evaluation than many people imagine. Carrying out an evaluation requires careful thought and planning before you begin testing. In this chapter we have highlighted the sorts of issues you need to think about during planning. Most development is carried out using an iterative cycle in which a formative evaluation is carried out during each cycle. The information that comes out of the evaluation can then be used to inform development during the next cycle of development. It is therefore important that you clearly understand what sort of data you should collect, and why. You also need to think about whom you will collect the data from, and the environment in which you will collect them.

Once you have the basic plan, you can start to think in more detail about how you will collect the data (and how you will analyze them, although we have not covered that issue here). There are many methods that you could use, and your final choice may be determined by factors such as how much time is available, what resources are available, and how many (potential) users are accessible to take part in the tests. We have briefly discussed several evaluation methods that are available, and touched)on the importance of making sure that you are aware of the need to treat the participants in your evaluation in a way that is ethical.

Evaluation is important because it produces feedback on development as it is progressing. If you can get real users to take part in your evaluations, their feedback will help make sure that the system is more likely to be usable and acceptable when it is delivered. In other words, it will reduce the risks that the final system will be a failure when it is delivered.

13.8 Other Resources

There is a web site devoted to the subject of evaluating adaptive systems: EASy-Hub (which stands for Evaluation of Adaptive Systems Hub) is available at http://www.easy-hub.org.

If you are designing a usability laboratory, Jacob Nielsen edited a special issue of the *BIT* journal about how to create and use usability laboratories. Although it is now somewhat dated, it still contains several useful nuggets of information:

Nielsen, J. (Ed.). (1994). Special issue: Usability Laboratories. *Behaviour & Information Technology 13*(1–2).

If you are not experienced working with studies with human participants, useful guides include:

Ritter, F. E., Kim, J. W., Morgan, J. H., & Carlson, R. A. (2013). *Running behavioral studies with human participants: A practical guide.* Thousand Oaks, CA: Sage.

Shadbolt, N. R., & Burton, A. M. (1995). Knowledge elicitation: A systematic approach.

In J. R. Wilson & E. N. Corlett (Eds.), *Evaluation of human work: A practical ergonomics methodology* (pp. 406–440). London: Taylor and Francis.

Stanton, N.A. & Young, M. (1999). *A guide to methodology in ergonomics: Designing for human use.* London, UK: Taylor & Francis.

One of the best introductions to user focused evaluations is by Elizabeth Goodman, Mike Kuniavsky, and Andrea Moed (also recommended in Chap. 2). They cover basic techniques and methods that will help you design better interactions. They also offer case studies and examples that you can compare to your own design situations:

Goodman, E., Kuniavsky, M., & Moed, A. (2012). *Observing the user experience: A practitioner's guide to user research.* San Francisco, CA: Morgan Kaufman

Another highly recommended text is Kim Goodwin's *Designing for the Digital Age*, published in 2011:

Goodwin, Kim. (2011) *Designing for the digital age: How to create human-centered products and services.* Wiley.

Finally, it is worth reading Gilbert Cockton's "Usability Evaluation" published online by the Interaction Design Foundation.
    http://interaction-design.org/encyclopedia/usability_evaluation.html

13.9 Exercises

13.1 Design a usability test for comparing two makes of mobile device (such as a smartphone), using at least two of the ways of measuring usability described above. You should include details of how many participants you would use, and an explanation of why you chose your selected ways of measuring usability.

13.2 Design a study to evaluate the usability of an advanced photocopier/printer, using at least two of the ways of measuring usability that were described above. You should include details of how many participants you would use, and an explanation of why you chose your selected ways of measuring usability.

13.3 Design a usability test for evaluating the web site of an on-line retailer, using at least two of the ways of measuring usability that were described above. You should include details of how many participants you would use, and an explanation of why you chose your selected ways of measuring usability.

13.4 Summarize the evaluations in Exercises 13.1–13.3, comparing and contrasting how the devices being evaluated influence the number of participants and the choice of evaluation methods.

References

Berg, M. (1997). *Rationalizing medical work: Decision support techniques and medical practices.* Cambridge, MA: MIT Press.

Brooke, J. (1996). SUS: A 'quick and dirty' usability scale. In P. W. Jordan, B. Thomas, B. A. Weerdmeester, & I. L. McClelland (Eds.), *Usability evaluation in industry* (pp. 189–194). London: Taylor & Francis.

Brown, C. M. L. (1988). *Human-computer interface design guidelines.* Norwood, NJ: Ablex.

Calfee, R. C. (1985). *Experimental methods in psychology.* New York, NY: Holt, Rinehart and Winston.

Campbell, D. T., & Stanley, J. C. (1963). *Experimental and quasi-experimental designs for research.* Boston, MA: Houghton Mifflin.

Card, S. K., Moran, T., & Newell, A. (1983). *The psychology of human-computer interaction.* Hillsdale, NJ: Erlbaum.

Carroll, J. M. (2000). *Making use: Scenario-based design of human-computer interactions.* Cambridge, MA: MIT Press.

Carroll, J. M., & Rosson, M. B. (1992). Getting around the task-artifact cycle: How to make claims and design by scenario. *ACM Transactions on Information Systems, 10*, 181–212.

Churchill, E. F., Nelson, L., Denoue, L., Murphy, P., & Helfman, J. I. (2003). The Plasma poster network: Social hypermedia on public display. In K. O'Hara, M. Perry, E. Churchill, & D. Russell (Eds.), *Social and interactional aspects of shared display technologies.* London: Kluwer Academic Publishers.

Endsley, M. R. (1995). Toward a theory of situation awareness in dynamic systems. *Human Factors, 37*(1), 32–64.

Ericsson, K. A., & Simon, H. A. (1980). Protocol analysis: Verbal reports as data. *Psychological Review, 87*, 215–251.

Ericsson, K. A., & Simon, H. A. (1993). *Protocol analysis: Verbal reports as data* (2nd ed.). Cambridge, MA: MIT Press.

Feurzeig, W., & Ritter, F. (1988). Understanding reflective problem solving. In J. Psotka, L. D. Massey, & S. A. Mutter (Eds.), *Intelligent tutoring systems: Lessons learned.* Hillsdale, NJ: Erlbaum.

Goodman, E., Kuniavsky, M., & Moed, A. (2012). *Observing the user experience: A practitioner's guide to user research* (2nd ed.). Waltham, MA: Morgan Kaufmann.

Hart, S. G., & Staveland, L. E. (1988). Development of the NASA-TLX (Task Load Index): Results of empirical and theoretical research. In P. A. Hancock & N. Meshkati (Eds.), *Human mental workload* (pp. 139–185). Amsterdam: North Holland.

Hock, R. R. (2002). *Forty studies that changed psychology.* Upper Saddle River, NJ: Prentice Hall.

Howell, D. C. (2010). *Statistical methods for psychology* (7th ed.). Belmont, CA: Wadsworth.

Kukreja, U., Stevenson, W. E., & Ritter, F. E. (2006). RUI—recording user input from interfaces under Windows and Mac OS X. *Behavior Research Methods, 38*(4), 656–659.

LaPiere, R. T. (1934). Attitude versus action. *Social Forces, 13*, 230–237.

Lazar, J., Feng, J. H., & Hochheiser, H. (2010). *Research methods in human-computer interaction.* New York, NY: Wiley.

Miles, M. B., Huberman, A. M., & Saldaña, J. (2013). *Qualitative data analysis: A methods sourcebook.* Thousand Oaks, CA: Sage.

Molich, R., & Nielsen, J. (1990). Improving a human-computer dialogue. *Communications of the ACM, 33*(3), 338–348.

Monk, A., Wright, P., Haber, J., & Davenport, L. (1993). Apendix 1—cooperative evaluation: A run-time guide. In *Improving your human-computer interface: A practical technique.* New York: Prentice-Hall.

Monk, A. F. (1998). Lightweight techniques to encourage innovative user interface design. In
    L. Wood (Ed.), *User interface design: Bridging the gap between user requirements and
    design* (pp. 109–129). Boca Raton, FL: CRC Press.
Mosier, J. N., & Smith, S. L. (1986). Application of guidelines for designing user interface
    software. *Behaviour and Information Technology, 5*, 39–46.
Müller, M. J., Haslwanter, J. H., & Dayton, T. (1997). Participatory practices in the software
    lifecycle. In M. G. Helander, T. K. Landauer, & P. V. Prabhu (Eds.), *Handbook of human-
    computer interaction* (2nd ed., pp. 255–297). Amsterdam, NL: Elsevier.
NASA. (1987). *NASA Task Load Index (TLX) V 1.0. Users Manual.* Retrieved 10 March 2014,
    from http://humansystems.arc.nasa.gov/groups/TLX/downloads/TLX_comp_manual.pdf.
Navalpakkam, V., & Churchill, E. F. (in press). Eyetracking: A brief introduction. In J. S. Olson
    & W. Kellogg (Eds.), *Ways of knowing, HCI methods*. Heidelberg, Germany: Springer.
Nielsen, J. (1993). *Usability engineering*. Chestnut Hill, MA: AP Professional Press.
Nielsen, J., & Molich, R. (1990). Heuristic evaluation of user interfaces. In *Proceedings of CHI
    90* (pp. 249–256). New York: ACM.
Nielsen, J., & Pernice, K. (2010). *Eyetracking web usability*. Berkeley, CA: New Riders.
Ray, W. J. (2008). *Methods toward a science of behavior and experience* (9th ed.). Belmont, CA:
    Wadsworth Publishing.
Reeves, B., & Nass, C. (1996). *The media equation: How people treat computers, television, and
    new media like real people and places*. New York: NY Cambridge University Press.
Ritter, F. E., Kim, J. W., & Morgan, J. H. (2009). *Running behavioral experiments with human
    participants: A practical guide* (Tech. Report No. 2009-1). Applied Cognitive Science Lab:
    The Pennsylvania State University, College of Information Sciences and Technology.
Ritter, F. E., Kim, J. W., Morgan, J. H., & Carlson, R. A. (2013). *Running behavioral studies with
    human participants: A practical guide*. Thousand Oaks, CA: Sage.
Smallman, H. S., & St. John, M. (2005). Naïve realism: Misplaced faith in the utility of realistic
    displays. *Ergonomics in Design, 13*(Summer), 6–13.
Todd, Z. (Ed.). (2004). *Mixing methods in psychology: The integration of qualitative and
    quantitative methods in theory and practice*. Abingdon, UK: Psychology Press.
Tullis, T., & Albert, B. (2008). *Measuring the user experience*. Burlington, MA: Morgan
    Kaufmann.
Whiteside, J., Jones, S., Levy, P. S., & Wixon, D. (1985). User performance with command,
    menu, and iconic interfaces. In *Proceedings of CHI'85 Human Factors in Computing Systems*
    (185–191). New York: ACM.
Woods, D. D., & Dekker, S. W. A. (2000). Anticipating the effects of technological change: A
    new era of dynamics for human factors. *Theoretical Issues in Ergonomic Science, 1*(3),
    272–282.

Part IV
Summary

Chapter 14
Summary: Putting It All Together

Abstract This chapter recaps some of the many things that you have learned about users in terms of their anthropometric, behavioral, cognitive, and social aspects. You have been provided with a lot of information, so we describe a number of different possible ways you can organize it. One way to organize and apply the information is with user models. These models span the range from implicit descriptive models, such as guidelines, through to explicit information processing models, which can be executed to produce behavior and predict performance. Another way is to organize the information based on how to use it. So we finish by looking at one system development process model—the Risk-Driven Incremental Commitment Model—as an example of how you can integrate knowledge about users into the system development life cycle. Failure to consider the users and their tasks during development leads to increased system development risk.

14.1 Introduction

Human centered-design is about putting humans at the center of system design. If we want to design systems that are both useful and usable, we need to understand humans—users, in particular—and this is not a trivial undertaking. If we do not take appropriate account of the users there is an increased risk that the project will be a failure: the users could refuse to accept the system if it does not fit into and support the way they work, or the users may end up wrestling with the system trying to make it behave as they expect it to, possibly with fatal consequences (e.g., Baxter et al. 2007), or it could just not be fully adopted by users.

Developing systems is an inherently interdisciplinary practice. The knowledge that we have presented here should make software and system engineers at least aware of the sorts of issues that human factors engineers routinely discuss. In this book we have tried to highlight the capabilities and limitations of humans but, really, we have just scratched the surface. We are not expecting software engineers to become human factors experts as a result of reading this book. We hope,

F. E. Ritter et al., *Foundations for Designing User-Centered Systems,*
DOI: 10.1007/978-1-4471-5134-0_14, © Springer-Verlag London 2014

however, that it will enable them to communicate with human factors engineers, and develop a shared understanding of the issues as they affect system development and use.

We conclude our discussions with a brief summary of what we have presented in this book. You will want to organize it yourself in some meaningful way to be able to make effective use of all the information about users that we have presented. How you decide to organize it will partly depend on how you intend to use it. You might find the metaphors in Chap. 12, those of the Gulfs and Cognitive Dimensions, to be useful. There are also methods and techniques that can help you. A few of these have been implemented as computer programs that are fairly easy to use, and encapsulate summaries of user behavior that can be applied in a range of ways. These models are just one way of applying what we know about humans to system design; they can also be used to help teach designers and developers about users as a sharable representation.

We finish by describing how you can take forward what you have learned here and incorporate it into system development. We would contend that you should always apply this knowledge, because a lack of knowledge about users nearly always constitutes a risk to system development. We illustrate this argument using an extended version of the Risk-Driven Incremental Commitment Model (Pew and Mavor2007).

14.2 Organizing What We Have Learnt About Users

If your aim is to build systems that are both useful and usable then the best way forward in many cases is to focus on particular people doing particular tasks in particular contexts. The knowledge that we have provided you will help. Whether a system can be described as usable or not depends on factors such as the shape and size of the users (anthropometric factors), external body functioning and simple sensory-motor concerns and motivation (behavioral factors), internal mental functioning (cognitive factors), and external mental functioning (social and organizational factors). It therefore makes sense to consider organizing your knowledge about these different factors in terms of the types of user characteristics that we introduced early in the book: Anthropometric; Behavioral; Cognitive; and Social—the ABCS. You should be aware that there are other factors too, which we have not addressed in this summary such as legal liability, and physiological factors which will often also be important.

14.2.1 Anthropometrics

Users vary. One obvious way they can vary is in physical size, as Chap. 3 noted. Different people of the same age and gender may have different heights and different weights, for example. Users also change over time as they develop and age. The physical attributes of the user will affect how they use a particular artifact, so you need to consider aspects such as whether they can reach the controls, whether they can operate the levers, whether they can push buttons, and so on.

The way that people use artifacts can also affect the well-being of the user. Upper limb disorders, for example, can arise from having to carry out the same task repeatedly over extended periods of time, and from the user failing to adopt the correct posture.

Anthropometrics is an important consideration in interfaces where touch) plays a central role. Probably the most obvious and widespread examples are smartphones and tablet computers. In addition, it is important when thinking about keyboards: conventional keyboards are still widely used with most personal computers, and many people use their thumbs to type on the keypads of some cell phones, for example.

14.2.2 Behavior

The user's behavioral characteristics are mostly related to perception, and the most important of these are vision and audition, as noted in Chap. 4. Users will also differ in terms of their perceptual capabilities. As people get older, for example, their vision and hearing often diminish and there are people who have permanently impaired vision or hearing.

When you are designing systems it is therefore important to realize that all users will not always behave in exactly the same way. Their performance will vary across a range of behavior which is approximately normally distributed, as shown on the left in Fig. 14.1. In those situations where the distribution cannot be two tailed, such as where reaction times (which cannot be negative!) are being measured, performance more closely approximates a gamma distribution, as shown on the right in Fig. 14.1.

Understanding the way that people perceive things is important, because this understanding can be used to create artifacts that more closely match the way that users behave. Knowing about red–green color deficiency, for example, is important because it will influence the way that colored items are used in an interface. At a higher level, knowing the Gestalt laws that describe the way people perceive groups of objects (Chap. 4) can be used to help you work out the layout of objects in an interface.

When it comes to designing audio outputs, knowing the way that hearing works can help you determine what sort of sounds to use for alarms, for example. We also know that people are poor at localizing sound, but it is easier to localize high pitch sounds than low pitch ones, and that speech conveys more information than sounds.

All users, from novices to experts, make errors and in some cases make the same errors as noted in Chap. 10. One of the main differences between novices and

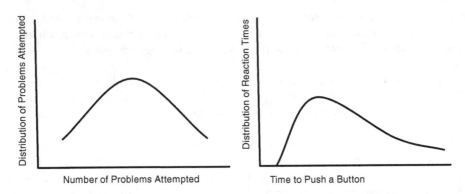

Fig. 14.1 A normal curve (*left*) [Strictly speaking, number of problems cannot go below 0 either, but for most practical examples, this distribution will be well represented by a normal curve when 0 is more than three standard deviations from the mean (the peak).] and a gamma curve (*right*) showing typical distributions for tasks attempted and response times for a task. These curves illustrate that users will have a distribution of behavior, and not always perform a task or have knowledge in a single way

experts is that expert users can often (but not always) detect and correct errors before any adverse consequences arise. When you design systems, you need to remember that all users will make errors. Some of these errors will be preventable, but others may not. You will therefore need to decide which errors you will prevent (using risk assessment, for example). For the other errors, you will need to include support to help the user spot errors and, in particular, to support the ability to correct errors, ideally before any adverse consequences arise.

Where the users have physical limitations, however, or there are contextual limitations (low lightinglevels, for example), these limitations will constrain what the users can and cannot do.

14.2.3 Cognition

Users' cognition is limited, at both the tactical level (e.g., limited working memoryand some difficulties in storing and retrieving items from memory) and at the strategic level (e.g., how to decide which are the important and long term issues), as noted in Chaps. 5–7. In some cases, the effects of these limitations can be ameliorated through learning, or through social processes, particularly where skills are pooled to perform particular tasks.

Attracting, managing, and maintaining the user's attention are all important. Users have limited attentional resources. This means that in busy contexts, where lots of things are happening or several tasks have to be performed simultaneously, they are unlikely to be able to attend to all of them. In other words, they will find it difficult to consciously control how they perform all the tasks. With practice, users can learn to perform some tasks with little or no conscious control (i.e., with little or no attention). The classic example that is usually quoted is that of riding a bike: when you first start out, you try to think of lots of things at once—keeping your balance, remembering to pedal, keeping the handlebars straight, being aware of the traffic around you, and so on—but as you learn how to do the task, you will focus more on just keeping the bike going in a straight line, and maintaining awareness of the traffic around you. We know that people learn in various ways, so you should design your system in such a way that it facilitates learning.

It is important to know your users, and to understand the language that they use. By doing so, you will be able to develop systems that they can more readily understand and use. The interaction between the user and their computer-based system can be considered as a form of conversation, which means that it can be optimized using Grice's maxims (Chap. 7). It is particularly important to know something about how people read and the ways that they seek out information (mostly through searching), because these are two of the most common user activities. You should design systems that present information in ways that the users can easily read, understand, and find. This means that you need to think about presentation (font choices, for example) as well as content issues.

Users have mental models of how things work, and the way they interact with an artifact is usually based on the (most) relevant mental model. These models develop over time as the user's knowledge and experience of using the artifact increases. As a system designer you should try to help the user to develop the right model of how your system operates. The mental model will help the users decide which action to take next. When they cannot see which action to perform, they will normally engage in problem solving behavior, which may involve reasoning from first principles, using trial and error, for example. On the basis of their problem solving, users will then make decisions. Decision making is usually sub-optimal because people do not take into account all of the relevant information that is available to them, and because their decision making processes are often biased in known ways. As a designer you can try to help users by making relevant information salient and by counteracting the known biases where possible.

The use of mental models also applies to users themselves. Across the range of behavior types, there are very few aspects of their behavior that users know about intrinsically. They can see their size, and this they know something about. Yet when it comes to choosing a chair, they have to sit in it to know if it fits. Many users do not sit in the best posture, and so we might note that many users do not know all that they could about themselves anthropometrically.

Many users do not know about their fovea, and most other aspects of perception are not available to consciousness—it is impenetrable. The results of vision are available when objects are attended to, but the parts that are not attended to are ignored or filled in. For example, most users will not know much about the blind spot on their retina, let alone see it. Most of perception is impenetrable. So, what they know about perception is mostly folk psychology.

Users (and untrained designers) think they know how they think. This is often misguided. While they are thinking about how they think, they are busy thinking. Imagine creating a computer that stored every action it took—but how can it do this? It would have to record actions while it was doing them. Users are basically like this as well. It is very hard to remember what you are doing when you are busy doing it. Ericsson and Simon (1993) laid out a fairly good theory of when users can talk aloud about what they are doing. It is even more difficult to talk about what you have done and be completely accurate. That said, sometimes the only data we can afford to gather is how users think they think, and sometimes users will choose systems based on such judgments, so we will often have to work with these judgements. You might wish to be more skeptical in the future about users' (and untrained designers') reports about how they do a task or whether they learn or not.

14.2.4 Social

Most tasks are carried out by teams of people interacting with one another. Sometimes they will be working directly with co-located people, but in other cases they may be working distally as a team. Individual users have limitations on how well they work together in teams: some people are natural leaders, whilst some are natural followers.

Chapters 8 and 9 note social factors that influence users, including distributed responsibility, and social influence on teams. For example, users (and system developers) will often misjudge social relationships. They will often send out one blanket email to ten people asking for one of them to volunteer, rather than sending out ten individual emails. The sorts of variations in performance that you see across users can sometimes be attributed to the context they are working in, as well as their own capabilities and limitations. If you put the same user in the same task and physical situation but vary the environmental conditions by increasing the temperature, or reducing the lightinglevels, for example, this may affect their performance.

14.2.5 The Role of Tasks and Environments

Knowing users' tasks will help design systems to perform these tasks in numerous ways as presented in Chap. 11. There are a wide range of uses and applications, and of ways to represent users' tasks and activities. Good designers can choose appropriately based on what is needed for a given design project.

Users' tasks are not always directly understandable by designers using their own intuitions, but there are ways to find what tasks users do and what tasks they want to do. However, there will still be surprises because it is difficult to know everything, particularly for new tasks and unexpected uses.

It is also important to understand the environment in which users perform their tasks. Usability studies help to provide a way to understand the tasks, the users, the environments, and how they interact.

14.2.6 Summary

Users can be viewed as having some aspects that are more uniform and some that are more unique. There are some communalities across levels that we can point out:

1. The ABCS note some of these aspects where users have shared communalities in how they think, interact with the world, and interact with each other; in some ways users are alike. So, when designing systems, you should not despair that all users are different.
2. There are also differences between users. There are simple differences in simple capabilities, such as different input and output speeds and capabilities. In more complex capabilities, like how to do a task and mental models of systems, users can vary widely based on previous experience and practice. In cases of goals and cultural beliefs they can vary the most. So, when designing, you need to keep in mind that, for some aspects of design, users can differ.
3. Users have limited capabilities. Across the chapters, limitations on how fast users can move, how fast and how they can think, and their abilities to produce perfect, error-free performance were noted. Most importantly, user limitations can be avoided by better design that does not make incorrect assumptions about users. Many of the bad web site design contests and bad and dangerous interface galleries are filled with designs that assumed something incorrect about the users' abilities or interests. So, when designing, you need to design for what people can do.
4. Users do not always know themselves. You can ask them, but they will sometimes not provide very accurate descriptions. Designers are also a type of user, and they suffer the same limitations about knowing users and themselves. So, when designing, do ask them but also think more broadly about users and their context. In addition, try to study the user as a domain. Have a theory of how they perform tasks, test this theory with data, and expand the theory as you learn and read more.
5. Systems can be helped in a variety of ways because of users. Users can learn, can then find new strategies, and can help each other. So, when you design, keep these less obvious changes in mind.

14.3 Models of Users

For the purpose of engineering design, it would be useful to model the human part of the overall system in a more formalized way, in the same way that engineering design specifications can be used to present a relatively clear and precise model for implementation. The model of the user would serve as a shared representation that could be used to support system design. From the human factors engineer's point of view, a user model captures the capabilities and limitations on user performance; from the software engineer's point of view, it would be used to illustrate how the system could perform when operated by real users.

Models of users therefore serve as a summary repository of our knowledge of users. It is important that this knowledge be captured in one place because it can lead to emergent behaviors where there are interactions between the different characteristics of users. The behavior of the models should be constrained in the same sorts of ways that human behavior is constrained (memory limitations, and so on).

We have seen throughout this book that humans are less predictable, consistent, and deterministic than computers. Defining a general, formal model of the human (as part of the broader socio-technical system) is not currently possible. Instead, a number of fragmentary and incomplete models of human information processing behavior have been proposed by cognitive psychologists and reinforced by empirical exploration. These models can be used to make predictions but do not provide details about how the system should be designed. Although the models are good at generating first-order effects, at lower levels of analysis their limitations and inconsistencies become apparent. The models are therefore useful at predicting gross behavior, such as error-free, expert behavior on unit tasks.

The most accurate, detailed models have generally been developed for those aspects of human performance that are easiest to test. Thus, models of the characteristics of the senses are well established (particularly vision and hearing), whereas there are very few models of some of the more intricate aspects of cognition that can only be indirectly observed and are less well understood.

14.3.1 Unified Theories of Cognition

There have been several attempts to integrate all that we know about human behavior into a single, unified theory of cognition (Newell 1990). The latest attempts have been realized as cognitive architectures, although they might be more properly described as human performance architectures because they deal with more than just the cognitive aspects of human performance. These cognitive architectures typically take the form of a computer programming language with special capabilities and limitations representing a (small) subset of the known capabilities and limitations of humans. Progress has been relatively slow, but the cognitive architecture developers are working towards providing a single coherent theory that ultimately accounts for—and predicts—human performance on all tasks.

A unified theory of cognition effectively forms a single repository of useful user-related information. This can be used in three main ways:

1. To help you remember theories and facts about users. You can use the schematic of the Model Human Processor (MHP, described below), ACT-R (also described

below), or Soar (Laird 2012), for example, to work your way through their hypothesized modules to understand how behavior will be generated. At this level of abstraction, there is a fair amount of agreement between the theories in that they all include modules for input, memory, cognition, and output.

2. To summarize user behavior. In time, architectures may be used more often during design as a way to conveniently capture theories of user behavior, and as a teaching aid to help designers understand users (Pew and Mavor 2007).

3. To apply what we know about users. In some cases, the models only offer fairly crude approximations of users, but they have been useful for populating computer games and military simulations. In other cases, they are being used to test interfaces and make predictions for designs (for a review, see any of these reports: Booher and Minninger 2003; Pew and Mavor 1998, 2007; Ritter et al. 2003).

14.3.2 Types of User Models

There are now more than 100 cognitive (and user) architectures if you include variants and different versions (Morrison 2003; Pew and Mavor1998; Ritter et al. 2003). They can be categorized into four types:

1. Implicit descriptive models. When you look at a car, for example, you can imagine some of the assumptions the designers have made about the driver. These assumptions are captured in an implicit model of the driver in which vision takes place in the top part of the body, and another part of the body operates the controls on the floor.

2. Explicit declarative models. These models describe the components or a structure in a system, but neither describe the mechanisms nor perform the task.

3. Explicit process models. The mechanisms and the way they operate are described, but the models, while perhaps supported by software, do not process information.

4. Explicit information processing models. These models include a full information processing architecture that produces behavior, and can predict performance times and the information processing steps that will be performed and their results.

14.3.2.1 Implicit Descriptive Models

Implicit user models appear in many systems, and some people would claim that all systems include a model of the user. For example, chairs assume a height of the user, and many file systems assume users can read and write English. Taken together, the set of assumptions used by the designer to create an artifact is an implicit model of the user, but it may be a particularly impoverished, incomplete, or incorrect model. There are certainly several tools and approaches that include models of users where the model is clear enough to talk about, but is not explicitly represented and may not be visible (or even known) to most people. Guidelines and web accessibility tools, for example, show that models can be useful even when they are not explicit, examinable, or even very modifiable.

Guidelines attempt to describe how to build a system to support users. The guidelines reflect an implicit model of the user (which may be more explicitly specified by the guideline developers). Guidelines that give advice about visual layout, for example, may assume that the users have normal (20/20) vision which, clearly, all users do not.

It would be difficult for designers to use these models and to manually apply tests against the guidelines. Where the guidelines have been encapsulated in software tools they are relatively easy to apply. Some of these tools only indicate compliance (or otherwise) with the guidelines, however, and do not explain why particular features are undesirable.

Where guidelines are implemented in software, for example, to test the accessibility of a web site, an implicit user model is employed to evaluate the interface against those guidelines. Tools like Bobby and Truwex (search online or see the book's web site), for example, assess the accessibility of web sites against the Web Content Accessibility Guidelines (WCAG, www.w3.org/WAI/intro/wcag.php). For a more extensive discussion of automated tools for evaluating interfaces see Ivory and Hearst's (2001) review that divides the tools into various categories and assesses their potential impact.

14.3.2.2 Explicit Descriptive Models

Explicit descriptive models describe the process and mechanisms that make up user behavior. These models include task analysis. Examples include models built with the KLM and with GOMS (Chap. 11) because they simply describe the behavior (a trace of the behavior) without describing in detail the inner workings of how the behavior is implemented in cognitive and other mechanisms.

These models can be very useful in system development. Examples of tools to help create such models include Interacting Cognitive Subsystems (ICS, Barnard 1987) and the Improved Performance Research Integration Tool (IMPRINT, Booher and Minninger 2003). IMPRINT has probably had the largest impact. It describes the tasks that users have to perform and how long each task should take. The resulting model is then used to predict how performance is degraded by fatigue and how many users are required to perform the set of tasks.

There are also tools that try to replicate the time course of the interaction, sometimes interacting with a simulation of the external world. The GOMS Language Evaluation and Analysis tool (GLEAN), for example, encapsulates the GOMS task analysis methodology (Kieras 1999; Kieras et al. 1995) in a way that makes it easier to use and apply GOMS models. This approach really sits halfway between descriptive models and process models that perform the task by processing information.

14.3.2.3 Explicit Process Models: Model Human Processor

Card et al. (1980, 1983) believed applying information processing psychology should be based on task analysis, calculation, and approximation. Their Model Human Processor (MHP) offers an early, simple, integrated description of psychological knowledge about error-free human performance relevant to HCI and system design. It was one of the first attempts to get away from the proliferation of descriptions developed to account for different psychological observations, and to provide a unified description of users. It started to create a quantitative methodology including average times. The MHP was an oversimplification, but it did provide a kind of prototype model that could be used as the basis for discussions.

The MHP was made up of a set of memories and processors, together with a set of principles, including the "principles of operation," which describe how the components functioned together. There were three interacting subsystems: the perceptual system, the motor system, and the cognitive system, each of which had their own memories and processors. These are shown schematically in Fig. 14.2. A detailed description of how the MHP would perform a task is achieved using either a KLM analysis or a GOMS analysis, described in Chap. 11. Examples of MHP analyses are shown in Table 14.1, and two more are on the book's web site.

Long term memory essentially does not decay ($\delta = \infty$) and has infinite capacity ($\mu = \infty$). Working memory has a visual store and an auditory store. Memories in both stores decay, but at different rates, and the sizes are different. Working memory outside the stores has a capacity limitation. The perceptual processor consists of sensors and associated buffer memories, the most important being a Visual Image Store, and an Auditory Image Store to hold the output of the sensory system while it is being symbolically coded. The cognitive processor receives symbolically coded information from the sensory image store into its working memory, and uses information previously stored in long-term memory to decide how to respond. The motor processor carries out the selected response.

Time predictions are generated by analyzing a task into the constituent operations that are executed by the subsystems. Then average times are associated with these operations based on the selected band of performance: Fastman, Slowman, and Middleman, which allows predictions to be made along the central and extreme points of the behavioral continuum of fast to slow users.

The MHP assumes highly idealized behavior (e.g., a single strategy to solve a task), and has trouble representing errors. The latter is important. Errors in text editing, for example, have been shown to account for 35% of expert performance time and 80% of the variability in that time (Landauer 1987, p. 151). Although the representations of the perceptual, cognitive, and motor subsystems were weak, the MHP did demonstrate the feasibility of the general idea and inspired later work on information processing cognitive architectures realized as computer programs, such as Soar (Newell 1990) and ACT-R (Anderson 2007).

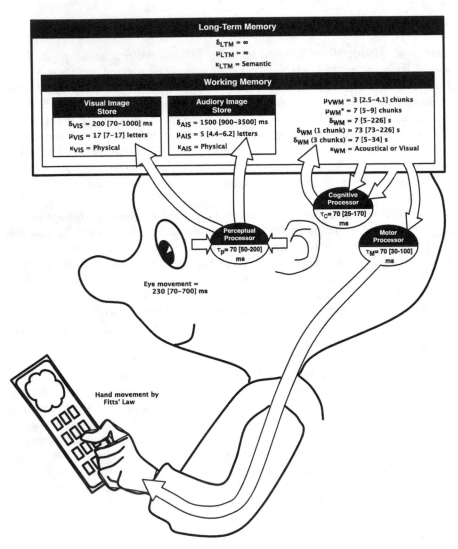

Fig. 14.2 A diagram of the model human processor (adapted from Card et al. 1983). δ indicates a half-life decay rate; μ is a capacity; κ is the modality of the storage; τ is the time to do something

14.3.2.4 Explicit Information Processing Models: ACT-R

There is now a range of cognitive architectures that take as input a descriptive task analysis that looks a lot like a computer program, and then simulate the cognitive aspects of task performance, often with limitations simulated from vision and motor performance. One of the most widely used architectures is ACT-R; others include EPIC (Kieras et al. 1997) and Soar (Laird 2012; Ritter 2003; Ritter and Bibby 2008).

Table 14.1 Example MHP analysis

MHP: example 1: motor skills, typing behavior

A manufacturer is considering whether to use an alphabetic keyboard on his handheld point of
sale (PoS) system. Among several factors influencing his decision is the question of whether
experienced users will find the keyboard slower for touch typing than the standard Sholes
(QWERTY) keyboard arrangement. What is the relative typing speed for expert users on the
two keyboards?

Typing rate = 152/ks (72 words/min)

Typing rate (alphabetic) = 164 ms/key (66.5 words/min)

MHP: example 2: cognitive, working memory

A programmer is told verbally the one-syllable file names of a dozen files to load into his
programming system. Assuming all the names are arbitrary, in which order should the
programmer write down the names so that he remembers the greatest number of them (has to
ask for the fewest number to be repeated)?

The fact that there are 12 arbitrary file names means the programmer has to remember 12 chunks
(assuming one chunk/name), which is larger than the storage capacity of working memory,
so some of the file names will be forgotten. The act of trying to recall the file names will
add new items to working memory, interfering with the previous names. The items likely
to be in working memory but not yet in long-term memory are those from the end of the
list. If the task is to recall the names from the end of the list first, he can snatch some of
these from working memory before they are displaced. The probability of recalling the
first names will not be affected because if they are available, they are in long-term
memory. Thus the programmer should recall the last names first and then the others
but will forget some

ACT-R has been continually evolved and updated—the latest version is
available at act.psy.cmu.edu. The structure of the latest version of ACT-R (see
Fig. 14.3) is somewhat similar to that of the MHP. The figure shows the modules
and mechanisms of cognition. It also attempts to show a mapping between the
mechanisms and the areas of the brain responsible for creating the behavior. This
correspondence is not perfect yet (Anderson 2007), but as technology advances
(brain scanning in particular) and becomes more sophisticated, it is becoming
more and more feasible to do this mapping.

ACT-R has been fairly extensively tested against psychology data to validate its
predictions. Like all information processing models, it has mostly been used in
thought experiments and as a research tool. ACT-R in particular, though, has been
used to create a large number of user models for several different domains
including driving (Salvucci 2006), human-robot interaction (Ritter et al. 2006,
2007), aviation (Byrne and Kirlik 2005; Gluck et al. 2007), air traffic control and
dual tasking (Schoelles and Gray 2001), and menu use (Byrne 2001). These
models are harder to create than GOMS or KLM models, but they make more
detailed predictions, including what information is required to perform the task,
and the results of the information processing. If an addition is performed by users,
for example, ACT-R can be used to predict their answers and the distribution of
errors in their answers (Lebiere and Anderson 1998).

Fig. 14.3 The schematic
block diagram of ACT-R 6.
Taken from Anderson (2007)
and used with permission

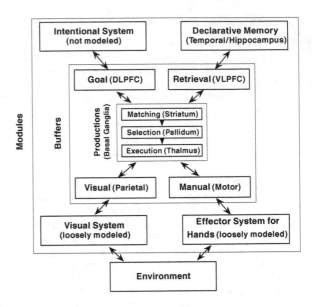

14.3.3 Summary

What is the purpose of user models? One use is that they can provide a way to create a shared representation of the user between interface designers, system designers, and others working on system development (Pew and Mavor 2007). They also be used as summaries of knowledge (Newell 1990), and are thus useful to people learning about users. These models are also useful in video games and other simulations where the more advanced types can serve as surrogate users, opponents, and teammates (Pew and Mavor 1998; Ritter et al. 2003).

User models provide frameworks, ways of seeing designs and targeting potential problems, and integrating psychological principles because the user's knowledge and capabilities are represented explicitly.

Which type of user model you choose depends on what part of the design you are working on and what you want from the model. For example, task analysis as a simple version of a user model is very lightweight and very useful, particularly for simple web site design. A more complex and formal model is useful as the complexity and impact of the system increase. For testing large numbers of interfaces (e.g., a web site), or for testing a site often or repeatedly, an automatic tool is useful. For high impact interfaces (e.g., aviation, automotive interfaces due to the large number of users, or space station interfaces), more complete and complex models are useful because they are more accurate, but currently come at a very high price.

The choice of which model to use can be based on what you want to learn about how users interact with your system. This can be seen as a way to reduce system development risks, and your choice of model can be based on the questions of what risks do you want to reduce, will the system be fast enough to use? Fast enough to learn? Will the error rate be too high? Using risk reduction in system design is taken up in the next section.

14.4 Risk-Driven Incremental Commitment Model

14.4.1 Introduction

There is now widespread acceptance of the fact that most systems development follows an iterative cycle, often represented by the spiral model (Boehm and Hansen 2001). It is only relatively recently, however, that human factors issues have been explicitly incorporated into the latest version of the spiral model (Boehm and Lane 2006) by the (US) Committee on Human-System Design Support for Changing Technology (Pew and Mavor2007). The revised model—the Risk Driven Incremental Commitment Model (RD-ICM)—encourages incremental development of systems in an ongoing spiral process comprising requirements specification, technical exploration, and stakeholder commitment. The process is shown in Fig. 14.4, where movement around the spiral represents time and commitment and work on the project.

The spiral is also sometimes shown linearly, as in Fig. 14.4, for discussion purposes. At each stage, the system development is assessed for risks to the system's success. The process is then targeted at reducing these risks. Where the risks are technical (e.g., Can we build it? Can we build it for that price?), technical work is performed to reduce the risk through increased understanding of the technical issues and how to deal with them. Other risks can arise from historical events, which are harder to reduce; and from financial matters, which can often be reduced by setting up contracts at a known price.

The RD-ICM has several key features:

1. Systems should be developed through a process that considers and satisfices the needs of stakeholders (it finds a reasonable solution that keeps in mind the costs of finding a (better) solution). This step is addressed by the Exploration and Valuation stages shown in Fig. 14.4.
2. Development is incremental and performed iteratively. These related aspects are shown in Fig. 14.4 by the multiple loops representing the increasing amount of resources committed to design and implementation, and in Fig. 14.5 by the five stages (Exploration, Valuation, Architecting, Development, and Operation). These stages are incremental because movement from one stage to the next depends upon a successful review to go to the next stage.
3. Development occurs concurrently, that is, multiple steps may be performed simultaneously—some people thus refer to this model as an Incremental Concurrent Commitment model. One part of the system may be implemented while another part is being tested. This is not immediately clear from Figs. 14.4

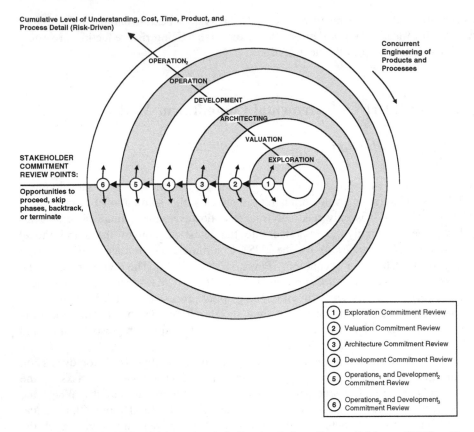

Fig. 14.4 The RD-ICM model as a spiral. Reprinted from Pew and Mavor (2007) with permission from the National Academy of Sciences, courtesy of the National Academies Press

or 14.5, but can be seen more clearly in Fig. 14.6. This figure shows how the amount of effort put into a given activity varies through the life of a system for a hypothetical example system. Some peaks occur on some activities when their phase is active (e.g., development), and some activities peak near the reviews (i.e., the Evaluation, Valuation, Architecting, Construction, and Operations Commitment Reviews). The level of activity will also vary within a phase, as iterations are done within that phase.

4. The process explicitly takes account of risks during system development and deployment. The level of risk is assessed at reviews between stages (shown holistically in Fig. 14.4 and explicitly in Fig. 14.5). Risk is used to manage the project—the level of effort and level of detail of work are driven by the level of risk (Boehm 2008 provides some nice additional information and examples). Where there is no risk to system development, there is no need for any effort to reduce risk. For example, if the system being developed is similar to an existing product, there may be no reason to explore further how to support users or how to manufacture that system.

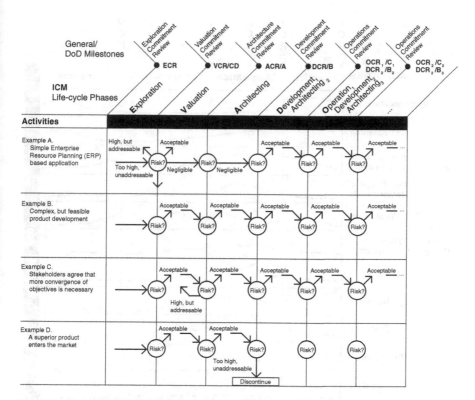

Fig. 14.5 The RD-ICM laid out linearly. This figure also shows the role of risk in system development, showing how different risk patterns yield different processes. Reprinted from Pew and Mavor (2007) with permission from the National Academy of Sciences, courtesy of the National Academies Press

Pew and Mavor (2007, pp. 91–133) provide three examples of using the Risk-Driven Spiral Model method to develop specific systems. These examples are taken from different domains and are different sizes. Their Chap. 5 (http://www.nap.edu/openbook.php?record_id=11893&page=91) covers the development of an unmanned aerial system (i.e., an unmanned aerial vehicle, a UAV) for the military, a port security screening system for homeland security, and an intravenous infusion pump for use in hospitals. Each example covers different aspects of the process, so together they provide fairly broad coverage of the approach.

The model is relatively complex, so we advocate that another way to understand it is through the viewpoint of concurrent activities. The standard way of presenting the model is as a spiral (as shown in Fig. 14.4), although the spiral can be unwound and the task activity levels can be represented in a linear fashion (Fig. 14.5), which makes it easier to recognize the concurrent phases of development, as well as concurrent activities that are out of phase and aspects like stakeholder commitment review points where the risks are assessed.

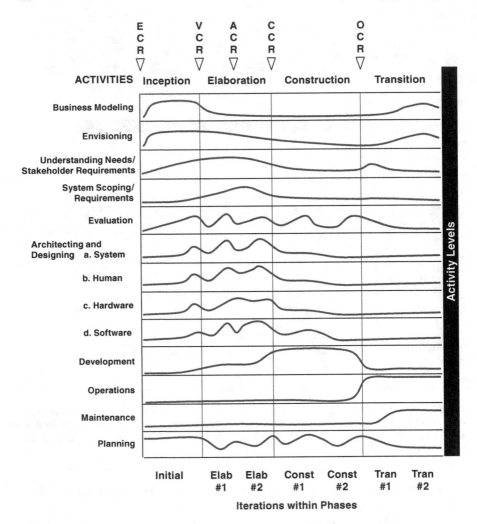

Fig. 14.6 The role of concurrency in system development, showing how different tasks may be performed concurrently and how activity levels rise and fall over the course of a project. It is similar to Fig. 2.3 in Pew and Mavor (2007) and incorporates ideas from Boehm's other work (e.g., Boehm 2008)

14.4.2 Insight 1: The RD-ICM Provides a Way to Organize User-Related Knowledge and Ways of Knowing

Experiences teaching and applying the RD-ICM to system design have led to a few insights and extensions. These are related to learning: learning through using this approach how to organize methods to reduce risks, learning by system development managers that there are sometimes risks related to humans using their systems, learning that designers are stakeholders too, and learning by designers as lessons from one design are applied to later designs.

Pew and Mavor (2007) report that the RD-ICM approach provides a useful way to organize usability methods. We have found that this approach also provides a useful framework for teaching this material. The three main areas that involve HIS activities are identified as:

1. Defining the opportunities and context of system use.
2. Defining system requirements and design.
3. Evaluation of the system.

There are several methods that can be used to reduce risk in these three areas. All of the HCI methodologies (not just the examples presented in the Pew and Mavor book) can be organized with respect to how much they can contribute to each stage of system development.

The RD-ICM has been very useful in discussing the relative merits of methodologies, and when to use each of the methodologies or techniques. Figure 14.7 highlights several examples of methods that are applicable across several stages of system development, as shown by the horizontal lines under each of the method names. The figure could be further extended by weighting the lines to emphasize where individual methods are more appropriate to a particular stage of development. If all the methods were included, the figure would also show that methods (and thus practitioners) could be grouped by usefulness at particular stages of development: some methods are best suited to the early valuation stage, for example, and some to evaluation.

14.4.3 Insight 2: RD-ICM is Descriptive as Well as Prescriptive

The RD-ICM formalizes to some extent what many people accept as perceived wisdom, i.e., that many system developers already recognize that several development processes are risk driven (or at least risk aware), incremental, and concurrent. Indeed, we believe that most system development processes are risk driven, and that systems developers are aware of the risks and adjust their development processes to reduce or mitigate the effects of the identified risks. We also believe that some parts of system development are often carried out in parallel. Furthermore, we believe that there is buy-in from at least some of the system stakeholders in nearly all projects. The RD-ICM is therefore not merely a normative model, prescribing what system developers should do, but instead captures and describes the practice of systems development. If the RD-ICM was described to systems developers, we believe many of them would claim that they already follow a similar process.

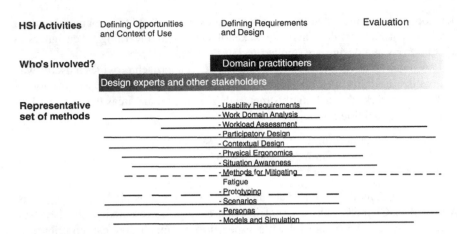

Fig. 14.7 Figure 7.1 from Pew and Mavor (2007) revised to show the approximate range of use of several methodologies across the development process. Reprinted with permission from the National Academy of Sciences, courtesy of the National Academies Press

There are two major areas of risk, however, that system developers and managers seem to be less aware of:

- The risks that arise from not giving appropriate consideration to *all* of the system stakeholders
- The risks that arise from not considering humans as part of the system.

Developers and managers are probably not effectively addressing these risks because they believe the risks have low probability or only lead to very minor consequences, perhaps because they lack formal training in these areas.[1] We believe that the developers and managers more fundamentally do not recognize the potential threat to the system's success from these two major areas of risk. Thus, we can either educate the managers, or provide other ways to highlight risks outside their expertise. It may be useful to bring in outside experts to evaluate the risks. The corollary of this is that it is probably worthwhile to include outside experts in the evaluation of all risks. They are likely to have greater awareness of a wider range of risks across a wider range of contexts, and to be more objective with respect to the project, so they will help to make the evaluation more comprehensive.

Irrespective of whether you are following some version of the Spiral Model (such as the ICM or RD-ICM) or any other life cycle model (waterfall, V-model, and so on), it is important that all stakeholders are considered. It is also important

---

[1] Engineers will see engineering risks, accountants accounting risks, and human factors engineers HF risks.

that they are considered from the start of the project. In other words, before we get to thinking about design issues.

There are several illustrations of why it is important to include consideration of users at the earliest stages of system development. Figures 1.1 through 1.4 in Chap. 1, for example, all showed that there are fundamental aspects of human behavior that designers are often unaware of. Some would argue that the consequences of these failures are irritating rather than severe, but the range and impact of the risks are exemplified in summary reviews such as those by Booher and Minninger (2003) and Casey (1998, 2006), in the regularly updated Risks Digest,[2] and in publicly reported incidents like that involving the USS Vincennes, where a civilian airliner was shot down by a US Navy ship because the airliner was thought to be a fighter plane. The examples in all of these reviews help to raise the visibility of the risks that need to be considered during development.

This approach is therefore not just prescriptive but also descriptive. Failures arise from not knowing risks. To fix this, we need to educate designers about human-centered risks and how to avoid them. This book can be seen as a direct step to address this problem.

14.4.4 Extension 1: Designers are Stakeholders Too

One of the insights that arose from teaching the RD-ICM is that a description of the development process reinforces the fact that designers are stakeholders too (see Steele et al. 2011 for one example). The success of designers is at least partially linked to the success of the project, and their needs and capabilities will influence the development process.

Designers are therefore stakeholders too, and, just like users, they have capabilities and limitations that can affect the outcome of a project. They have creative skills and experience of how to turn requirements into deliverable systems. More fundamentally, they will also have experience of the feasibility of whether a particular set of requirements can reasonably be turned into a deliverable system. In one sense, designers are users too, because they often rely on automated tools to help them to carry out and manage system development. If they are not supported or lack resources, including time, they will produce problems like that shown in Fig. 14.8.

If designers are stakeholders then there needs to be time allocated to soliciting their input, and to making sure that they are equipped with the appropriate skills and tools to do the design. This may mean that they need to be educated about the capabilities and limitations of users, for example, and to be provided with tools that can allow them to create design representations that they can share with other stakeholders as well as the users.

---

[2]   http://catless.ncl.ac.uk/Risks

Fig. 14.8 The question was,
"How did Robinson Crusoe
meet Friday?" The
duplication of the answer into
the extra information field
suggests that the interface did
not support a system
designer, and that the results
were not tested

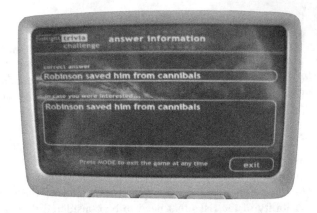

When designers (and implementers) push back against the discussion and management of risks related to human–system integration, this may be because they do not fully appreciate the risks in this area. Explicitly including designers as stakeholders should focus on helping them become more cognizant of the issues and context involved that is outside their training. Giving them this broader context should ultimately lead to better integration and greater risk reduction, including the reduction of system implementation related risks.

14.4.5 Extension 2: Learning Within and Between Projects

Given the multidisciplinary nature of system development, and the importance of involving all the stakeholders, it is obvious that communication is important. The various disciplines that need to talk to each other during system development all have their own history and culture, which includes their own terminology. One of the easiest ways of facilitating communication is through the use of representations that help to make ideas and concepts more tangible. Pew and Mavor (2007) explicitly recognized this in their call for research on shared representation and integration across the design process. In some ways this can be regarded as an extension to the idea of software design patterns which provide generic templates or descriptions of solutions to problems that can be applied in different situations (e.g., Gemma et al. 1995).

One of the major results from using simulation in CAD/CAM is that the lessons learned about one design can be applied to subsequent designs as well as to the current design. For example, in printed circuit boards, traces (printed wire paths) can be positioned too closely together. Tools like Spice (Thorpe 1992) help to highlight effects such as cross talk between the traces and short circuits that can be caused by the manufacturing process. After these design lessons are learned on the first design, they can be used to steer subsequent designs away from the problem rather than forcing the designer to start from scratch each time, modifying their designs based on a new analysis of the problems. Similar effects of transfer will happen after computing Fitts' Law a few times or comparing mouse movement times to keystroke times.

To facilitate learning, shared representations need to be made available within projects, across the system development team and across the different stages of the design process for a single project. We extend this, though, to re-using representations across multiple projects. This may mean that the shareable representations have to be able to reflect different levels of abstraction (based on their dependency on their context of use) so that they can be learned from and re-used. The corollary of this is that those people developing the shared representations are likely to need to document the shared representations with information about context.

In addition to sharing representations within projects, it may be possible to re-use these representations across projects. This would increase the value of these representations, and achieve the re-use that is called for by Pew and Mavor (2007). This would also broaden the audience for the shared representations to include managers and developers on future projects who may be able to learn about potential risks and which stakeholders to consult.

14.4.6 Summary

The RD-ICM model is just one way of creating systems that are useful and safe. It involves identifying the stakeholders—including the designers—and coming up with a system through satisficing their different requirements, finding the best solution matching their constraints, including the cost to find better solutions as a constraint. If stakeholders' needs are not adequately supported, they may not participate in the system development process fully, and may either obstruct the process or even refuse to accept the final system. An advantageous side effect of using the RD-ICM is that it can provide new ways of summarizing HCI methods and, more broadly, Human-System Integration (HSI) as an integral part of design and development.

In the vast majority of systems, a failure to consider the users as stakeholders, and a lack of understanding of the abilities, capabilities, and limitations of users will constitute a risk to system development and use. The main exceptions are where the system being developed is not novel, so the risks in these areas are likely to have been considered and dealt with on other projects. Where there are risks, however, work has to be done to manage them appropriately, given the available resources, and to balance all of the identified risks (user related risks will need to be balanced against technical risks, for example).

Managers and developers are usually familiar with the technical risks associated with software and hardware. To make them more aware of user-related risks, they are likely to require some level of education and training about the capabilities and limitations of users. This education and training should take them to a level where they feel comfortable discussing these sorts of issues with people from the other disciplines involved in systems development.

Shared representations are an important part of the development process, but they can be expensive to produce. It is therefore important to find ways to make them more valuable through reuse, for example. One way of doing this is by applying lessons from one design to subsequent designs on related projects.

On the surface, the RD-ICM may appear to encapsulate a relatively complex theory of how systems should be created. It attempts to capture best practice and what many developers already do, highlighting that development is not a simple, linear, one-size-fits-all process. There are enough facets to the RD-ICM that it appears to have the same sort of level of complexity as a programming language or even a cognitive architecture. Although learning to use the RD-ICM approach takes time and effort, the fact that it takes explicit account of human factors currently makes it possibly the best model to use for development.

14.5 Building on the Foundations

At this point you should know much more about users than you did when you started reading this book. We hope that we have convinced you of the importance of understanding users and that, as a result, you are now more sensitive to the ways that users think and behave.

There *is* a lot to learn, and while we have presented you with a lot of information, we continue to learn more about users as new technologies emerge and give rise to new ways of working. Even with the new technologies and new ways of working, it is important to think of them in terms of *particular* users doing *particular* tasks in a *particular* context. The information we have presented in this book should allow you to start to do that in a principled way, enabling you to design usable systems *and* to justify why you have designed them in a particular way. The *Implications for system design* sections should help here. Note, however, that in this book we have only really scratched the surface of what there is to learn about people, tasks, and contexts. If you want to find out more about any of the topics we mention, the lists of *Other resources* should provide a good starting point. Cynics might say that "Keep in mind that a year in the lab can save you an hour's reading. That is, spending a little time looking at previous work can save a lot of time needlessly duplicating known results.

One implicit lesson that we hope you have learned is that developing systems draws on multiple disciplines. We are not expecting software designers to become fully fledged psychologists, but we hope that our book sensitizes software designers to the psychological issues (about users) that need to be considered. We also hope that it provides a foundation for useful dialog across disciplines during system design.

You should also have tools for finding out information when the information is not yet published. The short exercises at the end of most chapters on gathering data and Chap. 13 on usability studies should provide you with a way to find out more about particular users, particular tasks, or particular aspects of a task. There are important topics not included here because of space, such as emotions, and these you are now well equipped to learn on your own, or through further formal study

As you start to use and apply your knowledge of users to systems development, you are likely to find that it leads you to raise several questions. When you address these questions to human factors engineers, you will often find that their answer is "It depends." If this book has achieved nothing else, it should at least have helped you to appreciate *why* "it depends": system performance is all about particular people doing particular tasks in particular contexts, and those people are all different individuals, they have different skills and abilities, and they may work in different physical, social, and organizational contexts.

The importance of appropriately integrating what we know about users into system design is becoming increasingly widespread. The revised version of Boehm and Hansen's (2001) incremental commitment model of system development, for example, includes explicit consideration of users (Pew and Mavor2007). The new model provides a principled way for deciding when you need to know more about your users. It explicitly acknowledges that not knowing enough about your users is a risk to the successful completion of a system development project. If this lack of knowledge about your users (their tasks and the context in which they work) poses a significant risk, then you need to invest more time and effort in addressing those issues until the risk is reduced to an acceptable level.

We have now shown you what sort of things you will need to know about your users, and how to go about finding out that information. In doing so, we have provided you with the foundations for designing user-centered systems.

14.6 Other Resources

Pew (2007) has written a history of models in this area. In it he provides a summary as well as a description of the relationships between the various families of models.

Salvucci has some nice models of how people drive (Salvucci2006), and some tools for predicting how secondary tasks will impair driving (Salvucci et al. 2005). Byrne and Kirlik (2005) have provided similar lessons in aviation.

We have previously laid out a vision of future work that is needed to help designers create models routinely (Ritter et al. 2003). It is available online and notes about 20 projects that remain to be done with computational models of users.

Pew and Mavor's (2007) book is available on line, and you can purchase it or register and download it. Their book provides useful pointers to a range of methodologies for reducing the risks to system success that are caused by not understanding users or their tasks. It could be and has been used to teach a separate class on HCI methodologies. There was also a special issue of the *Journal of Cognitive Engineeringand Decision Making* related to the topic published in 2008.

A short, easy to read technical report is available online that lays out a taxonomy of system development risks and a method to perform a risk analysis:

Carr, M., Konda, S., Monarch, I., Ulrich, C., & Walker, C. (1993). Taxonomy-Based Risk Identification (Tech. Report No. CMU/SEI-93-TR-6, ADA266992). Pittsburgh, PA: Software Engineering Institute, Carnegie-Mellon University.

14.7 Exercises

14.1 Consider a smartphone, either a specific one or a composite one, or a simple cell phone. Note all the limitations that will preclude users from performing well with it. Organize these by the ABCS framework.

14.2 Choose an existing interface. Note the tasks that users will want to use it for. Note the types of users and their characteristics. Run two small studies examining how well your theory of use fits the data. These studies could be to find out what tasks users really do, how well they do it (time and errors, and strategies), or characteristics of the users.

14.3 Choose an interface or system to create, such as a new application for a smartphone, such as a game, or book reader. Note what risks there are in developing such a system, with particular attention paid to the technical risks and those related to the user. Prioritize them. If you had 100 h, how would you allocate that time to reduce these risks?

14.4 Go back and read the Appendix on the Kegworth air accident again. Read the supplementary material referenced (e.g., the AAIB report) or other reports you can find. Identify four more factors (events, processes, or mistakes) that can be considered as causes of the accident. Describe how these things could have been avoided or ameliorated. Address the question of whether it was 'pilot error' that caused that plane to crash.

References

Anderson, J. R. (2007). *How can the human mind exist in the physical universe?* New York, NY: Oxford University Press.

Barnard P. J. (1987). Cognitive resources and the learning of human-computer dialogues. In J. M. Carroll (Ed.), *Interfacing thought: Cognitive aspects of human–computer interaction* (pp. 112–158). Cambridge, MA: MIT Press.

Baxter, G., Besnard, D., & Riley, D. (2007). Cognitive mismatches in the cockpit: Will they ever be a thing of the past? *Applied Ergonomics, 38*, 417–423.

Boehm, B. (2008). Making a difference in the software century. *IEEE Computer,41*(3), 32–38.

Boehm, B., & Hansen, W. (2001). The spiral model as a tool for evolutionary acquisition. *Crosstalk: The Journal of Defense Software Engineering, 14*(5), 4–11.

Boehm, B., & Lane, J. (2006). 21st century processes for acquiring 21st century systems of systems. *Crosstalk, 19*(5), 4–9.

Booher, H. R., & Minninger, J. (2003). Human systems integration in Army systems acquisition. In H. R. Booher (Ed.), *Handbook of human systems integration* (pp. 663–698). Hoboken, NJ: John Wiley.

Byrne, M. D. (2001). ACT-R/PM and menu selection: Applying a cognitive architecture to HCI. *International Journal of Human–Computer Studies, 55*(1), 41–84.

Byrne, M. D., & Kirlik, A. (2005). Using computational cognitive modeling to diagnose possible sources of aviation error. *International Journal of Aviation Psychology, 15*(2), 135–155.

Card, S. K., Moran, T. P., & Newell, A. (1980). The keystroke-level model for user performance time with interactive systems. *Communications of the ACM, 23*(7), 396–410.

Card, S. K., Moran, T., & Newell, A. (1983). *The psychology of human–computer interaction.* Hillsdale, NJ: Erlbaum.

Casey, S. M. (1998). *Set phasers on stun: And other true tales of design, technology, and human error.* Santa Barbara, CA: Aegean.

Casey, S. M. (2006). *The atomic chef: And other true tales of design, technology, and human error.* Santa Barbara, CA: Aegean.

Ericsson, K. A., & Simon, H. A. (1993). *Protocol analysis: Verbal reports as data* (2nd ed.). Cambridge, MA: MIT Press.

Gemma, E., Helm, R., Johnson, R., & Vlissides, J. (1995). *Design patterns: Elements of reusable object-oriented software.* Boston, MA: Addison-Wesley.

Gluck, K. A., Ball, J. T., & Krusmark, M. A. (2007). Cognitive control in a computational model of the predator pilot. In W. D. Gray (Ed.), *Integrated models of cognitive systems* (pp. 13–28). New York: Oxford University Press.

Ivory, M. Y., & Hearst, M. A. (2001). The state of the art in automating usability evaluation of user interfaces. *ACM Computing Surveys, 33*(4), 470–516.

Kieras, D. E. (1999). *A guide to GOMS model usability evaluation using GOMSL and GLEAN3.* AI Lab, University of Michigan. Retrieved 10 March 2014 from http://web.eecs.umich.edu/~kieras/docs/GOMS

Kieras, D. E., Wood, S. D., Abotel, K., & Hornof, A. (1995). GLEAN: A computer-based tool for rapid GOMS model usability evaluation of user interface designs. In *Proceedings of the ACM Symposium on User Interface Software and Technology (UIST'95)* (pp. 91–100). New York, NY: ACM.

Kieras, D. E., Wood, S. D., & Meyer, D. E. (1997). Predictive engineering models based on the EPIC architecture for a multimodal high-performance human-computer interaction task. *Transactions on Computer–Human Interaction, 4*(3), 230–275.

Laird, J. E. (2012). *The soar cognitive architecture.* Cambridge, MA: MIT Press.

Landauer, T. K. (1987). Relations between cognitive psychology and computer systems design. In J. Preece & L. Keller (Eds.), *Human–computer interaction* (pp. 141–159). Englewood Cliffs, NJ: Prentice-Hall.

Lebiere, C., & Anderson, J. R. (1998). Cognitive arithmetic. In J. R. Anderson & C. Lebière (Eds.), *The atomic components of thought* (pp. 297–342). Mahwah, NJ: Erlbaum.

Morrison, J. E. (2003). *A review of computer-based human behavior representations and their relation to military simulations* (IDA Paper P-3845). Alexandria, VA: Institute for Defense Analyses.

Newell, A. (1990). *Unified theories of cognition.* Cambridge, MA: Harvard University Press.

Pew, R. W. (2007). Some history of human performance modeling. In W. Gray (Ed.), *Integrated models of cognitive systems* (pp. 29–44). New York, NY: Oxford University Press.

Pew, R. W., & Mavor, A. S. (Eds.). (1998). *Modeling human and organizational behavior: Application to military simulations.* Washington, DC: National Academies Press. Retrieved from 10 March 2014 http://books.nap.edu/catalog/6173.html

Pew, R. W., & Mavor, A. S. (Eds.). (2007). *Human-system integration in the system development process: A new look.* Washington, DC: National Academies Press. Retrieved March, 2014 from http://books.nap.edu/catalog.php?record_id=11893

Ritter, F. E. (2003). Soar. In L. Nadel (Ed.), *Encyclopedia of cognitive science* (Vol. 4, pp. 60–65). London: Nature Publishing Group.

Ritter, F. E., & Bibby, P. A. (2008). Modeling how, when, and what learning happens in a diagrammatic reasoning task. *Cognitive Science, 32,* 862–892.

Ritter, F. E., Shadbolt, N. R., Elliman, D., Young, R. M., Gobet, F., & Baxter, G. D. (2003). *Techniques for modeling human performance in synthetic environments: A supplementary review.* Wright-Patterson Air Force Base, OH: Human Systems Information Analysis Center (HSIAC).

Ritter, F. E., Van Rooy, D., St. Amant, R., & Simpson, K. (2006). Providing user models direct access to interfaces: An exploratory study of a simple interface with implications for HRI and HCI. *IEEE Transactions on System, Man, and Cybernetics, Part A: Systems and Humans, 36*(3), 592–601.

Ritter, F. E., Kukreja, U., & St. Amant, R. (2007). Including a model of visual processing with a cognitive architecture to model a simple teleoperation task. *Journal of Cognitive Engineering and Decision Making, 1*(2), 121–147.

Salvucci, D. D. (2006). Modeling driver behavior in a cognitive architecture. *Human Factors,48,* 362–380.

Salvucci, D. D., Zuber, M., Beregovaia, E., & Markley, D. (2005). Distract-R: Rapid prototyping and evaluation of in-vehicle interfaces. In *Human Factors in Computing Systems: CHI 2005 Conference Proceedings* (pp. 581–589). New York, NY: ACM Press.

Schoelles, M. J., & Gray, W. D. (2001). Argus: A suite of tools for research in complex cognition. *Behavior Research Methods, Instruments, & Computers, 33*(2), 130–140.

Steele, M., Dow, L., & Baxter, G. (2011). Promoting public awareness of the links between lifestyle and cancer: A controlled study of the usability of health information leaflets. *International Journal of Medical Informatics, 80,* e214–e229.

Thorpe, T. W. (1992). *Computerized circuit analysis with SPICE: A complete guide to SPICE, with applications.* New York, NY: Wiley.

Appendix
The Kegworth Air Accident (1989)

Introduction

The Kegworth air accident is used to illustrate several points in this book. We chose this particular accident because it is well known and has been widely analyzed over the years (e.g., see Besnard et al. 2004). The full accident report is very comprehensive, and covers all aspects of the accident as well as the human factors issues. It is available from the web site of the UK's Air Accidents Investigation Branch (AAIB).[1] The AAIB are responsible for investigating accidents that occur within UK air space.

Description of the Accident

On 8 January 1989 a British Midland Airways (BMA) Boeing 737-400 plane crashed into the embankment of the UK's M1 motorway close to the village of Kegworth in the East Midlands, during a flight from London Heathrow to Belfast. Of the 126 people on board, 47 lost their lives.

Both members of the flight crew were highly experienced. The Captain had logged over 13,000 flying hours, whilst the First Officer had logged over 3,200. Both pilots were rated for the B737-200, -300, and -400 series aircraft. They had a combined experience of 76 flight hours in the Boeing 737-400 series aircraft. Furthermore, they had not been trained on the new plane's controls, but had only received a 1-day audio–visual conversion course on the B737-400, which has a glass cockpit, i.e., the information is presented on digital displays rather than the vast array of analogue instruments and electro-mechanical displays that appeared in the cockpit of its predecessor, the B737-300. In addition, the B737-400 series was fitted with a newer variant of an engine which could generate slightly more thrust. The engine had been certified by the appropriate authorities after undergoing testing.

During the flight, a fan blade broke off in the #1 engine. This resulted in an increase in vibration above what is considered normal, and which was strong

---

[1] http://www.aaib.gov.uk/sites/aaib/publications/formal_reports/4_1990_g_obme.cfm

F. E. Ritter et al., *Foundations for Designing User-Centered Systems*,
DOI: 10.1007/978-1-4471-5134-0, © Springer-Verlag London 2014

enough to be felt by the crew. This happened shortly after 20:05 h. At the same time as the increase in vibration was felt, smoke and fumes were drawn into the aircraft through the air conditioning system. In their analysis of the problem, the flight crew mistakenly identified the right hand (#2) engine as being at fault and therefore reduced its power accordingly.

An analysis of the data from the cockpit voice recorder (CVR) showed that there had been a slight hesitancy in determining which of the engines was at fault. When the Captain (the senior officer on the flight deck) asked the First Officer which engine was faulty, he replied 'It's the le… it's the right one.' As a consequence, the power to the right hand (#2) engine was throttled back and the engine was eventually shut down.

The actions taken on the right hand engine coincided (as it later turned out) with a reduction in vibration, and the smoke and fumes emerging from the left (faulty) engine also stopped. The flight crew therefore decided, erroneously (again, as it later turned out), that the correct engine had been shut down. They decided to put in motion the plan to make an emergency landing at East Midlands Airport, which involved talking to Air Traffic Control (ATC) to make sure they could get the appropriate clearances to land. Although the left engine continued to show a higher than normal level of vibration for several minutes, the crew did not notice this at the time.

When the crew began their descent towards the airport they reduced the power to the left engine. This led to a further reduction in the vibration in that engine to the point where it was not much higher than what would normally be expected. About 10 min later the crew decided to increase the power to the left engine once more, in order to maintain the aircraft's altitude in the final stages of descent. The vibration levels increased once more to very high levels, power was lost in engine #1, and a fire warning sounded. At this point the crew tried to restart the #2 engine but did not manage to achieve this before the aircraft crashed into the ground 0.5 nautical miles short of the runway shortly after 20:12 h.

An Analysis of Possible Contributory Factors

It is often very difficult to single out the exact causes of an accident after the fact. Where lives and machinery are lost, the best attempts involve a reconstruction of events based on the available evidence. In the case of aircraft accidents, this includes the information captured by the Flight Data Recorder, and the CVR. These are what you often hear referred to as "the Black Box" although they are usually a highly visible shade of orange!

In the Kegworth accident, the crash was ultimately attributed to the way that the flight crew managed a mechanical incident in the left (#1) engine. The events unfolded very quickly: from the vibration being detected to the crash took less than 7 min 30 s. As is often the case, there were several contributory events that happened which contributed to the accident. These occurred at different levels within the system. We pick out examples of several types of these below. Rather than providing an exhaustive analysis (which you can find by reading the accident report in full, and consulting the many papers that have been published about the accident), our intention is to illustrate the points of particular interest. We start at a level that is some distance away from the point at which people are interacting with technology, as a way of highlighting the importance of understanding the wider context in which people make decisions and take actions. When you have finished reading the book, you should be able to come back to the accident description above and identify further examples (this is Exercise 14.4).

Regulatory Level Issues

The B737-400 was fitted with a new type of engine. As with all aircraft engines, it had to undergo extensive testing before it could be certified for operational use. The engine in this case was a variant of an existing engine (which is common practice in the aero-engine industry), and it was thoroughly tested on the ground before being certified by the FAA (and ratified by the CAA). The engine was not, however, tested either in an altitude test cell (which simulates the conditions of flying at high altitudes) or in flight. If it had been so tested, this may have highlighted the fact that there was a flaw in the design which led to a turbine blade failure under certain patterns of vibration. This scenario illustrates how decisions that are made at remote distance from the user interface in a system can have an impact on the way that the users behave. If the engine had still been certified, and both the airline and the flight crew had known that this was a potential (even if very rare) problem, they could have included a checklist to deal with it in the Quick Reference Handbook (QRH) that is used by all pilots to deal with known situations, such as smoke in the cockpit.

Organizational Level Issues

The B737-400 was what is known as a glass cockpit aircraft, in which the information is presented on digital displays rather than the vast array of analogue instruments and electro-mechanical displays that appeared in the cockpit of its predecessor, the B737-300. The airline (BMA) did not have a glass cockpit flight training simulator for the B737-400, so pilots could only gain experience in using the new glass cockpit when they were actually flying it (i.e., on the job). The only training the pilots were given about the B737-400 was a 1-day audio–visual conversion course.

ATC offered the pilots two places to land. On company instructions, they chose to land at East Midlands airport, which was on their flight path, and the closest airport. This reduced the amount of time that they had available to reflect fully on the decisions and actions taken so far to deal with the engine problems. While the pilots were trying to get ready for descent and landing, they were also in receipt of regular communications from ATC, had to talk to the operating company (BMA), keep the passengers informed of the situation, and complete the appropriate checklist in preparation for landing with one engine. The problem was made worse by the fact that the First Officer struggled to reprogram the Flight Management System (FMS) successfully with the details needed for landing at East Midlands airport. The way they had to use the FMS was unusual and rarely practiced. This is another area where the lack of appropriate recurrent training contributed to the accident.

Flight Crew Level Issues

During the flight the pilots announced to the crew and passengers that there had been some trouble with the right engine but it had now been shut down. While some passengers could see the evidence of an engine fire, they did not inform the pilots that they had shut down the wrong engine. This appears to be an example of the problem of social distance, where the passengers perceive the pilots as being highly trained professionals, so they *must* know what they are doing, which means that the passengers do not feel in a position to correct them. The smell of smoke had dissipated by the time the announcement was made, too, which may also have had an influence on the passengers' thinking.

Three members of the cabin crew also reported having seen evidence of the fire in the #1 engine but they did not report this to the pilots. This seems to have been a failure in what is called Crew Resource Management, a procedure designed to ensure that all the members of a flight crew (pilots and cabin crew) communicate with one another and work together as a team. So the cabin crew should not have felt that there was a large social distance between them and the pilots, and should have not felt intimidated about telling the pilots about what they had seen even though it appeared to contradict what the pilots had said. This could have been attributed to a lack of CRM training.

Cockpit Level Issues

The first indication that there was a problem with the engines came when the flight crew felt excessive vibrations in the aircraft and detected smoke in the cockpit. When both pilots were interviewed after the accident, neither could recall having seen any indication of the abnormally high vibration levels on the Engine Instrument System (EIS). The Captain noted that he rarely scanned the vibration gauges because he had found them to be unreliable in other aircraft in the past. Experts, like pilots, have a highly developed mental model of the world in which they normally operate, and this helps them to perform the tasks they are supposed to. In pilots, this mental model will help guide where they need to look to find appropriate information about the current state of the aircraft. In this case, the

Captain appears to have eliminated the vibration gauges from his mental model, because he has found that they do not provide any useful information (because they are unreliable). If the captain had looked closely at the EIS, he may have observed information about the engines that would have changed how the flight crew dealt with the engine problems.

Technology Issues

The EIS which was fitted to the B737-400 used digital rather than analogue displays. A subsequent survey showed that nearly two-thirds of BMA pilots believed that the new EIS was not effective in drawing their attention to rapid changes in the engine parameters, and nearly three-quarters preferred the old EIS. Thus, the system designers of the EIS and the training could be deemed to have contributed to the accident. It appears that the pilots of BMA (at least) were not involved in carrying out any evaluation of the new EIS before they had to use it in flight.

External Issues

When the aircraft was in sight of the airport, the #1 engine finally failed completely. There was not enough time to restart the #2 engine, and the aircraft ended up landing on the M1 (one of the UK's main motorways). This road had had noise abatement embankments (small hills) put up to shelter the surrounding land from motorway noise. This caused the plane to bounce, and probably compounded the crash.

Summary

The formal accident investigation attributed the cause of the accident to pilot error. As you look through the description of what happened, and the list of contributory events, you should start to appreciate that maybe it was a series of mistakes, errors, and bad luck from a wide range of people who were part of the broad system. During a normal flight there are several things happening at the same time at different levels within the air transport system, and the flight crew has to deal with many of them. In the vast majority of cases, all the tasks are performed successfully, and the flight arrives safely at its destination and in a timely manner. It is often only when things go wrong, however, that you really begin to understand just how complicated getting a plane full of passengers from its original airport to its destination can be.

Reference

Besnard, D., Greathead, D., & Baxter, G. (2004). When mental models go wrong. Co-occurrences in dynamic, critical systems. *International Journal of Human-Computer Studies,60*(60), 117–128.

Glossary

ABCS Anthropometric, Behavior, Cognition, and Social factors: the high-level constructs which are useful for organizing the knowledge about people that is relevant to system design.

ACT-R A cognitive architecture used to model human cognition.

Aesthetics Relates to the characteristics of an object or system that make it pleasurable to use. Sometimes called Esthetics.

Affordance The intrinsic property of an object that suggests actions that can be performed with it, e.g., a handle affords grasping and pulling.

Anthropometrics The study of the shape of the body and how it influences what is designed. It takes into consideration the physical characteristics of intended users such their size and their muscular strength.

Attention A term that refers to the selective nature of perception which functions in such a way that at any given time a person focuses on some feature(s) of the environment to the exclusion of others.

Attribution theory Describes the tendency of people to attribute their own actions to external situational causes, whereas external observers attribute the same actions to causes that are internal to the person carrying out the actions.

Availability bias Arises because users tend to recall those items that are easier to recall even when they may not be most representative of a particular situation.

Blunt end The part of the system that is furthest away from where the user interacts with the technology. Normally refers to the level at which regulations and laws are applied. Often used in contrast to the sharp end.

Closed loop behavior A pattern of behavior in which users take some actions, and look for feedback on those actions before deciding how to proceed. Also referred to as feedback control.

Cognitive architecture A framework that supports the modeling of human information processing under different conditions. Cognitive architectures include mechanisms designed to help model human cognition.

F. E. Ritter et al., *Foundations for Designing User-Centered Systems*,
DOI: 10.1007/978-1-4471-5134-0, © Springer-Verlag London 2014

Cognitive dimensions (of notation) A common ontology used to name specific aspects of design as well as the associated design trade-offs.

Cognitive dissonance Cognitive dissonance occurs when a person holds two or more beliefs that are in conflict at one time, as in when people do not get what they want.

Cognitive modeling Using computer programs to simulate human behavior, usually within the framework of a cognitive architecture.

Cognitive task analysis (CTA) An extension of traditional task analysis techniques to facilitate the collection of information about the mental processes that underpin observable task performance. Usually comprises several methods.

Computer supported co-operative work (CSCW) The study of how people work together using technology.

Cones A type of light receptor cell located on the retina. Cones are sensitive to color. See also Rods.

Confirmation bias Arises because users tend to look for information that confirms their understanding of a particular situation, and hence have difficulty seeing things that conflict with their understanding of the world.

Content strategy Content strategy relates to the planning for the creation, publication, and governance of content that are both useful and usable. It covers which content to publish as well as why. Mostly used when referring to the web, but applies to all media, platforms, and devices.

Co-operative principle Basically refers to trying to say the right thing at the right time—the co-operative principle can also be seen as a description of the way that people normally conduct conversations. See also Grice's maxims.

CREAM (Cognitive reliability and error analysis method) Method for iteratively modeling and analyzing erroneous performance in a prospective or retrospective manner. The CREAM assumes that the context is a major influence on human performance. See also THEA.

Decibel A logarithmic measure of sound pressure: a tenfold increase in sound pressure (e.g., 10–20 dB) sounds twice as loud.

Declarative memory A hypothesized store which holds facts or statement about the world, e.g., the earth is flat.

Designers People who design systems or technology.

Diffusion of social responsibility When a group of people are held jointly responsible for dealing with a particular situation, the responsibility diffuses across people: several people may decide not to do anything in the belief that someone else in the group will.

Distributed learning Learning that occurs when practice is distributed over time in such a way that there are gaps between practice sessions.

Efficiency A system property that can be measured through its use of resources such as processor time, memory, network access, system facilities, disk space, and so on.

Einstellung *Einstellung* is related to Functional Fixedness but refers to the situation where a person gets fixated on a strategy to solve a problem.

Ergonomics The field that is concerned with providing a good fit between people and their work or leisure environments. Often used interchangeably with human factors.

Error The part of the system state that may lead to a subsequent failure.

Esthetics Relates to the characteristics of an object or system that make it pleasurable to use.

Event tree An inductive method for analyzing errors using a graphical binary tree representation.

Explicit memory A hypothesized store of items that can be explicitly reported. Most declarative information can be explicitly reported. Often used in contrast to Implicit memory.

Extrinsic motivation Motivation that arises from factors outside the individual, such as being paid to do something.

Eye-tracking A method for recording where the user's eyes are looking using a dedicated device (an eye-tracker).

Failure Something that occurs when the service that is delivered by a system or component is judged to have deviated from its specification.

Fault The adjudged cause of an error within a system.

Fault tree A deductive method for analyzing the causal factors that contribute to an error or accident, using a graphical tree representation.

Feeling of knowing Refers to the feelings an individual has about their knowledge on a particular topic, and particularly whether or not that knowledge exists within memory. It normally relates to making judgments either prior to recalling the target item, or after failing to recall it. The focus is on whether an individual *feels* that they know the answer, rather than what the answer actually is. Often used in the context of metacognition.

Field experiments Field experiments are trials of technologies in real world settings.

Field studies Evaluations that are carried out in the field, that is, in real world settings.

Figure and ground Figure is the term used to refer to the objects being focused on; ground is the rest of the perceptual field.

Fitts' law A method used to predict the time it takes to move a pointer to a target.

Flesch reading ease score A calculated value that reflects the readability of a selected piece of text.

Forcing function A mechanism for physically constraining actions to prevent the user from proceeding to the next step in task performance. To start most cars, for example, you are forced to put the key into the ignition.

Formative evaluation A type of evaluation that is used to help designers refine and form their designs. The focus of formative evaluation is to identify problems and potential solutions.

Fovea A small area of the retina (covering about 2° of visual arc). This is the area of clearest vision.

Framing effects Refers to the fact that the way that potential outcomes of a particular situation are presented (framed) has a powerful influence on how users choose between alternatives.

Functional fixedness Functional fixedness occurs when a person becomes fixated on a particular use of an object.

Functionality What the system does. Usually specified by the functional requirements.

Fundamental attribution error The belief that our own behavior can be attributed to extrinsic factors in the environment, and that the behavior of others is attributable to their intrinsic properties (e.g., they are a bad person).

Fundamental attribution error of design The belief, held by designers, that users act and behave in the same way as designers when using technology.

Generic error modeling system (GEMS) An approach to modeling errors based on interpretation, planning, memory, and acting.

Gestalt principles of visual grouping Can be used to explain how groups of objects are interpreted. The principles were developed as a rebellion against the simplistic notion that perception could be structurally analyzed into its component parts, and that complex ideas were the result of associating together simpler ones.

GOMS (Goals, operators, methods, and selection rules) A method of task analysis that can be used to describe the details of error-free, expert task performance using Goals, Operators (actions), Methods (procedures), and Selection rules (to choose between methods).

Grice's maxims The four basic maxims underlying the co-operative principle. These maxims make strong suggestions about how people should communicate with other people. When these suggestions are followed, communication is more successful and more satisfying.

GUI (Graphical user interface) A user interface that is made up of graphical objects, such as icons.

Gulf of evaluation The gap between the concepts used in the physical system and the user's psychological representation of those concepts.

Gulf of execution The gap between the user's (psychological) goals and intentions and the physical actions they need to take to achieve those goals.

Habituation Becoming so used to a stimulus that it becomes unnoticeable. (This is very similar to desensitization.)

Haptic devices Devices which utilize touch and tactile feedback. Most haptic devices only support interaction using the hands or fingers, even though users could use any part of their body. There is a growing number of devices that support input using the feet.

Hard mental operations One of the cognitive dimensions. It relates to the fact that users find some kinds of operations harder to perform than others, so they prefer easier mental operations.

HCI (Human–computer interaction) The study of how people interact with technology. The abbreviation is also sometimes used to refer to Human–Computer Interface.

Heuristic evaluation A relatively informal way of analyzing the usability of an interface design in which a small select number of people are asked to judge the design based on a set of guidelines or principles together with their own knowledge.

Hicks law An equation that is used to describe the time to make a decision based on the number of available choices. Also called the Hick–Hyman Law.

Hidden dependencies One of the cognitive dimensions. They show how visible the relationships between design components are, describing the number and direction of those relationships.

Hierarchical task analysis (HTA) A method for analyzing in detail how tasks are performed by decomposing goals into subgoals. It is often described in terms of decomposing tasks into sub-tasks.

Human factors The field that is concerned with providing a good fit between people and their work or leisure environments. Often used interchangeably with Ergonomics.

Human-centered design (HCD) An expansion of the User-Centered Design approach which extends the focus from the user's interaction with the system to considering how human capabilities and characteristics are affected by the system beyond direct interaction with the interface or system itself.

Iconic memory A store where perceptual images are held for a short period of time. Visual iconic memory, for example, holds only a few items and these decay fairly quickly.

Ill-structured problem Some problems are more difficult than others because they are ill-structured, that is, they are not clearly defined in terms of states, goals, and actions that are available. Also called ill-defined or messy problems.

Implicit memory A hypothesized store of items that cannot be explicitly reported. Most procedural information cannot be explicitly reported. Often used in contrast to Explicit memory.

Information Information can be thought of as organized data.

Information architecture A term used to describe how on-line information is structured to support usability by both its creators and its users.

Information scent Information scent is what leads a user to spend more time exploring a web page (or menu item) to find what they are looking for because the content effectively smells like the thing they are looking for. The idea is to make sure that objects and links appear to smell like the content they contain and do not smell like content that they do not contain.

Insight problems A class of problems where novel behavior or understanding is required to solve them. Sometimes called "Aha" problems.

Interaction design (IxD) An approach to designing interactive products and systems to support the way that people interact and communicate.

Intrinsic motivation The motivation to do something that arises directly from a person's inherent needs and desires.

Introspection The examination of your own mental experiences. It can be a source of insight but has been proven to be unreliable in general.

Just noticeable difference (JND) The smallest change in a perceptual stimulus that is noticeable by a user.

Keystroke level model (KLM) A simplified version of GOMS. It provides a quick and approximate way to calculate how long users will take to perform a cognitively manageable (unit) task.

Kinesthesis Kinesthesis (or the kinesthetic sense) generates an awareness of static and dynamic body posture based on information coming from the muscles, joints, and skin, along with a copy of the signal sent to the motor system.

KSA (knowledge, skills, and attitudes) Individual (or team) competencies that influence behavior.

Learnability How easy it is to learn to use the system.

Learning curve A graphical representation of performance that is assumed to reflect the learning that has occurred through practice. The shape of the curve reflects how response time changes with practice on a task. The curve is often described by a power law function and sometimes as an exponential function.

Loftus effect Refers to the fact that when people are presented with misleading information between the encoding of another piece of information and its later recall, the recall of the original information is altered by misleading information. Often referred to as the (Loftus) misinformation effect.

Long term memory An unlimited capacity store for items that have been processed or interpreted and permanently encoded.

Maintainability How easy a system is to maintain and upgrade over its lifetime.

Massed learning Learning that occurs when the practice is relatively or completely located within a single time period.

Mental model A user's mental model is a representation of some part of the world that can include the structures of the world (the ontology of the relevant objects), how they interact, and how the user can interact with them.

Metacognition Literally cognition about cognition. It includes knowledge about when and how to use specific strategies for problem solving and learning. See also Feeling of knowing.

Millisecond (ms) Abbreviated ms, this is one thousandth of a second.

Mistake A failure in planning. Refers to an action that was performed correctly but in the wrong circumstances.

Mnemonic Mnemonics are techniques that help to increase the amount or quality of information that can be stored, or the speed at which can it be retrieved.

Model human processor (MHP) One of the first simple integrated descriptions of psychological knowledge relating to error-free human performance in HCI.

Need for cognition Refers to the fact that some users like to think, and seek out opportunities to think, problem solve, and learn.

Normative behavior A term used to describe what people *should* do, rather than what they really do.

Open loop behavior A pattern of behavior in which users anticipate what will happen next in a particular situation, and take actions on that basis. There is little or no need to monitor the results of the actions. Also described as feedforward control.

Operators Generally used to refer to users who work in industrial settings such as nuclear power stations and chemical plants.

Parafovea The area of the retina that immediately surrounds the fovea. It provides a lower level of visual acuity than the fovea.

Periphery The area of the retina beyond the parafovea. Visual acuity is at its lowest in the periphery and vision is only in black and white.

Pop-out (effect) Refers to the effect that some stimuli appear to 'pop out' of a visual field based on color, size, shape, or other unique and easy to distinguish features.

Post-completion errors Errors that arise when the main goal for a task has been accomplished, but the goals of the subtasks have not.

Power law of learning A mathematical description of how learning takes place over time. Usually represented by an equation of the form $RT = aP^{-b} + c$, where RT is the response time for a particular trial, P, and a, b, and c are all constants.

PQ4R A method of studying designed to help readers retain more from what they read. It stands for Preview, Question, Read, Reflect, Recite, Review.

Premature commitment One of the cognitive dimensions. It relates to the situation where design decisions have to be made before all of the required information is available.

Primacy effect Refers to the fact that the items presented at the start of a list of items to be learned are subsequently better recalled than items in the middle of the list in a free (unprimed) recall situation.

Priming Used with respect to learning to refer to the presentation of a particular experience which makes the responder more sensitive or responsive to a wide range of stimuli.Used with respect to memory to refer to the triggering of the recall of related items, e.g., "yellow" would prime the recall of "banana," "custard," and other items that are yellow in color.

Problem solving Problem solving essentially involves working out how to get from the current state of affairs to the goal that you are trying to achieve by taking appropriate actions. More formally, this can be described as applying operators to states to reach a goal.

Procedural memory A hypothesized store which holds procedures that encapsulate how to do a particular task, such as how to move a knight in chess.

Programmable user models (PUMs) A psychologically constrained architecture which an interface designer programs to simulate a user performing a range of tasks with a proposed interface.

Recency effect Refers to the fact that the items presented at the end of a list of items to be learned are subsequently better recalled than items in the middle of the list in a free (unprimed) recall situation.

Recognition-primed decision making (RPDM) An approach to decision making which suggests that experts do not do problem solving, but that they recognize the particular situation (through perception) which directly leads them to make decisions about the correct actions to take.

Reliability When referring to evaluation, reliability describes the ability of a particular measure to produce consistent results when the same things are measured under different conditions. Often used in the context of test–retest reliability.When referring to systems, it refers to a dynamic property of the eventual system which relates to the ability of the system to function under stated conditions for a specified period of time.

Repetitive strain injury (RSI) A condition arising from upper limb disorders.

Retrieval biases Describes the inherent biases within people that affect what they recall from memory. They include primary effects, recency effects, and the von Restorff effect.

Rich pictures A component part of Soft Systems Methodology. Used to represent graphically the work context based on the roles, responsibilities, and concerns of the system stakeholders.

Risk-driven incremental commitment model A revised version of the spiral model which encourages incremental development of systems in an ongoing spiral process comprising requirements specification, technical exploration, and stakeholder commitment. At each stage the system development is assessed for risks to the success of the overall system.

Rods A type of light receptor cell located on the retina. Rods are very sensitive to motion. See also Cones.

Role-expressiveness One of the cognitive dimensions. It describes the extent to which a system reveals the goals of the system designer to the user.

Satisficing A method that finds a reasonable solution taking into consideration the costs of finding a (better, more optimal) solution.

Search engine optimization The process of increasing the visibility of a web page or web site in a search engine's organic (unpaid) search results.

Sensitivity A term used to describe how much a particular measure will change as other factors change.

Serial position curve A graphical representation of how the position of an item in a list affects its recall from memory. Often used to help show primacy and recency effects.

Sharp end The part of the system where the user interacts with the technology. Sometimes used in contrast to the blunt end.

Short term memory (STM) A relatively limited capacity store for items that have received a limited amount of processing or interpretation. STM is somewhat analogous to the registers in a computer.

Signal detection theory (SDT) A mathematical theory of the detection of physical signals based on the assumption that sensitivity to a signal depends on its intensity, the amount of noise, the user's motivation, and the criterion set for registering responses to the signal. Sometimes referred to as the Theory of Signal Detection (TSD).

Slip A failure in the execution of an action. Refers to performing the wrong action in the right circumstances.

Social capital A concept that highlights the value of social relations and the role of cooperation and confidence in establishing trusts and norms to get collective results.

Socio-technical systems Systems that involve a complex interaction between humans, machines, and the environmental aspects of the work system. (Nowadays this description applies to most enterprise systems.)

Soft systems methodology Essentially an analytical approach, mostly focusing on organizational aspects of the system. It does not purport to support systems design.

Spiral model A model of the system development lifecycle, which uses an iterative development process.

S–R (Stimulus–response) compatibility Refers to the fact the response should be compatible with the stimulus that causes it. This is typically exploited in the way that physical aspects of an interface (e.g., buttons) and displays (e.g., GUIs) are mapped onto the world that they are representing. It also explains why the call buttons for elevators are situated with the "up" button above the "down" one.

Stimulus–response mapping The mapping between the stimulus that the users see to the responses that they produce. Mappings that are simple and similar to previous mappings lead to faster, less error-prone interactions.

Subitizing The ability to determine directly the number of objects the user is looking at without counting them. This only works for small numbers of objects.

Summative evaluation A type of evaluation used to assess the success of the finished system or product, summarizing its overall impact and effectiveness.

Task-action mapping Describes the relationship between the domain of the task and the domain of actions. Ideally there should be a simple and direct mapping between the two.

THEA (Technique for human error assessment) Method for analyzing erroneous performance using an iterative process. Like the CREAM it assumes that the context is a major influence on performance.

THERP (Technique for human error rate prediction) An approach to modeling errors in human performance. The probability of errors occurring is conditioned by performance shaping factors as a way of taking into account the context in which the error happens.

Threshold The smallest energy level in a stimulus that can be detected by a user.

Tower of Hanoi A task used to study problem solving. It has three pegs or posts, and disks, typically three to eight, but in theory there could be any number of disks.

Transfer (of learning) Where learning on one task has an effect (either positive or negative) on a task that is performed later.

Upper limb disorders (ULD) Aches, pains, tension, and disorders that involve any part of the arm from fingers to shoulder or neck. They include problems with the soft tissues, muscles, tendons, and ligaments, as well as with the circulatory and nerve supply to the limbs. Often caused or exacerbated by work and, particularly, repetitive work. They lead to conditions such as repetitive strain injuries.

Usability A multi-faceted concept used to represent how easy a system is to use, how easy it is to learn to use, how safe it is, how effective (and efficient) it is, and how satisfying it is to use.

Usability testing A term usually restricted to describe the evaluation of the usability of a system under controlled (laboratory) conditions.

User experience (UX) The user's perceptions and responses that result from the use or anticipated use of a product, system or service. Some people regard UX as representing a broader view than usability.

User-centered design (UCD) An approach that focuses on the user's needs, carrying out an activity/task analysis as well as general requirements analysis, performing early testing and evaluation and designing iteratively.

Users Generally refers to people who use artifacts (systems, devices, and so on). There are several types of user, including operators, pilots, and drivers.

Validity A term used to refer to whether the particular measure that you are using is really measuring what it is supposed to be measuring. There are several types of validity.

Viscosity One of the cognitive dimensions. It reflects how hard it is to change something within a system.

von Restorff effect Refers to the fact that a single item that is made distinctive in a list of otherwise similar items will be easier to learn and subsequently recall.

WIMP (windows, icons, menus, and pointer) A shorthand description for a type of graphical user interface, using the elements that appear in that interface. Sometimes used interchangeably with GUI, but, strictly speaking, not all GUIs are WIMPs.

Working memory A hypothesized temporary store (an audio or semantic scratchpad) with associated mechanisms for rehearsing, refreshing, and using the stored information. It also includes a mechanism of central or executive attention that regulates the contents of that store based on performing a task.

Index